## Advanced Praise for *Helping Grieving People—When Tears Are Not Enough*, Second Edition

"This second edition of Jeffreys' best-seller is a work packed with plenty of practical pointers for professional helpers, and one that is guaranteed to sharpen one's skill as an 'Exquisite Witness' to the anguish and achievements of those whose lives are touched by loss. It offers grief professionals a helpful handbook that is keenly observant, well grounded in innumerable stories of loss and eventual gain, and one that continues to draw on the growing edge of grief theory to suggest relevant forms of assessment and intervention."

From the Series Editor Foreword by Robert A. Neimeyer, PhD

"Making an excellent book even better, Jeffreys' updated edition richly integrates professional and personal information to provide caregivers with the tools to best enable coping in the dying and bereaved. A superb resource!"

Therese A. Rando, PhD, BCETS, BCBT, The Institute for the Study and Treatment of Loss, Warwick, Rhode Island; Author of *Treatment of Complicated Mourning*

"In *Helping Grieving People*, Shep Jeffreys provides a great tool for clinicians and a gift for individuals struggling with loss. This book offers compassionate observations and insights tempered by experience as well as an integration of the most contemporary theories and research."

Kenneth J. Doka, PhD, Professor, The Graduate School, The College of New Rochelle, New York; Author of *Disenfranchised Grief*

"This is a wise, helpful, accessible book with excellent grounding in the literature and the author's practice and personal experience. It is an invaluable foundation for beginners at helping the bereaved, and there are also many riches for experienced helpers."

Paul C. Rosenblatt, PhD, Professor of Family Social Science, University of Minnesota; Author of *Parent Grief: Narratives of Loss and Relationship*

"Shep Jeffreys models admirably his own ideal as an 'Exquisite Witness' care provider for grieving people, drawing upon lessons learned from his own loss experiences, sharing his knowledge of experiences of grieving people in diverse life circumstances, and guiding providers toward useful and reassuring responses to the broad range of needs of the bereaved. The world would be a better place if more counselors put themselves in his able hands, and became like him."

Thomas Attig, PhD, Past President, Association for Death Education and Counseling; Author of *The Heart of Grief*

"Having already made a significant contribution to the field with his first edition of *Helping Grieving People*, Shep Jeffreys, in this second edition, offers more resources and richer ways for assisting people through the grieving process. The additional research adds greater breadth and depth to an array of outstanding clinical and pastoral resources. As an accomplished practitioner in the bereavement field, Jeffreys provides a plethora of insights that invite the care provider to serve effectively as an 'Exquisite Witness' through the dimensions of the 'heart, head, and hands.' As with the first edition, *Helping Grieving People* (2nd edition) will prove to be a valuable clinical and pastoral reference."

Reverend C. Kevin Gillespie, SJ, PhD, Associate Professor,
Loyola University of Chicago's Institute of Pastoral Studies

"In *Helping Grieving People*, Jeffreys artfully combines theory and research with clinical and personal experience. The result is an easy-to-read book that captures the complexity of the grief process and offers useful and practical guidelines for anyone supporting the bereaved. This second edition brings in the latest research and further elaborates on the concepts presented in the first. This book should be required reading for anyone wishing to understand grief and ways to help the bereaved."

Carol Wogrin, PsyD, RN, Director, National Center for Death Education,
Mount Ida College, Newton, Massachusetts

"Shep Jeffreys has presented a clear and unmistakably informative resource for any caring adult working with the grieving population. His work personifies an experienced professional from the heart quality of this book, to self-awareness exercises, grieving principles, and useful interventions and resources. I highly recommend *Helping Grieving People—When Tears Are Not Enough* for any professional, friend, or family member who hopes to become that 'Exquisite Witness' when being with a bereaved person."

Linda Goldman, MS, LCPC, FT, Private Practice, Chevy Chase, Maryland;
Author of *Raising Our Children to Be Resilient*

"Some books hook a reader early. This one hooked me with a story—a story of a boy named Steven who died too young and a family who chose to embrace grief. Only a professional who has experienced grief so 'close up,' and who has spent his career caring for grievers, can write so powerfully and so authentically. It is a book to be read, reread, and kept within an arm's reach for consultation. For someone new to this field and for those who have 'heard it all,' Jeffreys offers a page-turner and a book that you will dog-ear."

Harold Ivan Smith, FT, Grief Educator

# Praise for the First Edition

"Alternatively personal and poetic as well as professional, *Helping Grieving People* draws with equal comfort on the author's own rich trove of experience, on an artistic sensibility for capturing the poignancy of reflective moments, and on a range of contemporary theories that usefully inform our quest to understand bereavement and the needs of those subjected to it."

From the Series Editor Foreword by Robert A. Neimeyer, PhD

"With not one ounce of overstatement, it can be said that [this] book is one of the finest resources ever written to explicate the experience of loss and what can be done—and, in many cases, must be done—to effectively enable persons to cope with it. I cannot recommend it highly enough."

Therese A. Rando, PhD, BCETS, BCBT, The Institute for the Study of Treatment and Loss, Warwick, Rhode Island

"In his very readable, highly personal, and broadly informative book, Jeffreys reminds us, gently but firmly, that we all must listen and hear with our hearts if we are to competently and compassionately perform our obligations as care providers to those facing loss."

Ellen S. Zinner, PsyD, Assistant to the President, Salisbury University, Maryland; Past President, Association for Death Education and Counseling

"From sound theory to remarkable case studies, on to highly useful tools, this book works. It works because Jeffreys has been there and back. You walk away with a tool box, filled with all you will ever need to know."

Sidney B. Simon, Professor Emeritus, Psychological Education, University of Massachusetts; Creator of Values Realization

"*Helping Grieving People* does just that—and it does it masterfully. It is a gift to both counselors and bereaved persons. It may well become a classic in the field."

Kenneth J. Doka, PhD, Professor, The College of New Rochelle, New York; Senior Consultant, The Hospice Foundation of America

"*Helping Grieving People* is a rich conversation with the challenges and hidden gifts of one of the most overwhelming processes people must encounter at different points in their lives."

Robert J. Wicks, PsyD, Professor, Department of Pastoral Counseling, Loyola College, Maryland

"Well written and thoroughly researched, this is a book that will engage you in new ways so that others may engage you afresh."

Reverend Richard B. Gilbert, BCC, PhD, Executive Director,
The World Pastoral Care Center

"This volume overflows with good advice and good sense, clearly the work of someone who has known both ends of the healing process, as a healer and as one who needed healing and found it."

Rabbi Harold Kushner, Author of *When Bad Things Happen to Good People*

# Helping Grieving People –
# When tears are not enough

# THE SERIES IN DEATH, DYING, AND BEREAVEMENT
## ROBERT NEIMEYER, CONSULTING EDITOR

# FORMERLY THE SERIES IN DEATH EDUCATION, AGING, AND HEALTH CARE
## HANNELORE WASS, CONSULTING EDITOR

# Helping Grieving People –
# When tears are not enough

## A Handbook for Care Providers

## Second Edition

# J. Shep Jeffreys

Routledge
Taylor & Francis Group
New York   London

Routledge
Taylor & Francis Group
711 Third Avenue
New York, NY 10017

Routledge
Taylor & Francis Group
27 Church Road
Hove, East Sussex BN3 2FA

© 2011 by Taylor and Francis Group, LLC
Routledge is an imprint of Taylor & Francis Group, an Informa business

Printed in the United States of America on acid-free paper
10 9 8 7 6 5 4 3 2 1

International Standard Book Number: 978-0-415-87701-5 (Paperback)

### Library of Congress Cataloging-in-Publication Data

Jeffreys, J. Shep (John Shep)
    Helping grieving people : when tears are not enough : a handbook for care providers / John Shep Jeffreys. -- 2nd ed.
       p. cm.
    Includes bibliographical references and index.
    ISBN 978-0-415-87701-5 (pbk. : alk. paper)
    1. Grief. 2. Bereavement--Psychological aspects. 3. Death--Psychological aspects. 4. Loss (Psychology) I. Title.

BF575.G7J45 2011
155.9'37--dc22
                                                                        2010047312

**Visit the Taylor & Francis Web site at**
**http://www.taylorandfrancis.com**

**and the Routledge Web site at**
**http://www.routledgementalhealth.com**

*Both editions of this book are dedicated to the memory of Steven Daniel Jeffreys, who died at age 8 in 1975. His illness and subsequent death have created major and ongoing changes in our family's life and in the development of my own understanding of the human grief response.*

*These waves of change led to my focus on working with grieving people and to the writing of this book.*

*To the extent that my clinical and teaching efforts have assisted others who are grieving, Steven's illness and death are a gift to their healing.*

# CONTENTS

# SERIES EDITOR FOREWORD

"As an 'Exquisite Witness,'" wrote Shep Jeffreys in the first edition of this book, "we observe more than act, listen more than talk, and follow more than lead. 'Witnessing' celebrates the dignity and authority of the grieving person." And indeed, in the current edition, Jeffreys exemplifies the sort of witnessing he advocates, offering grief professionals a helpful handbook that is keenly observant, well grounded in innumerable stories of loss and eventual gain, and one that continues to draw on the growing edge of grief theory to suggest relevant forms of assessment and intervention. What emerges from these pages is not only a keen respect for the authority of the mourner, but also a sense of Jeffreys' own authority, as he winnows the lessons he has learned from his own losses and those of the countless people he has supported in their quest to move beyond the death of a loved one to a life again worth living.

Beginning with sociocultural and evolutionary foundations for an understanding of grief, Jeffreys proceeds to construct a scientific scaffolding for the work to follow. Central to this effort is a consideration of attachment theory and the ways in which various patterns of insecure attachment predispose to complicated bereavement, a discussion that is deepened and broadened by a review of contemporary work focusing on tasks of grieving, coping orientations, grief styles, and processes of meaning reconstruction. Layered onto this primarily individualistic level of analysis, Jeffreys adds a consideration of family structures and transitions that influence the grief of surviving members when a loved one dies. What keeps this from becoming an academic tome is his penchant for distilling relevant procedures for aiding the bereaved person, in the form of numerous lists of factors to consider in evaluating children and adults dealing with the death of a loved one, and concrete patterns of questioning that can prompt them to engage the loss in a healing fashion.

What follows is in many respects the clinical core of the book: a detailed treatment of the distinctive challenges of various groups of grievers, from children to parents and from bereaved elders to the dying themselves. In every instance, Jeffreys orients the reader to unique factors that exacerbate the distress of the relevant subgroup, condensing his intelligent discussion of illustrative cases into easily assimilated bullet points to remind the helper of the most relevant considerations in working with each. Personally, I found Jeffreys' discussion of the loss of a child especially evocative, perhaps because—as he acknowledges in the book's opening pages—it is a grievous loss that he knows so intimately from personal experience. As he goes on to offer a host of tangible guidelines for responding appropriately to the pain, guilt, and complications of such losses, adding to this edition extensive coverage of prolonged grief disorder anchored in recent research, and deducing from the literature and his own experience, guidelines for its treatment. In coverage of specialized interventions, it becomes evident that Jeffreys is equally at home with the psychotherapeutic promotion of forgiveness (of both self and other) and the recruitment of broader supports—sometimes in ritual form—for those most aggrieved by a particular loss. In this respect, this edition of the handbook struck me as equally relevant to the secular and spiritual helper, essentially assisting each to supplement her or his core disciplinary strengths with the complementary resources of other perspectives.

Finally, I would be remiss if I did not draw attention to the style that pervades much of the book. Alternately personal as well as professional, *Helping Grieving People* draws with equal comfort on the author's own rich trove of experience and on a range of contemporary theories that usefully inform our quest to understand bereavement and the needs of those subjected to it. This second edition of Jeffreys' best-seller is a work packed with plenty of practical pointers for professional helpers, and one that is guaranteed to sharpen one's skill as an "Exquisite Witness" to the anguish and achievements of those whose lives are touched by loss.

Robert A. Neimeyer, PhD
*Series Editor*
*University of Memphis, Tennessee*

# PREFACE TO THE SECOND EDITION

Five years have passed since the publication of the first edition, and my life has pulled and tugged and pushed and shoved.

I think of 34 years ago, just days after Steven had died of sarcoma, and a group of high school friends of our daughter Deborah were sitting on the floor of our family room in a circle, holding hands and singing. One boy looked over at her and said, "I'm going to find a cure for that cancer, Debbie." On July 7, 2010, a press release announced that a new clinical trial has had success in shrinking sarcoma tumors.* The principal investigator, Timothy Cripe, MD, PhD, Professor of Pediatrics, Cincinnati Children's Hospital Medical Center, is the boy who made that promise. He wrote to me saying, "My experience with your son set me on my current path and he has remained a rock of inspiration for me throughout the years."

One of the gratifying aspects of a traumatic loss is that it not be wasted. This revised edition of *Helping Grieving People* is a tribute not only to Steven but to the rest of our family as well, for it has been a family effort. Naomi Remen, MD,† said, "Every great loss demands that we 'choose life' again." We have, the four of us, been able to turn toward the suffering of others in our family, our community, and beyond via this book.

Although the basic goals of *Helping Grieving People* remains the same, much new research in support of additional understandings in the areas of cultural diversity, religiosity and healing, complicated grief, elder grief, forgiveness, and other clinical supports have been added. I have been gratified to learn that many academic instructors and staff development

---

* "Reprogrammed Herpes Virus Given Systemically Before Antivascular Drug Shrinks Distant Sarcomas," www.drugs.com (accessed July 7, 2010).
† Remen, N. (2000). *My Grandfather's Blessings* (p. 38). New York: Riverhead Books.

trainers have adopted the book as a training text. I was especially grateful to hear from a number of grieving people who informed me that the book enabled them to "know I'm not crazy!"

My wish is that you, the reader, regardless of your training level or purpose for reading this book:

- Will be increasingly mindful of your own personal loss material

- Will find comfort and satisfaction in knowing what to expect from grieving people

- Will know why grief is so natural and valuable—*it's what we humans do*

- Will have the confidence to offer your words, actions and comfortable presence to join them as an *Exquisite Witness* care provider "when tears are not enough"

# PREFACE TO THE FIRST EDITION

It was 1972. My wife and I would frequently remark, "Our cup runneth over." We had a wonderful marriage, three beautiful children, a new home, a new doctorate, and my recent promotion to head the state education department's program of pupil services—truly we were blessed.

The phone call came late one afternoon from my wife telling me that our pediatrician wanted to see us immediately. Our youngest, 5-year-old Steven, had viral pneumonia, and when it had run its course, a follow-up chest x-ray showed that the original dark patch on his lung had grown twice its size. I knew then that our lives would never be the same; and when the lymph node biopsy indicated lymphosarcoma, "our cup ran dry."

For 3 years we became part of the pediatric cancer subculture at Johns Hopkins Hospital. We learned about medications, radiation, and about their terrible, but necessary, side effects and those painful procedures. We learned and lived in the constant nightmarish fear of losing our child. Steven's sister and brother suffered during his illness and after his death from their own grief as well as from our unavailability.

When Steven took his last breath on Sunday night, November 23, 1975, we held him, talked to him, and some hours later, when his body had grown cold, we let go of him physically. We went home and the four of us bundled into bed, wept, and eventually slept.

Thus began a massive rewrite of our lives.

Five years later, as a practicing psychologist preparing a program for parents with children in the pediatric oncology service, I attended a weeklong residential workshop on life, death, and transition given by Elisabeth Kübler-Ross, MD. My unfinished grief emerged like underground waters coming to the surface.

I later became a member of Elisabeth's workshop and training staff. My general practice of psychology transitioned through the years to focus on increasing numbers of bereaved people and those coping with life-threatening and life-limiting medical conditions. In 1990, our family and a group of friends formed The Steven Daniel Jeffreys Foundation, Ltd. Its programs have included grief counseling, "Healing Through Loss" workshops, professional conferences, community education programs, and "Tears and Smiles"—bereavement groups for children and their parents.

In 1988, I began offering seminars and ongoing support groups for the staff of Johns Hopkins' AIDS Service and joined the psychiatry faculty of Johns Hopkins School of Medicine. My work also now includes teaching a course in loss and bereavement in the Pastoral Counseling Department of Loyola University in Maryland. The impetus for this book comes from the need for a resource handbook for my graduate students at Loyola College, the psychiatric residents at Johns Hopkins, and the many professional and volunteer providers and family caregivers who over the years have asked me, "What do I do to help grieving people?"

The effect of Steven's death on my life has moved me into an area that I would likely have never chosen. My work and this book are truly the gift of his loss. His loss makes the blessings we have in our life feel even more precious.

To that extent, "our cup runneth over" again.

# ACKNOWLEDGMENTS

Each of us comes to our own self-discovery through life events. I have had the blessing of not only a wonderful partner in my wife, Helane, who has shared the pain and joy of this life journey and has been at my side throughout the preparation of both editions of this entire project—thank you forever. Our children, Deborah and Ronald, have been an essential part of who we were and became as a family during and after our son Steven's 3-year illness and death.

For an incredible job of editing I am so happy to again thank Roberta Israeloff for her special understanding of this work and her wonderful talents. My deepest appreciation to Mary Cadden for her meticulous bibliographic citation expertise. Very special thanks to Dr. Ron Jeffreys for his medical review and suggestions in Chapter 8, and to both he and my daughter, Deborah Hurley, for their "siblings speak" memories. Thanks again to Patricia Wudel of Joseph House Hospice for the use of provider deathbed suggestions in Chapter 8. My appreciation to the staff of the Howard County Office of Aging (Maryland) for their continuing help.

A special thanks to Dana Bliss of Routledge, editor and friend, for his steady, supportive style of doing his job. Sincere appreciation to two additional members of the Routledge team: Chris Tominich, Senior Editorial Assistant, for excellent coordination of so many aspects of this project; and to Linda Leggio, Project Editor, whose rigorous copy editing is brilliant and instructive. Finally, my sincere appreciation goes to Professor Robert Neimeyer, colleague, friend, and teacher, who as the Routledge/Taylor & Francis Series Editor has encouraged me beyond that which I would have encouraged myself.

I would also like to acknowledge the education I have gained over the years from my private clinical clients, students in the Pastoral Counseling Department at Loyola University–Maryland, and the psychiatric residents who attend my seminars at the Johns Hopkins Department of Psychiatry and Behavioral Medicine. I also wish to thank the many bereaved parents I know at Bereaved Parents of the USA for their open sharing of pain.

My entry into this field of work was largely influenced by the late Elisabeth Kübler-Ross, MD, with whom I staffed over 12 years of workshops on life, death, and transition, and from whom I learned much about my own grief and how to help others heal from loss. I have no doubt that she already knows about this book and the continuation of her work by so many of her former staff members.

# HOW TO USE THIS BOOK

For many people, tears, prayers, loved ones, friends, and the passage of time will support their grief journey of healing through loss. This handbook is intended for professional care providers, trained volunteers, family caregivers, and caring friends who supply varying levels of help for grieving people—the bereaved, the dying, the chronically ill or disabled, and their families—when tears are not enough. During the 5 years that have elapsed since the first edition was published, I have been grateful to learn that many grieving people themselves have found this book useful for understanding their own reactions to loss or the threat of loss.

Starting with Chapter 1, we follow a pathway to understanding the three aspects of the *Exquisite Witness grief care provider*—the "heart" dimension (self-awareness), the "head" dimension (understanding the human grief response), and the "hands" dimension (supportive and clinical interventions).

The "heart" dimension is concerned with the care provider's own unfinished loss material. This is addressed with *self-awareness exercises* placed in the text as a mechanism to alert you to unfinished personal loss material—*Cowbells*. I ask you to take these seriously and complete them. They are not clinical assessment tools but rather exercises that can help to stimulate your thinking about your Cowbells. To further assist with the heart dimension, I suggest that you begin a diary or journal of physical and emotional reactions to the exercises and any memories that are triggered as you read and reflect. Talk to a trusted friend or colleague, spiritual advisor, or counselor. These reactions are like buried gold. Walking away from this book without examining your feelings can limit the value of the work you can do for grieving people—or for yourself.

The "head" dimension, which is concerned with the understanding of what the complexities of human grief are, is contained in each of the chapters of this book. In Chapter 2, we review the cultural and social impact on how people grieve and the death-related rituals they use. This is followed by a review of theories and explanations of human grief in Chapter 3. The role of family in the shaping and healing of human grief follows in Chapter 4. The unique needs of three populations of grievers—children, parents, and older adults—are given special attention in Chapters 5, 6, and 7, respectively. Chapter 8 is devoted to an understanding of the dying, chronically and terminally ill, and their families.

The "hands" dimension is concerned with care provider interventions. Look for recommendations that have been placed in *Care Provider Boxes* at the end of didactic material in the text. These represent general suggestions regarding a particular issue and should be modified to fit the unique needs of an individual or family. This dimension is further elaborated in Chapter 9, where we consider a continuum of supportive and clinical strategies for family caregivers, volunteers, and professional care providers. Chapter 10 reviews complicated grief syndromes as well as associated psychiatric disorders, and includes suggestions for the professional care provider following each description of complicated grief syndrome.

In Chapter 11, by way of reviewing the learning experience of readers, seven case studies are presented. Five of the cases are provided with recommendations for initial interventions and two cases have the recommendations omitted for the reader to address.

The Epilogue contains a story about people who help others, and who "don't turn their eyes away." It is also a time for saying "good-bye, for now."

Appendix A is a list of organizational resources, and Appendix B is a model of an advance medical directive discussed in Chapter 8.

This is a book to be read with a pen or pencil in hand so you can respond to the personal exercises and record some reactions and memories in a journal. This can be incredibly helpful.

Bon voyage.

CHAPTER

# The Exquisite Witness
# Grief Care Provider

When you go through the tumbler of life, you can come out crushed or polished.*

Elisabeth Kübler-Ross (1981)

## ☐ Chapter Preview

- You Never Know …

- Yet You Can Become …

- The *Exquisite Witness* Defined

- The *Heart, Head,* and *Hands* Dimensions Defined

- Cowbells

- Summary

---

* *Kübler-Ross, Elisabeth. (1981). "Death, Transition Workshop," Richmond, VA.

# ☐ You Never Know ...

What is going on inside someone else's mind—the person walking by you on the street, standing behind you at the checkout stand, waiting at the stop light in the car next to you, smiling hello as you enter the elevator, serving you coffee or sitting across the aisle in the commuter train— what he or she is thinking.

How much pain or rage is tearing at a person's heart or how much a grieving individual is struggling just to make it through another day at work.

Who or what a person has lost and how much that man, woman, or child is obsessing about the loss every waking minute of the day.

How much grief and anguish is being held inside or with how much longing that person wishes that it were just a bad dream.

What else may surface when you are helping a grieving person.

Which of your own losses will be triggered when you help grieving people through their grief and how this may affect your ability to help.

What another's pain is like even if the loss seems just like your own.

How unprepared you can feel as a provider until you experience the sense of "I don't know what to say or do right now."

How truly prepared you are until you relate to the grieving person more as a human soul in pain and less as a diagnosis or the object of a particular clinical skill to be used.

# ☐ Yet You Can Become ...

One human soul sitting with another who is suffering the pain of grief.

A care provider who understands that the grief journey is different for each individual.

A care provider who is sensitive to different cultural and religious/ spiritual backgrounds, and understands that your function is to support the journey and not control it.

A care provider who embraces the "heart, head, and hands" system for providing care.

A care provider who, as an Exquisite Witness for a grieving person— whether you are a trained professional, volunteer, or a family caregiver— provides what so many grieving people hope for.

The goal of this book is to point the way for grief care providers to learn how to become such an Exquisite Witness.

# ☐  The *Exquisite Witness* Defined

The *Exquisite Witness* is a health care, pastoral, or volunteer care provider who enters the sacred space between two human souls—having the deepest respect for the yearning, seeking, and wishful hopes of the other to diminish pain and survive in a new world after a loss.

The term *Exquisite Witness* encompasses my beliefs regarding the role of anyone who steps forward to help a grieving person. A medical or mental health professional; teacher; funeral director; fire, police, or rescue personnel; employee assistance counselor; medical receptionist; or family member who becomes the home caregiver can assume this role. An Exquisite Witness might be a friend, someone from the faith community who comes to visit the family, or the surgeon who stops by the recovery room after removing a tumor and then proceeds to reassure the waiting loved ones. What distinguishes an Exquisite Witness is not one's level of training but one's willingness to approach another human being with compassion and deep respect for that person's needs, fear, and grief.

The exquisite nature of the interaction is measured in terms of respect, care, honesty, and the ability to truly hear and understand the grieving person's anger and confusion. It may take very little time. A gifted psychiatrist whom I accompanied on rounds for medically ill patients at The Johns Hopkins Hospital was able, during a 10-minute conversation, to answer patients' concerns and make them feel cared for, respected, and hopeful. I have also seen a member of the housekeeping staff on an inpatient AIDS unit calm an agitated patient with a smile and casual conversation about the Baltimore Orioles' lineup.

The term *witness* directs the care provider to understand that the grief journey belongs to the grieving person—whether he or she has lost a loved one, has a chronic or terminal illness, has been admitted to the hospital for tests, has a loved one who is ill or dying, or has new job responsibilities in a reorganized workplace. As a witness, we *observe more than act, listen more than talk, and follow more than lead.* Witnessing celebrates the dignity and authority of the grieving person.

## Characteristics of the Exquisite Witness …

Has a commitment to self and is attuned to stored personal loss material. Such a care provider can, therefore, accompany grieving people into painful places on their journey, confident in knowing where his or her limitations in professional and personal availability are. This care provider also knows how to access the professional and spiritual resources available for personal growth.

Is more than a good listener, more than knowledgeable, and more than a skilled intervener. This care provider can join with a person deeply in grief and is generous with time and energy.

Draws from personal life experience to join with grieving people; whose own grief is healed in part through service to others—a "wounded healer."

Has a comfortable command of the psychological and sociological phenomena of human grief and its varied and changing forms.

Has a repertoire of intervention skills, including exquisite listening, to facilitate the healing of grieving people.

Has a commitment to a religious/spiritual pathway or personal growth journey that provides continued resources, emotional health, personal growth, and professional development.

Is not simply a matter of "This is what I do because this is what I have trained to do," but rather "This is what I do because this is part of the meaning of who I am and how I choose to live."

## ☐ The *Heart, Head,* and *Hands* Dimensions Defined

An Exquisite Witness must address personal loss issues (the heart dimension), is knowledgeable about what to expect from grieving people (the head dimension), and has the skills to respond both usefully and reassuringly (the hands dimension).

### The "Heart" Dimension

> [N]othing can be written about ministry without a deeper understanding of the ways which the minister can make his own wounds available as a source of healing.*

The "heart" dimension represents the process whereby old loss material may rise to the surface and interfere with the ability of a care provider to be available to a grieving person. This recall may be triggered by

---

* Nouwen, Henri J. M. (1972). *The Wounded Healer* (p. xvi). New York: Doubleday.

## COWBELLS

*Cowbells*—The way unfinished business is stored and its subsequent effects on a provider's own grief experience is illustrated by the following personal story.

When I was 4 years old, I attended a preschool program in a community center just across the street from where my family lived. Each morning the children would line up and get a tablespoon of cod liver oil—all from the same spoon! After some indoor games, we were sent outside to the playground. This was an area with a chain-link fence separating us from the sidewalk and the street beyond. I could see our building and as soon as we got outside, I would run directly to the fence, stick my little fingers and nose through the fence, and look longingly, yearningly toward my home. The image of my mommy was clearly in my mind, and I missed her and ached to be back with her.

At that same time every day, a junkman with a pushcart filled with old clothes and items he had been collecting came by ringing a cowbell roped to the handlebar of the cart to announce his presence in the neighborhood. The sound of that cowbell and my yearning, grieving feelings became connected.

Throughout my life when I have had aching, grieving feelings come up, the look on my face prompts my wife to ask, Cowbells? And I answer, Cowbells. Throughout the years, a symphony of Cowbells has rung out. Every one of us has our Cowbells. They accompany us to the bedside of every patient, to our interactions with counseling or pastoral clients, to parishioners, to staff meetings, to treatment planning, and to every human contact we engage in. As care providers, it is our responsibility to be sufficiently aware of them so that our own Cowbells do not drown out our clients. *Ask not for whom the Cowbells toll; they toll for thee ... and me!*

Personal self-awareness exercises are provided throughout this book to assist with discovering the reader's Cowbells and should be a regular part of all provider training and in-service education. Professional health and pastoral care providers are also advised that surfacing personal Cowbells can be a valuable means for informing their counseling, therapy, and spiritual guidance with grieving people. (For a detailed discussion of countertransference responses in end-of-life and bereavement care, see Katz & Johnson, 2006; Nouwen, 1972.)

circumstances of the case that are similar to the care provider's current or earlier life grief experiences.

When professional or volunteer care providers do not identify their own personal loss issues, they may consciously or unconsciously avoid areas of interaction that could have been of help to the grieving person. As human beings who attach and bond, we all have loss material, and the grieving person we are working with may trigger some unfinished grief. *No one is untouched.*

The nurse or physician who avoids a particular patient's room, a caseworker who limits the depth of information seeking, a counselor who keeps the conversation at a superficial level, or a hospice volunteer who becomes overly involved with one family may be dealing with old, unfinished loss material.

To be truly available to grieving people, care providers must examine their own unresolved loss and grief. This is the heart dimension of the Exquisite Witness care providing.

## The "Head" Dimension

The "head" dimension refers to knowledge of the phenomenon we know as grief; including its many subcategories as well as its dynamic shifts and changes over time. This includes understanding the biological and instinctual basis for grief reactions, the expected feelings and thoughts of grieving as well as behaviors derived from our social environment over time.

Providers also need to appreciate both the traditional and more recent explanations regarding the nature of grief and its predictable patterns. Knowing what can be expected from grieving people will not only enable care providers to give the highest level of service but will also increase provider comfort.

## The "Hands" Dimension

The "hands" dimension represents what the care provider says and does to help the grieving person engage in the process of mourning in the healthiest way possible. It includes the way providers interact, gather information, make decisions and suggestions, and gauge the level of appropriate intervention. Many grieving people in my clinical practice simply want to tell their story to someone who won't interrupt them, look at their watch, or change the subject. A grieving person may need to be heard over and over again without receiving any advice, interpretations, or words of wisdom.

As discussed in Chapter 3, the telling and retelling of the story of a grieving person's loss is an important part of his or her healing. In this context, the provider agrees to be a nonjudgmental Exquisite Witness. It is more than being a skilled listener. It means hearing with the heart and knowing that you, the Exquisite Witness care provider, are engaged in a healing process with another human being and can feel the joy of this healing. When people share their pain and fears, we are on sacred ground.

## ☐ Summary

The "heart," "head," and "hands" dimensions direct the Exquisite Witness to know his or her own grief issues, to understand the human grief response and its variations, and to have a repertoire of support and clinical skills to use for helping grieving people.

When Adam and Eve were sent from the Garden of Eden, they were informed that a gift awaited them outside. They wept and wept as they looked back at the sealed gates and were aware after their weeping subsided that they felt comforted. This was their gift—the tears of healing.

But sometimes tears are not enough.

That's when grieving people need you.

# The Social–Cultural Influence on Grief Experience

We are all tattooed in our cradles with the beliefs of our tribe.

Oliver Wendell Holmes, Sr. (as cited in Fenchuk, 1994, p. 2)

## ☐ Chapter Preview

- Introduction

- The Humanness of Avoiding Grief

- Statistical Realities of Death and Illness

- Cultural Legacies and Societal Values Affecting Grief

- Cultural Diversity and Cultural Competence

- Religion/Spirituality and Healing Grief

- Death-Related Rituals: Funerals, Memorials, Burials

- Conclusion

# ☐ Introduction

> Life changes fast. Life changes in the ordinary instant. You sit down to dinner and life as you know it ends.
>
> Joan Didion (2006, p. 3)

Many factors affect the nature of each individual's grief reaction. The purpose of this chapter is to give the care provider a sense of the social and cultural environments in which grieving people live, and to convey the importance of respecting their diverse legacies. Everybody grieves: old and young, incarcerated and free, religious people and nonbelievers, both foreign- and native-born, rich and poor. Death and traumatic loss are part of being alive, and as we shall see, not wanting to talk about it is a common human trait.

How do we develop our concept of dying and death? At what point in our development does the notion of death enter our realm of knowledge about life and the world we live in? Whatever bits and pieces of sights, sounds, smells, and bodily feelings we internalize and store may surge forward into consciousness when triggered by a new traumatic loss experience. Sometimes we recall a memory and its associated feelings, but sometimes we experience an old grief feeling without a connected memory, and it ends up merging with our current grief reaction.

## Death as Entertainment: Effects of the Media on the Formation of Death and Dying Attitudes

Children and adults are exposed to and affected by references to scenes of dying and death in stories, news reports, advertisements, cartoons, movies, TV nature shows, violent electronic war games, religious settings, and the visual arts. Daily, the media bombards us with images depicting the horror of large-scale natural disasters, terrorist threats and violence, and military actions, as well as regaling us with the stories of the deaths of well-known entertainment and political figures. Our reactions to this media barrage of stories about loss and grief add to what we know about death and dying from our society and culture. We differ and are similar in the ways we express and cope with loss depending on the ways these impressions affect us.

We usually associate grief with death and the loss of loved ones. But grief comes from many causes other than illness, death, and the process of dying. Traumatic changes—loss of employment, financial security, and sense of well-being—create additional deathlike losses for millions of people.

## ☐ The Humanness of Avoiding Grief

Avoiding grief amounts to avoiding the words, sounds, or sights that conjure up the idea of loss. We will discuss the natural origin and important function of the human grief response in the next chapter. However, there is an almost reflexive natural reaction that causes so many of us to withdraw from and run the other way from human suffering. The goal of this book is to enable those who help grieving people to turn toward that suffering—through emotional availability, knowledge, and skill. We will now look at the way Western cultures use avoidance or denial as a response to death, dying, and loss.

In Western society, we frequently hear people talking about death, injury, and loss with a twist of humor. This enables us to release some of the tension we feel about this topic by laughing. Death, loss, and aging supply material for many stand-up comics, newspaper comic strips, and situation comedies. We often use humor to soften, cover up, and avoid facing the full impact that acknowledgment of our own mortality and that of our loved ones has in our lives. Search for the phrase *death jokes* on the Internet, you will find thousands of jokes from a variety of Web sites. We see further evidence of our need to avoid the unpleasant reality of death by the wealth of euphemisms we use to refer to it. We say "we lost" someone, or they "kicked the bucket," "bought the farm," "bit the dust," "are pushing up daisies." When we can poke fun at mortality, we can almost feel some small degree of control over its possibility. This can comfort speakers and listeners alike. I still chuckle when I recall George Carlin's crack that he never says he's growing old, he says he's growing *older*. He might have more time that way!

Another way to keep the painful reality of death and loss away is to simply not talk about it or avoid the subject. For example, we don't visit the neighbor who is in hospice care, we don't attend the funeral or burial, we cut short the visit to a bereaved relative, we put off spending time with a dying patient, or we don't provide a counseling client with the opportunity to talk about old losses. These are very human behaviors and do not make a person wrong or bad. They can, however, limit a grief care provider's availability to the grieving person. The Exquisite Witness care provider (see Chapter 1) helps us learn how to turn toward the suffering.

I have heard the following ancient Persian folk tale in many different versions. It illustrates the very human need to run away from suffering and death.

> A wealthy prince was preparing for a magnificent banquet and sent a servant out into the garden to gather flowers for the tables. When the young man entered the garden he shrieked with horror for there stood Death. It raised its hands. He raced back into the palace and begged his master to save him from Death. The prince said, "Run to the stables and take my fastest horse and flee to Damascus. It is very far from this place, you will be safe there!" The prince watched as the servant boy ran to the stables and quickly emerged on a fine racing horse. He soon disappeared in a cloud of dust toward Damascus. The prince angrily strode into the garden where Death stood with its hands still raised and demanded, "How dare you enter my grounds and frighten my servant?" "But Sire," Death replied, "I was only expressing my surprise at seeing him here, for you see I have an appointment with him tonight— in Damascus."

No matter how far we run away from the inevitability of death and other life changes and losses, we cannot outrun them. They occur every day, to all of us. (See Table 2.1.)

# Avoiding Grief

We need our denial system to allow ourselves time to get used to the idea that the loss is irreversible, that the biopsy is malignant, that the company has been taken over, or that life as we have known it will never be the same. *Denial* is present when patients and doctors avoid talking about the gravity of an illness; when family does not want the loved one to know how serious things are; or when talking about death, grief, and painful change is simply avoided. It is important to note that some avoidance and use of humor are actually healthy responses to loss. Denial is the shock absorber for painful loss and crisis; it allows us to digest the agonizing truth in small bits. But the question remains: How much denial is healthy?

Some writers have labeled us a "death-denying society," which is simply saying that we are humans and it is human to avoid pain. Who wants pain? No one does. As care providers, we must respect the rights of a grieving person, family, or a workplace group to formulate some form of a denial system. However, denial can be problematic when there is failure to (a) get medical attention, (b) take needed health or safety precautions, (c) make necessary legal arrangements, (d) follow medical advice, or (e) maintain vigilance against suicidal or other harmful behaviors.

TABLE 2.1.  U.S. Total All Causes of Death—2008: <u>2,472,699</u>

(Past Total Deaths:  2002 = 2,447,862;  2006: 2,426,264)

| Total Children Deaths | 2001 | 2002 | 2006 |
|---|---|---|---|
| Under 1 | 27,568 | 27,977 | 28,527 |
| 1–4 | 5,107 | 4,862 | 4,631 |
| 5–14 | 7,095 | 7,169 | 6,149 |
| 15–24 | <u>32,252</u> | <u>33,075</u> | <u>34,887</u> |
| Total | 72,022 | 73,083 | 74,194 |

| Type of Death | 2001 | 2002 | 2006 | 2008 |
|---|---|---|---|---|
| Cardiovascular | 700,141 | 695,754 | 631,636 | 617,527 |
| Cancer | 553,768 | 558,847 | 559,888 | 566,137 |
| Cerebrovascular | 163,538 | 163,010 | 137,119 | 133,750 |
| Pulmonary | 123,013 | 125,500 | 124,583 | 141,075 |
| All accidents | 101,537 | 102,303 | 121,599 | 121,207 |
| Diabetes mellitus | 71,372 | 73,119 | 72,449 | 70,601 |
| Alzheimer's | 53,852 | 58,785 | 72,432 | 82,476 |
| Flu and pneumonia | | | 56,326 | 56,335 |
| Motor vehicle | | 41,804 | — | |
| Kidney disease | | | 45,344 | 48,282 |
| Septicemia | 34,234 | | | 35,961 |
| Liver disease | | 27,555 | | 29,963 |
| Suicide | | 30,646 | 33,300 | 35,933 |
| Hypertension | | | | 25,823 |

*(Continued)*

TABLE 2.1. (Continued)  U.S. Total All Causes of Death: 2008: 2,472,699

| Type of Death | 2001 | 2002 | 2006 | 2008 |
|---|---|---|---|---|
| Parkinson's | | | | 20,507 |
| Homicide | 20,308[a] | 17,045 | 18,573 | 17,837 |
| All other causes | | | 469,284 | |

Source: U.S. Centers for Disease Control and Prevention, National Vital Statistics
    Reports: 2001, 2003, 2004, 2006, 2010.
[a] Includes deaths from September 11, 2001.

If a person does not want to "talk about it" or even have a conversation about advance directives, these wishes need to be respected. Sensitive caregivers will gently reintroduce the topic during a later conversation. For many in our society, especially health care providers, death represents failure and defeat. It yields guilt and self-reproach as part of the grief response. It is easier simply not to talk about it, distract ourselves, and get to it later. Some people hold on to the hope that a very sick or dying person is going to be okay in spite of medical information to the contrary and the obvious worsening of the patient's condition.

In a family where a man was rapidly losing ground to cancer, his wife and children were able to continually adjust their expectations about his level of participation in family activities. Yet his own parents and siblings steadily maintained that he would be fine and that there was no cause for concern. The unfortunate result of this strong resistance to the reality of the man's medical condition was that his wife and children received little or no support from those relatives. The lack of support left this family with continuing major conflicts in the aftermath of this man's death.

In another case, the family was very aware of the rapid deterioration and it was the patient who was in denial.

A man with advanced cancer came to see me. He was very optimistic about a new chemotherapy treatment his doctor had told him about. His weight had recently dropped drastically, but he remained confident he would be much better after the new treatment began. His wife privately informed me that he was unrealistically positive and had no chance of surviving even if he was able to tolerate the new chemotherapy. She was unable to get him to have a conversation about advance directives in the event that he would not benefit from the new chemotherapy.

The man came to see me two more times and resisted any discussion of any possibilities other than remission. Before he was able to keep his next appointment, he was hospitalized. When I visited him, he told me that he and the doctor had agreed that the new chemotherapy would not be useful and he was not going to have any more treatment. He returned home and continued to avoid any discussion of dying or saying good-bye. A short time later, he simply lay down in bed and within an hour he died. This man remained true to his desire to leave life on his own terms. However, the family was left feeling very sad that they hadn't had any conversations with him at the end of life.

## Denial of Survivors

People who lose a loved one require their own timing as to when and to what extent they accept that the deceased is gone and is not coming back. It is not unusual for a family member to return home after the burial and pick up a ringing phone with the hope that it "might be Mom." "But we just buried Mom!" the person says to himself, only to think, "I know, I just thought maybe it was a mistake." This is not crazy or unusual. The head knows, but the heart is not ready to let go yet.

Holding on to that which has been lost may take the form of keeping the room, house, clothing, and other personal effects exactly as they had been. Denial of the terrible truth is what many grieving people do. We think, "She's just on a long trip" or "He's still away at school." Adults as well as children can engage in "magical thinking," and it serves a useful function by buffering the painful reality. In her book, *The Year of Magical Thinking* (2006), Joan Didion describes her attempt to make the death of her husband to not have happened. She relates how she repeatedly reconstructed the events seeking to find a flaw or mistake so she could have him back.

Repeatedly reviewing the death or other loss is a way people strive to make some sense of what happened. If the circumstances of the loss are ambiguous (e.g., when no body has been recovered), as in war, explosions, earthquakes, mudslides, tsunamis, and air and sea disasters, the denial may last a lifetime. The lack of a physical body and the inability to know that life has truly ceased for the loved one leaves survivors with an eternal question that may never be answered.

## Denial: A Personal Story

During the early months of my son Steven's cancer treatment, Elisabeth Kübler-Ross came to my hometown to give a lecture. Our friends all bought her book, *On Death and Dying* (1969) and went to hear her. I did not go. I did not need to go and hear the "death lecture" because Steven was going to get well. We would get him into remission and keep him there until he was clear of cancer. As each recurrence of the disease shattered hopes and plunged us into new panic, I would obtain the new statistics and hold onto the percentage for survival. I did the same when the odds dropped to 1%. Even on the day he died, I hoped that another blood transfusion would create a miracle.

I needed that denial to continue my role in the family and in my work, and so I could continue to care for and emotionally support Steven each day. Denial did not end even after the funeral and burial had taken place. I was in such great denial that I needed help from any outside source to express the grief that was locked up within me. Five years later, however, at a Kübler-Ross grief workshop, I exploded with the grief I had stored not only from Steven's illness and death but also the old grief related to the sudden death of my mother when I was 16. I worked to release my pain, anger, and fear of losing anyone else. This eventually restored my energy so that I could begin to reclaim life in the strange new world without Steven.

Some denial and humor are necessary responses to loss. We need our denial to allow us time to get used to the idea that our loved one is gone forever, that the lump is malignant, the business is bankrupt, the economic disaster has reached into our lives, or that our prayers were not answered. It's what we humans do.

## ☐ Statistical Realities of Death and Illness

In spite of how fast and how far we physically or psychologically flee from the troubling reality of our own mortality and that of loved ones, the fact is that over 2,400,000 Americans die annually. See Table 2.1 for the U.S. Centers for Disease Control and Prevention's National Vital Statistics Report (Heron et al., 2009) of selected causes and totals of deaths registered in the United States for 2010. The data have been drawn from several issues of National Vital Statistics Reports (Heron et al., 2009; National Center for Health Statistics, 2001). Based on 2,400,000 annual deaths for all causes and estimating five bereaved relatives or close friends per death, we can expect about 12 million or more people will join the ranks of the existing bereaved. Within this group, about 145,000 will be parents who lost a child. Additionally, over 1,700,000 people die annually of illnesses lasting for months or even years, resulting in ongoing grief reactions of the family before the final death. Sadly, the statistics reflect the ongoing realities of loss due to illness and death. No amount of denial or magical thinking can change this.

# ☐ Cultural Legacies and Societal Values Affecting Grief

Over the ages and across cultures, spiritual beliefs and practices have anchored and nourished families and their communities at times of death and loss.

Froma Walsh (2004, p. 182)

Myths, culture, beliefs and thoughts from the past "line the walls of our interior system of belief, like shards of broken pottery in an archeological site."

Joseph Campbell (1988, p. xiv)

Broad norms regarding how we generally think, feel, and behave regarding death, loss, and serious illness spread from the culture of mainstream society via educational and other institutions—media, literature, films, and theater—to families and individuals. These attitudes and practices may be blended or modified by the attitudes and practices of the diversity of religious and ethnic subcultures within society.

## Death Happens

Death is a natural part of human life. Through the ages, every society has shaped various cultural behaviors to acknowledge and celebrate the death of one of its members. "We are not born with our attitudes toward dying and bereavement, the way we are born with our needs for food, drink and sex" (Morgan, 1995, p. 25). We learn these attitudes from the cultural legacies and societal value systems into which we are born. Religious belief systems typically have a set of customary activities—chants, prayers, dance, and ceremonial items—related to the death event. Burial sites, tools, and the artwork of human cultures as far back as the Ice Age have revealed the variety of human beliefs regarding death and dealing with our bodies when we are no longer alive. This awareness of death and the expectation of a transition to some other existence are shown in the preserved items found in the ground, in caves, and in the drawings and writings of earlier civilizations.

The rites and practices surrounding death in our society are largely associated with a religious belief system, although military and other organizational rituals, from fire and police departments, unions, and fraternal societies, for example, may also be a part of the ceremony. Many religions also specify appropriate family practices during the period of active dying, at the time of death, and following death. Varying beliefs in an afterlife are presented in tribal theologies as well as in the more widely practiced faiths of today.

Each civilization provides for this natural part of life. Although the behavior of mourners is affected by their particular religion or other cultural influences, the outcome of living is the same—death happens.

## Grief Happens

When death happens, grief happens. But grief does not wait for death or some other loss event to happen in order to make its entrance. Grief gets an early start. It will very likely occur as soon as we form an image of the death or other loss that *could* happen. Further, grief is an equal opportunity human condition; grief affects everyone. However, *there is no one right way to grieve.* Although there are many similarities in grieving behaviors, individuals show their grief in many different ways. It is also true that grief does not appear only in the face of death or the threat of death. We can have a grief response for losses other than loss of life. Many of these losses have a death-like quality (aging, disability, workplace change, separation and divorce, and financial crises).

Here is a personal story relating how I became increasingly aware that aging was a loss issue for me.

> When I reached the age of 60, I felt an irresistible need to scan the obituary columns every day. What was I looking for? My students typically answer this question with "Your name?" or "People you know?" What I actually find myself drawn to are the ages of the people who died. When I read about people who died in their 60s, I quickly turn the page and keep looking. When I read about people who die in their late 90s, I say, "I'll take that one!"

We live in a society that places a very high value on youth, physical fitness, sexual attractiveness, and affluence. The shifting pictures of ourselves as well as the physical, mental, social, and financial limitations of aging, are specific and highly visible reminders of how we once were and how we have now changed. For a long time I could beat my son at racquetball. Eventually, we were evenly matched. Too soon the time came when I barely offered him competition. We recently shared a chuckle when my son found that he could no longer beat his daughter at tennis.

As we age, we may be faced with the death of a spouse, siblings, or other contemporaries; changes in work status; and altered family roles resulting in a massive list of losses with which the older adult members of our society must cope. Staying alive guarantees multiple losses and grief—grief happens.

To help get a sense of the many faces of loss in each of our lives, please complete the following exercise. Use a separate sheet of paper if desired.

### EXERCISE 1: WHAT DO WE LOSE?

Take a moment to list five types of losses other than death or serious illness—such as house fire, divorce, workplace change, relocation, relocation of a friend, financial crisis, rejection by a friend, job loss, being turned down from a job or school—that triggered a grief reaction in you or someone else you know.

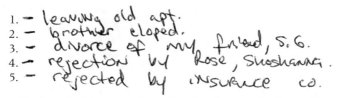

1. — leaving old apt.
2. — brother eloped.
3. — divorce of my friend, S.G.
4. — rejection by Rose, Shoshanna.
5. — rejected by insurance co.

Review the losses you have listed and note which would seem minor and which have more significant consequences. The traumatic loss experienced by a grieving person will occur against a background of many other losses. Even the flow of time that brings expected changes contains the potential for grief. I call this "passage of time grief."

People already grieving become painfully aware of the additional transitional loss factors going on in their lives. Additionally, they may also have financial, occupational, academic, and relational losses occurring at the same time as the primary loss. These other losses can each generate their own grief response adding to the intensity of the current grief reaction.

## Change = Loss = Grief

As we will see in greater detail in Chapter 3, any change can make us feel a sense of loss with a resulting grief reaction—even desired change. The reality is that things are always changing; we are constantly connecting to people, places, roles, and routines and having to let go of some of them at some point. When attachments we have made are lost or threatened, the result, for most people, is the pain of grief. There is no way around it. This is how it is for human beings: *Change = Loss = Grief.* Whenever there is change there is loss and when there is loss there is a grief reaction (Jeffreys, 2005).

Remarkably, although death and other traumatic losses are inextricably bound up with human existence, they continue to be taboo topics in much of Western society. Despite the growth of the death education and grief counseling fields, the enormous increase in self-help books dealing with the subject, and the growth of hospice and palliative medical care programs, we still do not want to talk about it. The view of death as a "failure by those who give care" (Sakalauskas, 1992, p. 84) and grief as a subject to be avoided exists in all components of society—schools, government, hospitals, religious institutions, and families.

The goal of this book is to ask and answer the question of how we can learn to turn toward the suffering when the rest of the world is running the other way. In the same way that societal values impact on our reactions to loss, religious, and family values substantially shape how we think and feel about life and death, loss, and grief. It is also important to note that those who serve as care providers for individuals and families who are grieving also bring with them their own personal histories, and cultural and family influences regarding death and dying.

Looking closely at the nature of the effects of various cultural and family traditions on grief reactions, we see that these can be classified. Kroeber and Kluckhohn (1952) think of culture as providing influences via traditional rituals, roles, problem-solving means, shared ideas, and organizations within the culture. These categories of influence are also found in societal subcultures that cut across ethnocultural lines: institutions (schools, hospitals), workplaces, age subgroups (older adult, young adult), types of loss (parental and spousal grief groups), and worship communities. The nature of an individual's grief will be influenced by his or her membership in various cultures and location in subcultural grids. These various cultural structures serve as containers for human grief.

As Exquisite Witness mental health and medical care providers, clergy, hospice volunteers, support group facilitators, employee assistance and human resources personnel, and any other person stepping up to help grieving people, we must be aware of cultural and family differences in order to be able to connect with and be trusted by those grieving. This is what is meant by *cultural competence.*

## ☐ Cultural Diversity and Cultural Competence

As a result of profound worldwide demographic change, grief care providers will increasingly care for people from cultural backgrounds other than their own (Crawley, Marshall, Bernard, & Koenig, 2002). Although cultural ties provide a source of comfort for families with a dying loved one, these differences in attitudes and custom that do not match traditional health care practice can create conflicts between provider and clients. For example, there was the case of a dying Spanish-speaking woman who seemingly was nodding in approval of what her physician was telling her. However, the physician learned later from the interpreter that she was actually nodding out of respect for him but disagreed with what he was saying (Crawley et al., 2002, p. 673). Attention to and knowledge of cultural differences are necessary to provide compassionate care for persons at end of life as well as for bereaved individuals.

"Serving dying and bereaved people from other races and creeds provides us with the privilege of learning from them" (Parkes, Laungani, & Young, 1997, p. 7). Bowlby (1980) views the value of understanding cross-cultural grief reactions as vital to providing help. As culturally competent care providers, we must grasp the importance of knowing and respecting a family's cultural heritage, mourning rituals, and customs for expressing feelings. *Cultural malpractice* has been defined as the lack of knowledge and sensitivity regarding client cultural variations by professionals (Hall, 1997). The variations affect not only death-related rituals, but also the way that family members communicate with each other and with others outside of the family about their loss and feelings of grief. For example, in some Asian cultures, medical and other healthcare providers may need to speak to family members rather than the patient. Grief care providers must be alert to such cultural diversity in the people they are serving.

In some families and ethnic traditions, talking about the deceased is typically not done. In my practice, for example, I saw a young Middle Eastern man whose father had been accidentally killed. The family was devastated. However, because he shared with me that in his family's tradition, feelings about the loss of a loved one were not discussed openly, I was unable to work with the whole family and help them to support each other by listening to each other's grief. He sought grief counseling because he had no one else with whom to talk about his father and his feelings. I became his only support until we were able to locate a person in his faith community who could also help him with appropriate rituals. Care providers must be "cautious when relating to people from other ethnic backgrounds than their own, avoiding any advance presumption of what an appropriate response, diagnosis, or treatment might be" (Irish, 1993, p. 10).

A report by the National Alliance for Caregiving indicates that "racial and ethnic minority populations are projected to represent 25.4% of the elderly population in 2030, up from 16.4% in 2000" (Talamantes &

Aranda, 2004). As our communities become increasingly multicultural, it is vital that care providers have a good grounding in the unique features of the grieving person's culture. How we view and respond to a family of one tradition may be vastly different from a family from another tradition (Klass, 1999). Further, studies show that when clients felt a therapist was not aware of their culture and the issues they confront as members of a minority population, the clients viewed the assistance as not responsive to their needs (Bloombaum, Yamamoto, & James, 1968; Nickerson, Helms, & Terrell, 1994; Sue & Sue, 2003). Other studies find significant differences in the way people of a number of nationalities respond to loss (Klass, 1999). What one culture's tradition considers an extreme grief reaction may be quite normal in another. "Grief is expressed so differently from culture to culture that it is absurd to use notions of pathology from one culture to evaluate people from another" (Rosenblatt, 1993, p. 18). It is impossible to include the multitude of cultural variations in one volume. The American Psychological Association's Diversity Guidelines (2003) state that care providers must be responsible and ethical in (a) recognizing cultural diversity, (b) understanding the role that culture and ethnicity/ race play with individuals and groups, and (c) understanding the socioeconomic and political factors that impact these groups. Diversity is not only a social issue but is a professional issue as well (Hall, 1997; Sue & Sue, 2003).

The Spiritual Care Work Group of the International Work Group on Death, Dying, and Bereavement (1990) has developed a series of principles and assumptions regarding the care provider, and the grieving individual and family. Several of these, which provide specific direction to providers with regard to cultural diversity concerns of grieving people, are presented next.

Care providers must seek information about and be sensitive to the cultural and/or family traditions of populations they serve and adjust care efforts accordingly. This information can be gathered casually by observing and asking questions of the family and friends, by contacting a colleague who has experience with a particular ethnic group, by speaking to a spiritual leader or elder of the family's religious community, or by reviewing the literature on cultural diversity.

# Principles and Assumptions Regarding Cultural Diversity

- Caregivers working with dying and bereaved persons should be sensitive to the interrelationships among the spiritual, mental, emotional, and physical aspects of the grief reaction.

- Caregivers should be clear that in a culturally diverse society no single approach to spiritual care is satisfactory for all.

- Caregivers must be sensitive to multicultural differences as well as to the individual's particular interpretation of them.

- Caregivers must be sensitive to the divergent spiritual insights and beliefs that an individual and the family may have.

- Caregivers must be aware that spiritual needs and concerns may change over the course of terminal illness or bereavement.

- No one caregiver should be expected to understand or address the entire spiritual concerns of individuals and families.

**Note:** The Spiritual Care Work Group uses the term *caregiver* in the same way that *care provider* is used in this book.

# ☐ Religion/Spirituality and Healing Grief

Yea, though I walk through the valley of the shadow of death, I shall fear no evil for Thou art with me.

**Psalm 23:4 (King James Version)**

Scientific studies of religion point to persuasive documentation of the positive relationship between religious involvement and physical and mental health outcomes.

**Doug Oman and Carl E. Thorensen (2005, p. 435)**

Overall, results suggest that relations between religion and adjustment to bereavement are generally positive but inconsistent and vary depending in part on how religion/spirituality is measured.

**Jennifer H. Wortmann and Crystal L. Park (2008, p. 734)**

Attempts to relate religiosity to level of adjustment to loss must be based on more than attendance at religious observances or identification with a particular spiritual or faith pathway. Religion and spirituality must be measured on many specific dimensions (attendance, affiliation, spirituality, belief in afterlife, and religious social support) as these each affect grieving people differently (Pargament, 2002; Wortmann & Park, 2008).

Care providers must have a sense of the wide variation of beliefs as well as the differences across age groups and other subsets within specific religious denominations. A cross-cultural CBS news poll taken in 2006 indicated that 82% of Americans believe in God (Hoar, 2006). In a survey report of 312 adults who were one year into their bereavement and studied over a 6-year period, 77% reported their religious beliefs were a significant help in their grief and the opportunity to say good-bye to the deceased was appreciably related to positive coping and outlook (Frantz, Trolley, & Johll, 1996). However, compared with their elders today, young adults (18 to 29) are much less likely to affiliate with any religious tradition. Yet in other ways they remain fairly traditional in their religious beliefs and practices. For instance, their beliefs about life after death and the existence of heaven, hell, and miracles closely resemble the beliefs of older people (Pew Forum on Religion & Public Life, 2010).

## Meaning Making

The free fall into helplessness can be stopped through religious involvement (Frantz et al., 1996). Grief care providers need to understand how grieving people view their faith and how it can help them adjust—to understand and cope with the post-loss world. "Can religion be a source of solace for grieving people? For example, does belief in an afterlife, engagement in cultural rituals or the chance to say good-bye have an impact on bereavement?" (Frantz et al., 1996, p. 151). Meaning making has been shown to be an essential component of the process of adapting to life after a loss (Frankl, 1977). The "potent influence" of a religious or spiritual belief system on an individual's health and well-being is "due in a large part to its provision of meaning" (Park, 2005, p. 299). People exposed to death, illness, and other traumatic loss can experience a crisis of meaning when "questions about the purpose of life, the nature of suffering and justice in the world" arise (p. 299). Perceptions of loss events may be altered to fit a person's religious beliefs (Pargament & Park, 1997).

Meaning making becomes "a tool for adaptation, for controlling the world, for self-regulation, and for belongingness" (Baumeister, 1991, pp. 357–358). Meaning is central to human existence and provides the basis for understanding the nature and consequences of loss or the threat of loss. Grieving people strive to make sense of what has happened. When a traumatic loss event can be integrated into a spiritual world-view or faith system, a meaning can be assigned to the loss and it can be contained in the religious faith context. In my clinical experience, this spiritual integration is associated with a decrease in feelings of bewilderment, hopelessness, and devastation.

Many religious teachings involve themes of loss, death, and an afterlife. Rituals associated with death—funerals, memorials, and burials—usually contain religious components such as reading from scriptures, prayers, clergy participation, and practices that come from a particular faith tradition. Religion therefore offers a way to address important issues regarding dying and death, and provides mourners with a framework of meanings for the loss experience. Grieving people turn to sacred rituals and practices that provide structure and organization at a time of disorganization (see Bowlby, Chapter 3, this volume) and emptiness. New meanings may be critical for those who have had their assumptions about life, fairness, and prayer severely shattered by a tragic loss (see Neimeyer, Chapter 3, this volume).

Other positive effects of belonging or subscribing to a religious system come from the social support of fellow congregants as well as the benefits of organizational services, for example, clergy contact, outreach programs, and grief counseling. Several studies have shown that mourners who have strong religious beliefs systems report greater social support, increased ability to find meaning in the loss, continued connection and belief in eventual reunion with the deceased, and less grief distress (Davis, Nolen-Hoeksema, & Larson, 1998; McIntosh, Silver, & Wortman, 1993).

There are many references in the Bible and Koran to death, the hereafter, mourning behaviors, burial practices, and the raising of the dead (Isaiah 61:13; Samuel 18:13; Matthew 5:4; Ecclesiastes 3:4, 7:2; John 11:1–44; Genesis 23, 37:34, 49:29, 50:22; Holy Koran 6:60, 26:55; 29:57, 40:46). The Hindu *Upanishads*, the *Egyptian Book of the Dead*, and *The Tibetan Book of the Dead* also contain many references. These scriptures reaffirm that people will suffer less pain from loss as a result of their belief in God. Grievers also find comfort in the belief that those who are deceased will continue to exist in a new place. Many of our current mourning and burial practices have been derived from these holy books and other ancient writings. To the extent that a belief system includes an afterlife existence, the hope and expectation of reunion with a deceased loved one offers some level of solace to grieving people.

For many people who are grieving and feeling empty inside, with no answers for their myriad questions, their spiritual and religious beliefs assume tremendous importance. Many of the people for whom I have provided care have told me when there was nothing else to turn to, there was always their faith. The rituals and practices that follow a death can provide substantial support and the earliest sense of hope for healing. "The earthquake may be over by the time of burial. But the aftershocks and the survey of destruction have barely begun" (Ashenburg, 2002, p. 50).

Kaddish (the Jewish prayer recited at the grave, and throughout and after the mourning period) has been called one of the earliest forms of bereavement support groups. It is believed to have begun in 12th century France and Germany (Ashenburg, 2002). Mourners recite a prayer that makes no mention of death but rather is a reaffirmation of faith. The community may stand and join in the prayer or give certain responses as the mourners recite the Kaddish. For many, the process of reciting prayers three times each day with other worshippers during the mourning period supplies a given structure and a healing action in which to engage.

In other religious systems, prayers, meditations, or wakes serve a similar function of providing activities in which to engage immediately after death and after burial or cremation. Communities engage in a host of other healing activities such as organizing social calls, bringing in meals, attending special prayer services or meditations, and visiting the grave. The Catholic tradition acknowledges a deceased loved one by celebrating a special Mass on death anniversaries and at other important occasions. Such acknowledgment in religious services helps family members remain continually aware of the loved one's presence in their post-loss lives (see Klass, Chapter 3, this volume). Coping with a loss within the context of a religious belief system allows mourners to search for significance or meaning of the death as they connect with sacred values (Pargament & Park, 1997).

A large part of the healing comes not only from participating in structured actions, but also from very the communal aspect of rituals and prayer services. The ancient procedure of the tribe or clan gathering after a member has died began because it offered visible proof that the community is still intact and will survive. For many mourners, the presence of other people gives them a sense of support and the knowledge that they are still part of a larger, protective social group. There is also an expectation by others that when they suffer a loss, there will be similar community support. Some families who are grieving a socially stigmatized death—related to drugs, crime, suicide, or AIDS—may find their faith communities unwelcoming and must create their own rituals. (See Chapter 9 for use of rituals for healing.)

For many, the funeral represents an opportunity for touching the mystery of the unknown. Here is a time when people can be physically close to their deceased loved ones, see and touch them, or touch the casket. They can assist or observe the deceased being taken out to the burial place or crematorium, accompany the loved one on the last steps of his or her transition to the place beyond this earthly life. This may also be a metaphor for the mourner's own transition into the post-loss world.

However, not all individuals follow their own traditional faith beliefs or rituals. They may modify the traditional service or create one that completely departs from their customary rituals. Frequently, the younger, second generation of immigrant groups may reject the "old ways," which can create conflicts with their more traditionally minded elders. The care provider may serve as a mediator and help to forge a compromise in such situations.

"There is very little research conclusively demonstrating that one particular mourning practice produces a better outcome than another" (Ashenburg, 2002, p. 17). *It is the availability of structured rituals and the presence of community in support that offers the healing potential of death-related rituals.* Postfuneral rituals, whether preexisting or created for the occasion, provide an action to take at a time of helplessness and immobility that may emerge after a death. This provides the opportunity to begin internalizing the reality of the loss and start the letting go process. Nevertheless, as always, we respect the needs of grieving people to engage in as many or as few ritual practices as fits their own personal circumstances. It is not unusual for some people to desire only a brief, simple graveside service and have a member of the family serve as leader. Others create elaborate services with music, readings, prayers, and dance that may also incorporate the rituals of veterans' organizations or other societies of which the deceased was a member.

# ☐ Death-Related Rituals: Funerals, Memorials, Burials

Weeks (2004) divides death-associated rituals into three groups:

1. *Predeath rituals*—Prayers, chants, life review, gifting others (giving away belongings), spiritual journeys, and reconnecting with others

2. *Immediate postdeath rituals*—Body preparation, the wearing of certain clothing and accessories (black armband, cut black ribbon), wakes, body viewing, funerals, burials and cremation, sitting Shiva, visitation with mourners

3. *Long-term postdeath rituals*—Visiting the grave; placing flowers, flags, and other items at gravesites and memorials; creating roadside flower memorials; selecting special commemorations during prayer services; and acknowledging the departed during holidays, birthdays, and anniversaries

Rituals enable us "to remain connected with the past, the future and with each other ... they also serve to provide us with comfort and security" (Weeks, 2004, p. 114).

If you have attended funeral services outside of your own religious tradition, you have probably noticed the wide diversity of behaviors. At some services, the volume of mourning is loud; at others, you can hear a pin drop.

Some families do not take an active role in the design of the funeral, leaving this entirely in the hands of the clergy or funeral director. Others create the service by selecting music and readings, offering eulogies, and encouraging those present to share remembrances. In many funerals, memorials, and cremation services, the clergy and the family will develop and lead services together. There are many funerals that are wholly designed by the faith system the family is connected to; in some memorial services God is never mentioned.

Some burial rituals end as the casket is lowered into the grave and the family and friends pour symbolic soil into it. Some families (Muslim) wash and prepare the body, dig the grave, lower the coffin, and completely bury the deceased. In other traditions, the coffin is left above the grave on the lowering device, with a mound of soil covered with artificial grass to the side. As the family is ushered away from the grave and out of the cemetery, cemetery workers do the actual burial. This is also the practice followed in military cemeteries. Several traditions (Hindu, Buddhist) use cremation as an ending ritual. Increasing numbers of people are selecting cremation even though several religions forbid this (Orthodox and Conservative Jewry, Islam). Cremation continues to grow in popularity largely due to its lower cost. Clearly, there is no universal or right way to conduct the final arrangements to lay to rest the body of a loved one.

Funerals and the funeral business are sometimes derided in the press (Mitford, 1963; Newman, 2002). However, they provide a very important function for the loved ones of the deceased. Funerals also provide a confrontation with the terrible reality of the loss not only for the family but also for community members. They too have an opportunity to express grief, say good-bye, and reestablish a sense of communal support and continuity.

Care providers may find that conflicts arise between older and younger generations regarding the degree of ritual desired at the end of life. Those who want to honor the dead as customary in their culture may experience the desire for new, more simplified rites as an additional loss. Time-honored rituals provide a familiar structure for the mourners, guide them through the bereavement period, and even stipulate when the mourning behaviors should come to an end.

It is important for the provider to remember that families from the same religious or cultural background may not approach the funeral in exactly the same way. Spiritual advisors may need to be called in. Be prepared by knowing who to call and how to contact such resources, and offer this option to a family confused over the nature and format of rituals. The provider must also be aware that there may be several subgroups within any given culture that have their own approach to death-related rituals.

During funeral rites, family members begin the saying good-bye process, officially begin their period of mourning, and begin a continuing connection with their deceased loved one (Bowlby, 1980). Highlighting the need for continuing the bonds with the deceased, many Korean American and Chinese American families bring the remains of dead family members from their original overseas burial sites to the United States to be reinterred; in this way, they keep the family together and have the remains available so that rituals can be performed and the sense of connection maintained (Fears, 2002).

There are many variations within every religious and cultural group. It is impossible to provide a truly comprehensive listing of the different practices within the many subgroups. For example, there is no one Native American, Buddhist, African American, or Asian set of rituals for death. Further, many individual families will adapt their traditions to complement personal preferences and meet their financial needs.

Following is a list of funeral practices for several religious and cultural groups. Though by no means exhaustive, it demonstrates the great diversity in death-associated practices. In preparing this material, I have drawn on my own personal and clinical experiences as well as from clergy and funeral directors.

Care providers must learn how to ask questions about a particular ethnic group's death practices as well how members of the group communicate their reactions to death and dying. In some cultures, such as among Asians, Latinos, and Roma (Gypsies), the oldest family member is the spokesperson, and the provider must communicate through this person to the family and often to the patient as well.

Care providers must also determine the nature of cultural guidelines as well as the individual person's or family's wishes regarding end-of-life and after-death rituals. For many families, culture serves as a framework, not a set of restrictions. The care provider must also be aware of how a family expresses itself emotionally regarding death and how its members have coped with and accommodated to past traumatic losses. For some people, certain deaths carry a social stigma, and they may have certain taboos regarding who can and cannot participate during rituals. Gender and age difference may influence these limitations. It is also useful to have a clear sense of the family's need for someone to hear confession at the end of life and to understand the family's ideas regarding afterlife.

When working with individuals who have no religious belief system, a care provider may be able to help them create their own understanding of dying and death that is not based on a specific theology. The provider can offer an opportunity to discuss the individual's philosophy or theories regarding life, end of life, and death, or refer them to another resource person. The provider's own belief system should be kept out of the discussion.

# Funeral Practices

## *Buddhist*

- Many Asian communities in the United States practice Buddhism.

- Buddhism has over 500 varying schools of thought with a variety of rituals regarding death.

- Buddhists do not believe in one God or Creator; Buddhism resembles a philosophical belief system.

- Buddhists seek increased awareness of all aspects of life to reach a state of enlightenment called Nirvana.

- The Tibetan Buddhist belief in rebirth is widely held.

- Buddhists have special meditations to be used at the time of death; families may request a limited morphine dosage for a dying person so that the person can remain conscious for meditation.

- Cremation is usual, and a family member typically officiates.

## Christian

- The concept of an afterlife is widely held as an important goal for the living to attain.

- Mourners can be comforted by the thought that the deceased is being reunited with loved ones and will be in the presence of Jesus Christ in the Kingdom of Heaven for eternity.

- The time between death and the funeral provides an opportunity for viewing the body, visiting with the family, and giving consolation and social support.

- The casket is typically lowered into grave after mourners leave.

- Dark clothing is typically worn.

## Roman Catholic

- The dying person makes confession to the priest.

- Last rites performed by a priest are very important; all dying Catholic patients must be given the opportunity to have a priest available to administer Last Rites. This serves as a comfort to the family as well.

- The priest officiates at the funeral and burial services.

- Families who have a Catholic heritage but do not have any affiliation to a parish should be given the option of contacting a priest.

## Protestant

- Confession and prayer can be made directly to God.

- There is life after death and the person who has faith will reach eternal life.

- Funeral sermons emphasize that the deceased is now in a better place.

- There are many denominations of Protestant churches with varied funeral traditions.

## Hindu

- Many gods and goddesses make up the Hindu religion and they all represent the One God with whom all dead will join.

- Hindus' fate in the next life will depend on how they have lived this life.

- Families wash the body and prepare it for cremation, which should take place on the day of death. State laws may dictate the length of waiting period before cremation.

- A Hindu priest officiates at the ritual; white is traditionally worn.

- During the 13 days of official mourning, friends visit to offer condolences.

- There are many sects in Hinduism with varying religious practices.

## Humanist

- Ethical humanism is a commitment to a way of life that is based on one's relationship to others.

- Funerals acknowledge loss and celebrate life without the use of religious rituals.

- Funerals are tailored to wishes of the deceased loved one's family.

- Funerals, burials, and cremation memorials may be held in a variety of locations.

## *Jewish*

- Funeral and burials usually occur within a day or two; cremation is not practiced among Orthodox and most Conservative families.

- Families place symbolic shovels of soil on the lowered casket; a rabbi or cantor officiates.

- A 7-day (or less in some families) period of mourning called Shiva is observed. Shiva prayers focus on the sanctification of God's name; talking about the deceased is part of Shiva.

- It is customary to visit and bring food during this period. Check the family's kosher food observance before bringing or sending food to the house.

- Sending flowers is not typically a Jewish custom; sympathy cards and charitable donations are the usual practice.

- Jewish theology includes the concept of a hereafter but it is not a primary focus in mourning.

- Attitudes regarding heroic measures and life support vary among Jewish families; traditional families generally request that life not be prolonged artificially if there is no possibility of recovery.

- For traditional families, hastening death is typically unacceptable, and a family will seek the presence of a rabbi to hear a special prayer or confession at the end of life.

- Forgiveness is an important aspect of saying good-bye to the dying person.

## *Muslim*

- Allah is just. He will judge all people according to their deeds, and they will be either rewarded with heaven or punished with hell.

- Dying is not the end of existence; thus, body preparation is designed for this purpose.

- The mourners carry the coffin to the grave, lower and bury it.

- Burial takes place as soon as possible.

- Cremation is forbidden, and males do the burials.

- The Imam or Holy Man leads funeral and graveside prayers with the mourners joining in.

- Official mourning lasts for 3 days; 40 days for the surviving spouse.

- Young children are typically not present at the burial rituals.

### Native Americans

- Practices vary within individual Nations.

- Some groups avoid contact with the dying.

- Many groups, such as the Hopi culture, adopt a very positive attitude in the presence of the dying person; grieving is done privately, away from the dying person.

- Some tribal groups include Christian beliefs in their practices.

## Summary

Funerals, memorials, burials, cremations, wakes, Shiva, farewell events, and transition ceremonies are all useful rituals that acknowledge the loss of a person or some other significant change in life circumstances. They also bring people together as a supportive community. Even in families in which some members are estranged, attendance at funerals usually overrides the conflict—at least temporarily.

Care providers may be asked to help a family organize death-associated rituals or obtain resources for the family. Grieving people should be encouraged to participate in memorial events to whatever extent is possible. Funerals, memorial ceremonies, dedications, candle lighting, and even moments of silent reflection provide them with a sense of involvement and an opportunity to say good-bye, reminisce, and digest the reality of the loss.

The death-related rituals we have each experienced throughout our lives make up our own information base and contribute to our understanding of what grieving people may experience. Some ritual events in our own experience may have been useful, whereas others may have lacked value or may even have been negative experiences. As a care provider, you may be asked to advise grieving people about loss rituals.

The following exercise is designed to help you recall your own experiences with death-related rituals.

First, let yourself reflect back, even to childhood, on past death-associated rituals and recall your impressions and level of participation.

### EXERCISE 2: DEATH AND LOSS RITUALS EXPERIENCE

1. What is the earliest memory you have of a death-related ritual, such as a funeral, memorial, burial, or cremations? Indicate your age and the setting (e.g., home, religious facility, funeral home, graveside, or other). What do you recall that was positive about this experience? What was negative?
2. Very briefly state the elements of your ideal memorial service.
3. How is this information helpful in your work with grieving families?

## ☐ Conclusion

The Exquisite Witness is a care provider who knows that the grief journey is different for each griever, understands each family's cultural background, and knows that the function of the provider is to support this journey and not control it. Such a provider guides the client through "the cave of darkness" (Wicks, 1995, p. 127) and accompanies the client on the passage to healing. The care provider must help to equip the grieving person and prepare him or her for this journey of healing through loss. Ask questions and listen to the answers. Know your client and know your client's culture. The clinical behaviors of the care provider as an Exquisite Witness will be explored more fully in Chapter 9.

Although cultural and religious legacies define the behaviors of grieving people, there are other explanations that underlie the variations in the nature and intensity of the human grief reaction. Chapter 3 will address the psychological ideas that will further reveal how natural and necessary is the human grief response.

CHAPTER

# The Human Grief Response
## Origin and Function

Should you shield the canyons from the windstorms you would never see the true beauty of their carvings.

Elisabeth Kübler-Ross (1978, p. 155)

## ☐ Chapter Preview

- Introduction

- Key Concepts

- Defining Grief

- Common Myths

- Denial: Friend or Foe

- The Seven Principles of Grief

- Origin and Function of the Grief Response

- Experimental Research and Human Attachment

- Attachment Theory and the Human Grief Response: The Drive to Survive

- The Three Conditions of Grief

- The Four Components of Grief: Psychological, Physical, Social, Spiritual

- Past Loss Survey

- Grief Process Theories: From Bowlby to Neimeyer

- The Path to Healing

- Conclusion

# ☐ **Introduction**

We now look at other mechanisms—beyond societal attitudes and cultural environments—that shape the nature of the human grief response. Understanding the underlying biological and psychosocial basis for human grief provides the Exquisite Witness with perceptiveness regarding its normalcy as a human reaction. This constitutes the head dimension of the heart, head, and hands approach to helping grieving people.

Knowing the usual and customary patterns of grief over time and being alert to the individual differences among grieving people will give the professional and volunteer care provider a sense of security and clarity in addressing the range of possible grief reactions. We begin with a list of important concepts.

# ☐ **Key Concepts**

Listed next are key concepts that an Exquisite Witness needs to know before working with grieving people. This listing is followed by an elaboration of each concept.

- Grief is a universal occurrence among human beings.

- Grief is expressed for both tangible and intangible losses.

- Grief is a natural reflex that exists to enhance survival.

- Grief is generally an adaptive response, although it may be character-ized by temporary disruptions of life.

- Grief is a natural phenomenon, although complications and illness can develop from it.

- Grief is complex and dynamic and varies between individuals and among cultures.

- Avoidance and denial are typical ways people soften or keep out the reality of painful loss.

- Grief has both predictable and unpredictable features.

- Grief support can come from professional health and pastoral care providers, friends, family, and trained organizational volunteers.

## Grief Is a Universal Occurrence Among Human Beings

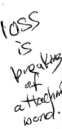

A reaction to loss, that is, the breaking of an attachment bond, is com-mon to all peoples. In a world where television and the Internet bring the tragedies of people from various cultural locations into the immedi-ate space of millions of others, the universal similarity of the anguished faces of loss is apparent. The skin may be of a different color, the clothing may be unusual to the viewer, the funeral rites may be unfamiliar, but the wailing lament of a mother holding a dead child looks and sounds the same everywhere.

## Grief Is Expressed for Both Tangible and Intangible Losses

We usually think of grief as a response to death. Death is only one of many forms of loss. Many other "faces of loss" can trigger a grief reac-tion. Loss is experienced when anything we have become attached to is no longer there. A friend who moves away, a job that is downsized, a pet that dies, a stolen wallet with credit cards, physical functions we can no longer perform, vanished dreams, a loss of our sense of trust and safety—many loss situations can cause grief.

Change in circumstances creates a loss condition that results in a grief reaction, even when the change is seemingly positive, for example, a promotion, marriage, or a new baby. All are positive yet they render the loss of a previous state or life condition, and this frequently carries a grief reaction.

## Grief Is a Natural Reflex That Exists to Enhance Survival

At its most primitive level, the human organism acts to reconnect when separated from another upon whom it depends for survival. When this reconnection is not possible, the reaction is grief. Animal offspring who are separated from the mother will utter a cry and seek to restore proximity in order to maintain safety, keep warm, and receive nourishment. Without this natural reflex, the chance for survival would be drastically reduced. The human grief response contains within it the basic drive to restore the attachment to the lost object. Examples of such behavior are looking in places shared, calling out the name, agitated movement, and sounds of distress. When reattachment is not possible, the individual exhibits despair and associated mourning behaviors: crying, sighing, withdrawal, depression, and, at times, disorganization of usual life activities.

## Grief Is Generally an Adaptive Response—Although It May Be Characterized by Temporary Disruptions of Life

Grief reactions may initially appear to be maladaptive—crying, raging, confusion—but they are actually attempts to restore that which is gone and no longer part of the person's world. The grief reaction presents a departure from normal life functioning and may be characterized by some as a form of maladaption. However, in the same way that a physical wound or illness requires a period of reduced function, pain, and change in usual life activity, and perhaps accompanying demoralization, the psychological wound of loss begins a similar period of the individual being "out of commission with life."

# Grief Is a Natural Phenomenon —Although Complications and Illness Can Develop From It

Although it is expected and important for people who have suffered a terrible loss to grieve, the reactions may become dysfunctional under certain circumstances and require special professional assistance. Natural grieving can go wrong when levels of depression become extreme and prolonged, or when anxiety, rage, and guilt reach proportions that severely limit life activities and place the grieving person at risk for physical and emotional illness.

# Grief Is Complex and Dynamic and Varies Between Individuals and Among Cultures

Human grief reactions are varied and contain many subparts. Grief is complex and as such may manifest as physical pain and discomfort, as psychological distress—both emotional and intellectual—as social dysfunction, and spiritual discontinuity. Grief is dynamic because it changes from morning to nighttime, from day to day, or from week to week.
The complexities of an individual's grief are also influenced by loss history, personality, family, and ethnic and cultural traditions associated with death and the expression of the feelings of grief. Additionally, *individual patterns of grieving* have been identified along a continuum including *intuitive style* (affective focus) and *instrumental style* (cognitive/behavioral focus) (Doka & Martin, 2010).

# Avoidance and Denial Are Typical Ways People Soften or Keep Out the Reality of Painful Loss

Denial enables us to take in the harsh reality of loss in small doses so that other requirements and obligations can be attended to. The reality of our own mortality is kept at bay by the use of humor and simply not talking about it. This is a normal and very human characteristic that enables us to go on with living without obsessing over the inevitability of our own death. It is human to push away thoughts that may cause pain. Some people describe this as feeling numb.

## Grief Has Both Predictable and Unpredictable Features

Although much has been written about the nature and course of human grief, many factors affect the actual resulting feelings, thoughts, and behavior of grieving people. When we look at cross-cultural or universal patterns of grief, we see that most people cry when a loved one dies. The pictures of people around the world burying their dead after natural or human-made disasters look fairly similar. African, Asian, European, and American families who are mourning loved ones look very alike. The faces, sounds, and body language of people in grief around the globe have a uniformity that lets us know that the person is grieving. Yet there are life circumstances that differentiate them from one another. Such determining factors are preexisting morbidity, personal coping styles, influences of personality type, and social–cultural factors. Such additional influences as nature of loss, age and role of deceased, level of support, and the mental health of the mourner will stamp uniqueness into any one individual's grief reactions.

## Grief Support Can Come From Professional Health and Pastoral Care Providers, Friends, Family, and Trained Organizational Volunteers

Many individuals provide care and comfort to grieving people. Some have medical or nursing backgrounds; others may come from mental health or pastoral care. Still others may be trained volunteers or family caregivers. Funeral directors, school personnel, and community agency outreach staff may also serve grieving people in some capacity. Providers use their own level of knowledge and skills to make their unique contributions to the grief support system.

Grief is a global phenomenon and any person who develops the heart, head, and hands dimensions of providing care has the potential to become an Exquisite Witness to the journey of a grieving person.

## ☐ Defining Grief

The term *grief* may be used in a variety of ways. Some use grief to mean the behavior seen when people are mourning a death or other tragic loss.

Grief is also used as a way of indicating that a person is having a hard time: "The umpire is getting a lot of grief from the fans since that last call." Some view the word as a set of internal psychological reactions to loss or the threat of loss. From a theological perspective, grief may be seen as a life condition that has the potential to bring a person closer to his or her faith. Some may see grief as a condition to be cured.

Many intermix the word *grief* with *mourning* and *bereavement*; others distinguish among the three as follows: (a) grief—internal reactions, (b) mourning—observable behaviors, and (c) bereavement—as describing the cultural/social role of one who has had a loss. The varied and overlapping uses of the term grief remind me of the five blindfolded men attempting to describe an elephant. Because each of them touched a different part of the elephant—the trunk, the tusk, the ear, the tail—they individually arrived at a different idea of the animal they were experiencing.

Counselors, theologians, experimental psychologists, academic lecturers, cultural anthropologists, and funeral directors all view the concept of grief from their own perspective. Yet each perspective provides a special and useful addition to the understanding of this very complex, dynamic, and human experience known as grief.

In this book, I will use the following definitions:

*Grief*—A system of feelings, thoughts, and behaviors that are triggered when a person is faced with loss or the threat of loss. Emphasis is on both internal (thoughts and feelings) and external (behavior) reactions.

*Mourning*—The behaviors that are part of the human grief response and serve to differentiate mourners from others in a person's social network. Emphasis is on external behaviors, expressions of grief, and manner of dress.

*Bereavement*—A cultural/social role or condition for a person who has experienced a death and engages in cultural rituals and behaviors associated with death. Emphasis is on behaviors or restriction of behaviors dictated by cultural norms.

## ☐ Common Myths

In my years of clinical practice, teaching, and consulting, I have encountered several myths about grief that people may fall back on when coping with loss or the threat of loss (Jeffreys, 2005, p. iv):

*I can handle this on my own.*

*I don't need to talk about it.*

*They can't tell how upset I am.*

*My pain, anger, and fear will just go away.*

*Bad things happen to other people.*

*If I don't think about it, nothing happened or will happen.*

The first four myths are examples of the human impulse to hold off the pain any way that we can. We tend to bend reality to protect ourselves from the pain of loss. The last two myths are examples of keeping bad news at arm's length to prevent us from experiencing pain.

These and other myths that we tell ourselves are part of the human defense system, which consists of all ideas that a person may use as "trenches [to defend our] existence, or as scarecrows to frighten away reality" (Ortega y Casset, 1957, p. 147). Sometimes we need to hold off the pain any way we can. Making use of these myths is a form of denial and is very normal.

## ☐ Denial: Friend or Foe?

> Being aware of death is "like trying to stare the sun in the face: you can stand only so much of it."
>
> Irvin Yalom (2008, p. 5)

We use denial to keep out or soften terrible news. Too often the use of denial is criticized as running away from reality. That is, we are perceived as weak and lacking the ability to face the painful truth of what has or is going to happen. Families with a very sick loved one in the hospital may overhear staff saying, "They really don't get how serious this is; they're in denial." However, unless denial creates medical problems or family dysfunction, it serves as a very important and useful shock absorber. Denial allows us to absorb the horrible reality in small doses or push it away, at least for a while. It provides us with the freedom not to deal with a grief reaction right away so that we can take care of other needs. Denial can be a useful way to cope over time throughout the grief journey.

Many grieving people are able to compartmentalize their days so that they focus their attention on life activities other than the loss. Practical requirements, such as child care, household chores, religious activities, workplace tasks, and social interactions, draw and hold their energy and concentration. Grieving people describe themselves moving back and forth between periods of painful memories about their loss and being able to be distracted by behaviors and thoughts associated with practical and spiritual matters.

We also use denial when we avoid grieving people. A year after our son Steven died, my wife and I were approached by a man who we knew, as we were driving out of a community center parking lot. He told us that he had yet to offer us any condolences about our tragic loss because it was too painful for him to talk about it.

I was told a story about a man in a bereaved parents support group that demonstrates one way that people react to the grief of a neighbor:

> After his son was killed, he noticed that people he knew in the community would play a game he called the "Safeway Samba." When he went shopping, for example, people he recognized would quickly slip into the next aisle. At first, he assumed that they had not seen or heard him, but gradually he realized that they were avoiding him. People in the group nodded, smiled, and recalled similar experiences. This "Safeway Samba" became our code word for being shunned by others who were not able to allow themselves to make contact.

Such avoidance is actually typical and understandable, and people who cannot cope with other people's grief are not bad. Contact with grieving people can eat away at a person's own denial system, and their avoidance serves the function of keeping a painful reality out of conscious awareness. We flee the horror of tragic circumstances that remind us of what could happen to us. Often, people just do not know what to say. Sadly, this can result in painful isolation for grieving people. The grieving person may need help to connect with neighbors, friends, and colleagues regarding their loss.

Care providers need to anticipate this avoidance and be prepared to spend time helping the grieving person cope with this sense of isolation when there is a lack of support from friends and family. This lack of support and contact becomes another loss to be grieved. Faith communities, fitness centers, and community events are settings in which the grieving person can begin to casually engage others. Support groups offer a place for expression of grief and a sense of acceptance and specific ways to respond to questions in social situations. (See Appendix A.)

_responsibility_

Denial can become problematic when it prevents necessary medical interventions and care provisions, interferes with completing advance directives and other important legal and financial arrangements, and precludes opportunities for final good-byes and forgiveness.

# ☐ The Seven Principles of Human Grief

The seven principles of grief give care providers an overall blueprint for further understanding grief reactions and what to expect from grieving people.

*Principle One*: There is no one right way to grieve.

*Principle Two*: You cannot fix or cure grief.

*Principle Three*: There is no universal timetable for the grief journey.

*Principle Four*: Every loss is a multiple loss.

*Principle Five*: Change = Loss = Grief.

*Principle Six*: We grieve old loss while grieving new loss.

*Principle Seven*: We grieve when a loss has occurred or is threatened.

## Principle One: There Is No One Right Way to Grieve

Everyone grieves differently. With some, tears are visible; with others, tears are invisible. We must respect the different ways we each grieve. Each culture has its own norms about how grief is expressed; grief reactions also depend upon one's family, personality, and gender.

People's grieving is based on stereotypes of gender, age, and other social–cultural identifications, for example, men don't cry, women cry, or older adults contain their grief. However, lack of crying is not a sign of being disloyal to those who have died. Childhood messages about whether it was acceptable to express sadness, fear, and anger continue to affect how we react to loss and crisis throughout life.

## Principle Two: You Cannot Fix or Cure Grief

While grief is as normal as the common cold, it is not an illness that needs medical attention. You cannot scrub it out like a stain on a shirt or fix it like a leaky faucet. The human grief reaction is a combination of thoughts, physical and emotional feelings, and behaviors that enable us to survive. It is, therefore, a normal way of reacting whenever we have already lost or are afraid we will lose someone or something important to us. The losses that create a grief response can be of a person, place, job, work routines, physical objects, dreams, or sense of safety and trust.

Although grief cannot be fixed or cured, one thing we can do is listen to it. The Exquisite Witness does not have to say something at every juncture in the conversation. The Exquisite Witness is an "exquisite listener," providing a safe place and the time and permission for the grieving person to express what is going on internally.

## Principle Three: There Is No Universal Timetable for the Grief Journey

The answer to the question how long will it take is "as long as it takes." We do not heal on anyone else's schedule but our own. Many years after our son Steven's death, my wife and I met an old acquaintance. After the usual small talk, this highly educated individual blurted out, "Are you two *still* grieving over that son of yours?" We were stunned at his harsh and insensitive question. "Yes," I finally said, "and we will, probably for life." People may get impatient with another's grief and after a while encourage them to be OK, stop crying, and be "happy again."

## Principle Four: Every Loss Is a Multiple Loss

When we lose a job by being laid off or by having our job description changed, we lose more than our familiar routine. We lose our social contacts, identity, status, financial security, career dreams, sense of well-being, and dreams for the future.

We incur secondary losses whenever we lose a person or place; loss ripples outward the same way a pond surface does when a stone is dropped into it. We lose not only the body and being of our loved one but also the part of ourselves that was bonded in relationship to the deceased, as well as the various roles he or she played in our life.

We are also affected by the grief of others. When our nation was attacked on September 11, 2001, we lost the sense that we were safe. These layers of secondary loss add to the intensity of the grief reaction as it moves outward from the nuclear family to other relatives, friends, coworkers, and neighbors.

## Principle Five: Change = Loss = Grief

Change is a part of life. Our physical and social environments change daily. Whenever there is change, we lose what we left behind and begin to connect with what comes next. Any change, even good change, can bring about a sense of loss and thus a grief reaction. Even happy life-cycle transitions—leaving school and being hired for your first job, getting married, having a baby, retiring—can trigger a grief reaction because we left one lifestyle behind as we moved on to another. When the change is death or a serious illness or an unexpected, traumatic, and sudden disaster, the grief reaction may be very intense and painful. As indicated in Principle Four, change in the workplace also creates loss and grief as employees must let go of a familiar work world and adjust to new beginnings. In fact, any notable change in the way things have been results in the loss of how it used to be. Any loss can result in many spinoff or secondary losses.

## Principle Six: We Grieve Old Loss While Grieving New Loss

As we move through the transitions of life and experience losses, we accumulate the loss material referred to in Chapter 1 as Cowbells. It is not uncommon for us to be reminded of a death that took place years ago when a loved one dies or a significant new loss or trauma occurs. In spite of our previous grieving, some unfinished and unaccommodated grief may remain. When a new loss occurs, the old, stored grief mingles with the new, intensifying the grief reaction.

## Principle Seven: We Grieve When a Loss Has Occurred or Is Threatened

We do not need an actual death or diagnosis of serious illness to begin to grieve; even the threat of loss can invoke the grief response. Think of how you feel when your loved one is extremely late arriving home, when you hear rumors that your company is downsizing, or when your doctor tells you to go for more tests. The beginning of a grief reaction will vary for each person, but often the process begins well in advance of the actual loss event.

# ☐ Origin and Function of the Human Grief Response

It is a curious paradox of the human condition that perhaps the most painful experience a person will suffer in life is also, at its primitive roots, the most necessary for survival, not only for the individual but for the continuation of the species as well. An Exquisite Witness care provider must understand the origin and function of attachment theory as the basis for understanding the human grief response in order to provide effective care for grieving people.

In the following section, we will review the biological and psychosocial basis of the human grief response, from the neurological separation distress signal to the role of attachment in survival. We will also cover the formation of attachment styles that influence relationships and ultimately the nature of how we grieve a loss.

# ☐ Experimental Research and Human Attachment

The nonverbal music of grief comes out through the body.

P. D. MacLean (personal communication, October 12, 2001)

## Separation Alert Signal

In the 1950s, National Institute of Mental Health neurologist Paul MacLean, MD, introduced the concept of a limbic system in the mammalian brain that governs emotional reactions, fight–flight response, and sexual behaviors (MacLean, 1952, 1955a, 1955b; MacLean & Pribram, 1953). MacLean (1973) later wrote about the limbic system's role in three functions: (a) the separation distress call, (b) maternal nursing behavior, and (c) play or social affiliation. Each of these processes is designed to protect and enable the survival of the individual to reproductive age. Of special interest is the separation or isolation alert signal that MacLean (1985) characterizes as probably the "earliest and most basic mammalian vocalization" (p. 405).

A young mammal senses the distance between it and its mother by changes in the intensity of smell, a drop in temperature, the loss of tactile contact, or critical visual distance from the mother. Acting like a security system, the limbic part of the brain sends an automatic message, resulting in a *distress cry*. When the mother receives this signal, her own brain connections trigger her protective reaction to restore physical attachment to the baby; then she leads it to safety and comfort.

## Survival Basis of Attachment

A baby may reach out, grasp, seek its mother's nipple, utter continued sounds of distress, and engage in searching actions in order to restore the physical proximity. These behaviors are what Bowlby (1969, 1982) calls *attachment behaviors*. The agitation generally subsides when reunion is accomplished. Mammal babies whose genes did not provide a well-developed separation alert system were eaten, died of exposure, or starved to death. MacLean (personal communication, May 6, 2003) theorizes that of the earliest little mammals on the dark forest floor, only those who had this alerting system survived. The neurological process that drives the offspring to maintain attachment for survival is the basic level of the human grief response (K. Pribram, personal communication, July 16, 2003).

I have composed the following tale to further illustrate the work of MacLean (1973) on the primitive survival basis of attachment, the foundation for understanding the normalcy of the human grief response.

On the Dark Forest Floor

Many, many years ago there lived on the dark forest floor a tiny little baby mammal named Dino. He looked a lot like his great-great-grandfather—the one they called "lizard face." Dino had a longer snout than his cousin Tina, who was also very young. Dino had clawlike feet and could run faster than Tina, but he was unable to make a sound with his throat. One day, Dino wandered away from his mother. He heard a commotion and turned to see a big, hungry lizard coming toward him. He began shaking his long snout from side to side; but his mother, in the dark forest-floor world, could not see this visual signal for help. Tina was nearby and heard the noise of the hungry lizard too. She immediately squealed out her vocal distress signal. Her mother came running and led her quickly to safety.

Tina tells this story to her grandchildren, who were all born with the ability to emit vocal distress call signals that bring their mothers whenever they are too far from her body. Dino was never seen again; and all the other baby mammals that looked like great-great-grandfather "lizard face" also disappeared.

As the little mammals, Dino and Tina, in the story demonstrated, the development of the human grief response is a matter of survival.

## Psychobiological Attunement in Attachment

Experimental psychologist Tiffany Field (1985) has further contributed to the understanding of learned behaviors associated with attachment and separation by identifying the psychobiological attunement process in the mutual feedback loop of actions and reactions between mother and baby. As mother and baby learn a series of signals and cues by which they modify their behavior, their bond develops beyond their initial instinctive behaviors. These cues take the form of crying, clinging, hearing and repeating sounds, feeling the comfort of being held and caressed, and seeking and greeting actions. "Each partner provides meaningful stimulation for the other and has a modulating influence on the other's arousal level" (Field, 1985, p. 415). For example, a mother's smile and cooing may stimulate sounds or facial reactions from the baby, and this causes the mother to pick up the baby and cuddle it. Although babies initially focus on bonding with their mother, they eventually include their father, siblings, and later, as the individual matures, peers, life partners, other family, and friends.

The nature of earlier bond formation will influence future adult pair bonding as the individual matures. It is the pattern of individual attachment style that affects the character of the relationship, and this has a direct bearing on features of grieving when the attachment bond is severed or threatened (Bartholomew & Horowitz, 1991; La Guardia, Ryan, Couchman, & Deci, 2000; Mancini, Robinaugh, Shear, & Bonanno, 2009; Peters, 2008).

We have much to learn about the complex nature of attachment and maternal care behaviors. The role of organic brain function in the underlying attachment behavior has been given increasing attention in the laboratories of experimental psychologists investigating the role of brain chemicals in stimulating receptors for separation distress (Insel, 2000). Clearly, an understanding of how and why we attach to others is essential to understanding how and why we grieve.

# ☐ Attachment Theory and the Human Grief Response: The Drive to Survive

Attachment theory is based on findings from ethology (the study of behavior in different species), evolutionary biology (the study of the transmission of instinctive behaviors from parent to offspring), and psychological studies of both animal and human behavior. The human grief response is a complex set of feelings, thoughts, and behaviors following the loss or threat of loss of an attachment bond. In addition to brain researchers, several writers have contributed to our understanding of human attachment behavior. Foremost among these is the work of British psychiatrist John Bowlby, considered by many as the father of attachment theory.

Bowlby (1969, 1973, 1979, 1980, 1982) has written extensively on how and why human beings attach to each other, and what happens when we are faced with separation or even the threat of separation and loss. His work, often in collaboration with Mary Ainsworth (Ainsworth & Bowlby, 1991), focuses not only on the nature of early attachment bonding between the very young and their maternal caregivers but also on adult attachment throughout the life cycle.

According to Bowlby (1969, 1973, 1979, 1980, 1982), young mammals maintain a close physical tie to the mother to survive predation, starvation, and other physical harm that would prevent the baby from reaching reproductive age. Attachment behaviors (as well as sex drive) are therefore a *mechanism for individual survival and continuation of the species*. This *drive to survive* is carried forward from birth to death (Bowlby, 1979), manifesting itself later in life as adult pair bonding.

Utilizing direct observational studies of children, Bowlby (1969, 1979, 1982) and Ainsworth (1973, 1978) identified typical separation behaviors of very young children and their mothers at the time of separation and upon reunion. These observations form the basis for modern studies of adult attachment patterns (Fraley, 2002; Fraley & Shaver, 1999; Hazen & Shaver, 1990; Rholes & Simpson, 2004; Simpson & Rholes, 1998; Wayment & Vierthaler, 2002). Studies investigating adult attachment styles strongly suggest that the way an individual makes and breaks social bonds in childhood is carried forward into later relationships throughout life (Fraley, 2002). Making the connection between attachment styles, nature of the relationship, and impact on grief reaction will inform best clinical practices for helping grieving people (Peters, 2008).

When an individual with a history of secure attachment bonding is unable to restore the contact with a person or other significant lost object, the result is typically protest, agitation, and separation distress—the behaviors we identify as a grief reaction. A very young child who has been separated from its mother will cry, scream, look in the direction she was last seen, stand up in the crib, shake the crib framing, and possibly flail and throw things. Where the attachment bond is secure—mother has consistently returned and interacted warmly upon return with the child—this agitated distress will abate upon mother's return and reinvolvement with the child. Some of us may recall hearing or singing this song to a child: "Mommy always comes back, always comes back, she always comes back to you." But what if the mother or caregiver seldom or never returns, and there is no consistent surrogate as may be the situation in orphanages and similar institutions? In these cases, the period of agitated hyperdistress will often continue and initiate the beginning of mourning.

Abandonment or a history of inconsistent caregiver return and loving involvement sets the stage for *insecure attachment bonding.* This impacts on the nature of future relationships and subsequently on the nature of grieving the loss of a primary attachment bond. The ability of a mother or other caregiver to identify and seek out the baby when it is in distress or threatened with danger is part of a reciprocal system of relationship and protection (MacLean, 1973). Attachment bonds form the basis of several clinical interventions for problematic psychological conditions, including reactive attachment disorder (Mayo Foundation for Medical Education, 2009). Couple issues (Johnson, 2002, 2004) are based, in part, on the nature of attachment bonds. In addition to the three attachment prototypes identified by Bowlby (1982), Bartholomew and Horowitz (1991) have described the four adult attachment styles:

| Childhood Attachment Styles | Adult Attachment Styles |
| --- | --- |
| • Secure attachment | • Secure attachment |
| • Anxious–ambivalent attachment | • Anxious–preoccupied attachment |
| • Avoidant attachment | • Dismissive–avoidant attachment |
| | • Fearful–avoidant attachment |

## Secure Attachment Bonding

When a baby in distress has been responded to promptly by the mother (or other primary caregiver) and receives a rich set of caring behaviors—holding, caressing, singing, talking, feeding, cleaning—a secure bond will be formed. Such a child can eventually create a stable inner image of the attachment figure, is able to tolerate periods of separation, and is confident enough to explore the environment. A set of expectations or "working models" of the possibilities of response from the primary attachment person develops over time. "If I cry, I will be picked up and held." Adults may expect that, "If I am sad, my partner will reach out to me with loving support." Bowlby (1973) also pointed out that the child's inner representations of attachment fall into one of two categories: (a) the attachment bond figure will be supportive and protective when needed or will not; and (b) am I someone who an attachment bond figure would be likely or not likely to respond to with support and protection. Additionally, the attachment style of adult caregivers will influence the way the child bonds with them. These core principles of attachment apply to both child–mother bonding as they do to adult pair bonding.

## Anxious Attachment Bonding

When the response to a child's distress signals is consistently delayed or absent, and the nature of maternal interaction is also limited, the child is unsure of the availability of the mother and how much protective caring she will actually provide. Infants with anxious-ambivalent attachment bonds make unsuccessful and unrewarded attempts to connect with the mother or other caregiver (Hazen & Shaver, 1990; Parkes & Weiss, 1983). As adults, such individuals generally have a pattern of relational anxiety, may be insecure about the other's commitment (She loves me, she loves me not; Does he or doesn't he still want me?), and are possessive and controlling. This adult attachment style is called an anxious-preoccupied attachment.

Mikulincer, Shaver, Bar-On, and Ein-Dor (2010) found that adult attachment insecurities are associated with uncertainty regarding the relationship. Typically, they may fear abandonment and hold on to the attachment figure through clingy, possessive, and controlling behavior (Feeney, 1998). They also possess an underlying fear that their bond partner cannot be counted on for safety and support in times of distress. However, changes in these patterns are subject to interpersonal learning throughout the lifespan. Adults with anxious–preoccupied attachment patterns are typically at high risk for chronic grief complications when a bond is broken (Hazen & Shaver, 1990; Parkes & Weiss, 1983). They are likely to become stuck in grief due to their inability to alter their inner

Care providers may find it necessary to help these couples decrease their emotional distancing and enhance their communication as well as build the level of support skills of both parents. For example, couples that learn active listening techniques and schedule time for conversations often discover that the ambivalent partner becomes less anxious over time.

representation of the lost attachment figure. They typically have great difficulty letting go of the deceased loved one as a living bond mate. See Chapter 10 for a discussion of complicated grief.

I have found that when one member of a couple who has lost a child has an anxious-ambivalent attachment style, there is often conflict because the anxious person perceives the other as not being available. Individuals with this attachment style may resent the lack of attention to his or her grieving needs—listening, holding, close proximity. The result can be the development of painful relationship conflicts.

## Avoidant Attachment Bonding

This type of bonding results when infants make no attempt to secure the mother figure's attention or social interaction because they have learned that such an expectation will be unmet. Subsequently, they develop an internal style of coping with distress. These children typically seek emotional distance and independence, and resist help from others during and following a crisis.

Adults can have an avoidant attachment style in which they seek safe emotional distance and flee from intimacy. *Dismissive–avoidant* attachment individuals are motivated to distance in order to satisfy their needs for autonomy, whereas those identified with the *fearful–avoidant* attachment style are remote in order to protect themselves from the pain of rejection. Such people have learned to consciously or unconsciously suppress or deactivate the attachment system in a time of distress (Fraley, Davis, & Shaver, 1998). They can appear to be resilient in the face of the loss of a partner.

In either of the nonsecure attachment types (anxious–ambivalent or avoidant), grieving people are not to be condemned for being too demanding or too distant. They are simply engaging in those attachment behaviors that have been shaped by their early life experiences.

Care providers need to obtain a thorough relationship history to understand how best to support bereaved individuals with a history of insecure attachments. The care provider can invite the grieving person to relate the story of his or her relationships. This can yield some insight into how this individual will grieve. A clingy, anxious person may be more likely to suffer prolonged and debilitating grief. A bereaved avoidant, distancing individual may be more likely to suffer physical complaints.

# ☐ The Three Conditions of Grief

Grief reaction is a result of the loss of an affectional bond or the threat of such a loss. The following three conditions associated with attachment bonds result in the human grief response.

## Broken or Altered Bond

We grieve when a bond has been broken or unalterably changed (as in Alzheimer's disease). Death or permanent separation from an attachment figure brings on the grief response as we have described in the previous section on attachment theory.

## Threat to Bond

We also grieve when there is a threat to the attachment bond. A relationship that is at risk, a loved one with a terminal illness, a workplace undergoing massive reorganization, a recently detected breast lump, a child late coming home from a party—all these can bring on a grief response as intense as it would be if the loss had already occurred.

## Unestablished Bond

Finally, we grieve for that which never has and never will happen—the relationship you never established with an alcoholic father or mother, the child you were never able to conceive, the promotion you never obtained, or the partner you were never able to court. These ongoing

The care provider must gather information about the multiple sources of grief impinging on the grieving person. What old and other current losses may be adding to the person's grief reaction? What Cowbells are ringing for the grieving person? This can be accomplished by taking a comprehensive loss history that is discussed in Chapter 9.

grief issues may become linked with more current, acute losses, intensifying the grief reaction.

## ☐ The Four Components of Grief: Psychological, Physical, Social, Spiritual

Grief is expressed in feelings, thoughts, and behaviors. These manifest themselves within four aspects of an individual's life: the psychological, physical, social, and spiritual components of grief.

### THE PSYCHOLOGICAL COMPONENT

*Emotional Aspects of Grief—Feelings of Grief*
 Sadness
 Anger
 Fear
 Guilt
 Shame

*Cognitive Disturbances of Grief*
 Memory
 Concentration

*The Physical Component*
 Health Factors
 Physical Symptoms

*The Social Component*
 Family and Other Relationships
 Society and Attitudes Toward Grief

*The Spiritual Component*
 Faith Resources and Life Philosophy

# The Psychological Component of Grief

The psychological component of grief is divided into two parts:

- Emotional (feelings)

- Cognitive (thought process)

The role of the Exquisite Witness care provider is to be fully present and to accept and normalize all feelings and thoughts that the grieving person wishes to express. As discussed earlier in the section on attachment, the human grief response is a normal response to loss or the threat of loss. Normal grief is not an illness to be cured but, for most persons, an expected pattern of behaviors that are necessary for healing to take place.

In some cases, grief may become complicated and even have associated psychiatric disorders. Such grief may be overly prolonged and intense, filled with debilitating anxiety, depression, or physical symptoms. (See Chapter 10 for further details on complications of grief.)

## *Emotional Aspects of Grief*

### *Sadness*

*Sadness* and *grief* are terms that many people use interchangeably. The pain of grief is usually associated with crying, sobbing, sighing, blowing the nose, wringing hands, shaking the head, and verbal expressions of pain and hurt. You can expect anything from soft sobbing to vigorous wailing. I have heard clients say things, such as (a) *This is going to kill me*! (b) *I will never get over this*! (c) *I don't want to live without her*, (d) *It hurts so much*, (e) *When will this awful pain stop*? (f) *I feel so empty inside*, and (g) *I'm afraid I will never stop crying*. We recommend that care providers never shove a tissue at a crying person. This may send the message that we want the crying to stop. Instead, I suggest placing easily accessible boxes of tissues around the room so that grieving people can reach for one when they need to. Grieving people will often say that they have very little opportunity to express their sadness because others in their lives do not want to hear or see them cry. Sad, hurting, and aching hearts may need to weep and sob. As one client once told me as she cried copiously, never once reaching for a tissue, "I want to feel the wetness on my face and know that I am really grieving."

Sadness often comes and goes in waves. People will feel good one day and awful the next. There is no straight line on the graph of grief feelings, and not all people will express sadness in the same way. I have met some bereaved persons who show little or no outward expressions of grief. Some individuals who have had a nondeath loss believe they are not entitled to cry and mourn. For example, the losses connected to the workplace—mergers, downsizing, and reengineered work roles—can feel very much like a death loss. Those affected may withhold their grief feelings because of workplace culture expectations. However, we endorse their entitlement to grieve and recommend company provisions of grief support measures (Jeffreys, 2005).

There are also individuals who show none of the usual and customary emotional reactions to a loss due to death (Bonanno et al., 2002; Wortman & Silver, 1989). Such persons are described in the literature as *resilient* "people who after a loss have positive emotional experiences and show only minor and transient disruptions in their ability to function" (Bonanno, 2004, p. 20).

Although there is continuing research to determine the reason for what is believed to be nonpathological absence of the symptoms of grief, the people I have worked with in clinical practice, hospitals, and workplace settings who suffer a loss continue to demonstrate the natural and expected expression of sadness and other feelings of grief. Where these reactions were absent or minimal, there have been adequate explanations for such absence. These include but are not limited to restrictions on expression of feelings learned in childhood, fear of loss of control, resistance to acknowledging the painful reality of loss, and intervening practical responsibilities to others that place the person's grieving on "hold." These may be based on the nature of attachment styles developed in childhood and further shaped in their adult versions.

There are also mourners who do not grieve because the nature of the relationship with the person who died was abusive, controlling, or sufficiently negative to leave them feeling liberated. For such persons, the loss generates positive feelings, which are contrary to the feelings and thoughts friends and family may have been expecting. Absence of grief reactions have in the past led to the diagnosis of complicated grief and the person had to deal with others wanting to know why they showed no sadness but rather a sense of freedom and an enthusiastic view of their new future (Elison & McGonigle, 2003). Further, many persons caring for a very ill loved one for months and years feel very relieved when the ill one dies. Care providers must help to normalize these feelings and assist with any guilt that may follow from the feeling of relief and freedom from burden.

## Anger

Take a rattle away from a baby and the baby cries—a quavering vibrato, which is usually accompanied by a reddening face. This is the cry of anger, a natural reaction to loss. Missed out on a good parking space when another driver slipped in ahead of you? Anger! Lose your car keys or a contract bid? Anger is not unusual in any of these cases. But when life, a relationship, or a job is at stake, anger can take on frightening proportions.

A grieving person's anger can be intimidating. He or she may scream out, bang fists, slam doors, or have hostile outbursts. The care provider needs to view this as part of the grief response and be available to the person despite the expression of rage. Anger may be directed to anyone connected with the death, diagnosis, layoff, or other loss situation; or to God or a belief system. Anger may even be directed toward the care provider who then becomes a part of the safe space for the grieving person. An Exquisite Witness will understand that this is part of the grieving process for this individual and will provide a space for release of such anger. However, this does not mean that physical violence against the care provider (or others) is to be tolerated. (See "Externalizing the Feeling of Emotional Pain" in Chapter 9.)

Anger also has a quiet side. It may go underground and cause internal emotional and physical damage. A client may sit in your office gripping the armrests with white knuckles and deny feeling angry or claim that his anger will go away on its own. But anger does not simply disappear; it has to be acknowledged, accepted, and released safely.

## Fear

Many grieving people will express specific fears and general anxiety as part of their grief reaction: (a) *I don't believe I can make it on my own*, (b) *I'm afraid I will be alone for the rest of my life*, (c) *Maybe I (or a loved one) will get sick and die too*, (d) *I'm afraid I will go crazy*! and (e) *I don't know why I am frightened but I just am*. Underlying all of these statements are fears about one's physical and emotional survival.

One woman who lost her baby told me, "I'm afraid my husband won't come home alive from work." She also feared that she would never get pregnant again. Children who lose a parent usually express fear for the health of their surviving parent. Children who lose a brother or sister may fear that they will die of the disease that killed their sibling. In general, it is not unusual for bereaved people to feel threatened by any possibility of losing another loved one.

## Guilt

"Guilt is a normal and expectable aspect of the grief experience" (Rando, 1984, p. 31). Much of the guilt we see in grieving people is related to the "imperfection of human relationships" (Raphael, 1983, p. 45). Guilt is often most pronounced in bereaved parents and survivors of suicide but is not unusual for any type of loss.

Guilt usually comes from two sources: the nature of the death and its preventability, and from relationship issues (Archer, 1999). Some grieving people may have a clear and valid reason for their guilt—they were responsible for another's death or severe injury through neglect or error in judgment. In other cases, the guilt comes from "shouldisms," that is, from what they believe they should have done or not done in the relationship while the deceased was still alive: (a) *I didn't visit her enough,* (b) *Why did I not hear his call for help?* (c) *I should have called 911 sooner,* (d) *I should have insisted on a third opinion,* or (e) *I should have visited her more often and taken a greater role in her care.*

Sometimes, the guilt has no rational or tangible source: "I just feel guilty because I am still alive and he or she is not." Other clients focused on self-reproach as a way of creating some meaning in a situation that has no precedent or suitable explanation. Bereaved parents often express profound guilt at not having protected their child. Though there usually is no basis in reality for such feelings, parents may go to great lengths to find cause for self-blame. Here is a personal reflection:

> As have many other parents who have lost a child to a protracted illness, we agonized many, many times over what we might have done differently. We wished we had let Steven stay home from school more often, helped him and his siblings to better understand his medical condition, and made more time for our two other children.

In cases where the death may have been prevented, or where the grieving person was somehow responsible, guilt is a reasonable reaction and must be approached differently than guilt that is obviously not rooted in reality (see Chapter 9 for helping with guilt issues).

A special type of guilt arises when the relationship being mourned was characterized by ambivalence, conflict, or distance. Such conflicted relationships feed later grief and may require focus on past issues and forgiveness. A mourner may ruminate, replaying the times he or she was angry or unkind to the deceased or very ill person. A woman I saw professionally had frequently quarreled with her adolescent son about his hair and dress. After he was killed in a car crash, she nearly suffocated in self-reproach for not resolving her relationship with him when she had the opportunity.

## Sibling Guilt

Similarly, surviving siblings often feel plagued by guilt if they were jealous of or angry with a sister or brother who was ill and later died. They may also suffer from *survivor's guilt*, the guilt of having survived while a sibling died. Bereaved parents may also suffer survivor guilt. Many employees who survived layoffs carry a sense of guilt as well (Jeffreys, 2005). Another type of guilt arises among caregivers or family members who devoted themselves to the care of another and now feel relief when the death finally occurs.

According to Worden (2009), "Most often the guilt is irrational and will mitigate through reality testing" (p. 20). However, grieving people who have continuing distress and dysfunction due to complications arising from guilt must be given special attention to facilitate healing. (Chapter 9 provides suggestions for helping with guilt issues.)

## Shame

Shame is related to guilt. People who feel shame are often concerned about their social status. When ashamed, people say things like: (a) *I can't admit to anyone that my husband died of a drug overdose*, (b) *I do not want the funeral service or the obituary to reveal that our son died of AIDS*, (c) *It's so hard to be with our friends since John killed himself*, or (d) *I just know the whole neighborhood is talking about my being laid off*.

Certain types of loss are more prone to producing shame as a part of a grieving person's emotional reaction: death by suicide or drug overdose; criminal behavior such as driving while intoxicated; losses due to failure at school, layoff, bankruptcy, divorce, or legal misconduct; and stigmatizing illnesses and conditions such as AIDS or schizophrenia. When persons or families feel ashamed or disgraced, they may isolate themselves from

Care providers working with people who are blocked in this way need to assess the extent to which the individual is blocked and the basis or reasons for the emotional withholding. Therapy can focus on facilitating insight and the opportunity for the release of feelings. Methods for assisting with the release of feelings (externalization) are presented in Chapter 9.

their customary social support systems. They should be directed to support groups composed of others who have similar situations.

## Summary of Emotional Aspects

The degree to which grieving people feel comfortable expressing the emotions of grief is related to the emotional climate of the family of origin and their culture. Some ethnic traditions inhibit the expression of anger, sadness, or anxiety at a time of crisis. About one-third to one-half of the audiences I address indicate that they did not feel free to be emotionally expressive as children. Typically, I have found that people who were inhibited from expressing themselves as children will have more trouble expressing their grief as adults. They may know that giving in to their feelings would be helpful, but they cannot shake the messages they heard when they were young: "Don't cry! Act like a big boy or girl." Sadly, such grieving people may want desperately to cry out but cannot.

## Cognitive Disturbances of Grief

People who are grieving may find that their thought processes are also affected. The unreality of their new situation violates their assumptions about the world. Loved ones are gone or are terminally ill, careers have been aborted, and lifestyles and dreams have vanished, but the individual's inner picture of the old preloss world does not match the painful new external post-loss world reality, and a discrepancy exists. Matching pre- and post-loss is really hard to do for most people and can fatigue and disorient the mind.

Some common cognitive disturbances to this inconsistency include the following:

- *Responding sluggishly to questions*—A long lag between question and answers

- *Difficulty concentrating*—Easily distracted from tasks; lack of focus

- *Memory loss*—Unable to locate things, recall appointments

- *Loss of interest in usual activities*—Avoids work, sports, games, collecting, social clubs, hobbies

- *Loss of pleasure*—Avoids sex, entertainment, food, and social events

- *General numbness*—Shutdown of reactions to social stimuli, no pain, and no joy

- *Intrusive thoughts about the loss*—Constant barrage of thoughts, images associated with loss

- *Confusion and disorientation*—Difficulty with time sequences, location

- *A sense of futility about life*—"What's the use?" and "Why bother?" apathetic attitude

- *A sense of helplessness*—"Can't do anything to help myself" sense of impotence

- *Uncertainty about identity*—"Who am I now?" and "How do I present myself to others now?"

- *So-called crazy thoughts*—Hearing or seeing the lost loved one; feeling like they can communicate with them

- *Mental fatigue*—Too tired to figure things out, mind just won't work

Many of these symptoms, especially those relating to confusion and inability to concentrate, naturally dissipate over time. However, questions associated with personal and social identity may persist and require continued support. As grievers confront the question of meaning and identity in the post-loss world, they may ask: (a) "Who am I now?" (b) "What do I do now?" (c) "Why did this happen?" (d) "If I have been a good person, why am I being punished this way?" or (e) "Where was God?" For some, absorbing the traumatic loss event into a larger worldview, such as a religious or philosophical belief system, can help make sense of a tragedy. Others may be driven to review police or medical records. Those coping with workplace change and trauma may initiate grievance actions to obtain answers to the questions of "why" and "how."

Some people simply need to tell and retell their stories. Frequently, time with the care provider is the only time when they have the

Care providers should be aware that cognitive changes are frequently associated with depressed mood, and there is a tendency to diagnose a grieving person as depressed. Providers need to determine whether the level of depression requires special treatment or a referral to a mental health professional. When in doubt, make the referral. Further discussion of grief and clinical depression is provided in Chapter 10.

opportunity to do this. It is through the process of *meaning making* that people come to grips with the cognitive aspects of grief (Frankl, 1977).

# The Physical Component of Grief

## Health Factors

Nerves, muscle, bones, hormones, viscera, senses, the immune system, the heart, and circulation—all of these parts of our physical being are affected by the trauma of loss or threatened loss. According to Klerman and Clayton (1984), bereaved children and adults are "at greater risk for a variety of adverse health consequences" (p. 15). In addition, grieving people have been shown to be at increased risk of mortality; aggravation of existing medical conditions, especially cardiovascular problems; and such health-threatening behaviors as substance abuse, smoking, and poor nutrition (Klerman & Clayton, 1984; Parkes & Weiss, 1983). Further, continued grieving is stressful, and chronic stress lowers the ability of the immune system to protect the body from infection. Vulnerability to colds is not unusual among grieving people (Hirsch, Hofer, & Holland, 1984).

## Physical Symptoms

Grieving people complain of various combinations of the following physical complaints. These symptoms are not unlike those experienced by depressed persons.

- *Lack of energy*—Physical fatigue, too tired to do daily activities

- *Stomachaches*—Cramps, spasms, burning

- *Chest pain and tightness*—Dull ache or throbbing twinges

- *Shortness of breath*—Awareness of breathing, cannot catch their breath

- *Dryness or lump in throat*—Continued need to drink, throat muscle spasms

- *Multiple pains and other muscle aches*

- *Dizziness*—Head spinning, difficulty with balance

- *A perception of empty space within the body*—A "hole" or sense of something missing

- *Frequent colds*—Lowered immune function and colds, coughs, fevers

- *Nausea*—Feeling like they could vomit or simply a low-level queasiness

- *Sleep and appetite disturbance*—Unable to fall asleep, waking during the night, overeating, lack of appetite

- *Body change*—Loss of weight or weight gain

- *Sexual dysfunction*—Lack of desire, inability to engage in sexual behavior

## The Social Component of Grief

### Family and Other Relationships

Grief changes the individual's face to the world. Social roles, family relationships, and identity are all modified by significant loss. Some individuals shrink from social contact, whereas others overextend themselves socially.

Here is a personal recollection regarding the effect on my life of the death of my mother.

Care providers can help by advising good eating and sleeping habits, physical relaxation, physical exercise, and specially designated time-outs from active grieving. At the same time, care providers need to take clients' continuing physical symptoms seriously and refer those with lingering problems to their physician. This not only treats the grieving person with utmost respect but also enlists the medical practitioner as part of the grief support team. For example, grievers who develop clinical depression need to be evaluated to determine if antidepressant medication is indicated. Those exhibiting features of posttrauma stress should likewise be assessed for possible medical treatment.

I was 16 and the only kid in my group of teenage friends whose mother had died. Every time one of the guys said, "My mother says ..." I would feel a stab in my heart and become silent and withdrawn.

The death of my mother from cardiac arrest following surgery was a major change-producing event in my life. I was 16 and my sister was 10. My mother was 36 and her death put into motion a number of life-altering changes, as premature deaths frequently do.

The remarriage of my father during the early stages of our grief introduced a new person into the family system and limited our ability to talk comfortably about our loss. We moved out of state, away from friends and family, and what support may have been available was then cut off. The grief for my mother was buried deep within, and the priorities of college, military service, as well as later becoming a husband and father, filled my time and attention, further burying my grief for my mother.

Five years after our son Steven's death in 1975, I attended a "Life, Death, and Transition" workshop given by Elisabeth Kübler-Ross. As I began to work on my pain over his death, I found myself weeping for my mother. It took two workshops, as well as personal grief therapy, to get back to Steven and obtain some relief from the stored, unfinished grief material from my mother's death. I say "some" relief because my own awareness of grief and my clinical work with grieving people have shown me over and over that we never completely expunge grief from our hearts. Rather, we learn to manage and live side by side with grief as a part of who we are as we reclaim a life in the strange new post-loss world in which we find ourselves.

The death of my mother severely shifted the course of my life, and this is true to some extent of all loss in life. We are pushed, pulled, buffeted, seek, and find places of satisfaction and even joy. Yet, pain of loss can also serve to highlight the times of blessings and peace.

Care providers can help by normalizing much of the social discomfort a grieving person experiences and by identifying support groups where such experiences are shared and discussed. The provider can also bring family members of the bereaved together to educate them about how to be supportive to their relatives in the post-loss world. Further, the care provider can assist the grieving person by suggesting ways to respond to unwanted advice and hurtful words.

## Society and Attitudes Toward Grief

In a similar way, people react in special ways to a person whom they know has suffered a loss. Some individuals in the griever's social network avoid them—remember the "Safeway Samba" reported by a bereaved father? Others are overly solicitous, seeking out mourners and offering "should" advice.

Regrettably, some well-intentioned people say very hurtful and inappropriate things to grieving people. A couple who lost their first baby to SIDS was told, "Maybe you will be more careful with your future children." A mother whose son was shot and killed was asked after 6 weeks, "When are you going to stop crying?" A woman who suffered a miscarriage was told, "It was just a fetus. Why are you so upset?" I spend a good deal of time helping clients to cope with the avoiders, the advisors, and the hurters.

Grieving people are also hurt by lack of attention to their loss. One newly widowed woman was bewildered when no one at the family Thanksgiving dinner mentioned her recently deceased husband. Families frequently do not know what to do about "poor cousin Sue" who is now a widow, has three young children, and is sad and tired all the time.

Many fathers mourning children are hurt by the assumption of others that they need less sympathetic support than their wives. They hear comments such as, "This must be so terrible for your wife." Or, "How is your wife doing since the baby died?" as if their loss and pain were unimportant.

# The Spiritual Component of Grief

## Faith Resources and Life Philosophy

The human grief response is typically bound up with spiritual considerations. Many people suffering loss will turn to their belief system for help with death-related rituals, prayer support, comfort, and for advice on placing the loss within a greater spiritual context. Families and friends are usually drawn together to participate in funerals, burials, and memorials. It is a time when many reach back to their traditions for connection with some sense of comfort and understanding. Others may reject any notion of God or a Higher Power because they see their tragedy as incompatible with such a concept. Many ultimately reconnect with their faith systems, and some never do. There are also people who may have no particular faith system and seek comfort and answers in nontheological, humanistic, or other secular philosophies of life.

Care providers can help by determining the grieving person's desire for religious or other spiritual support and assisting in locating clergy or other spiritual advisors in the community. This should be done as a respectful offering of such resources and with the understanding that some grieving people may not wish this area of help.

# ☐ Past Loss Survey

One of the best ways to learn about grief is to use our own loss material as part of the subject matter. This is an opportunity to look for our own Cowbells. Let yourself become your own consultant to that part of you that may still be holding unfinished loss material. Understanding our own loss material—the heart dimension—provides personal data that can be related to the theoretical material on the grief process. Please complete the following exercise to help you identify some of your unfinished grief material or your Cowbells. (This can be done on a separate sheet.)

### EXERCISE 3: PAST LOSS SURVEY

1. List two important losses you have experienced. In addition to death, illness, and separation, consider other losses (e.g., pets, a home, dreams, jobs). Choose one from childhood if possible.
2. Locate the degree to which you still have feelings and thoughts concerning the two losses and mark the spot on the line between 1 and 10 to indicate to what degree each is still having a continued effect on your daily life. Please also list one or two feelings (if any) that still come up about this loss.

**LOSS**

1: ~~Another~~ *special* relationship w/ mom

*No Current Effect*                    *Major Current Effect*

1                         ⑤                         10

Feelings raised: Sadness, anger, hurt, loss

**LOSS**

2: _____

*No Current Effect*                    *Major Current Effect*

1                         5                         10

Feelings raised: _____

3. Briefly describe the ways in which your own loss experiences have helped or hindered your own personal or professional growth. Please be specific. (For example, does any particular loss make it uncomfortable for you to work with others who have experienced the same type of loss? Does your own loss experience give you a sense of comfort with a particular type of loss?)

You can use this survey for purposes of stimulating thinking about your own Cowbells. The exercise is a technique to start the process of uncovering unresolved grief material that may be interfering with your comfort in working with certain loss situations. It is not a clinical diagnosing instrument but rather a thought-provoking exercise.

You can do this survey repeatedly and get new material each time. The material that comes up can be placed in a journal and added to the Cowbells that you are gathering for self-discovery purposes. I have used it in training programs for care providers and also with grieving people who are seeking to identify the extent that old loss material is affecting current grief. If feelings have been stirred up by this exercise, this is gold for you. Do some journaling or talk to a trusted friend before continuing.

## ☐ Grief Process Theories: From Bowlby to Neimeyer

Understanding the nature of normal grief and how it heals is the foundation of the Exquisite Witness's head or knowledge dimension. This understanding enables the person who is helping grieving people to have a sense of the range of reactions to expect from grievers as well as being aware of the variety of explanations addressing the complex variations of the human grief response. These have direct implications for the development of various supportive and clinical interventions (hands dimension) for helping grieving people—when tears are not enough. (See Chapter 11.)

The literature on loss, grief, and the healing of grief contains the work of several important contributors who have studied and written about this human phenomenon from several perspectives. The following summary will highlight the main features of each writer's contribution to the understanding of grief and healing. This will be followed by a synthesis of seven conceptual points on the path to healing.

**Note:** While various writers have used different formats and emphasized one aspect of healing grief over another, the purpose for all of the explanations is to arrive at an understanding of how grieving people can be helped to heal. I have divided the theoretical material into two groups of writers: those who use a stage or phase design (Bowlby through Rando), and those who do not (Stroebe through Neimeyer).

## John Bowlby: Four Phases of Separation

John Bowlby (1969, 1973, 1980, 1982) outlined a four-phase process of what happens when a human being is separated from an attachment bond figure, such as mother, lover, sibling, friend, and pets. He includes symbolic losses (such as future dreams) as well as loss of youth, health, function, roles, and home.

*Phase I—Numbing*: An initial period of shutdown, denial, and unreality lasting for a few days to several weeks. Grieving people may appear to be doing very well during this time because they do not grieve outwardly.

*Phase II—Yearning and Searching*: A time during which the grieving person attempts to recover the person or other loss object. This is "attachment behavior." Mourners experience agitation and distress as they seek contact by calling out the name of the deceased loved one, wearing items of clothing that belonged to the deceased, and ruminating about that which was lost.

*Phase III—Disorganization and Despair*: A sad time during which hopes for reunion fade and the mourner acknowledges, "She or he is never coming back." Despair, fatigue, loss of motivation, and apathy are common. One bereaved father called this "the bleeding stage of grief."

*Phase IV—Reorganization*: A new definition of self is established as grieving persons create new patterns of thinking, feeling, and acting. "Who am I now?" "How do I fit in with others now?" "What new ways do I have to adopt?"

## Elisabeth Kübler-Ross: Five Stages of Loss

Elisabeth Kübler-Ross (1969) suggests five stages of loss as an outgrowth of her work with over 200 dying cancer patients and their families. These stages are still perhaps the most familiar to the lay public and should be referred to as descriptions of observed behaviors rather than required steps for healing grief.

*Stage I—Shock and Denial*: "No! It can't be!" "There must be some mix up with the x-rays." "Let's get another blood test." These expressions of shock and denial are common immediately after a loss or the threat of loss.

*Stage II—Anger*: Rage, resentment, bitterness, irritability, hostility, and violence are all expressions of the anger that grieving people may feel and express. Anger may also take the form of passivity, stubborn refusal to eat or comply with medical advice, or even to speak with family or medical staff.

*Stage III—Bargaining*: "If I start praying again, or pray more, maybe I will get well." "Maybe if I come in earlier and stay later, I will survive the next layoff." These are examples of bargaining through which a person seeks an extension of time or at least freedom from pain and discomfort.

*Stage IV—Depression*: Many individuals withdraw to prepare for the final act of dying. During this stage, patients may literally turn their back to visitors and staff in an attempt to conserve energy. They may spend time thinking about their lives, the meaning of life and death, or religious or other spiritual truths.

*Stage V—Acceptance*: This is perhaps the most misunderstood of these five stages. It refers to the fact that some terminally ill or bereaved persons may *intellectually* accept the unavoidable reality while at the same time remaining depressed, angry, and frightened.

## Colin Parkes and Robert Weiss: Tasks of Grieving

The three tasks outlined by Parkes and Weiss (1983) are based on data collected from the Harvard Bereavement Studies completed in 1973.

*Task I—Intellectual recognition and explanation of loss.* Mourners need to understand their loss, to have it make sense.

*Task II—Emotional acceptance of the loss.* In this phase the bereaved can recall the deceased without a resurgence of pain. To accomplish this, the bereaved must repeatedly confront memories and express feelings of pain.

*Task III—Assumption of a new identity.* This transition to a new way of thinking of oneself (e.g., as a widow, as an orphan, as unemployed) is often a turbulent time of painful reality testing.

These tasks provide for some of the basic requirements for healing: emotional release and the creation of a new identity in the post-loss world.

## William Worden: Four Tasks of Mourning

William Worden (2009) has made a major contribution with his conceptualization of four task-based categories of behavioral goals that must be addressed for healing to take place.

*Task I—To accept the reality of the loss.* A grieving person must realize intellectually that the loss has occurred before progress toward healing can take place. The primary objective at this time is to ultimately integrate the reality that the loss is irreversible and to neither deny nor minimize it. Examples of minimizing a loss include a teenage boy who told me, "My mom was sick for so long that I didn't get to spend much time with her anyway, so I don't miss her that much now," or an executive who reacts to being laid off by saying, "I knew it was time to move on anyway."

*Task II—To process the pain of grief.* Pain in this context refers not only to emotional pain but also to the physical and behavioral pain associated with loss. Worden (2009), as do Bowlby (1980) and Parkes and Weiss (1983), emphasizes the importance of experiencing this pain in order for grieving people to heal. Further, when this task is not sufficiently addressed because of avoidance or suppression of memories or images of the deceased, healing will be impeded, and the result may be emotional complications of grief or physical problems. Worden is clear that not everyone "experiences the same intensity of pain or feels it in the same way" (p. 44). However, those who do need to express their feelings should have the opportunity to do so in a safe and healthy way.

*Task III—To adjust to the world without the deceased.* Worden divides this set of tasks into three subsets: (a) external adjustments—adapting to such everyday functioning as cooking, shopping, and working; (b) internal adjustments—developing a new identity in a changed world; (c) spiritual adjustments—necessary changes in beliefs, values, and assumptions about the world.

*Task IV—To find an enduring connection with the deceased in the midst of embarking on a new life.* "Moving on with life," in this case, means being able to hold on to the inner picture of the person or other loss object and function in a changed world. The bond with the deceased or other loss is altered yet continues in the post-loss world. This relates to the concept of "continuing bonds" (Klass, Silverman, & Nickman, 1996).

In Chapter 9, we will use Worden's four tasks to describe how care providers can offer support and clinical interventions.

## Therese Rando: Phases and Processes of Mourning

Therese Rando (1984, 1993b) divides the responses of grieving people into three broad time periods or phases:

*Avoidance*—A time of denial, disorganization, and confusion.

*Confrontation*—A time of intense grief.

*Accommodation*—A time of diminished grief and reentry into the world as a changed individual.

Rando (1993b) describes six processes of mourning that are grouped into each of her three phases. She advises that these processes need to be addressed for healing to take place. When some interference prevents a process from occurring, a person is at risk for complicated mourning.

*Avoidance*

1. Recognizing the loss—Acknowledging and understanding the loss.

*Confrontation*

2. Reacting to the separation—Experiencing pain and feelings of loss and secondary losses.

3. Recollecting and reexperiencing the deceased in the relationship—Reviewing and grieving.

4. Relinquishing the old attachments—Both to deceased and to pre-loss assumptions about the world.

*Accommodation*

5.  Readjusting to move adaptively into the new world without forget-
    ting the old attachments—Revision of world assumptions, creating
    a new relationship with deceased, a new identity, and new ways to
    function in the post-loss world.

6.  Reinvesting energy formerly absorbed by the living bond into other
    relationships or activities, causes, or hopes.

The following writers describe the human grief process in a non-
stage-based format.

# Margaret Stroebe and Henk Schut: Dual Process Model of Grief

Stroebe and Schut's (1999, 2001a, 2001b) dual process model was developed as an alternative to stage-based models of human grief. In this view,
the grief response is explained as having two focuses:

*Loss-Oriented Focus*—Behaviors that express feelings of grief. These may
    include expressing a range of emotional reactions such as feelings of
    grief, as well as reviewing and reminiscing, yearning, and missing the
    lost loved one or prior condition.

*Restoration-Oriented Focus*—Behaviors that reorganize the self in the new,
    post-loss world. These include learning new skills, constructing a new
    identity, or relocating the inner image of the loved one. Feelings in
    this area of focus can range from pride of accomplishment to fear of
    the unknown.

Stroebe and Schut (1999, 2001a, 2001b) also describe an oscillation
phenomenon—the grieving person moves between engaging in the loss-
oriented focus and restoration-oriented focus in the post-loss world. In
this system, the care provider enables emotional release as well as confronting the new meanings in the post-loss world.

## Dennis Klass: Continuing Bonds After the Loss

Dennis Klass (1988, 1996; Klass & Goss, 1999) initially explains the healing of bereaved parents as the development of a new inner representation of the deceased child and an adjustment to a new social world.

*New Inner Representation*—Parents must ultimately revise the inner image of the child and find equilibrium with the new world reality. It is then possible to form a bond with this new image of the child, a bond that continues throughout the life of the parent. In a similar way, the continuing of bonds with other deceased loved ones facilitates healing in the post-loss world. This concept of continuing bonds has been extended to bereaved people of all ages.

*Reestablishment of Social Equilibrium*—In both the inner and outer worlds, parents must evolve an authenticated picture of who the lost loved one now is and who the bereaved parent now is to the outer world. The Compassionate Friends or Bereaved Parents of the USA support groups for bereaved parents and other grief support groups provide a social network where the bereaved parent, grieving child, or widow identity is normalized and accepted by others. In a similar way, groups for cancer patients, unemployed, and family survivors of homicide provide such acceptance and understanding.

## Kenneth Doka and Terry Martin: Patterns of Grieving

Doka and Martin (2010) have broadened the earlier concepts of gender-based styles of adaptive grief reactions. That is, women express with feelings and men express with intellectual and behavioral responses, to a continuum of grieving patterns that include intuitive at one end and instrumental at the other. The use of a continuum allows for the identification of grieving individuals at points along the scale without exclusive regard for gender. It also speaks to the reality of how human beings blend the two areas of grief reactions depending on several psychosocial factors. These include the nature and circumstances of the loss event, past loss experience, personality, family and social/cultural network influences.

The former use of women's versus men's style suggested a one-size-fits-all description of how people grieve and left no room for the complexity and range of individual differences in how people grieve. By shedding the male and female labels and using a universal application of intuitive (affective release focus) versus instrumental (cognitive/active focus), grief counselors and other providers helping grieving people can avoid the restrictions of stereotyping grief reactions according to gender or viewing one end of the grief patterns continuum as more favorable than the other for successfully adapting to the post-loss world.

## Thomas Attig: Relearning the World

Thomas Attig's work (1996, 2001) regarding the importance of the grieving person's need to relearn the world emphasizes the value of the care provider helping the grieving person to make sense of the post-loss world, to reinvent self in a world missing who or what used to be. Attig also endorses continuing bonds as necessary for healing grief.

## Robert Neimeyer: Meaning Reconstruction in the Post-Loss World

Robert Neimeyer (1998, 2001) emphasizes the need for many grieving people to restructure the meaning of their lives in order to reclaim them. He views each of us as developing a "self-narrative," defined as "an overarching cognitive-affective-behavioral structure that organizes the 'micronarratives' of everyday life into a 'macronarrative' that consolidates our self-understanding, establishes our characteristic range of emotions and goals, and guides our performance on the stage of the social world" (Neimeyer, 2004, pp. 53–54). Seen in this way, the basic meanings that constitute our life stories are not simply thoughts or cognitions, but are instead passionate assumptions that provide the existential, spiritual, social, and personal grounding for our unique life stories, for our sense of identity (Neimeyer, 2001).

When trauma or loss occurs, these meanings and assumptions are challenged and often profoundly disrupted, and have to be adjusted to help us find orientation in the new reality of the post-loss world in a way that secures the validation of significant others in our family, community, and culture. In emphasizing this quest to reaffirm or reconstruct a world of meaning that has been challenged by loss, Neimeyer (2001) would help the mourner seek answers to such questions as, "What do my loved one's life and death mean to me? Who am I now? What can I no longer take for granted in this changed world? What do I need to learn and who do I need to become in order to integrate this loss and move forward with my life?" In some respects, Neimeyer's (2001) theory recalls the work of Victor Frankl (1977), who urged those who suffered devastating losses to seek meaning in them in order for healing to take place.

## Summary of Grief Process Theories

The previous review of important explanations of the human grief response and how grief may proceed over time is a necessary part of the care provider's understanding of the predictable aspects of grief behavior—the head dimension of the Exquisite Witness. Understanding the origin and function of the human grief response demystifies the process and imparts to the care provider a sense of the normalcy of grief and its importance in the healing through loss of grieving people.

## ☐ The Path to Healing

The following seven basic concepts are drawn from this chapter and can provide a summary of the material for understanding grief and formulating a plan for helping grieving people.

1. *Attachment is an instinctive behavior* occurring from infancy throughout adulthood, which has as its purpose the protection and survival of the individual. Early individual patterns of attachment affect the nature of relationships throughout life as well as issues associated with mourning. The goal of attachment behavior is survival.

2. *Grief reactions are a normal part* of the human behavioral repertoire and will occur whenever attachment bonds are broken or threatened. Grieving people must be helped to see the normalcy of their grief responses. Under certain conditions, grief can become complicated and pathological.

3. *The human grief reaction* manifests in four aspects of an individual's living: psychological, physical, social, and spiritual. The thoughts, feelings, and behaviors that compose the grief response may include shock, avoidance, physical and emotional pain, confusion, and other

cognitive disturbances, withdrawal and other social disturbances, and spiritual questioning or seeking.

4. *The expression of emotional pain*—anger, fear, sadness, guilt, shame—surface in many grieving people as they confront the reality of their loss or threat of loss.

5. *The reconstruction of a grieving person's life story*, identities, and social meanings in the post-loss world is a critical part of the healing process.

6. As a grieving person *relearns the world* after a loss, the inner representation of the lost loved one or lost condition changes. This enables the grieving person to maintain a connection or *continuing bond* to that which was lost in a way that matches the new reality.

7. We can discern several *predictable patterns* in the way that people show their grief over time. However, the Exquisite Witness care provider needs to learn and respect the individual differences of grieving people that derive from personal styles of coping as well as from the person's family, culture, and society. Predicting the nature of any individual's grief is at best an estimate of what to expect.

## ☐ Conclusion

Whether you are a family doctor, a professional mental health provider, a hospice volunteer making a home visit, an oncology nurse, a pastoral care bereavement worker, school counselor, clergy, friend, or family caregiver, understanding the nature of the human grief response and its complexities over time will give you the comfort of knowing what to expect when working with grieving people.

There are many instances where the volunteer or professional care provider will just simply listen with heart and soul to provide a safe space for the grieving person to tell his or her story. The ability of a family to listen to a dying or bereaved person is an intrinsic part of the social support for grieving people. As providers, we must help family members learn to listen to one another.

Loss and grief typically occur within the context of family. The Exquisite Witness care provider must learn about current family relationships and dynamics to provide optimal care. These issues will be explored in Chapter 4.

**CHAPTER**

# Loss and Death in the Family

## ☐ Chapter Preview

- Introduction

- Death/Loss and Change in the Family: Primary and Secondary Factors

- Factors Influencing the Family Grief Reaction

- Family Life-Cycle Stages and Objectives

- Unfinished Grief and Emotional Inheritance

- Family Loss Genogram

- Healing Tasks for the Grieving Family

- Factors Interfering With Healing

- Conclusion

A universal task of all families, regardless of cultural diversity, is to resolve loss.

Pauline Boss (2004, p. 237)

# ☐ Introduction

## Family

Think family whenever you are working with a person who is faced with a loss or the threat of loss. Family is the basic social unit for the individual, and grief will play itself out among the members of that unit. Family members will typically be the most affected by a loss event, and their reactions will become part of the emotional climate of the grieving person.

## Family Change

Any significant change in a family creates a shift in its balance and a need for the realignment of relationships and responsibilities, and the reallocation of resources, including time, energy, and money. Death, divorce, separation, birth or adoption, chronic or terminal illness, disability, natural disaster, job loss, relocation, and the blending of families are all change events that require that a new balance be established. Even though some of these changes bring joy, they are always accompanied by a loss of the world that was; and this can generate grief responses. We will discuss the family as it is affected by such changes so that the care provider will have an understanding of how to help families who are coping with death, illness, and other significant loss or threat of loss.

In this chapter, we will look at the family as a system with its own needs and unique forms of grief reactions. Among the factors we will consider are the stage of the family in terms of life-cycle events and the role of unfinished grief that moves down through the generations to mix with new grief. We will also consider the needed realignments and shifts in the organization of the family as grief unfolds. These changes in family organization sometimes cause additional and ongoing grief for its members. Family tasks that must be addressed for healing to take place will also be reviewed. The special nature of the grief of children, parents, and older adults will be discussed in Chapters 5, 6, and 7, respectively.

## Family Defined

I define *family* as intentional as well as biological units. Therefore, groups of single people, gay couples, religious communities, and long-term neighbors who have developed a highly connected social network are considered families. In addition, long-standing workplace colleagues or those who bond through the intensity of their task, for example, fire, police, and military, can serve an extended and supportive family role. It is important for a care provider to learn who makes up the grieving person's support system so that they can play a role during the grief process.

## ☐ Death/Loss and Change in the Family: Primary and Secondary Factors

> The pain of death touches all survivors' relationships with others, some of whom may never have even known the person who died.
>
> Froma Walsh & Monica McGoldrick (1991, p. 3)

## Rippling Effects of Primary Loss

When a family is affected by a primary loss, such as death, divorce, disaster, or job loss, there is a painful transition from the world that was. The hopes, dreams, and predictions that could be counted on in the pre-loss world are shattered, and grieving people find themselves thrust into an alien world. Family members are propelled into a new life stripped of their old assumptions, identifications, and meanings. Their pre-loss world is simply gone. We may think our assumptions about the world will last forever but tragic loss shows us how tenuous our assumptions are. The flowing moments of life are fleeting, temporary, and fragile. It is scary for us to think about the impermanence of our life and that of our loved ones. Mortality—theirs and ours—is like "staring at the sun," we can only do this for short periods of time, and then must turn away (Triesman & Angelo, 2004; Yalom, 2008).

Family members must also cope with the sudden awareness of the end of or threat to existing plans for the future. Attending college, buying a new car or home, changing jobs, looking forward to familiar activities and routines—all these are either thwarted or put in jeopardy. When a beloved grandmother dies, a family may lose the sense of comfort they enjoyed that was associated with spending the holidays together at her house. Even expected and positive changes such as the children going off to college or taking new jobs bring an end to those great Sunday morning breakfasts together.

## Secondary Losses for Family Members

The secondary losses that result from the primary loss—death, illness, disability, and layoff—also create changes in the life activities of the family and a trail of loss and grief in their wake. When there is a death or other traumatic loss in a family, it is natural for each family member to evaluate the effect of the loss or threat of loss on his or her life. The following examples illustrate secondary losses that flash into the minds of the surviving loved ones:

- A newly widowed mother and her children have a session with a counselor to figure out how to reorganize their lives. The preteen daughter announces with anger and some anxiety, "How will I get to camp without Dad's paycheck to count on anymore!" Her older brother says nothing, but he is thinking about the bill for his next semester's college tuition that arrived a week after his father's funeral.

- A young man, recently a father, is about to be promoted to a much more responsible position at work when his wife is killed in an auto crash. He finds himself grieving not only for his wife but also for the likelihood that his single-parent responsibilities will end his chances for a promotion at work.

- A mother of two preteens is bedridden with severe cardiac dysfunction. At night in their room, the girls cry together over the afterschool club activities they will no longer be able to attend now that the household responsibilities fall on their shoulders.

- At a Bereaved Parents of the USA support group meeting, an elderly woman points out that the death of her 50-year-old daughter means not only the loss of her only child but the loss of the person she counted on to care for her as she aged.

When the primary wage earner has been laid off, the family must not only deal with the anxiety about the loss of financial support or health insurance but also the unhappiness of the person now out of work. Family members may also fear that others may view them differently as a result of the job loss. When a parent becomes seriously ill or disabled, children lose not only the attention of that parent but also find the caregiving parent much less available. Children of a chronically ill parent may feel painfully different from their peers. Many new widows and divorced women find themselves in a downward economic spiral that forces them to move into less expensive housing, curtail their children's activities, and to severely reduce their food and clothing budgets.

Separation and divorce bring many other changes besides the end of a marriage. Often children have to balance their time between two homes, cope with conflicts that continue beyond the physical separation of parents, worry about how they look to others, care for lonely parents, and adapt to new routines. The aftershocks of traumatic loss in the family continue to trigger grief reactions through the family's future generations (Bowen, 1991). The absence of one parent from the life of the children, from the grandchildren, and from special life transition events can have lingering effects on the family system through the years. Additionally, the lack of home-life stability and the associated limitations on financial resources continues to yield ongoing losses.

As a care provider, you will need to gather sufficient background information regarding the rippling effects of the secondary losses that flow from a primary loss event such as death, job loss, relocation, financial hardship, separation, and divorce in the family. Some people talk about their concerns over these secondary losses easily. Others have a harder time. Many feel guilty.

As a care provider, one of your most helpful functions is to assure family members that thinking "What do I lose?" is a normal reaction and part of the grieving process. When people understand the nature of secondary loss and accept that their responses are natural, they often feel more willing to share their grief experience with each other.

If family members are reluctant to talk about their concerns over what they have lost, care providers can initiate the discussion by making a general statement about how most people automatically inventory what will be different as a result of their loss.

Care providers can also give examples of how other grieving people have thought about losses and can even compile a master list of "What do I lose?" items as a teaching device.

# ☐ Factors Influencing the Family Grief Reaction

The family's grief reaction—their thoughts, feelings, and behaviors—will be influenced by the factors listed next. The care provider will need to be aware of these influences on grieving behavior and consider them when deciding how to help a particular family.

- Stages of the family life-cycle development

- Family values and belief systems

- The role of the dying or deceased person in the family

- The nature of the death

- The age of the person dying, deceased, or bereaved

- The nature of the attachments to family members

- The nature of the family's functioning

- Disenfranchised grief

- Additional factors affecting the nature of grief

## Stages of the Family Life-Cycle Development

A newly married couple with young children will have different needs than an elderly couple with grandchildren. At each stage in the life of a family, different goals are affected by a loss. For example, the death of a young father leaves a woman alone as a single parent with different issues than an older widow with grown children.

## Family Values and Belief Systems

Family values flow from social and cultural heritages and unique family traditions that develop over time. Attitudes toward life and death, dealing with death-related rituals, and patterns of communication about grief vary and require great respect and sensitivity from the care provider.

## The Role of the Dying or Deceased Person in the Family

Each role—wage earner, elder, patriarch, matriarch, problem solver, entertainer, social convener, mechanic, financial advisor, turkey carver, pie baker—has its own set of expectations that are lost along with the person. Care providers may need to locate additional resources for a family to fill the holes that have been left by the loss.

## The Nature of the Death

Grief varies with the circumstances under which the loss occurred. Some loss events can complicate the grief reactions; sudden, violent, and unexpected deaths, for example. Family members who have witnessed violent deaths are more likely to develop problematic grieving such as posttraumatic reactions. Lengthy illnesses can drain a family of energy, time, and motivation to engage in other aspects of life. Further discussion of types of death is as follows.

### Sudden Deaths

Sudden deaths do not allow for any preparation time for the family. There is no opportunity to have developed internal images (fantasies) of the future without the loved one. There is no chance to say good-bye, and survivors may feel guilty that they are still alive.

### Lingering Deaths

Lingering deaths do provide time to prepare, to begin the grieving process, to experience many changes, and to anticipate the changes to come. The family system is altered gradually. Painful medical procedures may be part of the experience, and resentment at the disruption of life caused by caregiving may occur. This anger and resentment may also be followed by guilt. Siblings may be jealous of the attention their sick brother or sister receives; this is normal. Opportunities for saying good-bye and having a dignified and spiritually affirming death are possible.

With the lingering death of a homebound terminally ill person, more than the body is lost. The after-death removal of the hospital bed, medicines, oxygen, or other medical support apparatus leaves a gaping physical hole; the departure of outside nursing help creates a sense of emptiness. Caregivers may also be physically and emotionally exhausted from the prolonged dying of a loved one. They may feel relief and it is not uncommon for guilt to follow this. Families, therefore, need to expect a reaction at the end of their caregiving role, and the provider can help to normalize this reality for them.

## Suicide

Suicide reportedly claims the life of more than 30,000 people each year in the United States (National Vital Statistics Reports, 2004). Families who have experienced the death of a loved one who has taken his or her life typically have a very difficult and complex grief journey. Parents bereaved by suicide have, in my experience, an enormous level of intense grief and may require long periods of provider support. Emotions range from rage to pain, guilt, shame, and fear. The unfinished business of the loved one who has completed suicide is left in the lap of his or her family. Families sometimes are reluctant to talk about the death as a suicide and even omit this fact from obituaries. Guilt is a prominently expressed feeling in a suicide death and must be listened to and not belittled. Later in the grief process, guilt can be gently reality tested. Should guilt or rage become a fixed part of the grieving person's sense of self, referral to a mental health provider may be required. Support groups for family survivors of suicide are available. (See Appendix A.)

## Homicide and Drunk Driving

Death by homicide presents its own sense of horror for family members. They are tortured by images of their loved one being terrified, in agonizing pain, and helpless. They may have rage at the perpetrators and have no way to express it directly. Legal procedures may keep the wounds open for a protracted period of time. This may also be true for survivors of drunk driving. There are a great number of homicides that go unsolved and often unprosecuted. Surviving loved ones of such deaths are at high risk for endless grief. There are special support groups for the family survivors of homicide and for victims of drunk-driving deaths. (See Appendix A.)

# The Age of the Person Dying, Deceased, or Bereaved

Grief reactions are typically influenced by the age of the person who has died. Normally, the death of an older aged adult is considered an expected death, whereas the death of a child has been labeled "unthinkable" by Rosen (1990, p. 61). However, the loss of an older adult can be just as painful. I've been with teenagers who sobbed as they recounted the loss of beloved grandparents and even great-grandparents. Here is an example from a family I know.

> I listened to the deeply sad words expressed by a bereaved great-granddaughter in a family discussion at her grandmother's home after the funeral of her great-grandpa. The teenage girl talked about her many visits to great-grandpa in the nursing home, how he loved to tell her of his early days in this country. She enjoyed this time and now sobbed as she expressed grief at missing his smile when she came into his room and also pushing him in his wheelchair around the floors and grounds.

Certain deaths—that of a child, the loss of a spouse on the threshold of retirement, or of a parent just before one's wedding—provide a sense of untimeliness that adds an additional thread of pain to the grief reaction. Why now we ask ourselves.

I have also heard women at Bereaved Parents of the USA meetings who have lost grown children question the intensity of the grief reaction of women who suffered miscarriage or neonatal deaths. They felt that the younger the child, the weaker the attachment bond, and therefore the more attenuated the grief should be. However, each type of loss has its own misery. Parents of deceased grown children mourn the people they knew and loved; parents of infants mourn the loss of the opportunity to be parents and the loss of the child they would never know. We cannot prejudge the effect of age or timeliness on the nature or intensity of grief.

Care providers can help a family and their friends to understand that there is no one right way to grieve. All grief is valid regardless of who, when, and how the loss occurred. Various examples of normal grief reactions can be mentioned, and it can also be a time to teach some of the psychological basics of the how and why we humans grieve. (See Chapter 3.)

The care provider can offer an opportunity to discuss these issues or arrange for a referral to a mental health provider. Problematic relationships can lead to complicated grief reactions such as chronic grief, distorted grief, or clinical depression. An awareness of past relationship and attachment history can provide necessary background information.

## The Nature of the Attachments to Family Members

The intensity of the attachment to the person who died, the degree of dependency, and the quantity of unfinished business with that person all affect how we grieve. If the surviving member of a couple was very dependent upon the other, or derived his or her self-image from the lost loved one, grief may be intense, prolonged, and interfere with daily functioning. Survivors of ambivalent or abusive relationships often have to deal with unfinished business before they can focus specifically on the loss.

## The Nature of the Family's Functioning

The degree to which the family members communicate with each other and with people outside of the family can have an impact on grief. The existence of social connections to various parts of the community—faith community, social clubs and recreational groupings, workplace friends, and neighbors—can yield rich levels of support. Some families choose to remain more secluded from their social surroundings or do not know how to express their needs and receive support. Family therapists have found that many Western culture families who have a more open style of communicating both within and outside of the family are generally more open to support and heal more quickly than families that have relatively closed patterns of communication (Walsh & McGoldrick, 1991, 2004).

Families with preexisting conflicts among their members may reflect this in their grief during and beyond the mourning rituals, and add additional stress to an already stressful situation. They may lack connection, fail to support each other, and even continue hostilities. The Melbourne Family Grief Study comparing families coping with death from cancer that were rated as adaptive (high cohesive, expressive) or maladaptive (low cohesive, low expressive) found that there is "a close link between family functioning and the psychosocial outcome of bereavement" (Kissane

Care providers should be aware that while many families can benefit from external support, individuals, families, and cultures vary in the function and value placed on sharing their feelings. This is true for communication within or outside of the family boundaries. The care provider can get a sense of the family's style of communication during informal discussions and by observing how the family interacts. Additionally, being with the family at home, in the hospital cafeteria, in the visitor's lounge, and in the hospital room can also yield important information on how family members communicate.

et al., 1996, p. 665). Low-communicating families had the highest intensity of grief, and maladaptive families had the highest levels of depression and overall psychological distress (Kissane et al., 1996). I have seen some families remain at odds and erupt in angry turmoil during discussions of inheritance and distribution of the deceased person's belongings. Other families are able to effect a temporary truce during the early period of mourning and have even been able to use the period of bereavement as an opportunity to begin the healing of old wounds.

## Disenfranchised Grief

"Every society and its sub-cultures have norms that provide expectations for how one is to behave but also how one is to feel and think" (Doka, 2002a, p. 6). The grief of certain groups—children, the mentally ill, the intellectually retarded, elderly, gay partners, ex-spouses, clandestine lovers, and legal offenders—is frequently invalidated (Doka, 1989, 2002a). Medical and pastoral care providers, schoolteachers, classmates, and work colleagues also may be overlooked as grievers. Not only can certain grievers be disenfranchised but also certain types of loss are open to invalidation. Grief for abortion, miscarriage, giving a baby up for adoption, pet death, and death of a friend are examples of disenfranchised losses. The grief of the disenfranchised has sorrow that may be hidden or unrecognized by the people in their lives. Such people grieve alone, painfully alone.

Some individuals disenfranchise themselves. Here is a personal story:

I participated in a local funeral for a husband, wife, and their daughter who were killed in a small plane crash. The community was devastated, and several close friends of the family gathered in a small room prior to the ceremony. I attempted to comfort a man I know who was especially distraught. He looked up and said, "Oh, I'm okay. I'm just a friend."

## Nondeath Losses

Zinner (2002) points to the need to take a broader view of loss and to legitimize the grief reactions to nondeath loss events. She cites a number of examples of disenfranchised nondeath losses gleaned from grief research: aging and dementia; childhood trauma; community disasters; chronic illness or disabilities; hearing, speech, vision, and other impairments; injuries; mental retardation; alcohol and drug abuse in the home; marital dysfunction; loss of romantic relationship; immigration; pet loss; and relocation.

## Terminally Ill, the Dying, and Their Families

So often the terminally ill, the dying and their families become "hidden grievers" as friends and neighbors become accustomed to the wheelchair, special equipment, the lack of visibility outside of the home, and gradually withdraw their attention to the family. Often, nondeath losses are not considered valid reasons for grieving. Families whose primary wage earner is laid off experience grief and mourn the loss of the sense of financial security they had before the loss. Children who overhear their anxious parents discussing financial concerns may carry the burden of uncertainty with them to school, playground, and the neighborhood. Teachers, guidance counselors, and other school staff must be sensitive to such loss events and the continued effect they may have on students.

Zinner (2002) describes how some people may determine the validity of a loss using the *Hallmark test*: "If Hallmark™ Cards has a card for it, then the loss is legitimate. If not, we tend to believe that people don't have a valid cause to mourn" (p. 391). Where does the ex-wife sit at the funeral? How does the partner of a man who dies of AIDS participate in the funeral that has been planned by the partner's parents? Adults may not want to listen to a young person grieve after a cat dies.

## Infertility

Couples who have tried repeatedly to have a baby and have been unsuccessful represent another group of hidden grievers who receive little social support. This is partly because infertility is not usually a topic of discussion. However, even when it is known that they are trying but have not gotten pregnant, family and friends are reluctant to call or somehow offer some support. The grief over what is not happening ripples outward to the couple's parents, grandparents, siblings, and close friends. It is very sad and frustrating for couples who are so very anxious to begin a family and lack consistent social support.

## *Ambiguous Loss*

"An ambiguous loss is defined an unclear loss—a loved one missing either physically or psychologically" (Boss, 2004, p. 237; see also Walsh & McGoldrick, 2004). We usually picture a situation where the body has not been recovered from war action; drowning; air, sea or ground disasters; fires; kidnappings; and other disappearances. Boss (2004) calls this *physical absence with psychological presence,* where there is continued holding of the image of the lost loved one because there is no tangible proof of death.

However, ambiguity occurs as well in other circumstances of loss often with resulting chronic grief reactions from family and friends. Such losses are referred to as *psychological absence with physical presence,* where a loved one is missing psychologically but is physically present. This takes place in families where there is dementia, depression, addictions, severe autism, organic brain disorder, stroke, severe homesickness after immigration, and chronic life-limiting mental or physical illness and disability.

Here are several examples: I recall a story in a documentary, *Death the Trip of a Lifetime* (Ambrose Video Publishing, Inc., 1993) where a mother is determined to keep the American flag flying outside of her Maryland home until she has final proof of the death of her son who was reported missing in action in the Vietnam War. A terminal cancer patient I worked with complained that he was receiving less emotional and social support from friends because of his presenting himself as cheerful, socially active and minimally anxious about the reality of his illness. His attempts to keep a positive outlook on his remaining life resulted in less contact and support from friends than he received when he looked and acted more in keeping with the seriousness of his medical condition. He decided to be more honest with family and friends regarding his pain, his extreme exhaustion, and the ever-present fear of death. Additionally, many of the international students in my Loss and

Care providers may have to help a couple struggling with the complex and financially draining infertility treatments to avoid displacing anger on each other and teach them how to keep lines of communication open.

Bereavement course report severe homesickness as a major loss issue and feel very alone in their grief.

I received a phone call in April 2010, from a Reuters reporter asking me to comment on a story he was preparing regarding the mixed reactions of 9/11 survivors and other citizens to the continued search for human fragments in the rubble remaining from the 2001 destruction of the New York World Trade Center. He wanted to know why it was so important to spend the money and time to keep on looking for DNA that could identify victims lacking definitive proof of death. Although there are some who are not in great need of confirmation of their loved one's death, there continue to be others who are having great difficulty coping with the unknown, the ambiguous loss of no body or fragment to bury or make a part of a memorial ritual, to say good-bye to. Part of the grieving process involves letting go of the physical being of someone who has died, saying good-bye. It's hard to say good-bye when there is nothing tangible to say good-bye to. The result is chronic or prolonged grief reaction.

Ambiguous loss has been described as the "loss that defies closure" (Boss, 2004, p. 239). The long-term effects are depression, ambivalence, anxiety, guilt, anger, and inability to adjust to some level of comfort in their lives. Inasmuch as we require some degree of meaning making or making some sense of the situation for adjusting to life, the ambiguity continues to eat away at the chance to reclaim some comfortable level of living. We will discuss some of the methods for helping families and individuals to cope with and find some meaning in their ambiguous loss grieving in Chapter 9.

### Adoption

Although adoption can be a wonderful and positive experience, it may sometimes present difficulties and represent another potential area of loss and disenfranchised grief. Some problematic areas are (a) the grief of the birth mother who lives with the loss of the child she gave up, (b) grief for those adoptive parents who continue to wonder what their own biological children and grandchildren would have looked like, and (c) the adopted child's grief at some point when he or she learns of the adoption and the loss of the birth parents.

## Additional Factors Affecting the Nature of Grief

Education level, economic realities, spiritual resources, cultural expectations, and available community resources will have an effect on how

The care provider's role is always to enfranchise, to empower the grievers to sigh, cry, and express their rage, their fears, and confusion. Frequently, other hidden losses impact on current grief and may be unrecognized as a factor in the intensity of their grief reaction. Providers can educate families about the ramifications of the added grief from such undercover losses as continuation of genetic legacy, stigmatization and lack of acceptance of the adopted child by others, and inability to locate birth family.

family members grieve. For example, people who are expected back on the job after a 3-day "bereavement leave" are not likely to have had time to sufficiently grieve. A family whose financial resources have been drained by caring for a terminally ill family member will have additional anxieties to cope with on top of their grief. Some families are isolated because they have had to relocate so many times and have no local family or long established friendships to count on for support. In other cases, family mourning behaviors will be affected by the traditions of their faith and cultural heritage. Some families may not be part of a religious group, and the care provider will have to help them seek available social support in the community. (See Appendix A for a list of support groups found in many communities.)

## ☐ Family Life-Cycle Stages and Objectives

### Family Life-Cycle Stages

As families develop, they pass through various transition periods during which certain tasks have to be accomplished for the health and well-being of its members. During some periods, there is a natural moving away of family members—from home to school, to jobs, to marriage, to retirement. The life-cycle stages presented in Table 4.1 provide a road map of the natural tasks that families will typically address at each stage. When a traumatic loss or threat of loss occurs, the objectives for a particular stage may be severely compromised. In some cases, traumatic loss or threat of loss has the effect of drawing people back into the nuclear family against the flow of natural developmental movement away from home. This disruption of the tasks in each stage creates yet another series of losses for family members (McGoldrick & Walsh, 1991a; Rosen, 1990).

**TABLE 4.1. The Family Life-Cycle Stages**

| Developmental Stage | Objectives Being Addressed |
| --- | --- |
| 1. Young adult moving between family of origin and new family | Become independent of parents; establish adult role in college or job; seek and obtain a mate |
| 2. Newly joined couple | Form new nuclear dyad; realign and modify attachments to family of origin |
| 3. Family with young children | Learn parent roles; integrate children into couplehood; further develop connections to family of origin |
| 4. Family with adolescents | Adapt to children who are beginning the move away from the family; redirect energy back into couple |
| 5. Empty nested | Adapt to new freedom as a couple and reconstruct the relationship; continued adaptation to children as adults, and to grandparent role; manage health issues for self and own parents |
| 6. Later life | Adapt to retirement; coping with physical decline and multiple losses of advanced age; facing death of spouse and own mortality |

The material in Table 4.1 has been drawn partially from concepts gathered from the work of McGoldrick and Walsh (1991a), Rosen (1990), and Walsh and McGoldrick (2004) as well as from my clinical practice.

## Effects of Traumatic Loss in Each of the Stages

The effects of traumatic loss in each of the stages of family development depend on whether family members are moving toward or away from the family unit in a given stage. A death, a frightening medical diagnosis, disability, financial or other traumatic loss event has the potential for thwarting the natural push outward of younger family members and creates a strong force pulling them back into the original family unit.

The care provider needs to understand how the disruptions to a family's natural developmental inclinations at each stage add additional stress to grieving. Realizing what is at risk for family members at each stage of the life cycle when there is a death, separation, or other loss will give the care provider a fuller understanding of the grief reactions of family members.

A college-age child, for example, may decide to attend a local school and live at home to help out in the face of an impending death or serious illness of a parent. An engaged couple may postpone its marriage. A young adult may turn down a good job opportunity in another city. This push–pull effect, described by Rosen (1990, p. 51), is at work in every stage but is more prominent during adolescence (Stage 4) or young adulthood. In Stage 5, family members who should be experiencing greater independence may resent being pulled back in at a time of crisis. Young adults, who have invested great energy in launching a career or a serious relationship may be heavily conflicted when a parent becomes terminally ill or dies, and leaves a surviving parent in need of assistance and care.

The anguish of a young person caught in such a conflict can result in resentment, guilt, and anxiety regarding the balancing of the push-pull equation as well as fear of sliding back into a dependent relationship with the parent. This may lead to chronic anger toward the parent.

People who are newly coupled (Stage 2) or creating a family (Stage 3) feel a strong pull into their young family unit, and they are establishing new boundaries with family of origin members (e.g., "Mom, please don't come over next week, we want to spend more time with just the three of us."). In Stage 5, couples also pull inward as they reestablish themselves as a two-person household once again (e.g., "Sorry, dear, we can't babysit; we're off on a trip for the weekend."). A death or other traumatic loss in these stages can impede the formation of newly independent family units (e.g., "I need Mom here all the time since I miscarried.").

The widowed or divorced midlife man or woman (Stage 5) may find that they are isolated in their grief. Their children are grown with families of their own and their friends may neglect or avoid them. "Single again" men and women frequently have referred to themselves as the fifth wheel at gatherings of family and friends. At a time when the couple should be enjoying their couple commitment, death or illness undermines the pull toward each other and may create a dependency on children or other relatives for managing grief and creating a new life.

Care providers may need to help bereaved individuals establish ground rules for visiting family, and find resources to assist in developing plans for personal growth and development as well as social activities, and financial independence. When desired, support groups for widows and widowers can do much to help them reenter the social world with their new identity. (See Appendix A.)

There is always the issue of how much time can be comfortably spent with married children, or a brother's or sister's family. Conjugally bereaved midlife individuals must create a whole new sense of identity to make sense of the new world in which they find themselves.

Older adults (Stage 6) have multiple loss issues to deal with when a spouse dies or when one becomes ill and perhaps has to live in a nursing home. The hopes for retirement leisure, increased freedom from work, and the pursuit of nonwork activities may be dashed when traumatic loss or illness occurs. Added to this is the disenfranchisement of elder grief that we will take a closer look at in Chapter 7.

# ☐  Unfinished Grief and Emotional Inheritance

Current grief is typically fueled, in part, from the leftover energy of old grief. This stored loss material is called "unfinished business" and can add to the intensity of the grief response. The unfinished business may come from the individual's own personal history (Cowbells), or it may have originated as unresolved issues passed down like a shock wave from earlier generations (Bowen, 1991). Care providers must have an appreciation of how such loss material has infiltrated the current grief response. Often, grieving people talk about older losses as they tell the story of a current loss. The grief care provider needs to attend to this old loss material to fully serve grieving people. Unfinished business from an older traumatic loss becomes an important part of the grieving person's story and part of the healing process.

## The Unfinished Business Model

The unfinished business model (Jeffreys, 2005) presents the three sources of unfinished material that are stored (Figure 4.1). Such old grief material may or may not be obvious to the grieving person or to the grief care

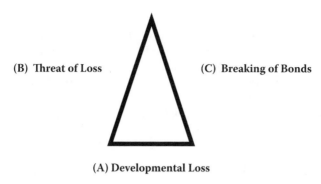

(C) Breaking of Bonds

(A) Developmental Loss

**FIGURE 4.1** Unfinished business model. (Reprinted with permission.)

provider. Compiling a thorough loss history using this model will help the clinical care provider and grieving person gain the best perspective so that the unfinished material can be addressed. (This will be discussed in greater detail in Chapter 9.)

## Developmental Loss

We naturally store loss material that is created by the normal and expected changes that occur throughout human development—moving from diaper to potty, from being at home with mom to going to school, from being a couple to welcoming home a new baby, or moving from work to retirement. Each time we make a transition to the next stage of development, we lose what went before—all that is comfortable and familiar—and this can create a grief reaction.

## The Threat of Loss

We store up loss material when we live under a constant threat of loss. The threat of loss can arise from having to cope with chronic financial insecurity, physical and emotional abuse, a life-threatening illness, a past history of traumatic losses, a loved one on military deployment, or living in a high-crime environment. Here the loss factor is the ever-present potential for a loss to occur and the chronic anticipatory grief reaction. This material is stored in the pool of unfinished business.

## The Breaking of Bonds

We also store up loss material when bonds we have made are broken or severely altered—when people die or leave, pets die, a beloved teddy bear

Care providers can help to identify unfinished loss material by taking a thorough loss history. This will alert the grieving person as well as the provider of old loss material that may need attention. This can also be addressed by having the person talk about the most difficult times of life or by having the individual compose an autobiography that includes a time line indicating losses and their life-changing effects.

is lost, we move to a new city, friends reject us, we are dropped from a team, we lose a job, or a loved one develops Alzheimer's disease. The distress of this loss is also added to the accumulated other loss material.

In summary, grief reactions that are not given the opportunity of expression and acknowledgment are stored as unfinished grief material. Grieving people are vulnerable to the reappearance of this material each time a new loss occurs. These are their Cowbells ringing. The goal for Exquisite Witness grief care providers is to sufficiently process personal loss material so that the inevitable ringing of Cowbells does not drown out the grieving client.

# ☐ Family Loss Genogram

Material in this section was drawn from Bowen (1991), McGoldrick (1991), McGoldrick and Gerson (1985), and Rosen (1990). The work of Murray Bowen provides us an understanding of the effects of past family deaths on current loss. He refers to unfinished business and tension left over from deaths in earlier generations as an *emotional shock wave* that moves down through the years and mingles with reactions to new deaths and traumatic loss. Some of the energy feeding such a shock wave is the result of lack of knowledge as to the cause of a death, secrets or suspicious circumstances around a death, lack of sufficient medical information regarding an old illness or death, relationship secrets, tensions, and breakups in earlier generations.

Again, to fulfill the heart dimension, the Exquisite Witness grief care provider must look first to him- or herself. The following family loss genogram exercise (Exercise 4) is included to provide you with an activity that can further inform you of illness and death-associated tensions coming from your own family system. Understanding how this is

**My Personal Genogram**

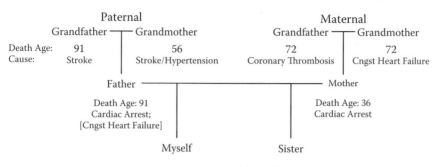

**FIGURE 4.2**

revealed in your own family loss genogram can be of assistance in working with individuals and families who need to understand the role of unfinished business on current grief.

I will very briefly summarize three generations of my own family in terms of health issues and age at death as a guide to this exercise. As I look back over the ages at death and the nature of serious illnesses of my parents and grandparents, and their siblings as well, a history of cardiovascular disease, cancer, and stroke are obvious. Our family has had its share of death due to illness, and I am aware that the fear of loss of a parent was very much in evidence in both of my parents. My first awareness of fear of loss of a loved one due to death from illness occurred when my mother's mother had been diagnosed with diabetes and was hospitalized for amputation of a gangrenous leg. I saw the fear in my mother's face as she prayed for the survival of my grandmother. I was 5 years old. The death of my father's mother at age 56 from a stroke threw me into the worst-case scenario we had feared when my other grandmother had her amputation. Now the reality of a loved one's potential loss was firmly in place. Four years later my mother, who had suffered from heart disease, died after surgery and the horror of my fears came true. All of this loss became a backdrop for the unthinkable: the death of my 8-year-old son from cancer.

When care providers work with an individual or with the family, information gathered from an exercise such as the loss genogram can yield history that bears directly on the nature of current grief. With this in mind, please complete Exercise 4.

### EXERCISE 4: FAMILY LOSS GENOGRAM

On a separate sheet of paper, compile the following information for three or four generations of your family following the directions and the model. Put males on the left and females on the right. Indicate miscarriages or abortions.

1. Starting with your grandparents' generation, list the names of living relatives and ages (or age at death and cause of death) of grandparents and current state of health.
2. Do the same for your parents and their siblings.
3. Do the same for you and your own siblings.
4. Do the same for your children.

Answer the following questions about the information you have recorded:

1. What was the earliest death in your family that you can recall?
2. Which deaths do you know the least about? Do you know why this is?
3. How many deaths did you list in this exercise? Is this a surprise?
4. To what extent were you included or excluded from rituals and conversations about death?
5. What patterns of cause of death do you notice?
6. How does the above material influence the way you respond to death?

In addition to insights you may have gathered by completing the genogram and answering the previous six questions, what images and feelings are you aware of? If you have been journaling or are willing to begin a journal, write down your images and feelings and keep a record of emotional reactions as you read this book.

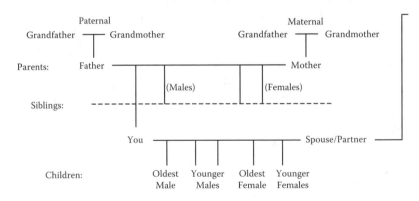

**FIGURE 4.3**

# ☐ Healing Tasks for the Grieving Family

Worden's (2009) four tasks of mourning have been adapted by family therapists (Rosen, 1990; Walsh & McGoldrick, 1991) to demonstrate a set of action-oriented behaviors and outcomes that will help families adapt to the post-loss world. I have drawn the following material from these sources as well as from my own practice of family therapy. The role of the care provider is to help the family address these tasks.

## Task I: Sharing Acknowledgment of Death or Other Traumatic Loss

### Denial Versus Acceptance of Reality

It is important that the family ultimately recognize that the loss is final and irreversible. Denial may be useful to permit the acceptance of reality in small doses; however, the goal of this task is to have family members share their sense of the loss. Funerals, memorials, prayer services, wakes, sitting Shiva, viewings, and other rituals can help achieve this.

### Closed Versus Open Intrafamily Communication

The more easily and openly a family communicates, the more they can engage in necessary sharing. Planning memorials and traditional rituals as well as other joint family events can help move people toward a more open discussion of the reality of a loss event. (Note: The degree to which a family communicates may vary greatly by virtue of cultural traditions, which may support or restrict open communication either within or outside of the family.)

### Inactivity Versus Activity

Although it is important for individuals to have private time to mourn their loss, healing is often eased when family members undertake a joint activity. Planning religious services, receiving visitors, sending appreciation cards, creating the obituary, and notifying others in their social network about the illness or death are all useful actions. Again, family and cultural traditions will play an important role in determining how this is accomplished.

## Closed Versus Open Communication Beyond the Family

Connecting with extended family, friends, faith community members, support services, and work colleagues can provide families with the opportunities to deliver the painful news and receive support.

# Task II: Sharing the Pain and Grief

## Storytelling

Much of the sharing of pain and grief will take place as the family engages in storytelling with one another and with extended family, friends, and others in the social network (Nadeau, 2001). Grieving people typically need to tell and retell the history, describe characteristics of the loved one, relate medical information, the circumstances of the death or other loss, and consider what they will miss and how different life will be.

## Conspiracy of Silence

In some families, however, there may be a conspiracy of silence, an unstated agreement that "We don't talk about it." Other families simply say, "We are all fine, thank you." The reluctance to share their needs with others may limit the family's support from outside sources. This may be a function of cultural or family customs.

## Expressions of Emotions

Sharing expressions of disappointment, helplessness, relief, guilt, anger, anxiety, panic, or the need for quiet withdrawal are all possible responses to loss; and useful for others in the family to hear and acknowledge. The expression of these emotions can vary widely among family members (Rosen, 1990, p. 90). Couples can show great astonishment at the level of pain felt by the other spouse. The family rule may be one of "keep your

It is not the care provider's role to confront resistance to open communication head-on, but rather to offer the family opportunities to share feelings or express emotions indirectly by delivering eulogies, telling stories, speculating on the future, using drawings, and creating personalized memory albums.

Care providers can help alleviate guilt, anger, and shame in the aftermath of a loss by enabling family members to discuss their feelings with one or two others and even doing some journal writing or letter writing to the deceased loved one.

Care providers must be prepared to raise questions in a family meeting about the future of the family—routines, finances, reorganizing responsibilities at some point when the family decision maker has died. All eyes may turn to the surviving spouse for answers to such questions. If the family is unable or reluctant to discuss their needs for the future, the provider can assist by having a meeting expressly for planning limited to the immediate future. This should concentrate on discussing how family members will take on new responsibilities.

pain to yourself." Lack of awareness of how others in a family are feeling can give the false impression that "No one else is as upset as I am" or "You don't really care so much about our child's death."

Guilt and anger are particularly difficult feelings to express to others in the family, but it can be an extraordinary relief for a family member to find out that he or she is not alone in having those feelings. Caution must be taken with those ethnic cultures whose customs restrict open communication.

## Task III: Reorganizing the Family System

### Realignments and Reallocations

The realignment of relationships and the reallocation of roles may begin as the family prepares for a funeral and other death-related activities. Who chooses the pallbearers? Should we have an open casket? Such decisions may need to be made as a very ill person fades from active participation in family life: "Who will make Thanksgiving dinner this year since Mom can't?" Everyday household responsibilities may be shifted. Who takes out the trash, pays the bills, and services the car? How do couples reestablish their relationship after the death of a child? What responsibilities are shifted to the middle child when the oldest has died?

Care providers can help guide families to consider when and how to reestablish rules and delegate roles as needed. This can be approached as a problem-solving/brainstorming session with the provider facilitating the creation of a proposed list of changes in family limits and rules. This may also be a time when outside support from extended family and friends can be sought.

How well do siblings bond with each other when the parents are focused on a dying child?

## Evaluation of Ambiguous Limits and Rules

Uncertainty may follow immediately after a death, life-threatening diagnosis, separation, loss of job, or disabling accident. Sustaining a loss can usher in a period of confusion in family life, and members may need to be guided into a process of setting limits for children and establishment of interim schedules and responsibilities for such activities as homework, household cleaning tasks, shopping, and meals.

## Adopting New Family Organization Structures

The opportunity to abandon old patterns and adopt new, functional structures in the family is available to grieving families, especially if the deceased was the dominant family member. Whenever there is a significant change, there is the opportunity to review old traditions and seek new ways to have recreation, family meals, create and implement a budget, and relate to others outside of the nuclear family.

The care provider can introduce the idea that new traditions can be established in the wake of loss. A note of caution: This idea should not be brought up before the family has had the opportunity to spend time mourning their loss. Some families may need weeks or even some months to be ready to create new traditions and routines for living. Approaching holidays typically prompts a family to consider other traditions and routines. Here again, a brainstorming session with all ideas accepted and listed for consideration can be helpful.

## *Starting a Subsequent Pregnancy*

The question of choosing when to start a new pregnancy at some point after a miscarriage or neonatal loss, and whether to have another child after a pregnancy loss or the death of a child is a very sensitive and highly individual issue. Many couples have been advised to wait a year or more so that they can complete the grief for the loss, but this is not a uniform requirement. I have seen young couples, for example, who have sustained a traumatic loss but were able to direct their attention and emotional resources to the joys and anticipation of a new baby much sooner than a year.

## *Other Replacement Concerns*

Other replacement concerns typically occur after the loss of a spouse or life partner. Social conventions and resistance from the family may influence when a grieving person should decide to resume his or her social life. Pressure from immediate family members may be for the widow(er) to find a new companion or to keep him or her unattached as long as

Care providers need to be particularly sensitive to the couple's emotional needs during the first several months of the new baby's life. This period can be filled with extreme anxiety and can complicate the grieving process. If complications in the grieving process arise—chronic acute grief reactions, extreme anxiety issues, clinical depression—the care provider needs to suggest a consultation with a professional mental health provider. There is no single formula for healing; much of how the couple reacts to a new baby after previous pregnancy loss or the death of a child depends on the coping resources and social support the couple receives from family and friends.

The care provider can work with bereaved individuals on specific areas such as relationship concerns, improving self-confidence, entering the current dating scene, and strategies for integrating a new partner into the family system. Support groups also can be helpful as others can share how they approached difficult or awkward situations.

possible. I have seen some individuals enter the social scene as soon as they are able and others who resist this indefinitely. For many, there is the awkwardness felt by existing family members and their resistance to accepting a new person into their lives. Children may resent Dad's or Mom's new friend. In-laws may be hurt by the daughter-in-law or son-in law having a new relationship. This may be especially difficult for grandparents who perceive a new spouse as replacing their deceased adult child; they may also fear being left out of their grandchildren's lives.

## Other Traumatic Losses

In the case of other traumatic loss—layoff, financial crisis, divorce, destruction of home by fire, or other disasters—families may be as devastated as if an actual death has occurred. The prospect of living with a severely reduced income, parents living apart, and the loss of a home and all personal belongings has secondary effects beyond the initial loss event. Children are especially vocal and blunt about their concerns for survival: "Where will we live?" "How will we pay for food?" "How will I get to school?" "When can I see my friends?"

Too often such nondeath losses are not viewed as legitimate causes for grief reactions. The survival concerns, the many secondary losses, and the traumatic experience are truly justifiable reasons for mourning. The losses and changes not only require reorganization to get the family restabilized but also provide windows of opportunity to create new patterns for the family to live by.

The care provider can help by arranging for resources to meet the immediate needs of the family and helping to reassure children—and adults as well—that they will not starve and will have shelter. Providers can help the family review and reorganize to meet the new realities. They can also direct the family to resources that can help them secure part-time jobs; develop careful budgeting; and provide for consistent childcare, fair custody arrangements, or temporary new shelter.

Providers are not expected to do all of this on their own. Faith-based organizations can be called upon. Local government and community service agencies have provisions for emergency assistance and can offer longer-term support. (See Appendix A for a list of support organizations.)

Care providers can help families achieve a balance between memory and idealization of the way things were. In this way, family members can stay connected to the past or the loved one while feeling free to explore new options and experience new possibilities. Providers can help family members to give themselves permission to explore such new options for living. Brainstorming sessions with the family can be held to review existing routines and schedules and list new ideas for these basic requirements, as well as for recreation, finances, and addressing holidays.

## Task IV: Creating New Directions, Relationships, and Goals

### Moving on in the Face of Loss

Moving on is usually accomplished slowly over time. People realize that they can continue to honor the memory of a loved one while making changes in their present-day lives. For instance, a surviving spouse can renovate her home as she and her late husband had planned, but may allow herself to make certain changes that she alone wanted. A child who felt pressure to attend his deceased father's alma mater may decide to attend the college he or she really wants to go to.

### Creating New Traditions

Sometimes, overidealization of the deceased or past traditions and routines may prevent people from initiating new ideas that more adequately meet the needs of the family as it is now. Many family members will keep certain traditions and routines because Dad or Grandma always did it that way. Some of these family customs may serve to keep the members attached to the deceased loved one, while others can be replaced by new and more satisfying ways of doing things.

## ☐ Factors Interfering With Healing

There are a number of specific issues arising from certain losses that may prevent family members from expressing grief emotions and thinking about how to reorganize their lives and create new meanings in the post-loss world. Following are a group of reasons that make it difficult to move ahead in the healing process.

1. Loss event is too painful to express grief.

2. Early childhood messages inhibit expression of feelings.

3. Relationship was problematic, engendering anxiety, anger, or guilt.

4. Old loss material overwhelms the current loss, creating an overload.

5. The mourner feels disenfranchised.

6. The mourner has preexisting psychopathology.

7. There is a lack of social support.

8. Lack of tangible evidence of death , no body recovered.

## The Loss Event Is Too Painful to Express Grief

Often a loss is too painful to talk about and denial is needed in order to survive each day. Denial serves a useful function and enables the grieving person to take in the awful reality in doses. Sometimes denial can limit the freedom to communicate with other family members and friends. The dread of "bringing it up" can keep mourners from communicating and create distance that may become problematic. The internalized pain of grief can also become somaticized and show up as physical health problems. Not everyone needs to express pain and talk it through with others. However, for those who have a need to express themselves and fear to do so, some assistance must be provided to help them slowly start the process of externalizing their emotional pain. (See Chapter 9.)

## Early Childhood Messages Inhibit Expression of Feelings

In many families it was not acceptable to show anger, express fears, or cry. These early childhood messages often linger in the inner core of our self-concepts and direct us to restrain our expression of sadness, anger, or fear at the very times when it would be helpful to do so. People who find themselves unable to express feelings may need to learn or relearn that they are entitled to express their pain and talk to others about their grief.

## Relationship Was Problematic, Engendering Anxiety, Anger, or Guilt

The level of guilt, anger, and pain that may still be present as unfinished business can interfere with the grieving person's expression of these upsetting feelings.

## Old Loss Material Overwhelms the Current Loss, Creating an Overload

Accumulated loss material (Cowbells) may overload the capacity of the grieving person to let much out. The old grief combines with current loss material and it can feel too unsafe to open up at all.

## The Mourner Feels Disenfranchised

When the grieving person feels unentitled to grieve or gets the impression that others around them do not see why they are so upset, it can shut them down. An ex-wife, a coworker, a neighbor, or a lover can all be given the message that their grief does not count.

## The Mourner Has Preexisting Psychopathology

Various emotional disorders make an individual highly vulnerable, and they may withdraw from active mourning. Some may be on medications that impede the expression of feelings. For example, people who have a history of depression and are extremely fragile may seek to protect themselves by avoiding active grieving. In some cases, medications may keep the mourner's mood at a consistent level and inhibit active expression of grief.

## There Is a Lack of Social Support

When the safety net of emotional and practical support is absent, the grieving person may be too preoccupied with practical matters of self and family care to take the time to express his or her grief. They may also feel isolated and unsafe for allowing strong emotions to surface. Grief may therefore be postponed.

## Lack of Tangible Evidence of Death—No Body Recovered

(See earlier section titled "Ambiguous Loss.") When there is no tangible evidence of death—missing in action, sea and air disasters, or explosions—there is no recovered body. Some simply remain unconvinced that their loved one will never return. Others cannot engage in the traditional funeral and other death-related rituals that allow for the grieving person to grasp the reality of the loss. During the aftermath of the disaster at the World Trade Center, a massive search continued for months to find any identifiable body parts so the families could have some tangible evidence of their losses.

Creative alternative rituals such as guided imagery funerals or saying good-bye exercises can be of some help to mourners who lack a body and any tangible evidence of the death.

The care provider, when taking a formal history or informally gathering background information about a family, must be aware of all of grief-complicating factors. If anyone in the family is having particular difficulty with the grieving process, the provider should try to determine if any of the aforementioned issues are the cause. Where the provider is not trained to address the issue of complicated or prolonged grief, a referral should be made to a mental health professional.

# ☐ Conclusion

In this chapter, we have considered loss in the context of the family system. We must consider the grieving person's family and family history to truly understand the realities in which they live out their mourning. The family's communication style, their cultural influences, the life-cycle stage of the family, and the nature of the intrafamily relationships all affect human grief responses.

Additionally, within the family system, there are members who require some special consideration as grieving people: grieving children, parents, and older adults. Chapters 5, 6, and 7, respectively, give special attention to these three groups of grieving people.

# The Grief of Children and Adolescents

## ☐ Chapter Preview

It takes a village to raise a child.

**African proverb**

It also takes a village to heal a bereaved child.

# ☐ Introduction: The Grief of Children

"The loss of a parent to death and its consequences in the home and in the family change the very core of the child's existence" (Worden, 1996, p. 9). Children are also influenced by the nature of the grief expressed by the adults in their lives.

Here is a clinical observation of the delicate interplay between the parent and child grief reaction:

> Two little girls sat in my office. I had already talked to Dad who was now sitting in the waiting room. The younger child, age 6, had an eager look, made eye contact, and waited to hear what I was going to say. The older girl, age 10, looked down at the floor, appeared sad and reluctant to have any conversation. Their mother had died 3 months earlier, and Dad was concerned about what he believed was his older daughter's lack of mourning. Many parents express such concern and bring their children into counseling or therapy with the hope that I can somehow "prime the grieving pump."
>
> In response to my questions about how things had been for them since their mom had died, the younger girl told me that she missed her mommy and that her daddy had to hold her when she cried. Her older sister was less willing to share information but did let me know that she was also sad. When I asked her if she ever cried like her sister, she said she did. She said she only cried in her bedroom at night. I expressed interest in these remarks and told her that her dad was concerned because he never saw her crying. When I asked what kept her from crying when her dad was nearby, she said, "I never cry in front of my dad; it upsets him too much."

Too often, adults expect children to grieve in specific ways. According to an African proverb, "It takes a village to raise a child." It also takes a village to heal a child. Grieving children need a supportive network of adults and, at times, adults who have expertise in working with bereaved children and who also understand the life experiences that influence the nature of their grief.

Children have rich internal lives, and their grief can be both similar and vastly different from that of adults. We form attachments in order to survive. When an individual loses the person whom he or she depended on for survival, the grieving person may react with panic, dread, bewilderment, despair, or rage. Even the threat of loss of our primary attachment figure (usually mother) can result in grief reactions. Children, no matter what their age, have an inborn drive to survive, and their grief response to loss is part of this drive. To help children who have lost loved ones, the adults in their lives need to be aware that

- Children do grieve,

- Their grief needs to be acknowledged, and

- The nature of children's grief varies widely with age and maturity.

All of these issues will be addressed in this chapter. (Loss of a sibling is discussed in detail in Chapter 6.)

## ☐ The Needs of Grieving Children at a Glance

Children need to be:

1. Allowed to grieve appropriately for their age.
2. Heard.
3. Part of the family's grieving process and participate in family grieving rituals.
4. Appropriately included in the information loop.
5. Assured that their usual schedules, routines, and limits will be maintained.
6. Hugged, held, and shown love by a parent or other caring adult, and reassured regarding safety and other survival concerns.
7. Reassured that their feelings are okay and have opportunities to express them.
8. Reassured that they are not the cause of the death or illness.
9. Allowed to have time-outs from grieving.
10. Able to ask questions and have them answered truthfully.
11. Prepared for questions and comments from neighbors and others in the community.
12. Not be singled out for special consideration by teachers and other adults.

# Children Need to Be Allowed to Grieve as Children

Children are often overlooked as credible mourners, and their grieving may be very unlike that of adults. Too often, their grief is evaluated on the basis of an adult's expectations for seeing and hearing adult mourning. Adults frequently expect children to grieve as they do, but children may appear not to be grieving according to this expectation. Children grieve in idiosyncratic ways: Some may not appear sad or distressed at all; others withdraw; still others may cry, sob, and talk about missing the parent or sibling and then go back to playing as if nothing has happened to change their lives. This shifting back and forth should not be misconstrued to mean that they are not deeply affected. Some children appear to put off their grieving for several months. This may alarm the parent and sometimes results in a request for counseling. Some children may regress by wetting the bed, becoming clingy, or acting out by hitting other children or by refusing to do schoolwork.

Doka (2002a) states, "When a loss occurs, societal grieving rules tell us not only how one is to behave but also how one is to feel and think" (p. 6).

Following are some basic guidelines for comparing the ways children and adults grieve.

- Children do not usually grieve continuously; they take breaks. They grieve in small portions and may actually delay much of their grief for weeks or even months.

  - Adults grieve fairly constantly and grief is usually not delayed.

- Children's grief behaviors may be mixed with play activity.

  - Adults typically separate grief from play.

- Children's understanding of death is limited to their cognitive development.

  - Adults are aware of the irreversibility of death.

- Children (preadolescents) may have difficulty retaining the image of a deceased person.

  - Adults have a more fully developed memory of the deceased.

Care providers may need to offer opportunities to talk or to simply be with children as they play. Providers can also coach parents or other family members on how to provide special alone time to talk about the deceased. Children can be helped to express their grief by drawing, playing games, and role-playing fantasies, or reading some of the many children's books about loss and grief.

- Children are dependent upon adults for support; they may not be able to articulate their needs.

  - Adults can seek help and are usually able to meet their needs independently.

    – Both children and adults need their grief to be heard and acknowledged.

    – Both need the support of caring people.

    – Both need to know it is normal and acceptable to mourn and express feelings.

    – Both may express similar feelings of sadness, anger, fear, guilt, and shame in their mourning.

## Children Need to Be Heard

It is not unusual for children to be excluded from participation in family rituals for burial and grieving. Too often, children are not fully appreciated as grievers in the family system, yet they are very much affected by the grief of others. The story of how I learned of my grandmother's death points out how easy it is to disenfranchise children's grief.

One early morning when I was barely 12 years old, my father's uncle and his son's pounding on the front door awakened us. I ran to the door and let them in. My uncle ordered me to get my father right away. I woke Dad and Mom up, and Dad went out to see what was happening. Suddenly my father began to cry. I asked Dad's uncle what was wrong and he said, "Figure it out!" This was the only answer I received. My dad was sobbing;

my mother was pale and holding him. I was terrified but not at what had happened. Seeing my father cry for the first time in my life alarmed me.

The sudden death of my grandmother from a stroke sent a stunning wave of horrible reality through my senses. Her funeral was my first. It was the first time I saw a dead body and attended a burial. I was mostly frightened, however, by seeing all of the important adults in my life crying, bent in pain and sorrow. People hovered around my grandfather, my dad, and his sister and brothers. No one seemed to be concerned about how my sister or I were feeling. I assumed that no one was supposed to.

## Children Need to Be Part of the Family's Grieving Process and Participate in Family Grieving Rituals

Children should be able to observe the surviving parent crying and realize that the parent can still function as a mom or dad. They may interpret a lack of evidence of mourning as, "We must hide our grief." Parents and other adults can let the children know that we are sad because our loved one has died and it's okay to cry and feel very upset.

Even though younger children may not grasp the permanence of death, it helps to have them participate in funerals, burials, and memorial services—if they are willing to go and the adults can prepare them, answer their questions, and offer reassurance. The funeral, the gravesite, and the cemetery not only provide visible evidence that death has occurred but also reassure children that "we are not alone in our mourning" and "that this has happened to others as well." For older children, these rituals "constitute proof and confirmation of the fact that the deceased has passed away from our world and will remain only in our memory" (Smilansky, 1987, p. 111).

Generally, young children will use only the information they need and block out or not register the rest, as the following example illustrates:

When my aunt died, we asked my 4-year-old grandson Zack if he wanted to see her at the family viewing. He agreed. Picking him up, I showed him the body in the casket, explaining that she was no longer living. Together we touched her forehead and felt the coldness. I asked if he had any questions. "What happens to her now?" he asked. I told him that the casket cover would be closed and then after the funeral service we would take her to a cemetery where she would be buried in the ground. "Okay," he said. "Can I go and play now?"

At the cemetery, Zack played with the pile of soil next to the grave and watched with interest as the casket was lowered and covered with shovels of earth. Zack participated in this ritual and played with the mound of earth. Back at my aunt's house, Zack asked me, "Papa, what was in that box anyway?" I explained that our aunt's body, the one we saw in the funeral home, was in the box. "Oh yeah, that's the one we buried." I felt as if he benefited from being with us and participating in the family ritual.

## Children Need to Be Appropriately Included in the Information Loop

"Parents and children need to know the facts about a loss. This information lessens fear and creates a foundation from which to grieve" (Goldman, 1996, p. 69). It is vital that children not be overlooked as part of the family's grief process and not be patronized or dismissed with clichés. I often hear complaints from adults who, as children, experienced the death of a parent or sibling and felt as if they were kept out of the information loop.

## Children Need to Have Usual Schedules, Routines, and Limits Maintained

Children need structure in times of crisis; therefore, bedtimes, curfews, mealtimes, and other familiar limits need to remain in place. These provide security, assuring children that there is a sense of control and that the family system will survive. When children don't feel as if structure exists in their lives, they may act out behaviorally until an adult provides the structure and limits they need.

## Children Need to Be Hugged, Held, and Shown Love by a Parent or Other Caring Adult and Reassured Regarding Safety and Other Survival Concerns

Caregiving adults should reassure children with loving physical gestures. This lets children know that, even though a terrible thing has happened, they are loved and will be taken care of. Children are very aware of and worry about how the family will survive financially. They must be given a sense that they are safe and that the family will continue to provide for their needs.

Care providers and family members can encourage children to express their feelings of grief by supplying them with paper and crayons, puppets, electronic recording devices, and other means through which they can emotionally express themselves through play. Care providers can help neighbors, friends, and relatives understand that it is not unusual for children to play and even laugh while adults are grieving in the next room.

## Children Need to Be Reassured That Their Feelings Are Okay and Have Opportunities to Express Them

Children need to see that their feelings of grief—sadness, anger, fear, guilt—are accepted as normal by the adults in their lives. They should not feel disapproved of when they are not grieving. Visitors to the family may judge the children or teens critically because they are playing games, watching TV, or even singing. Grieving children should be protected from those who want to interfere with how they grieve, such as family visitors who criticize them for playing or watching TV. An understanding adult needs to explain to these judgmental adults that the children are not being disrespectful or unfeeling but rather that they need to escape from the terrible reality from time to time. It's also important to remember that children often incorporate their feelings about their loss into their play, and adults can facilitate the release of such grief feelings.

## Children Need to Be Reassured That They Are Not the Cause of the Death or Illness

Young children may fantasize that they were bad or possibly had a bad thought about the loved one that caused the death. Some children carry these thoughts for years and are troubled by them into adulthood. Keeping the lines of communication open and asking children what questions or concerns they may have can encourage them to express these concerns. Play activities can also reveal these fantasies. For example, while engaging in doll or puppet play with the child, the adult can set up a story similar to the loss situation and work in statements indicating that the child in the play story is not at fault for his or her parent's death or illness.

# Children Need to Have Accepted Time-Outs From Grieving

Adults need to accept the fact that children often grieve intermittently. Some children can only allow themselves to feel the pain in small portions; others may have a short attention span; still others do not yet have the mental maturity to engage in prolonged episodes of painful grieving. For all of these reasons, they need time-outs from grieving.

# Children Need to Be Able to Ask Questions and Have Them Answered Truthfully

Children struggle as adults do with questions like, "Why, why did this happen?" "When will Nanna come back?" "Where is Aunt Rita now?" "Why do we bury dead people?" or "Will I ever see Papa again?" Questions are a way that children attempt to make sense of a situation at their own level of cognitive development. Answers, which are strongly influenced by cultural beliefs and customs, should be brief and as specific as appropriate. Excessive and detailed information will not be useful and could confuse the child. Lying is not only disrespectful but may haunt the parent at a later time when the child learns the truth. It's okay for a parent or other family adult to say, "I don't know the answer, but I will find out for you." Adults can also circle back to answer a question the child asked previously; this will provide an opportunity to have a conversation about other unspoken areas of concern—the child's guilt fantasies or anxiety regarding survival of the family.

Care providers can help by educating the family about the special loss needs and grieving patterns of children. Teaching the parent and other family members what to expect and how to help the child express his or her feelings can help create a comfortable and understanding environment for grieving children.

Care providers can help prepare children for questions from others by role-playing with them and helping them to find the words with which to respond to the questions of others. Family members can also benefit from such activities. For example, the provider can coach the child to say, "I really don't want to talk about my dad's illness now" or "You will have to ask my mom that question."

## Children Need to Be Prepared for Questions and Comments From Neighbors and Others in the Community

Children need help to know how and when to respond to other children and adults who ask them questions about their deceased parent or sibling. They will need to be prepared for this, especially if they experience comments and questions as upsetting.

## Children Need to Not Be Singled Out for Special Consideration by Teachers and Other Adults

As a rule, children seek conformity with peers and are uncomfortable being identified as the kid whose brother was killed or who has a dying or incapacitated parent, grandparent, or sibling at home. They may be reluctant to have friends over because of the need for quiet or because the home has a depressive quality to it. In fact, some houses of mourning may be off limits to playful children. Children may also be reluctant to invite friends over fearing that these friends may witness their parents in tears. All of these issues need to be discussed with children to help them cope with awkward situations as comfortably as possible.

## Summary of Grief of Children

As children mature, they become more fully aware of the painful changes in their lives occasioned by a loss. Grieving becomes more adult-like. Further, older children and adolescents may have unfinished business as a result of earlier losses or traumas that may be triggered by the current death or other circumstance of loss. Regardless of age, children need lots of hugs and kisses, and reassurance that they are not to blame for the death or because they survived the loss. It is natural for them to want to talk about their feelings. Adults should provide for this. Children also need to be aware that it is okay *not* to grieve.

## ☐ Developmental Stages and Children's Grief: Helping Grieving Children

The material in this section is drawn from the work of Bowlby (1980), Rando (1984), Raphael (1983), and Worden (1996) as well as from my own clinical experience. Goldman (2000) describes grief as a "normal, internalized reaction" to a primary loss (death of parent, sibling, or other loved one), which may also result in such secondary losses as disruption of routines, loss of sense of security, and fears about the future (Goldman, 2005).

The child's reaction to the death of a parent has two components: an emotional response and an intellectual processing of the reality of the loss. Younger children are able to respond emotionally before they are old enough to really grasp the implications of what has happened. The emotional feelings arise from the separation from a parent or other primary loved one. This reaction is usually referred to as *separation anxiety* and is related to the fear that comes from loss of proximity to the person who has ensured their survival. This response is reflexive and takes the initial form of crying out when the distance between child and mother reaches a point of alarm for the child.

This reflexive response is reminiscent of Paul MacLean's (1973) isolation distress call discussed in Chapter 3. It is a response to a loss or a signal for the threat of loss (mother is putting her coat on, wearing her "going out" perfume, walking toward the door) and does not entail intellectual processing. Behavioral responses to actual or to threatened separation include crying, reaching, screaming, moving toward Mommy, and looking and searching in the direction she has gone. These behaviors will vary according to the child's age and developmental stage. They represent the attachment behaviors Bowlby (1980) described as part of the "protest" phase of the grief process.

As children mature and are better able to comprehend the world around them, their understanding of the meaning and consequences of separation or threatened separation deepens. Thus, their emotional reactions to separation will be further intensified by the realization that Mommy or Daddy is never coming back and that a new chapter of their lives is beginning. The realization of the finality of the loss and the multiple changes that occur increasingly become part of the grief process as they get older.

These three anecdotes illustrate reflexive survival reactions:

- Jake was almost 4 when he and his older brother Zack were listening to me read them some bedtime stories. I began to tell the story of "Jack and the Beanstalk" with increasing drama. Jake was really engrossed when I got to the part where "Jack had quietly taken the magical singing harp from the table while the giant slumbered and snored. As Jack began to creep out of the window, the harp screamed out to the giant who awoke and reached out to grab Jack." At that point, acting as the giant, I thrust my hand toward Jake who screamed out in terror, "I not Jack! I not Jack!"

- A colleague was running a workshop in Northern Ireland for bereaved children who were given an opportunity to release pain and anger by beating on pillows and letting it "all come out." One 5-year-old was so angry at the circumstances of his life that he cursed and said he wanted to get rid of all of the grown-ups in his life "except for you" and he pointed to my friend. When they completed the session and went to lunch, my friend asked the boy why he had said, "Except you!" The boy answered matter-of-factly, "Well, somebody has to feed me."

- I was seeing a family with young children in which the father had recently died. During the course of the session, the 10-year-old daughter emphatically stated, "Well, what are we going to do now? We won't have Dad's paycheck to count on every week!"

As these three children contemplated the consequences of loss, the survival-oriented reactions ran the gamut from a reflexive "I not Jack!" to the more studied "Well, what are we going to do now?" Each reaction to loss or predicted loss is governed by the ability of the child to reason and evaluate circumstances. In the first story, Jake's knee-jerk screaming out "I not Jack!" is an example of remarkable self-preservation behavior. In the next story, the young boy was clear on the importance of knowing where his next meal was coming from. The young girl in the last story voiced a concern for the whole family. Children typically cut to the bottom line of survival needs. This is why it is so important that they be given early reassurances that they will be secure and cared for.

The following brief outline summarizes how children grieve at various ages and includes some recommendations for helping them. Although some grief reactions are particular to a certain age range, there is a great deal of overlap. Each child or teenager must be viewed according to his or her own personality, family situation and history, cultural influences, religious affiliation, and developmental stage, all of which result in unique grieving needs. We serve children best when we both take our lead and learn about their grief from them.

## Helping Children Under 2 Years of Age

Very young children, unable to understand the irreversibility of death, respond to the emotional reactions of the surviving parent or caregiving adult. They are specifically attuned to how much attention the adults in their lives can bestow upon them. If the emotional climate of the family becomes agitated or depressed, the young child will mirror this change. In the case of death of a mother or other primary caregiving adult, older infants may protest and search for the mother, alter their sleep and feeding schedules, and generally be fussier. (A substitute caring adult can offer comfort by providing continuity of attachment.)

## Helping Children Ages 2 to 5

The mourning behaviors of children in this age category are intermittent. These children still lack the capacity to view the loss as irreversible or understand feelings of distress. They may believe that the parent is still going to come back to them and take care of their needs again. Each sound of a car driving up, a door opening, or the dog barking may arouse their expectations that their mommy or daddy is going to walk through the door. Because of this, children may need to be told repeatedly and tenderly that their mommy or daddy is not there.

Children may exhibit regressive behaviors such as bed-wetting, acting out, becoming clingy, reverting to baby talk, or insisting on sleeping with the parent. They can be given a sense of security in spite of their loss with continuous and loving care from the surviving parent or a surrogate caregiving adult. If the surviving parent is not available due to his or her own grief, another caring adult can provide some level of structure, comfort, and continuity of care. Children will feel safer if caretaking adults observe established schedules and routines.

Other activities to soothe children this age include showing them photos of the deceased parent; this helps them to create an inner image of Mom or Dad who is no longer here with them. Children also need to be reassured that the other important adults in their lives—the surviving parent and grandma, aunt, or adult friend—are all okay and are able to take care of them. The message imparted in age-appropriate language, needs to be this: "Things are different now and you will still be safe and taken care of."

## Helping Children Ages 5 to 8

Early elementary school-aged children are better able to grasp the consequences of death, such as its finality, due to their increasing cognitive maturity. They may, however, use denial to avoid the reality they can now grasp. Grieving may be more internal than outward. Some regression may take place: bed-wetting, thumb or pacifier sucking, or seeking to sleep in bed with the parent or other adult. It is best to provide a patient and caring response to questions and accept the regression as normal and temporary.

Other children grieve in ways that are more external; they need to be helped to view these emotions as normal and acceptable.

Children often engage in fantasies or "magical thinking" associated with their belief that they somehow caused the death by bad or angry thoughts about the parent. They should be encouraged to discuss these fantasies and be reassured that they were not to blame for the death or illness.

They may repeat questions in an attempt to integrate the implications of the death. These children may also need to hear, often more than once, about the facts of death in age-appropriate language. Caretakers should avoid resorting to fictional explanations, such as "Daddy is away on a long trip" or "Mommy's working very hard at the office and can't come home yet." Questions should be answered calmly, accurately, and as completely as possible without overwhelming the child. Explain to the child that a part of the body stopped working because of the accident or illness, and that ended the person's ability to stay alive. If the child has lost a pet or an aged grandparent, and the loss was handled positively, the caregiving adult can refer to this incident of loss to help put the loss of a parent in context: "We were all sad when that happened, too."

Some children may want to believe that the parent will not stay dead and will come back to be with them again. To this, a caregiver can say, gently, "I know you would like that to happen and so would I, but that is not what will happen because when people die they don't come back, but it's all right to want that to happen."

When children's questions are answered this way, whether the answers come from the surviving parent or other caring surrogates, they can move forward in their development, secure in the knowledge that they are being well taken care of, loved, and cherished in spite of the absence of the deceased parent. In time, the concepts of finality and irreversibility will be integrated into their sense of self and they will be able to generate new meanings of the world without the missing parent.

## Normalizing Feelings

### Modeling Mourning Behaviors

Adults can help children at this age by modeling mourning behaviors—crying, sighing, expressing words of sadness, and using facial tissues. Tissue boxes can be left around to remind the child that this is what people do when someone has died: "We are sad, we cry, and we blow our nose." Children need to feel that they have permission to let the feelings of grief out; they may externalize some of their grief by playing with dolls or action figures. Art materials, dolls, puppets, a chalkboard, clay, or a sand table should be easily accessible for children of all ages, and they should be invited to use them.

### Helping With Anger

It's normal and acceptable for a 5- to 8-year-old to express anger; however, anger should never be allowed to become harmful to another or oneself. If anger takes a hurtful turn, an adult needs to step in and spend some time with that child, exploring nonhurtful ways to vent anger.

### Helping With Memories

To help children remember the deceased parent, caregivers and family members can reminisce with them. Together, families can create a memory book or album with photos and memorabilia, and write notes or add stickers on each page. Children this age can also be asked to draw a picture showing where they think their deceased parent is now. For many, this is a comforting activity. It can encourage children to explore their ideas about heaven.

## Helping With Current Family Conditions

Children also work out their feelings about the understanding of death by telling a story using dolls and props. A child may say: "The daddy doll is very sad and doesn't have time to play with the children," "The children are at the dinner table, and they hate the food their grandma is cooking," or "Their daddy doesn't know how to tuck the children in at night." Family members can then discuss what life is like in their home since their mommy died. Encourage children to talk about what is different now; invite them to teach Daddy how to do a proper tuck in or suggest that Grandma cook some other kinds of food. Other feelings can emerge during play or while informal conversations are taking place.

## Helping to Deal With Guilt

Children's guilt and regrets should be addressed so that children do not blame themselves or fall into despair. They can write a letter, for example, asking the deceased parent to forgive their misdeeds; this is a good way for children to let go of continuing guilt thoughts. Open discussions with other children may help grieving children realize their guilt feelings are normal. In addition, hospice, schools, religious, and other community organizations usually run bereavement groups for children.

Care providers can help 5- to 8-year-olds externalize their anger by encouraging the free expression of feelings through the use of drawing materials, or clay or other molding material; or by hitting a pillow or a punching bag. Children can also write and read aloud letters they have written about their anger; younger children can relate the story aloud and enlist an adult to write it down or record it. The goal is to make it clear that anger is an acceptable feeling to have and express but not in a way that will harm the child or someone else.

# Helping Children Ages 9 to 12

Children in this age group have the intellectual capacity to understand the finality of death and generally use less denial. Preteens may also exhibit behaviors that are similar to the 5 to 8 age group ("magical thinking" about the cause of the death, seeking parental attention, having fears associated with survival) and may also imitate some of those we typically see in adolescence (distancing, investing emotional energy in friends, seeking autonomy). It is a time when peers take on an increasing importance and the need to be like the other kids is a priority. Some of their needs may feel babyish to them, and they may therefore be reluctant to express feelings or ask for help. This holding back of feelings also helps them to maintain a sense of control. Preteens are often very aware of the family's vulnerability when the primary income-producing parent has died or is seriously ill.

For preteens, talking with other bereaved children will help them feel less isolated and different. They do not want to be singled out as the kid whose mother or father or brother died. School personnel should be advised to avoid drawing attention to bereaved children publically with special privileges and relaxed requirements.

The grief process will be helped along if children in this age group are included in family decision making (preparing and participating in the funeral service, reallocating household chores and responsibilities) and in creating family memorial projects that can help them remember their loved one. They also appreciate it when they are given the opportunity to mourn. Children this age need to feel free to have their grief unfold on its own course, which sometimes includes long periods of not grieving.

## *Helping Them Feel Normal*

Adults need to help preteens to feel normal not only in terms of their fears, sadness, and bewilderment about the tragic changes in their lives but also to assure them that they still have a place in the world. They often seek solace by escaping to be with their peers in formal and informal settings. Participation in school and religious group activities; athletics; and other extracurricular activities such as music, dance, and martial arts lessons helps preteens feel that they are okay. These activities should be continued and supported by the parent and other adults involved in the family.

In addition to separation anxiety and pain, the feelings of grief may be associated with their greater understanding of the consequences of

Care providers can suggest that preteens gather their thoughts and feelings in a journal or diary of what has been happening; doing "past, present, and hopes for the future" drawings; writing letters of good-bye; listing all the things that they are missing and what they feel they still share as a family; and sharing some of this material in family meetings. Creative children can make documentaries, create theatrical pieces, or compose music about how they are feeling.

the death. They may feel a need to withhold feelings as a way to defend against the pain of their grief and may deny that they are upset as a way of ensuring themselves that they won't regress emotionally or behaviorally. Very sensitive to the well-being of their surviving parent, they may also withhold their grief and anger out of the desire to shield this parent from worrying about them. In this vein, they may take on the responsibilities for younger siblings as a way of coping and also as a way of reducing Dad's or Mom's stress.

### Helping With Aggressive Behavior

Because preteens typically have more freedom to come and go, they may also find themselves acting out and getting into fights or trouble during class, recess, afterschool programs, or in the neighborhood. Releasing anger in this way can be an effective way to hold off the terrifying pain about what has happened and the fear of what the future will be like: "Does Mom have to get a job now?" "Is Dad going to start dating?" "How will we make it financially?" "Will we be able to buy food?" Though preteens may not articulate these questions, the issues should become part of a larger family discussion whose theme is, "How are we going to manage and reorganize to meet our needs?" If the parent is unable to do this, another caregiving adult should let the preteen discuss his or her survival fears.

## Helping Adolescents Ages 12 to 18

Adolescence is a time when children normally cope with great emotional turbulence as the transition to adulthood looms closer. The death of a parent creates a great conflict as the natural drive toward autonomy clashes with the teenager's need to be with his or her family in time of crisis. Teenagers who feel drawn back into the family by loss can experience

A care provider or other trusted adult who can hear a teen's expression of guilt, fear, anger, and frustration can normalize these emotions, assure and calm the bereaved teenager. What teens need most is to think, "I'm okay and I can manage this tough time."

Care providers can also inform the surviving parent about basic adolescent psychology. At each stage of development, the way grief plays out will be influenced by a variety of life conditions and past experiences, which all affect the meanings the child will place on a death and its consequences. There are a number of excellent books for teens and their parents. Surviving parents who are aware of teenage psychology can respond less with anger than with understanding and respect.

bitterness, depression, withdrawal, resentment, and sometimes guilt for feeling resentful. They may also experience physical aches and pains, and sleep and appetite pattern changes, which they do not identify as part of their grief response. They may seek to minimize the effect of the loss and bury their grief, or they may use anger to control an aching desire for the lost parent. Secondary losses that have to be faced relate to autonomy, future planning, and involvement with peers. If, in the course of normal adolescent rebellion, an adolescent had fought with the parent who died, he or she may also experience a residue of guilt. Additionally, adolescents may have a recurrence of grief when they acquire a more mature understanding of the consequences of their loss.

Bereaved teens are at high risk to experience an aggravated grief reaction. Boys especially sense that it is not cool to cry; they are more likely to show anger, an easier emotion to express because it maintains their recently acquired sense of maturity. Girls are more likely to seek comfort for their outward expressions of pain; however, both boys and girls this age may need to keep their grief private from adults, and feel as if their natural expression of sadness has no easy outlet. Young people in this age group can benefit from joining teen bereavement support groups in which they can release anger, sadness, and guilt.

The effect of the parent's death on the adolescent's plans, freedom, and purchasing power is no small issue. Teenagers often resent the fact that what should have been an enjoyable time in their lives is now complicated by loss. In addition to the pressures they would have experienced—academic and extracurricular requirements, the drive for peer acceptance, and their emerging sexual awareness—they now feel a need to be available to their families. All create a mix of pressure, already at a high pitch before the death of a parent or other loved one.

# ☐ Other Mediating Influences on the Nature of Children's Grief

Many factors mediate the intensity and duration of the child or adolescent's grief reaction. These are listed below.

## The Nature and Circumstances of the Death

- Who died? Father or mother?

- How was the child informed of the death?

- Was the death expected?

- Was the death the result of a long or brief illness?

- Was it sudden?

- Was it a violent death?

- Was the child present at the death?

- Did the child receive care and support after he or she learned of the death?

The death of Mother or other primary attachment figure will typically result in a more intense grief response. As a child matures, the nature of the evolving relationship with parents will play a large role in grief behavior. A child may feel more prepared for the death of a seriously ill parent if he or she was old enough to comprehend the possibility and was kept informed. Sudden and violent deaths—especially those which the child witnessed—may result in posttraumatic reactions (nightmares, high anxiety, phobias, extreme startle reactions, hypervigilance, engaging in reenactment of the traumatic event); these children may require special care from a mental health professional.

# The Nature and Circumstances Surrounding the Death-Associated Rituals

- Did the child see the body?

- Was the child at the funeral or memorial service?

- Did the child participate in the service or attend the burial or cremation?

- How was the child prepared for these experiences?

Seeing the grave and the other graves in the cemetery confirms not only that the death has occurred but has occurred in other families as well. "The irreversibility of death as well as its universality gradually penetrates the consciousness" (Smilansky, 1987, p. 112). In my own experience, increasing numbers of children attend funerals. One long-term study found that "95% of the bereaved children attended the funeral" (Worden, 1996, p. 23). Unless a child is vehemently opposed to attending the funeral or burial, every encouragement should be offered. Children should be prepared in advance for what the funeral service and burial will be like. Arrangements can be made in advance for them to leave early should they become unable to tolerate the experience. However, children should never be made to feel bad or guilty if they do not attend the funeral or if they have to leave early.

Participating in the preparations and the actual service can help the child acknowledge the death, honor the memory, and begin a different relationship with the deceased parent as well as feel included in the ritual event. Some children help to choose burial clothing; select flowers, music, and food to be served; and write and read the eulogy. In all cases, children need to be involved in deciding what role they will play.

# The Nature of the Family Relationships Prior to the Death

- What are the patterns of relationships in the family?

- How did people typically respond to each other and to crisis in the past? Were they open, intimate, and willing to share, or cold and withdrawn from each other?

- What, specifically, was the nature of the relationship between the parents?

- What were the family's attitudes toward death?

- How much did the family concern itself with what the neighbors think?

- How much were they invested in the status quo and aversive to change?

- What is the loss history and medical status of the surviving parent?

- What is the loss history and medical status of the child or children?

- How chaotic and unstable has life been in this family?

- Is the family financially solvent?

- Is this family connected to the community or an extended family, or isolated and without community support?

- What cultural, ethnic, or religious traditions are relevant to the family's grieving process?

"The child's responses to death and loss must be viewed in the family context," writes Raphael (1983, p. 114). The patterns of communication between family members, attitudes toward expressing feelings openly, level of support and caring in the parents' relationship, and connection to outside resources will directly affect the way a child grieves and feels permission to express his or her grief. If supportive community and extended family members are available to help, children often do well.

If there is a history of conflict between the parents, or if the home was disorganized, chaotic, nonexpressive, and insecure, children will be more likely to experience intense grief and also be at increased risk for social and psychological problems (Kissane et al., 1996).

## The Nature of the Family Conditions After the Death

- Is there a surviving parent? Is the surviving parent the mother or the father?

- What is the emotional condition of that parent?

- How intense is his or her grief reaction?

- What is the nature of the relationship of the child and that parent?

- Is the child going to reside with the surviving parent?

- How will the surviving parent balance work requirements with time for the child or children?

- To what extent are other family and friends involved in providing continuity of support and care for the child or children?

The emotional state of the parent who must care for the child will play an important role in how much the child feels able to express his or her grief feelings. Children will protect the surviving parent from their own pain and stifle their crying when the parent is present. This is done out of love and concern for the parent, as well as to avoid the discomfort of seeing the parent become upset and cry. If the surviving parent is overwhelmed with his or her own grief, and the responsibilities for maintaining a home and making a living for the family, the parent may not have much time left over to devote to sharing their feelings of grief. In cases like this, children may be literally on their own to cope with a multitude of feelings about the death of the other parent. Depending on the age and level of independence of the child, the surviving parent may need to seek support for the child from extended family, friends, the faith community, or from social service agencies.

The physical health of the surviving parent and other children is also of concern. Grief is very stressful and drains the body's capacity to withstand colds, flu, and other infections. Grieving families need proper nutrition and medical attention. This is a good time for friends, extended family, and members of a family's faith community to organize and step in to provide food and care for weeks or even months.

Children, like adults, harbor assumptions about the world. Losing a parent, sibling, or other important loved one shatters our assumptions and expectations. Children's hope for a cure or for a parent to return as well as the expectation that life is secure may evaporate with a death or other tragic loss. Children must be given a sense of safety and security in the post-loss world and an opportunity to restore the assumptions of survival and continuity (Goldman, 2002).

# The Role of the School in the Life of a Grieving Child

- To what extent has the school staff been informed of the parent's death?

- How are they preparing the classmates for the return of the bereaved child?

- How well do the teachers and other school personnel understand the grief of children?

- Do they know what age-appropriate grief behavior to expect?

- How does the school maintain communication with the surviving parent or surrogate caregiving adult?

- How will the school accommodate the needs of grieving children who do not want to be given special consideration or do not want to be seen as different from the other students?

When necessary, a mental health professional should be made available to the staff to orient them to the needs of grieving children and the nature of their grief. All of the child's teachers should be informed of the child's loss; this can spare the child being asked awkward or hurtful questions. Some method of communicating with the surviving parent should be established so that the child's educational progress is maintained.

# The Role of Peers in the Grieving Process of the Child

- Does the child have a friend or friends with whom he or she can maintain contact during this difficult time?

- If parental death was due to a lingering illness, was the child able to maintain contact with friends and peers during the period of illness?

- To what extent does the grieving child feel stigmatized by having had a parent die?

- Has the grieving child been able to express his or her pain and even cry with friends?

- Do friends feel comfortable mentioning the dead parent to the child?

- Do the grieving child's friends comfort him or her?

- Does the bereaved child hide or avoid the fact that he or she has lost a parent?

- Is the child ashamed because the parent died by suicide or homicide, or because of drugs or alcohol?

- Were friends present at the funeral or memorial service?

- Have friends visited the home since the death?

It is not easy to be a bereaved member of a peer group. Some friends may say things that are disturbing or describe an experience with their parents that can cause the grieving child to withdraw. It is also common for the child to feel envious or even angry with those who have two parents and an intact family.

## ☐ What to Expect From Grieving Children

Much of the outward signs of children's grief and adult grief are similar. Here are some of the ways that children express normal grieving:

- *Physical pain and health problems*—Headaches, stomach and intestinal disturbances, more than the usual number of colds, fatigue, sleep disturbance (too little or too much), and appetite changes

- *Regression to younger age behaviors*—Bed-wetting, soiling, thumb or pacifier sucking, baby talk, clinging and seeking to sleep in parent's bed, not wanting the parent to leave, playing sick in order to stay home, and seeking attention more than usual

- *Mood shifts*—Irritability; emotional lability; episodes of anger; periods of despair and withdrawal; anxiety; fears for safety and well-being; fighting at home, school, or in the neighborhood; being disrespectful; and blaming the surviving parent for death of the other parent

- *Poor school performance*—Drop in grades, misbehavior at school, failure to complete homework

- *Apathy and lowered self-esteem*—Helplessness thinking about the future, feelings of guilt and regret

- *Social changes*—Social withdrawal or overly invested in social life

# ☐ Clinical Concerns

Some children and adolescents need more than the type of support outlined. Parents should be on the alert for the following danger signals that their children are at risk for complications in the grieving process, in which case a mental health professional should be consulted. (See Chapter 10 for a discussion of complicated grieving.)

1. The complete and prolonged absence of any reference to the loss or evidence of sadness, crying, or questions about the absence of the parent.

2. Threats or actions of self-harm; suicidal ideas, plans, or attempts.

3. Physical abuse of animals or other children.

4. Inappropriate clinginess; the child is panicky or fearful of being without an adult present.

5. Extreme change in appetite, weight, and sleeping patterns.

6. The child states he or she has not been told the truth about the death.

7. The child had a conflicted, ambivalent relationship with the deceased parent.

8. The child is extremely withdrawn and refuses to make any social contacts.

9. Use of drugs or alcohol.

The care provider should alert the parent, other family members, or caregiving surrogates about these signs, and refer the child and family to the appropriate health care professionals.

10. Extreme and sudden change in behavior: failing in school, personality shifts (child becomes highly energetic or extremely listless), aggressive or delinquent behavior, extreme and prolonged regressive behavior (bed-wetting, soiling self, thumb sucking, returning to crib, baby talking).

11. Continued physical complaints: headaches, stomach pains, muscle spasms, and tightness in chest.

## ☐ Conclusion

This chapter has provided a brief overview of the nature of the grief of children and adolescents who have suffered the death of a parent. Unfortunately, until recently, children were expected to mourn like adults. Their unique needs as grieving people have been ignored. When we recognize their status as bereaved, we not only show children the respect they deserve, but we also make it more likely that children will undergo a healthy and healing grieving process. Adults need to know how children grieve, what to expect from bereaved children, and how to help them adjust to a world without their mom or dad. When the usual, normal process of grief goes off course, it is important that children and adolescents receive the special attention required to help them continue on a path to healing.

Chapter 6 will discuss the grief that parents, siblings, and others endure when a child has died.

**6**
CHAPTER

# The Grief of Parents
## An Upside-Down World

## ☐ Chapter Preview

- Introduction

- The Grieving Parent: A Look Inward

- Parents Whose Child Was Murdered, Completed Suicide, or Died From Other Violent Causes

- Impact of a Child's Death on a Couple's Relationship

- Sibling Grief

- Impact of a Child's Death on Grandparents, Extended Family, and Friends

- What Grieving Parents Ask From Care Providers

- Summary of Clinical Considerations

- Self-Help Support Groups

- Hope for the Grieving Parent

Be fruitful and multiply.

Genesis 9:1, 7

# ☐ Introduction

From a biological perspective, the parent is the physical agent whose function is to send the genes received from earlier generations into the future. This biological imperative intertwines the parent and child in a very special relationship. The essence of this is reflected in the way our culture and society defines the role of parents as well as the expectations placed upon them regarding the protection of their offspring. When a child dies, the generational continuity is cut off.

In addition to the biological attachment for survival, other factors—psychological, cultural, and social—impact on the attachment and create a uniqueness that is the parent–child bond. Over time, each becomes attuned to the other's needs and expectations so that a reciprocal system of actions and reactions is formed (Field, 1985).

The media and literature are filled with many powerful and evocative statements that reflect our strong intention to protect and nurture our children. We create laws nicknamed "Amber Alerts," and agencies like Child Protective Services; we invent "child safety seats." We tell each other "Woman and children first!" and "It takes a village to raise a child." Elliot Rosen (1990) calls the death of a child the "Unthinkable loss … no doubt the greatest tragedy any family can endure." John Bowlby (1969, 1982) said, "The attachment bonds of the nuclear family are linked to the very core of human existence" (p. 179). Beverly Raphael (1983) concluded that "child loss commonly evokes patterns of chronic grief and irrational guilt and that the deceased child is never forgotten." In Genesis 37:35, Biblical patriarch Jacob, after being told that his beloved son Joseph has been killed by a wild beast, says, "I will go down to my grave mourning for my son."

The loss of a child can refer to things as disparate as the loss of a fetus or the death of a middle-aged daughter who is already a parent herself. This tragedy shakes a parent's life to its very roots and begins a process of searching for meaning, often involving a review of past behaviors, of seeking to assign blame and catalog regrets, and of searching for details and explanations as to why it happened.

Parents frequently experience massive guilt when a child dies. Many explain their loss as a failure in fulfilling their own job description. Archer (1999) discusses the connection between family closeness and the level of involvement in ensuring the survival of the young. The closer the family member (parents and siblings), the more intimate the involvement in the care of the young. It follows then that we should expect that the more intimate the childcare role, the greater the intensity of grief if that child happens to die. Although this is understandable, parents and siblings aren't the only ones who mourn the loss of a child—grandparents, aunts, uncles, cousins, teachers and friends grieve as well. These close family members and friends should also be accorded the highest validity as grievers.

It is fair to say, however, that the parental grief response is the most complex. For in most families, parents are heavily invested in "providing and doing for children via the roles of provider, problem-solver, protector, and adviser" (Rando, 1984, p. 120). The losses that are grieved are much more than the death of the child; they are all the things that won't be shared for the rest of the parents' lives.

"When you lose a child, you don't heal." The late actor Carroll O'Connor (best known for his roles in the popular television programs *All in the Family* and *In the Heat of the Night*) said this at a televised press conference after his son's death, and it calls to mind an incident in my own family that took place years after my son Steven's death: My wife received a phone call from an old friend. During the conversation, the woman said, "I don't know how you survived the loss of your son. I would have died." My wife answered, "I did. The person I was is gone." Both my wife's and Mr. O'Connor's remarks reflect a sad truth. The title of "bereaved parent" reflects the parent's new and permanent identity. Healing typically becomes a lifelong process.

## ☐ The Grieving Parent: A Look Inward

O my son Absalom, my son, my son Absalom! Would I had died for thee, O Absalom, my son, my son!

> King David upon learning that his son had been slain;
> 2 Samuel 19:4 (King James Version)

Who is the grieving parent or parents? What is their life like now? What do they think and how do they feel? How do they cope with the upside-down world they now find themselves in? Many live in dread of being asked what sounds like an innocent question: "How many kids do you have?"

A bereaved mother sat in my office and shared her sense of dread about an upcoming meeting for parents at her daughter's new school. She ached with pain because she knew the other mothers would ask her "how many kids do you have?" Simply articulating the question brought back with ripping pain her memories of her younger son who was struck and killed the year before while playing outside. This woman's experience isn't unusual. Other grieving parents have expressed horror at the thought of being with people who aren't aware of the tragedy they sustained. Bereaved parents experience conversation about other people's children as a knife in the heart. It is enough to make many of them withdraw from social contact.

## The Upside-Down World

Not only is the world of the bereaved parent lonely, but it is also truly upside down. Parents are not supposed to outlive their children. The bereaved parent is forced through a crack in the universe into a world where expectations are turned inside out. The death of a child before the death of the parent goes against the grain. Here is an ancient folk tale illustrating this point:

> After waiting in vain for years, an emperor was overjoyed at the birth of an heir for his throne. He and the empress invited royalty from far and wide to attend a great celebration. The royal poet was commissioned to create a special poem for the occasion. On the day of celebration, the newborn son lay in a royal cradle between his parents. After all of the guests had eaten, the emperor called for the royal poet to deliver his poem. "Grandfather dies," the poet read; "Father dies; Son dies." The emperor was enraged at the poet for connecting death with his newborn child and called for the poet to be executed on the spot. But the poet interrupted. "Sire," he said, "is this not the best course for history? Each generation should die in sequence, the younger outliving the older."

Here is an entry from my personal journal, written 22 years after our son Steven's death, in which I try to address the devastation I felt of having my child die before me:

KADDISH—A MEMORIAL PRAYER, NOVEMBER 23, 1997

It seems so stupid to say Kaddish for a little boy.
Kaddish is a prayer of respect for the dead—for a dead parent
  usually,
Or an uncle or an aunt or a grandparent
Or maybe even for an older brother or sister.
But for an 8-year-old boy?
Who now has been dead for 22 years ...

It just doesn't fit.
I am sitting in front of a
Roaring fire in our living room.
When he died, we kept a fire burning
During the several days before
His funeral, and for
Many, many days after
He was buried.
Tending a fire gives me an
Activity, a distraction for the moment.
The hissing flames cry out
The pain that is still in me
Twenty-two years later.
I'm not sure why
I am so sad and listless
This year.
Last year I almost didn't remember it was November 23rd
  again.
I find myself irritable
And very sad at odd times throughout the day.
This year I just want to sit and tend to the fire,
And not say Kaddish
Or light a memorial candle.
It feels stupid to say
Kaddish for a little boy.
He should be saying it
For me!

(©1997, J. Shep Jeffreys)

I heard similar sentiments expressed at a regional The Compassionate Friends meeting (The Compassionate Friends is a support group for bereaved parents) during which some parents began to debate which was worse: losing a baby or an older child. I asked them, "When is the best time for a child to die?"

They answered, "After me!"

## Parental Guilt

Many bereaved parents experience a deep sense of guilt that flows heavily from the wound of loss. They engage in painful self-evaluation over what seems like their failure to keep their child alive. Their disturbing and demoralizing guilt is composed of:

- Regrets about the quality of parenting.

- Misgivings about medical treatment and other decisions involving the child.

- Unresolved conflicts with the child.

In short, just about every aspect of the parent–child relationship may be examined and used for parental self-blame.

Some view their grief as a possible punishment for their misdeeds as parents, whether sins of omission or commission. I hear them tormenting themselves with such questions as:

- *Why did I (or didn't I) let him go out that night?*

- *I should have checked who was driving the car.*

- *Why didn't I look in on the baby sooner?*

- *We should have gotten another medical opinion!*

- *I should have known she was so desperate.*

- *We had a terrible fight the night of the accident.*

- *I should have visited her more often in the hospital, been nicer to her, told her I loved her.*

This is just a small sample of the kind of painful self-evaluation that parents engage in when they feel guilty for "failing to keep their child alive," failing to fulfill their "job description." For most of the parents that I have worked with, the issue of guilt has been raised as a disturbing and demoralizing feature of grieving.

Guilt comes in a variety of forms and is a powerful influence on both physical and mental health (S. E. Johnson, 1987). Guilt may arise out of a parent feeling implicated in the death. For example, parents whose child died in the car they were driving or whose child died from drowning due to lack of supervision may relive the terror of the child's death over and over again. Still other parents feel guilty because they are not grieving enough, or even are enjoying rare moments of laughter and contentment. (See Chapter 9.)

## Survivor's Guilt

Many parents feel guilty because they are alive and the child is not, regardless of any possible connection to the cause of death. This is called survivor's guilt. Siblings and grandparents can be affected similarly. It is also not unusual for some women to feel survivor's guilt because they have a healthy newborn, and their sister or other close relative has suffered a recent miscarriage or is unable to conceive.

## Secondary Losses

Often children fulfill more than the role of child; they can also serve as best friends, business or fishing partners, and confidants. "Parents who depended heavily on a child for need-fulfillment can also experience complicated responses" (Solsberry, 1984, p. 82). These parents may have depended on their children physically, or psychologically, in the case of an absent spouse. Children also provide their parents with a sense of status or self-esteem. Mothers have said things like, "Once I gave birth to her, I really felt like I was finally important." For some people, having a child depend on them gives them a real sense of purpose in life: they

Care providers should anticipate the expression of parental guilt and listen to it, never agree with it, and confront it only when the parent is ready to work on this. Often, parents who find someone who will simply listen to him or her express their guilt feel unburdened and relieved of some of their pain. At an appropriate point in counseling, reality-testing activities—such as reviewing medical information if the death resulted from an illness, or police reports and eyewitness accounts if the death was accidental—helps parents relieve their guilt. Seeking forgiveness from our deceased child and others, as well as granting forgiveness to anyone we feel has caused us pain, anger, or suffering can also alleviate the intensity of remorse. (See section on "Forgiveness as a Healing Tool" in Chapter 9.)

undertake a great responsibility and feel as if they have a continuing job to perform. Having and nurturing a child also gives some parents the opportunity to lavish on another the love and care that they themselves were deprived of as children. When the child dies, the opportunity to fulfill these needs dies too, creating significant aftershocks.

Much of the guilt parents experience will melt away over time. When this doesn't happen, it may be that the grief has become complicated, yielding chronic despair, guilt, anger, and physical complaints that can linger for years. Continued guilt can give rise to prolongation and intensification of the grief process resulting in depression, low self-esteem, alcohol and drug use, self-sabotaging behaviors, and overextension of energy into work and other activities. (See Chapter 10 for details on complicated grief.)

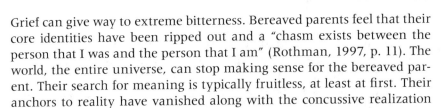

## Parental Anger

Grief can give way to extreme bitterness. Bereaved parents feel that their core identities have been ripped out and a "chasm exists between the person that I was and the person that I am" (Rothman, 1997, p. 11). The world, the entire universe, can stop making sense for the bereaved parent. Their search for meaning is typically fruitless, at least at first. Their anchors to reality have vanished along with the concussive realization

Regardless of the source of the bereaved person's anger, it is an expected component of grief. The care provider must provide a safe place for it to be expressed. It is not unusual for angry, bereaved people to lash out with rage, which in turn triggers aching feelings of grief that were lying just beneath the surface.

If the anger is directed at the care provider, he or she needs to internally reframe the outburst as a part of the process and realize that the grieving parent views the care provider as a safe person. The provider can also reflect this feeling back to the grieving person by saying, "Who else would you like to hear yourself express those feelings to?" This helps to put the anger in a more productive context. Providers who are not experienced in working with highly explosive individuals must exercise caution. When in doubt, get a consultation and consider referring the individual to a colleague specializing in rage issues. Techniques for helping the parent understand and discharge stored anger are discussed in Chapter 9 in the section "Externalizing the Feelings of Emotional Pain."

that their beloved child—an extension of their being, their stake in the future—is no more and will never be again.

In some cases, outward rage and bitterness is how some parents cope with depressed or hostile feelings toward themselves. Other parents direct their rage at people who are seen as having had some role in causing the death of the child—the driver of the car, a neglectful babysitter, a health care provider, or a spouse. Anger is sometimes directed at the dead child or at God. Parents who feel betrayed by their faith may reject any support from their religious community. Parents may even direct their anger toward surviving children, distancing themselves as a way of self-protection from additional losses, and in some cases protecting their children from parental sorrow.

## Coping With Other People

Sometimes a grieving parent will find it necessary to educate friends and family as to what is and isn't helpful in order to create a useful social support system. We have found that the bereaved parents' loved ones generally welcome such guidance. However, grieving people need to be aware that there are people in their lives, including parents or siblings, from whom they will never get the support they would have expected or desired. It is usually a shock for a bereaved parent to realize that even close relatives may not be able to be supportive and instead may distance themselves. Other people may be at a complete loss for words and not know what to say, or else say hurtful and destructive things, such as, "You will just have to move on," "When are you going to stop crying and

The care provider can help grieving people find tactful ways to respond to uninvited advice, judgmental statements, and other non-helpful comments from people who may be available for support if they had some direction. I have found that replying to insensitive comments clearly and firmly, without any sarcastic overtones, works well. Some examples include:

- "You can help me most by just listening to me for a while."
- "Advice is not what I need right now."
- "I really don't want to talk right now; I hope you understand."
- "That comment was not only unhelpful, it hurt me."
- "Can you just sit with me while I cry for a little while?"

get a life?" and "I really don't care to be with you when you are so down all the time." It's best for grieving people to avoid such individuals.

## Parental Fear

In addition to the hurt, pain, and anger expressed by grieving parents, another fear and anxiety often engulfs them: the fear of losing other children or any close person. We attach to survive; and when the critical parent-to-child (or sibling-to-sibling) bond has been broken, the individual may become sensitive to the reality that it could happen again. Sometimes bereaved parents overprotect surviving children, spouses, or other relatives and close friends, and can become a serious energy drain, causing problems in other relationships. Sometimes the anxiety-related overprotectiveness of grieving parents causes them to excessively worry about their own health.

## Meaning Making: A New Me in a New World

As bereaved parents search to define their new identities, they need to restore both their inner sense of the dead child and their ability to create a new social equilibrium—that is, to answer the question, "Who am I in the outer world?" (Klass, 1988, 2001). The inner representation of the lost child—whether it was a fetus, an infant, older child, or adult child—must be converted to the image of a child who exists within but is now no longer physically available as an external reality. An example of this is a parent who can say to herself, "I know I have the picture of my child in my mind, but I don't expect him or her to come to the table for dinner." The same is true for the dreams, hopes, and wishes they had for the future with this child.

Parents must also create a new internal picture of who they are in the outside world, a picture that includes grief at varying levels of intensity. Holidays as well as birthdays, graduations, weddings, and births will all serve as powerful reminders of loss as they confront who is not there, whose life story will never unfold, whose own marriage and family never happened. How do we act on Mother's Day or Father's Day, or at the graduation of the children our deceased child once went to school with?

Bereaved parents often point out how different they feel from other parents whenever they encounter them on the playground, at school events, during family occasions or any other social activity. Their loss and grief accompany them everywhere they go. Others may be aware of their loss but seldom bring it up. This often causes bereaved parents to feel as if they were wearing masks—they look fine to the outside world and feel like an impostor inside. One grieving mother told me how rejected she felt by family and friends in the months and years following her son's death because of their continued lack of sensitivity to her grief.

Making new meanings in the new world without the deceased child is an important part of reclaiming life. It involves making sense of something that does not make sense in the "upside-down world" of the bereaved parent. *Benefit making*, a term used by Neimeyer (2000; personal communication, 2010), is also important. Parents who were able to actively pursue a cause in their child's name are often able to eventually acknowledge the "gift of the loss." These activities benefit not only the receiver but the giving parents as well, who are able to say to themselves that their child's death was not wasted or in vain. In addition, benefit making provides a constructive distraction from active grieving.

Our family, for example, formed The Steven Daniel Jeffreys Foundation, Ltd., a nonprofit that provides grief counseling, workshops, community education, and professional conferences for mental health and pastoral care providers. We enjoy reporting to each other instances in which the foundation that carries Steven's name has helped friends or colleagues who are dealing with loss and bereavement. This serves as a positive outcome, which is a legacy of Steven's illness and death. Though my family suffered traumatic changes, we coped by extending the gifts of his loss to others. Other parents have created scholarships, planted memorial gardens or trees, worked in soup kitchens, built nature centers, collected funds for education about the consequences of drunk driving or drug use, and supported research on various fatal diseases.

## Painful Reminders

Seasonal reminders of loss are part of a bereaved parent's reality. Here is a personal journal entry that never fails to take me back to a painful time.

There may be many reminders each week; some you notice and others slip past the corner of your eye. Newly bereaved parents may suddenly find a little sock in the laundry that catches them unaware and causes them to wince, sob, or even scream. Over time, the parent reorganizes the inner picture of the lost child from one who was available in a real, physical sense to one who is available only in memory. As a way of maintaining the bond with the deceased child, many parents continue

---

**HALLOWEEN IS STILL PAINFUL—OCTOBER 24, 1995**

Ah, yes. It's pumpkin time again. Driving down the highway, I see them—in all their orange shapes and sizes dotting the road-sides. The sight snaps me back to the time of unrelenting terror when there was "no way out of this prison of pain." Halloween—twenty years ago. Steven just didn't have the energy to go trick-or-treating, and I so wanted him to; just as he did when he was well and not dying. He refused to let me carry him piggyback. He couldn't even put on his costume. Ghosts and goblins came to the door all evening. *They didn't know.*

(© J. Shep Jeffreyes, 1995)

---

to relate to the inner image of the child, reminisce with others about the child, and think about how life would be had the child lived.

Parents can continue to acknowledge the deceased child at family events such as holiday celebrations. They can also visit the grave and create religious ceremonies. Many parents want to hear their child's name spoken and may continue celebrating the child's birthday. Parents adapt to a world without their deceased child by incorporating the image and memory of the child into the post-loss reality. The parent can feel as if he or she is still connected to the child as life goes on—not necessarily without pain but with the knowledge that the memory of the child remains available. This is a very normal part of the healing process; it helps create a "new normal."

## Linking Objects and Continuing Bonds

One of the most common ways that parents maintain their relationship with their deceased child is by linking objects, locations, or events associated with the child. This helps reduce their anxiety and can be a source of comfort (Klass, 1997, 1999, 2001). Many diverse items have served as linking objects: toys, games, clothes, jewelry, photos, music, dried flowers, stuffed animals, dolls, a hospital identification bracelet, a strand of hair, prints from a child's hand or foot, coins, stones, a copy of the sonogram of the fetus, a blanket, stamps, sports cards or a coin collection, school artwork and homework papers, a pet, a plant, a garden plot, an infant car seat, and even a fragment of bone recovered from an accident scene.

   The Facebook page of one very popular and beloved teenager who died suddenly from an illness helps his parents and many friends stay connected to him as well as with each other. They continue to talk to and about him, tell him what they are doing, and express their ongoing love for him and grieve for his absence from their lives. The social networking capacity of the Internet provides unlimited opportunities to continue to bond with deceased loved ones.

   Various rituals are also beneficial in maintaining a continuing bond with the child. Parents can celebrate others' happy occasions by donating money to a worthy cause in the child's name, planting a tree or memory garden, creating a memory book or box to be displayed on special days and events, and planning and holding religious/spiritual ceremonies. In some cultures, the long-deceased loved one's bones are dug up and arranged in urns for ritual use. Some parents save their child's ashes, which they then mix with concrete to form a garden monument in order to have a place to connect, to pray, to cry. These links, whether through objects, rituals, or social contact, not only affirm that the child did live but also validates the existence and importance of the continued connection.

   Participation in events is another linking behavior. Frequently, parents will also attend school sporting events, graduations, and other community functions that their children would have participated in, as representatives of their dead child. They visit the site of the accident and mark it with flowers, cards, artwork, and religious symbols; they visit cemeteries, maintain ashes at home or in a special site, attend military parades and other memorials—all of which serve to maintain contact with their dead child.

   Robert Neimeyer (1998) states that grieving parents must ultimately "redefine the inner connection to the deceased while maintaining our relationship with the living" (p. 98). Some parental efforts to stay connected to their deceased children are more helpful than others (Barrera et al., 2009; Field, Gao, & Paderna, 2005). Maintaining bonds with deceased children is seen as optimally achieved by adjusting to the new reality and, concurrently, sustaining a level of connection to the deceased. However, some attempts to maintain the bond impede parental coping with the post-loss world, resulting in dysfunctional relationships at home, in the community, and at work. When dysfunction persists, complicated grief develops. (See Chapter 10.) Such unhelpful behaviors, which are often disturbing to other family members, include keeping the child's room exactly as it was for a prolonged period of time; talking, dressing and behaving in ways that the child did; and keeping clothes, toys, and other memorabilia in close proximity at all times. Because the nature and degree of how parents express their desire to maintain a bond with their deceased child will vary over time, I suggest caution against labeling these behaviors as maladjusted or irrational. It's important to remember that these behaviors are, at heart, efforts at adjustment motivated by agony and suffering. In Chapter 10, we present three evaluation criteria (Jacobs, 1999) for determining whether grief has become complicated, in which case parents should be referred to a mental health professional.

As the grief journey proceeds, many linking objects and activities lose their potency as the need for them diminishes. During these transitions, parents may keep linking items in a box kept in a nearby closet or night table drawer. Some items may be displayed, whereas others may be distributed to relatives, friends, and community organizations associated with childcare or hospital pediatric waiting rooms.

I experienced this transition firsthand. My son Steven wore a baseball cap when chemotherapy caused his hair to fall out. After he died, I placed his cap under my pillow. Each night I could reach under my pillow, touch the hat and feel some connection to Steven. It was always a good feeling. It remained under my pillow for a year and has been in the drawer next to my bed since. I seldom look at it now, but I know it is there.

The continuing spiritual bonds and linking objects support grieving parents as they gradually reconfigure their identities and the new ways of being in the world without their child. The bonds are thus not severed but rather remolded in a way that allows them to create a new relationship with the dead child in a new world. For many, this provides a sense of comfort and restores a sense of equilibrium, but not for all.

## Reunion Fantasies

I have heard many parents state that they simply do not wish to be in a world without their child. They may even express a desire to join their child. Although any self-destructive remarks must be taken seriously, this type of reunion fantasy usually exists without any plan for implementation. Parents need to know that it is safe for them to express such thoughts to the helping person. Many parents find the thought of reunion with their child a comfort and a way to diminish the painful anguish. (See Chapter 9 for suicide assessment procedures.)

## The Bereaved Parent Lives in Two Worlds

The feeling that the world "isn't right" after a child dies is directed not only inward, affecting a parent's sense of self, but also outward, affecting

Care providers may need to refer grieving parents to other sources of community support, such as Compassionate Friends, Bereaved Parents of the USA, religious or spiritual groups, or health care professionals. (See Appendix A for a list of support organizations.)

the couple's relationship, the deceased child's siblings, and extended family and friends. The waves of grief also flow out to school friends and teachers, health care providers, neighbors, workplace peers, the faith community, the people from whom the family buys food and services, mail delivery people, and anyone else who has regular contact with the family. Bereaved parents operate in two spheres. In one world parents grieve, connect with the internal image of the dead child, reminisce, engage in rituals, and attend to the legal and business affairs dealing with the child (insurance claims, tax accounting, estate law, and in some cases, courts and attorneys). But parents also live in the everyday world in which they must work, plan for the future, and care for other children, family members, friends and colleagues. Which world predominates? Neither. Families move between both, focusing on maintaining the inner image of the lost loved one as well as engaging in grief-related activities, and on accommodating to the new post-loss world (Rubin, 1996; Rubin & Malkinson, 2001; Stroebe & Schut, 2001a,b).

I realized this myself when I visited Steven's grave just before the anniversary of his death.

### Visiting the Grave Site—November 21, 2003

#### Walking Between Two Worlds

Leaving Steven's grave is like drawing away from grief.
Walking towards the car is facing away from one reality
And looking in the direction of the world without him.
Driving out of the cemetery and turning onto the street
Is reentering life as usual, life with traffic, people, stores.
A few minutes earlier I stood looking down at my son's grave.
I prayed, I told him how much I still loved him, missed him.
I sang a song he sang before he died and I also sang
"Morning Has Broken,"
The song we sang at his funeral 28 years ago.
Then I walked a few steps to the left and
Prayed at the duplex gravesite of my father-in-law and mother-in-law.

I sat for a while on an adjacent marble slab.
The sun was warm. It was peaceful, quiet and filling there.
Then I looked back at Steven's grave marker, got up and
Walked towards the car.
Leaving Steven's grave is like drawing away from grief,
Walking between two worlds.
I belong to both.

(© J. Shep Jeffreys, 2003)

# ☐ Parents Whose Child Was Murdered, Completed Suicide, or Died From Other Violent Causes

A family sits at the Thanksgiving dinner table happily awaiting the last arrival. Suddenly, the phone rings: It's the hospital chaplain calling from the emergency room. Their loved one was killed on the way to the dinner. Life changes in seconds.

Parents coping with a child's traumatic death clearly have special needs. If a child was murdered; took his or her own life; or was killed by a drunken driver, war, or a disaster, the suddenness of the death wreaks an abrupt concussive blow to mental and emotional balance. Their assumptions about the world are violently torn away, and familiar, grounded reality is gone. Their sense of safety, predictability, and personal identity is forever shattered in a moment. (See Chapter 10 for more on traumatic death of a child and grief complications.)

## Parents of Murdered Children

Homicide and suicide loss "as compared with other types of bereavement, renders a significantly pathological appearance" (Rando, 1993b, p. 537). Parents of murdered children often feel that losing a child in this way sets them apart from other bereaved parents. The unnatural elements surrounding homicide—intentional violence, possible violation or mutilation, and the thought that the child may have suffered—can yield a high level of parental anxiety and put them at increased risk for posttraumatic stress.

Care providers must be prepared to deal with the parents' sense that justice was not done. Providers can also educate these parents as to the typical emotional and cognitive reactions they may expect. It is not always easy for a parent to find friends who can be present and listen to the story of this type of loss, and also be comfortable with strong grief reactions. Most local prosecutors' offices run victim support programs that provide a climate of understanding, acceptance, and caring for families coping with homicide. (See Appendix A for community resources.)

Parents of murdered children may have lingering involvement with the legal system as the killer is sought, taken into custody, tried, and sentenced. They may need to attend trials and sentencing hearings, sometimes for long periods of time. The media may also become involved. All of these factors prolong and impede the healing process. If the killer is either not caught or not prosecuted, or receives a lesser sentence than the parents feel just, they are left with unfinished business.

## Suicide Completion

In 2006, suicide was the third leading cause of death for young people ages 15 to 24 (National Institutes of Health, 2009). Suicide completion by a child leaves the parents with guilt, rage, intense hurt, and frequently many unanswered questions. In these cases, parents may want to avail themselves of peer support groups in addition to individual care providers. (See Appendix A.) In my own work with very angry parents, I found that allowing them to release their pain and anger enabled them to connect with their child through rituals and forgiveness exercises. (See in Chapter 9 sections: "Externalizing the Feelings of Emotional Pain," "Forgiveness as a Healing Tool," and "The Use of Rituals for Healing.")

In more severe cases, in which there was substantial unfinished business between parent and child, parents may be at risk for complications of grief including posttraumatic stress syndrome and suicidal ideation. These parents may require special clinical help. (See Chapter 10.)

# ☐ Impact of a Child's Death on a Couple's Relationship

"When our baby was born, a mommy was also born," said a very sad woman who was sitting in my office one day. Her husband, who sat apart from her, without touching or looking at her, just looked down. My initial impression was that he was grieving the loss of his child. When he later spoke, I realized that he was not only grieving the loss of his child but also the loss of his wife who no longer seemed involved in their relationship. As his wife related her lament—a lament he'd heard many, many times in the several months since the sudden death of their infant—he slowly shook his head.

Just as the birth of a child has a major impact on the life of a couple, the death of a child has the potential to bring cataclysmic waves of change. Some couples simply lack the skills to make contact in the aftermath of such a tragic event in their lives. The hopes, dreams, and expectations for life's journey in the company of their child as a vital member of their family system were ripped out from under them. Whether the death was sudden or the result of illness, the empty space in the home and in their hearts frequently causes them to retreat into their private worlds of grief. Separately they struggle to emotionally keep their heads above water. Many report a sense of drowning. They are often suffering from a serious loss of control and uncertainty as to how to communicate with their partner; they hurt too much to do anything. "Where do we go from here?" couples frequently ask me.

Care providers must help couples set some outcome goals for counseling: They need to imagine a new direction and to envision a new structure to their lives. Even a brief homework assignment, like consenting to spend an agreed-upon interval of time together, can start the process of reconnecting. When a mother and father can redevelop a process for communication, they can begin to restore their sense of couplehood and support each other's grieving. Exercises that help the couple restore communication are important aids in reducing feelings of isolation.

Care providers can help a couple assess their own readiness to have another child by helping them understand the grief and healing process; in this way, they participate in their own evaluation. A variety of tools can be used for this, including Worden's four tasks, Rando's six processes, or Neimeyer's meaning reconstruction. (See Chapter 3.)

## Subsequent Pregnancies

In my experience, many couples who have suffered the loss of a fetus, infant, or older child, or sustained a stillbirth are often anxious to have another child fairly soon after the loss. They may seek guidance from a mental health or medical care provider to determine how long they should wait. There is no clear-cut answer, but care providers can offer them a way to evaluate their readiness so that they can make the most intelligent choice for themselves.

Several important issues must be resolved before making some recommendations. First, what is the medical status of the mother and what does her physician advise regarding her health needs? Second, and admittedly this may be difficult to ascertain, to what extent have they mourned the child who has died? According to Rando (1984), "The couple must have achieved some resolution of the loss of the deceased child" (p. 140). How can we find this out? I have used assessment via the four tasks of mourning as described in Chapter 3. Although the assessment process can be lengthy, most parents who seek guidance for this issue understand the importance of making this determination as thoughtfully and completely as possible. As Rubin and Malkinson (2001) state, "The need to maintain an ongoing attachment to the unique child who died, and to allow for the formation of a distinct attachment to the unique child who is about to enter the family, are important benefits of experiencing the grief and loss process" (p. 232).

## The High Divorce Rate Myth

Bereaved couples do not have a high divorce rate. A major study of bereaved parents reports that "overall, 72% of parents who were married at the time of their child's death are still married to the same person" (The Compassionate Friends, 1999, p. 11). Of the remaining 28% of marriages, 16% ended due to the death of a spouse, leaving only 12% truly ending in divorce. Of those couples whose marriages ended in divorce, only one out of four reported that the death of the child contributed to their breakup.

In addition, an extensive review of studies designed to measure the degree of marital discord and extent of divorce following a child's serious illness or a child's death from many different causes found that only a "relatively small percentage of bereaved parents do divorce in the aftermath of a child's death but many parents reported either no change in marital status or definite positive effects of the child's death on their marriage" (Schwab, 1998, pp. 460–463). Some parents described their relationship as being closer because of their mutual grief. It is important that care providers dispel the erroneous myth that marriages are necessarily doomed after a child dies.

However, in spite of the low rate of divorce after a child dies, many grieving parents do experience some considerable marital strain—many say that they feel like strangers in their own relationships—and have to make some readjustments in their marriages. Oliver (1999), for example, reports "most empirical studies have found that a substantial minority of couples experience marital difficulties after the death of a child" (p. 197). People who lose a child naturally turn first to their spouse (or even an ex-spouse) for support and at times to place blame. The trauma of child loss can escalate an anxious attachment that creates increased need for emotional support (Oliver, 1999). The parent who does not need high levels of emotional support may feel overloaded and withdraw just when

Care providers should expect some disruption of marital communication and help couples understand why their post-loss relationship feels strained and how this is normal. Providers should also give couples opportunities to reconnect, using techniques for building mutual support. Communication enhancement activities such as structured, scheduled periods of contact and sharing how each is feeling and what each needs, can be a focus of couple's counseling. Each person can be encouraged to keep a diary of feelings to share at the agreed-upon communication sessions. In this way, grieving parents learn to record their feelings in the heat of the moment rather than share them in ways that may be burdensome to the other partner. Friends and other family can become part of an inner circle of support. Self-help support groups can also help. (See Appendix A.)

the other has the greatest need for talking, physical contact, and reassurance. Those who feel as if they are not receiving the care and comfort they expected may detach and withdraw from contact. This then can lead to further hurt, distancing, lack of communication, and deterioration in the couple's functioning; counseling is indicated when this happens.

## Grief Varies in Timing and in Intensity

When couples feel out of sync in terms of their grieving styles and rhythms, breakdowns in communication occur. Let's return to the couple described at the beginning of this section. The bereaved father admitted that he was "tired of hearing his wife's grieving all of the time." They both complained that there never seemed to be time to talk because each seemed to be in a very different phase of the grief cycle. The father had spent the day in a nonchild environment with few painful reminders, and he was ready to relax. His wife, however, had spent the day at home trying to avoid the baby's room filled with never-used furniture and accessories, hearing the sounds of little children playing outside, glimpsing television shows interrupted by baby food and diaper commercials, and images of late-model vans loaded with happy, healthy children. She could not escape from her shattered dreams. The depth of his wife's grief made the husband feel helpless and unable to come to her aid. Before they left my office, I suggested that he not use his computer as an escape and that he and his wife engage in mutual information-seeking conversation.

## Men and Women Often Grieve Differently

The differences in styles or patterns of grieving as presented by Doka and Martin (2010) help to explain the basis for conflict in the grieving couple. (See Chapter 3.) At one end of the spectrum is the *intuitive* or affective expression style of grieving which is more frequently associated with women. On the other end is the *instrumental* or intellectual, action-oriented style, typically viewed as a male pattern. However, many individuals blend the two forms of grieving. The more alike in their grieving styles, the less conflict the couple will experience.

A summary of studies by Rosenblatt (2000b) on bereaved parents' styles of grieving indicates that fathers and mothers differ in the length, intensity, and degree of public openness of their grief. It was reported that mothers typically grieved longer and were more openly expressive than

The care provider must encourage the couple to be conscious of any distancing and help them to find ways to connect. Ground rules for communication can be developed to guide couples toward connecting and speaking. Couples can agree, for example, to let each other know how they are feeling, no matter how sad they are, even if it may cause the other to start to cry. Providers can help the partners to grasp the importance of "human presence." They can train men to be available without feeling as if they have to fix their wives' pain and suffering.

men. Couples interviewed by Rosenblatt frequently cited the communication problems resulting from these gender differences as causing stress in their marriages. How does this play out at home? A woman who thinks nothing of giving vent to her feelings may have a husband who does not know how to be with his sobbing, despairing, and sometimes bitter wife.

So many husbands say they "don't know how to make it better for her" and too often this fix-it, problem-solver role is what men believe they are supposed to assume. They often feel helpless because they don't have the magic words that will make their wives feel better. At the same time, the masculine style of grieving is often misinterpreted by women this way: "He has no feelings about this tragedy; he just doesn't care about me and goes on as if nothing has happened." This miscommunication can result in increased withdrawal, isolation, and bitterness on the part of both people.

On the other hand, women do not want solutions or magic words. Many wives report that they feel abandoned by their husbands when they fail to listen to them. "He wants to advise me or solve my problem," women typically say, "but all I want is for him to listen to me, even for 15 minutes!" What they don't take into account is some men resist expressing or talking about their grief because it causes them too much pain. As a result, women may seek out relatives or friends with whom to grieve, which may in turn create more distance between her and her husband. Although many women may need to confront their grief directly, many men elect to take a more indirect route. I've met men who work out their feelings of anguish by exercising, doing home improvement projects, and by throwing themselves into their work. A man may withhold his expression of grief with his wife so as not to upset her. This isn't a problem unless these different styles of grieving lead partners down such different paths that they don't spend any time grieving together or at least reporting some aspects of their grief to each

Care providers can help by assisting couples to understand the reasons for their isolation and the factors preventing them from communicating about grief. Further, couples should be helped to develop some simple, brief check-in procedures that will begin the process of reestablishing some workable mutual support. Couples can agree, for example, to phone each other once or twice a day just to say, "Hi, what are you doing now? I'm feeling …" or "What's been on your mind the past half-hour?"

other. Communication is the life energy of a relationship—when it goes, the relationship goes. To hold back reduces mutual grieving.

In my own life, after Steven died, my wife and I realized that we were sometimes unaware of each other's grieving. We discovered that both of us were holding back so as not to bring the other down. Many times her sadness made me cry, just as my tears broke her heart. But we made a pact not to hide our expressions of pain in order to protect the other; we resolved to make our grief part of our experience as a couple. Although we each still grieved alone at times, we also grieved together.

Not all differences in grieving are due to gender differences. Sometimes the differences result from the fact that each parent has a unique relationship with the child, which affects how each parent grieves. The primary caregiving parent will face a different set of secondary losses after the death of a child than the parent who has been significantly less involved due to work, travel, withdrawal, separation, or other causes of disconnection. It is also true that those parents who considered their children as companions, confidants, or business partners will feel additional losses and may grieve more intensely as a result.

Other times, in spite of the best of intentions, each partner is so emotionally drained from coping with personal grief that there is no energy left over to support each other (Bernstein & Gavin, 1996). This is especially true when there are other children to care for, and if one or both parents have demanding jobs outside the home.

## Old Childhood Messages Influence the Rate and Depth of Sharing Feelings

A couple's communication patterns are based on each person's life experience and the temperament with which each are born. Individuals who grow up thinking that they may not express feelings of sadness, anger,

A care provider must help couples like this build bridges to each other during the grieving process. Providers must continually remind couples to be respectful and tolerant of the different styles of grieving, explaining that each individual has a different pain and grief threshold at any given moment. Some need to give vent to grief; others need to limit or avoid these expressions. Care providers can also help couples realize that even though they may grieve in different ways, they still have opportunities to grieve together. They can create family rituals, visit the gravesite, review and arrange photo albums. They can also hold family discussions, include their children and talk about their grief. This can be an opportunity to learn how grief reactions are different for each person.

Care providers can help couples begin to gradually share their grief using letter writing (either handwritten or e-mailed to each other), sharing written diaries, and listening to audiotapes the other has prepared in private. Providers can also suggest specific homework assignments, such as asking that one partner tell the other how he or she is feeling or misses most; and what each thinks the other person is going through. These communications can be initiated by writing notes, which are first exchanged, and in time, read aloud to each other.

or fear may have trouble expressing these feelings as adults. If such a person marries someone for whom emotional expression comes easily, their communications styles conflict. Such conflicts can be exacerbated when grieving for a child.

## Some Parents Find It Too Painful to Express Grief Directly to Their Partners

Some grieving parents cannot grieve in front of each other because "It hurts too much!" or "I just can't let him or her see me like this," or "I feel judged when I cry with my spouse present." Many times, parents simply do not want to hear themselves cry and feel the devastation again. In such cases, the sound of the other parent's sobbing becomes so anguishing that the other partner distances or distracts him or herself.

Care providers can help couples talk to each other about what each wants sexually and how they can achieve their goals. It's helpful to determine what issues regarding sex predated the loss of the child ("What is different about their sex life now?"). For many couples, the return to an active and mutually happy sex life is a sign that they have reclaimed their normal marital life.

## Couples Experience Different Sexual Needs

For some men, sex may serve as a comforting and releasing activity, whereas women report that grief is inconsistent with lovemaking and that their pain makes this impossible for them. (In some couples, the roles are reversed.) As a result, the partner wanting sex ends up feeling frustrated, angry, and abandoned, whereas the other partner says, "How can you not know how I feel?"

## ☐ Sibling Grief

Each year approximately 1.8 million American children, from birth through 18 years of age, become bereaved siblings (Hogan & DeSantis, 1996). Many factors influence the nature and extent of sibling grief. A friend of mine in his early 60s told me that he had borne a painful guilt from the time he was about 9 years old regarding the death of his younger brother. He and his brother had gotten into a fight, and he kicked his brother in the stomach. Some months later his brother fell ill and died of an intestinal disorder. My friend remained convinced that he was the cause of his brother's death and kept this secret for decades. It became part of his deep memory, surfacing mostly upon hearing of the death of a child. During psychotherapy, the unfinished material about his brother surfaced. He felt much relieved and later discovered, after investigating his brother's medical records, that he was not at all responsible for his brother's death. He also told me somewhat ruefully how different his life would have been had he been able to talk to his parents about his fears and have them reassure him that he did not kill his brother.

The effects of living with a terminally ill sibling and the ensuing death of that sibling on brothers or sisters are too often neglected. This is unfortunate as the grief reaction of surviving siblings is a critical part of the emotional climate of the bereaved family. Adults need to help children deal with their own feelings of loss in age-appropriate ways.

## Information Flow

It's hard to keep secrets in a family, especially when a child is sick. Some children read signals and often ask difficult and evocative questions: "Is he going to die?" "Does she know how sick she is?" Other children may not ask questions because they fear upsetting their parents or because they don't really want to know the whole truth. When siblings are kept out of the information loop, however, they may fill in the gaps with troubling fantasies. They may, for example, worry that they themselves will take ill and die, or they fear that their parents will be killed in a car crash on a trip to the drugstore to fill a prescription. It is absolutely vital to consider the sibling's need to know what is happening with an ill child or what has happened to a child who has died. Children need to be encouraged to ask questions and to have these questions answered. The health and healing of the family depend on it.

Failing to keep siblings apprised not only makes children feel afraid and guilty but can also create a chasm between the sibling and parents. Many changes in the family are set in motion when a child's brother or sister dies. Rosenblatt (2000a), Fanos (1996), and Repole (1996) have shown that the death of a sibling can yield long-term effects on the mental health of an individual, especially when the experience has been a traumatic one and the child hasn't had an opportunity to express the feelings and thoughts of grief. Children have a right to know the facts regarding the illness or death of a brother or sister.

On the other hand, "just as one can err by trying to shield children from grief so one can err in the other direction and overwhelm them with grief" (Scherago, 1987, p. 3). Parents must be careful not to give children more information than they can use or that is inappropriate for them to have. Troubling details regarding sudden, violent, and mutilating deaths; those regarding agonizing pain of a degenerative illness; or any other potentially traumatizing details may need to be omitted from the information provided to young children.

## Availability of Parents

Children heal most effectively from the death of a sibling when their parents remain in their lives caring for them, playing with them, doing homework with them, and going out together. As indicated earlier, this may be difficult to achieve, particularly if the parents are consumed with their own fears for the life of a seriously ill child or are so devastated by

Care providers should remind parents that it is important to maintain continued communication with their children about how they feel and what they need from them. Parents who hold family meetings in which everyone can share feelings and concerns and ask questions will necessarily be more aware of their children's needs. Parents can also encourage children to share in family activities, such as creating memory albums, so that children feel included. If parents cannot meet the needs of their healthy, surviving children, then other adults need to be enlisted to meet these needs.

grief over a child's death that they have no emotional and physical energy to spare. Faced with demands from work and household responsibilities, grieving parents can be tempted to put the needs of the children off for another day. However, surviving children experience this as rejection, and it can lead to lingering resentment.

## The Nature of the Parents' Grief

Parental grief will have a direct effect on the reaction of siblings. Parents who don't cry or seem not to be distressed out of a desire to protect their surviving children can give children an unrealistic picture of grief. When parents grieve openly, children learn that it is normal and acceptable to feel and express grief. When parental grief is shared, children learn that grief is a natural emotion. Some families may have conflicts over how much and how deeply children should grieve the loss of a brother or sister. At these times more than ever, open communication aids the grieving and healing process.

## Nature of the Illness or Death

The nature of the illness or circumstances of the death of a sibling affects how surviving children grieve. If the death is prolonged by illness, or if it's sudden and violent, complicated grief reactions can occur. Risk factors for complicated grief are discussed in Chapter 10.

Death due to a lingering illness, characterized by numerous relapses and remissions, hospitalizations, painful treatments, debilitating medications, and drastic changes in the sick child's physical appearance, can

The care provider must be sensitive to ethnic and cultural differences about grieving. Behavior that is acceptable in one culture may be unacceptable in another. To offer appropriate care, providers need to seek out family members or friends who understand the family's traditions.

traumatize the surviving siblings. Some parents send their healthy children to stay with relatives or friends in an attempt to spare them from the harrowing details or so parents can spend more time at the hospital with the sick child. This can provide relief for parents but may severely diminish the healthy sibling's awareness of the seriousness of the situation and limit their participation in the grief process. Children who remain at home to witness long-term illness firsthand, however, will need to talk about their fears, anger, guilt, anticipatory grieving, and any other issues that they feel.

Sudden, violent, or avoidable deaths send shock waves through the family, creating the potential for complicated grief reactions in surviving siblings. Their anxiety and diminished sense of security may result in posttraumatic reactions, and they may become fearful, hyperactive, sleepless, or easily startled.

## Fear, Shame, and Guilt

Children with sick siblings may experience shame or embarrassment simply because their families are so different from those in which all the children are alive and healthy. Preteens and teens are particularly sensitive about feeling different. In addition, the resentment that naturally builds up as parents and visitors are absorbed with the ill brother or sister

Care providers must facilitate the flow of appropriate information to children and provide opportunities for them to ask questions and receive answers they can understand. This information may in fact help them begin their grieving process. They must also be reassured that they will be cared for and that they are still important to their parents. Parents can express these sentiments verbally, or through shared activities such as engaging in rituals, spending quality alone time with each child, reading to each child, playing board games, engaging in family art projects, going on outings, and having unstructured hangout time.

Care providers can help families to open up the lines of communication between parents and siblings—both during a child's illness and after a death has occurred. Because younger children have their own timetable and ways of grieving (see Chapter 5), the family should come together from time to time to engage in such activities as sorting through the deceased child's possessions; creating a memory/photo album; rearranging and redecorating the room, closet, or play area; creating a memory collage or family mural; writing letters to the dead child on his or her birthday (or other special days); and planting trees, flowers, or shrubs together in honor of his or her memory.

usually leads to feelings of guilt after the death has occurred. Siblings typically regret what they thought and felt and how they acted when their brother or sister was alive. This guilt can become part of unresolved grief that may surface years later. Further, many siblings express feelings of being medically vulnerable and fear that they too will either contract their sibling's illness or meet a similar sudden death.

Children should be given the opportunity to talk with parents and other siblings about what it was like during the illness or upon hearing the news of the accident, and how they are now feeling about the death of their sibling. Child/adolescent bereavement groups offer a grieving child the opportunity to learn that other kids experience guilt and regrets. (See Appendix A for resources.)

## Replacement Expectations

Some parents who lose a child may consciously or unwittingly communicate to surviving children that they are expected to assume the role of their dead sibling. Some parents may deify the dead child, enshrine his or her room, and focus on the dead child to the exclusion of the surviving siblings. When this happens, not only is the surviving child's grief process disrupted (Rando, 1984, p. 125), but also he or she can become resentful and experience mild or serious psychological disturbances.

## Siblings Speak

Birth order affects how surviving children picture themselves during a sibling's illness and after a death. Typically, the oldest child serves as a stand-in parent for the younger children and more closely identifies with the parents' pain. Oldest children typically express concern for the well-being of the parents and seek more information than younger children.

My wife and I have learned about this through talking with our own surviving children, who bravely agreed to share their stories with you. Thirteen years after Steven's death, when my daughter was 28, she recalls the time surrounding Steven's illness and death this way:

> I had a major issue with not being included in the realities of Steven's illness. I was aware of Mom and Dad getting more and more withdrawn from things. I remember how much he (my brother) hated going to the hospital and his screams of, "I don't want to go!" I felt incredible responsibility for both of my brothers, especially when we heard Steven screaming in pain. I felt reluctant to discuss my brother's illness with friends and felt great pain for my parents as well as a need to be strong for them and for my other brother. I was angry at receiving no information about when periods of remission began and ended. I felt cut off, and this scared me.
>
> I was angry that this was happening: Why him? Why this family? I remember waiting, always waiting in the hospital waiting room. I still feel angry that I was not told that my brother was going to die. I felt him distancing himself from me as he got sicker and sicker. He was in his own world of doctors and pain, and pushed us away. I feel cheated out of not having a brother who would be 20 now. I miss the friendship we would have had, and have dreams about him and feel his presence. I have painful memories when I see friends of his now. I wish we could have explored more alternative healing methods.
>
> I found that I was able to keep up my usual activities. My mom made a great effort to keep things normal around the house. My parents were there for the big things and supportive adult friends were there. I feel that other subsequent deaths have been easier for me. Now, as a brand new mother, I am aware of how horrible it must have been for them, and I have fears about losing my own son.

Steven's brother, 3 years younger than his sister, recalled his experience this way:

> My brother's illness became a way of life. I was jealous of his presents in spite of Mom's explanations. I still felt competitive with him in games. I worried when he was in pain and moaning when I was babysitting for him. I never pictured that he could be "dead." I just wanted him to get well, so we could play as we did before he got sick. I was frightened by his thinness and seeing his heart beat through his chest. I was not aware of the true life-threatening nature of his illness. I remember the music played at his funeral and always feel close to him when I hear it. When you have a younger brother, you always have a playmate. I am angry that I have lost

the older brother role. I feel cheated out of the experience of having him in my life. I had the protector role. I wanted to keep his room intact. I lost the availability of my parents when they took trips to the hospital.

I have guilt over fighting when we shared a room, when I tore up a club certificate in anger when he was well. I feel that I have more crying to do and want to visit his grave and fill in some memory gaps. I now feel different from others as a result of his illness and death. I feel that I know what life is really about and that I grew up faster. I feel guilty when asked about siblings and I answer "a sister." I find myself catastrophizing whenever I have physical symptoms.

Twenty-eight years after Steven's death, my daughter, age 43, says:

I think of him now whenever I see a kid with a baseball cap whose hair is cut short. I wonder how he would look if he were still alive today. What kind of uncle would he be? I feel cheated out of his kids. It gets harder to picture being with him and to remember the original experience. I wonder how much of my memories of him are memories of memories. I worry about my own health because I would never want my parents to go through that again.

We did not talk about it enough. I had a sense that it was bad but did not know he was dying until the last few months of his life. I thought what we were doing medically was going to make him better. Even on the night he died, I didn't believe he was going to die. I remember the ride home after he died. There were no pangs of pain from him when we hit bumps in the road. We all slept in the same bed that night.

I felt very responsible for my other brother and had to stay strong in order to not be another burden for my parents. We were absorbed with the death of my brother and still trying to maintain some kind of normal life. My teenage friends were crucial to my support. They listened to me and didn't judge me. I have had fears about my children as each of them reached the age my brother died. They have grown up hearing and knowing about their uncle. This has given them an awareness of death and life because of our talking about him and other loved ones who have died.

I am aware that I overreact to my children's illnesses for fear of losing them.

Here are the reflections of my son, at age 40:

I look at people who have brothers. A brother is a lifelong friend you can do things with. I have flashbacks when I play with my son, of being back with my brother. It's a neat feeling like unlocking a mystery as sudden memories surface—collecting cards, playing games. When my kids got a hamster, it took me back to my brother's gerbil and secretly buying him a new one when our cat Felix got the first one. Sad memories when I pass an area where my brother and my father and I took an overnight trip to an

The care provider must help parents achieve balance so that they apportion time for grief and time to attend to their surviving children. Parents need to be aware that surviving children who feel neglected may be at risk for developing feelings of unresolved anger and guilt and abandonment. If the parents are too emotionally bereft to function effectively, other supportive adults will have to be found and brought into the family system.

amusement park. He was weak and felt ill. I could see his heart beating. It rained all night. I still have a weird feeling whenever I see that amusement park. I still feel regrets over ripping up that certificate for a club we made up after a fight we had. He cried and we were mad at each other.

Sometimes my son's crying reminds me of my brother's crying. I remember my brother said, "I'm dying." Now, I take extra time with patients to see where they are with the issue of dying. My wife and I wonder what it would be like if he had lived. How would he be in our lives?

## ☐ Impact of a Child's Death on Grandparents, Extended Family, and Friends

### Grandparents

Much of what we have said about couples and their need to respect different styles of grieving also pertains to grandparents, other relatives, and friends (Rando, 1986). However, grandparents are unique because they are exposed to double pain when a grandchild dies: they grieve for their children as well as their grandchild. Grandparents have a stake in the future that is cut off when a grandchild dies, especially if the death represents the end of a family's lineage. Because grandparents are often seen as the stable entity within the family, admired for their courage and looked to for guidance, they may find it difficult to grieve on their own. This is especially true if they become parental surrogates when parents are unavailable due to their own grief. Unfortunately, they may also be left out of the information and decision-making loop and thus not have an opportunity to express their grief. Not many support groups specifically for grandparents exist, and little research has been directed toward this population (Galinsky, 2003). Sadly, "there remains a deficiency of specific information to assist grandparents to survive an event they never believed they would live to experience" (Reed, 2003, p. 1).

Care providers can encourage family meetings that can include the extended family so that all participants express their grief and their needs. All family members can also be encouraged to support each other as best they can by regularly communicating, listening, and being nonjudgmental.

However, grandparents are welcomed to participate in Bereaved Parents of the USA and The Compassionate Friends support groups.

## Extended Family

Family social systems include aunts and uncles, cousins, and close family friends. Their grief expressions are a vital part of the healing process. Conflicts need to be talked through as well. For example, family members may have strong feelings about whether caskets should be open or closed. Some issues that arise during illness and death are continuations and variations of conflicts that have troubled the family for years. If they are not allowed to express their feelings, unspoken tension within the family can create an emotional shock wave that will affect relationships for years to come.

## Close Friends

Close friends may easily be overlooked in the mourning process. Since they don't share a blood tie, they may not feel entitled to participate and remain on the periphery.

The Admission Ticket to Grieving Is Love

I was at the memorial service for a mother, father, and daughter who had lived in my community and died in a plane crash. When I joined the sole surviving daughter and several friends who were preparing for the funeral service, I noticed a man I knew was weeping, and I asked if there was anything I could do to help. He said, "No thanks, I'm okay. I'm just a friend."

This man had disenfranchised himself as an entitled griever, yet he was an invaluable emotional and practical support to the bereaved young woman and very much entitled to be part of the grief process.

Not all friends react in such helpful and heartfelt ways as he and his family did, however. Many of the parents I have worked with complained that some family and friends distanced themselves in the aftermath of the death of a child for various reasons. Some people feel the family's pain is too great. Some fear, superstitiously, that death may be catching. They may come to the funeral or memorial service and make an initial visit to the home, but beyond this, avoid the family. One mother said to me just a month after her child died, "Where did everybody go?"

Parents often say that the best support during bereavement came from neighbors and friends who were not that close. According to The Compassionate Friends study (1999), coworkers are another strong source of comfort. In addition, many bereaved parents turn to their faith communities and community groups for ongoing support.

Care providers can help bereaved couples by helping them identify their needs for support and by obtaining the support they ask for. In some cultures, families turn only to each other in times of grief; other families reach beyond the immediate family to a larger support network. Preexisting family conflicts must also be taken into consideration in determining who can play supportive roles.

Caregivers also need to determine which people will be helpful rather than hurtful. Many grieving parents ask for people who are ultimately not good resources. "Care providers can help sort out those friends and family members who can help from those who can't. This is an important distinction," says Paul Rosenblatt (2000b).

Care providers can also help parents judge with whom they can share information and who needs to be kept more at arm's length, as well as learn how to ask for and receive help. In addition, providers can help mourning parents discover creative and healing ways to include family and close friends in various rituals surrounding the death.

Finally, care providers can help devise networks composed of friends and family to greet visitors who come during the mourning period, to answer the phone and doorbell, and to tend to household needs. Keeping the lines of communication open and providing for the needs of all family members beyond the first month is very important. To provide this structure, the care provider may have to contact family, the faith community, and other available support systems.

# ☐ What Grieving Parents Ask From Care Providers

Bereaved parents are valuable sources of information about their various needs. Here are some of the comments I have gathered from grieving parents in support group meetings:

- It's very hard for the average person to understand what we are going through.

- Everyone, especially my family, has a different plan to help me, but the support I want is to have someone just listen.

- I don't want anyone to tell me that I should or shouldn't feel the way that I am feeling. It makes me feel discounted or dismissed. I don't want a judgment—just a listener.

- Members of the clergy should ask the family to inform them about personal traits of the child if he/she didn't know them or let a family member speak. Clergy should not make general comments that indicate that they didn't know the child.

- I am still a mom even though I lost my only child. I would have liked someone to listen. Don't ignore me. I am not invisible.

- I still miss him after 10 years. I wish others could acknowledge my pain about this.

- Friends whom I have known all my life are avoiding me. I wish they were here for me.

- I really would have liked to have the support of my family regardless of the geographic distance. I need the recognition of my daughter by friends and family.

- Other people give sympathy, not support. Sympathy is not what is needed. Moral support is needed very much at this time.

Many bereaved parents feel misunderstood by those who they feel should know better—family, medical and mental health providers, and clergy. The comment I hear most frequently from grieving parents is that they don't want sympathy or advice; they want another human soul to listen to them. Many parents want to talk about their child. They want to hear their child's name said at family events. Bereaved parents do not want to be treated as if they are not there.

## ☐ Summary of Clinical Considerations

Here are the principles of grief, explained in Chapter 3, adapted for grieving parents' specific needs:

*You cannot fix or eradicate grief.* Many grieving parents will ask the provider why. Why did this happen to us, to our child, to our family? Why is not a frivolous or obstinate utterance. It usually is asked with no real expectation that an answer, satisfactory or otherwise, will be forthcoming. Yet, you may be tempted to answer, to give a response—perhaps a philosophical or spiritual statement in lieu of a medical explanation. I welcome the question and find it to be an opportunity to reach into the heart of the grief. I often say, "Yes, the question why is so much on all of our minds. I wish there was an easy answer. Even though I cannot give you an answer, I can listen to what is in your heart." By listening, I learn that bereaved parents have many thoughts connected to the question of why this happened. In this way, asking why is like opening a door.

Some parents are pleading for relief from the despair that threatens to engulf them; they want their pain fixed or cured like a cold or headache. As care providers, you can normalize these reactions so that parents

Care providers can help by facilitating a flow of information to all who are connected with grieving people about what they need and what they don't need. A goal of the Exquisite Witness care provider is to disseminate information throughout the family's community about how to be most helpful and supportive in their relationships with grieving parents and siblings. This can be done informally at home, during hospital visits, or when death-related rituals take place. With permission from the parents, a care provider can also call other family members and/or friends, school personnel, or workplace associates to provide information about the needs of a family.

Providers can also give more formal presentations about the effects of the loss of a child at bereavement classes, PTA meetings, religious community programs, schools, and at workplace or community group events.

The care provider's goal is to educate grieving people about the variations in grief styles and to help each person respect individual differences. The provider also needs to arrange family meetings as conflicts arise and facilitate or secure a counseling professional to enable resolution of the disagreements.

feel less different, less "crazy." Assure them that these feelings are not unusual and that most parents say similar things. If medical symptoms persist, however, refer the individual to the family physician.

*Everyone's grief is different.* It may be helpful to identify the many grief reactions you encounter as falling somewhere along the continuum that has *intuitive grief* at one pole and *instrumental grief* at the other; the former connotes grievers who need to express their feelings, and the latter those who wish to "fix" things, gather information, and restore equilibrium. Most of us blend both approaches to varying degrees. Essentially, we all grieve differently, and this can lead to misunderstanding and conflicts.

*Every loss has multiple ramifications.* The loss of a child, at any age, means more than the loss of the body and being. It is also the loss of what was expected, looked forward to, and dreamed of. In addition, we lose that part of ourselves that has or would have interacted with that child. For many, understanding this multiplicity of loss can help to explain the intensity of their despair. When people know what is happening to them and what to expect, they may feel less acutely distressed and even comforted. This restores some degree of normalcy to their lives and the lives of their surviving children.

*There is no set timetable for the grief journey.* Personal grief does not unfold on a schedule or according to a calendar. We all have our own timetables and roadmaps; often, healing isn't linear. It may be two steps forward, one step back. Think of standing in ocean surf. At times, a wave knocks you down; at other times, it barely touches your feet. You can be flooded, overwhelmed with cold water and still remain standing upright. Parents need permission to take as long as they need to heal.

*We extend the boundaries of what constitutes "normal" grief behavior for bereaved parents.* "Do you think I am going crazy?" Bereaved parents often ask care providers this question because they dream of their child night after night, talk to a photo of their child, keep the child's baby seat in the car, believe they saw or heard the child calling out, feel the presence of the child, or think that the child is guiding their decisions. These experiences, whether they occur soon after the child has died or months later, are not unusual; they are evidence of the continuing connection the parent feels toward the child.

As an Exquisite Witness, the care provider must be available to meet the needs of the grieving parents in an authentic way. To be available means more than setting aside sufficient time for a consultation. It means being aware of our own Cowbells and processing our own unfinished loss material so that we are more available to enter the bereaved individual's space—a space that may be filled with pain, anger, fear, guilt, and shame. Further, the provider must be sufficiently aware of the special nature and range of parental grief so as to know what to expect from particular bereaved parents and have a repertoire of appropriate skills to apply. Availability to grieving parents is therefore affected by the head (understanding grief), heart (aware of personal losses), and hands (skills for helping) dimensions of being an Exquisite Witness care provider.

*Life changes bring about many losses, and this results in compound grief.* The loss of a child sets in motion a ripple effect in the lives of parents, siblings, other family members and friends, classmates, workplace colleagues, members of the faith community, and the neighborhood. Some of the changes are swift and obvious, whereas others are subtler and creep in over time. The empty crib or car seat, the crashing silence in the house, the absence of hearing the child's name spoken, the unoccupied seat at the table, the cessation of treatment and trips to the hospital, the restaurant reservation for three instead of four, the lack of an answer when you call out the child's name, and the nightmare of all questions: "How many children do you have?" These are all reminders of the depth and breadth of one's loss.

## ☐ Self-Help Support Groups

Parents, siblings, and grandparents need a safe place to share with other people—people who are grieving the loss of a child. This gives the griever a sense of belonging, of identification: "I don't feel like such an out-of-place weird person when I am in here."

Self-help support groups for bereaved parents such as The Compassionate Friends programs and the local chapters of Bereaved Parents of the USA, as well as programs operated by hospice, religious organizations, community social service organizations, hospital pastoral care, and private care providers operate around the world. Many special support subgroups accommodate those with special needs, such as parents

Care providers should familiarize themselves with the various programs by attending some of these meetings. Visiting groups will
give the provider insight into the appropriateness of the group and
its helpfulness to a particular set of parents. The care provider will
be better able to explain to parents what they can expect should
they desire to attend. It is also useful for the care provider to get
acquainted with the contact persons for the various support programs and to receive the organizational newsletters.

who have suffered miscarriage, SIDS, suicide, homicide, or other forms
of child loss. (See Appendix A, and consult telephone directories for local
phone numbers and more information.)

In the safe haven of a self-help group, parents typically discuss their
grief, their children, and how they cope—with birthdays, death anniversaries, holidays, and life in general. The Compassionate Friends and
Bereaved Parents of the USA groups use rituals, such as candle-lighting
memorials to help members survive difficult times (like the holidays)
and birthday cake and photos when their child's birthday falls in the
month of the meeting. Members share feelings, pictures, and memories,
providing parents with the opportunity to deepen their bond with their
deceased child in a very accepting environment.

Not all bereaved parents benefit from group meetings (sometimes,
one parent appreciates this type of support but the other does not). Some
feel overwhelmed by the level of pain in the group. In this case, they
need to be respected for their opinion, and given the option of returning in a few months when they may be more open to the group sharing
experience or of seeing an individual support person (a counselor or spiritual adviser).

## ☐ Hope for the Grieving Parent

For many grieving parents, hope is sometimes around the next bend, but
not quite within their grasp. In the early experience of grief, parents can
seem lost in helpless despair and apathy. To tell them "hang in there" and
that "it gets better over time" rings hollow. What can you say to comfort
people whose light of life has gone out?

In the most despairing times, I might simply offer parents something
to read with a spiritual message, a beautiful piece of music to listen to,

or some lovely artwork to contemplate. Even books designed for children that are about nature and the cycle of life can comfort grieving adults.

I include this poem of hope that I wrote the day after I'd been to a bereaved parents' meeting as I walked around a nearby lake on a snowy, wintry morning in March.

### HOPE IS A ROBIN IN THE SNOW—MARCH 11, 1999

I move into the day,
Once more.
The sky is blue and
The bright sun stretches down
To touch the fringes of brilliant
Snow around the lakepath.
And the air is frigid,
Almost painful, as I
Breathe it into me.
Signs of winter's retreat
Surround my walk,
And I hear the aching words of
Parents in grief—
"Oh how I hate spring!"
What a contrast
What a paradox.
Who doesn't feel some excitement stirring
From the prospect of warmth,
And green growth's return?
For grieving parents renewal of life is soured, and
Inner pain screams out against
The coming rebirth of earth.
And then,
I see nearby
In the cold whiteness ...
A robin in the snow.

(© J. Shep Jeffreys, 1999)

We may not be able to change reality, but we can help to move some of the pain aside and start the process of turning the upside-down world right-side up.

Chapter 7 will address the realities of bereaved older adults and consider the needs of family caregivers.

# Older Adult Grief

## ☐ Introduction: Realities of Aging

An 88-year-old woman came to see me because her only child, her 55-year-old daughter, had died. There were no grandchildren. She had been a widow for many years and had no family left. Though she was in good health, she wanted very much to die. "Why hasn't God taken me?" was the question constantly on her mind. She had expected her daughter to be part of her final years; now, she had no one.

This woman's story is the story for many older aged grieving people. The deaths of close relatives and friends leave many elders wondering why they are still here. Even though the loss of an older adult's spouse is considered by society to be an expected or "normative" death, the survivor typically enters a world that is strange, lonely, and sometimes unfriendly.

The grief of older people is unique because of the multiple and sequential nondeath losses that are a part of aging. These include physical changes, changes in family, occupational and social roles, and shifts in cognitive functioning.

Death becomes a much greater part of life's experience for aging people than it is for those in childhood and young adulthood (Marshall, 1996). This issue needs serious attention because the population of people over age 65 has been increasing for decades, and the post-World War II Baby Boomers are joining the ranks of seniorhood at a very rapid pace. The number of persons 65 years old and older is growing, and it is estimated that this portion of America's population will have risen from 35.6 million in 2002 to 63.5 million in 2025. Some researchers predict that the older age "death rates will decline resulting in even faster growth of this population" (Corr, Nabe, & Corr, 2006; U.S. Census Bureau, 2009).

Approximately 2.4 million people die annually in the United States, and close to 1.76 million people over age 65 died in 2006 (Heron et al., 2009). This means that although people over 65 make up only 12% of the population, the percentage of people in this age bracket who die is 73% of total annual deaths. Clearly, more well-trained and emotionally available grief care providers are needed to serve the growing population of older grieving adults.

Many older adults have been learning the "language of loss" over time. In fact, we are all introduced to changes in our bodies very gradually during the initial phase of midlife. We become aware of the need for various aids that make it possible for us to be able to hear, read, chew, or manage chronic back pain. Perhaps we have had to cut down on certain foods to curb weight gain or keep cholesterol, blood sugar, or blood pressure readings in the normal range. These gentle reminders of the deterioration of our bodies gather momentum as we age and little by little scoop away energy and our ability to heal quickly as well as our overall physical functioning. Of course, it is important to distinguish the symptoms of treatable disease and physical malfunctioning from normal changes, wear and tear, that accompany the aging process.

Transitions and losses in later years occur against a backdrop of recurring and cumulative physical and cognitive limitations. The older the person, the more likely it is that these limitations will have an impact on coping abilities.

However, not all older people are frail, confused people. The range in physical and cognitive limitation is wide, and many senior citizens lead active and healthy lives. The purpose of this chapter is to help care providers understand the needs of the older members of our communities who experience the death of a loved one or a close friend. Additionally, we want to alert the care provider to the special circumstances that in-home caregivers (frequently a spouse) may face.

## Defining Old Age

There are a number of terms used interchangeably to define people society deems old: *elderly, old, older adults, senior citizens,* and *young-old* as well as *old-old.* The actual age at which old age begins is continually shift-ing as the age at which "middle age" begins creeps upward. This upward drift is affected by longer life spans and the cultural exhortations to eat healthy, keep fit, and stay active. Age and stage of life are less defined by a number and increasingly defined by a person's state of mental and physical health and degree of social activity. In addition, older adults can bring a richness of life experiences and a depth of insight about them-selves and others to the challenges they face in later life. The term *elders* connotes wisdom, of having negotiated and survived transitions and problems of earlier years.

As I review my professional experience with older adult clients, both in my clinical practice as well as in workshops on loss and grief, I often ponder the question of the role of age in the response to loss or the threat of loss. Does aging increase one's vulnerability to loss or does lon-gevity bestow the benefits of increased resilience to loss? So many times I have heard people comment that older bereaved people are "used to loss" and therefore need less support as grievers. In fact, studies of spou-sal loss in older adults point out that there is more intense grief and more adjustment problems among the younger than older bereaved (Hansson & Stroebe, 2007; Parkes, 1972/1996).

Regardless of the differences reported in research studies, each case of older age bereavement must be viewed in the context of the life cir-cumstances of the bereaved. Are they living independently, with family, or in a retirement facility with assisted-living services? Are they close to family, or geographically or psychologically distanced from their chil-dren and grandchildren? Are they physically healthy or dealing with chronic medical problems? What level of support are they able to obtain from their faith beliefs and faith communities or other continuing social groups? What is their situation in terms of finances, transportation, mobility, and nutrition? How lonely are they? To what extent is the nature of their bereavement influenced by their ethnic culture or spiritual/religious belief systems? All these factors influence how older people experience loss or even the threat of loss.

# ☐ Factors Affecting Grief of Older Adults

## Physical Health Factors

As older adults enter the later years, health conditions and physical limitations affect their quality of life. Some are biological, a function of wear and tear. Basic body systems, such as our cardiac, neurological, digestive, endocrine, muscular-skeletal, and immune system, naturally break down. Some limitations are related to sudden events such as a fall; others result from a disease process that might have begun earlier in life or are the result of multiple chronic conditions. Many of these disease processes and conditions can and should be treated.

Other changes in health that may influence grieving include:

- Decreased ability to heal and restore the body after injury, illness, or surgery.

- Increased vulnerability to chronic infectious disease.

- Changes in physical appearance due to loss of muscle tone, wrinkling, and loosening of facial skin and other visible skin changes.

- Decrease in range of joint flexibility and spinal curvature due to arthritic processes.

- Decrease in muscular strength and physical endurance.

- Loss of balance.

- Loss of bowel and bladder control.

- Diminution of the senses—smell, taste, touch, hearing, and vision.

Care providers must also be aware of the extent to which an older person uses alcohol use for self-medication since it can cause negative effects when it interacts with prescription medication. Counseling for alcohol abuse may be required.

- Dental changes that cause nutritional problems.

- Side effects or interactions of multiple prescription and over-the-counter medications.

- Undiagnosed depression or other mood-altering conditions.

## Cognitive Factors

Cognitive changes also take place in the later years of life that can affect the performance of familiar tasks and make people feel inadequate. They may find themselves confused trying to drive to the home of an old friend or trying to fill out a health insurance form. Short-term memory loss, slowed-down reaction time, decreased alertness, or decreased ability to select appropriate words are also common. Some cognitive change is reversible if caused by inadequate hydration, drug interactions, or urinary tract infections. For other people, small strokes or the beginning of a disease process such as Alzheimer's disease may be the underlying cause of memory loss or other cognitive changes. The care provider should not assume that reduced cognitive ability is either permanent or a normal sign of aging unless the older adult's primary physician has verified the diagnosis.

## Social Factors Affecting the Grief of Older Adults

Many social issues and conditions have an impact on older people's grief reaction.

### Isolation

Limited social contact is a reality for some older adults regardless of where they live. Even those in assisted living and nursing homes can be

Care providers should help older adults be active in the community. They need opportunities to connect with others and have the benefit of social interaction. Intergenerational work opportunities can also be sought as this helps older adults feel as if they're still contributing members of society. Information about social activities and work or volunteer possibilities can be found in local senior centers or regional offices on aging. Providers should also be aware of programs offered by religious organizations and other community human service agencies.

very lonely. Seniors living independently may be isolated because of the lack of transportation; limitations on their physical mobility; or the loss of family, friends, and neighbors after a move. Even those seniors who live close to children and grandchildren may still feel isolated because of family conflict or because the family does not visit often enough.

Some older senior citizens may experience isolation because so many of their friends have died, leaving them no one with whom to reminisce. At the same time, many older people have fewer opportunities to meet new people and make new friendships. Finally, loss of the role created by work or volunteer involvement can result in social isolation when not replaced.

## Disenfranchisement

Older adults are frequently not credited as experiencing the same depth of grief and fearfulness about death as younger people do. I have heard younger members of a family take the view that an elder is used to people dying because he or she has lived for such a long time. This lack of validation can cause the older adult to withhold his or her grief expression, which in turn can lead to physical, mental, and emotional problems and conditions.

## Social Devaluation

In many cultures, older people are highly respected, valued, and revered. But in the United States, the term *elderly* conjures up stereotypical images

Care providers can assure seniors and their families and friends that age doesn't diminish the grief response and that our elders are entitled to all of their feelings as well as the opportunity to share them. Efforts must be made to include all seniors in death-associated rituals.

Care providers need to encourage older people to share their considerable wealth of family history. Families can create opportunities for their elders to impart their memories in ways that involve grandchildren such as in jointly creating journals, family photograph albums, and oral histories.

of people who are frail, unproductive, sexless, and unimportant. In our society, older adults are viewed as unattractive and cognitively impaired; we think of them as requiring medical care and as being depressed or grieving. They typically no longer work. They might need the radio or TV volume turned very high, and may have difficulty with mobility. They may like to talk about the "old days" and the "way we used to do things when I was growing up." It's not simply that their values may conflict with those of the younger generation but that older people's values are generally devalued.

We forget that people of advanced years are an invaluable resource; they have stories to tell and wisdom to share. Some of this wisdom consists of their recollection of family members and friends who are deceased, which is lost if not passed on to the next generation.

## Multiple Losses

A bereaved elder experiences death within a web of other losses. These losses may include:

- *Fiscal independence*—Loss of income and purchasing power can create a sense of helplessness and dependence.

- *Work role and status*—When some older people stop working and retire, they not only may lose an income but also a sense of their self-identity and self-worth, status, social connection, and the sense that they are productive members of society.

Care providers need to be aware that multiple losses are incurred whenever an older adult sustains a loss. Providers can help grieving elders by arranging for them to have family contact and for them to participate in bereavement-related rituals and activities, such as attending religious services, being visited by clergy, and enjoying activities with grandchildren and social activities with peers. Additionally, older adults need help finding and developing new and meaningful roles in the community. They can be encouraged to join community organizations, participate in holiday commemorations, or volunteer in hospitals or schools. Even planning for and helping to set up for meetings, lunches, and trips can give older people the sense that they are making a contribution to others.

- *Community roles*—Older people resign from community leadership positions because of declining health, lack of transportation, or because they move, which also forces them to relinquish the role of neighbor.

- *Mobility*—Older people who stop driving or who have trouble walking are dependent on public transportation, family and friends, or social organizational outreach programs to help them get around.

## ☐ Losses of the Older Adult

## Death of Spouse

"Late life spousal bereavement is the most common form of spousal loss" (Carr, 2008). The Changing Lives of Older Couples (CLOC) study (Carr, 2008) found that older bereaved spouses are far from uniform in their reactions to their loss. Reactions range from severe depression and grief to resilience. The nature of post-loss responses is viewed as being "contingent on characteristics of the bereaved, the late spouse, the context of the death, the quality of social support available and nature of the marital relationship" (Carr, 2008, p. 417). Four medical conditions comprise the bulk of current older adult deaths: heart disease, cancer, stroke, and chronic obstructive pulmonary disorder (COPD) (Carr & Jeffreys, in press). Surviving spouses typically will have served as primary caregivers for some period of time—weeks, months, or even years.

Individuals married for many years create a closed system in which they have each become each other's primary attachment figure. This is "a system of roles, traditions, and mutual experiences, which are in turn reflected in an identity shared by the couple" (Moss, Moss, & Hansson, 2001, p. 246). The loss of one partner may literally leave the other without an anchor in reality. Widowers find themselves anxious at the prospect of having to step into the homemaker role formerly occupied by their wives. Widows are now responsible for making unfamiliar financial decisions or for physically demanding home repair that the spouse may have handled. Additionally, prior to the actual death, spouses may have provided care for an extended period of time, compromising their own mental and physical health (Schultz, Boerner, & Herbert, 2008.) In this light, the process of becoming widowed may begin at the onset of the spouse's illness or disability (Carr, 2008).

One study found that anxiety was the dominant grief reaction for older men who had lost their spouses, more so than loneliness or depression. This is explained as *separation anxiety*, the loss of their primary attachment figure and difficulty adjusting to living alone (Byrne & Raphael, 1997). There are many men who were so dependent on their wives that they had very limited relationships with friends outside of the marital dyad. The shock of the death of the long-term "bond-mate" and subsequent anxiety response pattern is reminiscent of *isolation distress behavior* discussed by MacLean (1973) and the *agitated protest behavior* of Bowlby (1980). (See Chapter 3 for a discussion of attachment theory.)

Older women frequently have women friends and may not suffer as great a level of isolation distress as a result. Women who go to senior centers and participate in other community activities often arrive with one or more female companions, whereas men are more likely to arrive alone.

Yet, both widowed men and women say things like: "What will I do without her/him?" "How can I go on?" "I'm so used to being with

---

Care providers (or a family member), at an appropriate time, can introduce the widow(er) to the idea of participating in one of the many structured senior citizen activity programs in most communities such as exercise classes, current-event discussion groups, and lecture and lunch programs. Many older seniors can benefit from being coached on determining who to call for information about these activities: the area agency on aging, religious organizations, town recreation departments, and the AARP. The goal is to minimize isolation, reduce anxiety, and provide social interaction to reduce loneliness. (See Appendix A.)

Care providers should be aware that the trauma of losing a mate might aggravate other existing loss conditions as well as trigger old loss material (Cowbells). Individuals may need referrals to support groups that provide support and encourage productive physical as well as mental activity.

Some older people who resist participating in structured support groups enjoy the meetings when they do attend. Care providers and family members need to acknowledge that not every elder will be either physically healthy enough or psychologically inclined to make the effort to participate in a support program. For some who have never been "joiners," the inclination to attend is simply not there. Home visits from various community volunteer organizations may be helpful in such cases.

Many older adults find great solace in their religious affiliations. According to Weaver and Koening (1996), "the religious community is central to the lives of most older Americans" (p. 496). It is estimated that 80% of older persons are members of a religious community. The services and ritual observances provide an ongoing set of meaningful activities, and the spiritual comfort they find in such affiliations can help them develop a sense of meaning in their new lives.

him/her that I can't get a grasp on who I am or what I'm supposed to do now." It is a considerable challenge for such individuals to engage in creating new meanings for personal identity and figuring out how they will adjust to this strange, new post-loss world. Others may withdraw into the silence of despair and become clinically depressed or ill. In families in which the adult children and other relatives are geographically distant, the bereaved elder may be without social support after several weeks or even as soon as a few days after the funeral. Unless other social support resources are in place, the individual can be isolated and become very lonely. This is especially true for same-sex older couples. When a life partner dies, the surviving person may lack the social support traditional couples have. Care providers must also be sensitive to the variations in death-associated rituals and communication patterns due to the growing cultural diversity of our population.

## Death of an Adult Child

Adult children play a major part in the social and emotional world of parents throughout their lifetime (Moss et al., 2001). The death of an

Care providers can help families recognize the bereaved parents' status as mourners, and find ways for them to help plan and participate in family memorial rituals. Caregivers can also help older adults balance their lives so that they can interact with their spouse, surviving children, and grandchildren. If the deceased adult child has children, the caregiver can help grandparents and grandchildren stay connected to help each other through the grief process.

adult child, while engendering all the reactions detailed earlier in relation to a child's death, poses special challenges for those older adults who think of their adult children as caregivers. They typically verbalize fears that their future needs will not be met.

Older adults who lose adult children adjust to their post-loss world if they can hold on to an internal picture of the child and think of the bond between them as continuing. Photos and memorabilia, talking about the deceased child, and acknowledging him or her in memorials and other family rituals can bring the lost loved one into the present. The surviving parents of adult child loss may receive less support than the mourning wife and children, a disenfranchisement that has to be addressed by other family members and care providers.

# Death of an Adult Sibling

"Perhaps the most frequent death of a close family member in later years is the death of a sibling" (Moss et al., 2001, p. 245). However, many older adult siblings are disenfranchised as grievers. When a brother or sister dies, attention and support is usually directed to the sibling's spouse and children who are commonly considered the inner circle of mourners. Elders are often not included in the inner circle of mourners along with the sibling's spouse and children. There are no grieving elder sibling support groups. Typically, the only support most bereaved older siblings may find is from their surviving brothers and sisters when they take the time to review the past and reminisce together.

Care providers can make every effort to encourage the families with whom they are working to include older adult bereaved siblings in memorial services and rituals.

## Death of a Grandchild

In a study reviewing the differences between the grief of parents and the grief of grandparents, Ponzetti (1992) found that "grandparents' concerns focused on their children" (p. 69). Grandmothers are generally more involved with the bereaved parents than grandfathers. Grandparents' grief was found to be threefold: They grieve for the loss of life their deceased grandchild has suffered, for their own child's grief, and for their own loss of the grandchild. (The grief of grandparents has been discussed in greater detail as part of the death of a child in Chapter 6.)

## Older Adults and Suicide

Research indicates that "older adults who attempt suicide die from the attempt more often than any other age group" (Miller, Segal, & Coolidge, 2001, p. 358). Older people tend to choose lethal weapons to end their lives; hanging themselves and discharging firearms are the most common (Miller et al., 2001). They are less prone than younger persons to inform others of their suicidal thoughts or plans, or to seek out crisis hot lines and mental health services. Many suicides, however, are believed to be a result of undiagnosed or untreated depression. Since the primary care physician most likely has frequent contact with the older adult, medical providers need to become more aware of the signs and symptoms of clinical depression so that adults at risk can be more accurately screened

Care providers must assess bereaved older people for suicide risk because suicide rates increase with age and are highest among Americans aged 65 years and older. Also, suicide rates among older individuals are highest for those who are divorced or widowed (Kochanek & Smith, 2004). When the clinical picture of the grief response includes diagnosable psychiatric disorders—major depression, anxiety, thought disorder, confusion, and social phobia—a treatment plan in the best interest of the bereaved spouse will be developed. (See Chapter 9 for assessment procedures for suicide risk as well as other clinical details. See Chapter 10 for criteria regarding complicated grief.) Referral to a physician should be made when there are chronic physical symptoms. Post-assessment follow-up contact by care providers is critical with elders at risk.

(P. Madachy, Director, Howard County Office on Aging, Maryland, personal communication, December 19, 2003).

# ☐ Helping the Bereaved Older Adult

Can an aging bereaved person learn to hold on to the past while connecting to the changed present? To do so, is to embrace opposites. But this is what aging people should try to achieve: to become aware of their strengths as well as their weaknesses, to embrace their post-loss life while acknowledging how different it is from their old life, to hold on to their memories while facing the challenges of today and tomorrow (Fischer, Norbeerg, & Lundman, 2008). They can do this by sharing memories of those who have died with those who still survive. The Exquisite Witness care provider can help connect older people to their post-loss world in several ways. As we will discuss in Chapter 9, these interventions can be supportive, clinical, or a combination of interventions.

## Supportive, Clinical, or Combined Interventions

Supportive helping is generally preventative. Care providers can make a friendly home or residence visit, facilitate attendance at a senior center activity, do grocery shopping, help to prepare food, or help to plan for future needs. Other activities that help the elderly bereaved are looking at photos, preserving objects that link them to the deceased love one, talking about the loved one, creating memory albums, listening to favorite music of the deceased, saying prayers, and engaging in specific rituals that help the bereaved maintain a spiritual bond with the deceased loved one.

Clinical help includes encouraging bereavement counseling, prescribing medication, or making an assessment of cognitive or emotional functioning. During this time, the bereaved older adult can be helped to develop ways to maintain the bond with his or her lost loved one. (See Chapter 9 for additional details.)

Self-help support groups, grief and loss workshops, and discussions about grief combine supportive and clinical interventions. During these group experiences, attendees learn that their grief is normal and discover ways to grow despite the loss. In the remainder of this chapter, we will concentrate on the combination of supportive and clinical interventions. (For more detailed supportive and clinical interventions when grieving becomes problematic, see Chapter 9.)

**Note:** No bereaved elderly person should automatically be referred for grief counseling or other clinical treatment simply because he or she has sustained a loss. Grief is not a disease (Raphael, Minkov, & Dobson, 2001). There are many people who can provide a first line of care and support for the bereaved as they grieve and work on the four tasks for healing (see Chapters 3 and 9). In addition to family and friends in the community, volunteers, clergy, or other spiritual advisors should be in contact with the bereaved if the family welcomes such contact.

## Support Groups

When the time is appropriate, an older bereaved person can be made aware of various community resources available. There is no single best time to introduce the idea of attending a support group. However, sometime during the first or second month of bereavement, the concept should be suggested. The family member or care provider can introduce the group as "people who share the same or similar losses and are able to receive and give help to each other."

Many support groups are self-help groups, that is, other similarly bereaved persons make up the group and serve as facilitators. Other groups engage professional facilitators to lead them. Some bereavement support groups are specific to the nature of the loss (spouse, child, suicide, homicide), whereas others are mixed. Some widow-to-widow groups are organized by age, which is preferable since similarly aged people generally have similar needs and concerns. A growing number of services are provided by regional offices of aging, hospice, and other community service organizations available in many local communities. Family members and their support persons should avail themselves of these resources.

Here are some resources for locating support groups. (See Appendix A for additional details.)

- Local hospice

- Area agencies on aging

- Senior centers

- Churches, synagogues, mosques, and other faith communities

- Religious-affiliated social service organizations

- Funeral homes

- AARP

- Red Cross

- Alzheimer's Association

- National Caregivers Association

For a child's death or deaths due to drunk driving, suicide, or homicide, contact:

- The Compassionate Friends

- Bereaved Parents of the USA

- Mothers Against Drunk Driving

- Homicide victim support programs run by local district attorneys' offices

- Parents of Murdered Children

- SEASONS suicide support

- Survivors of Suicide

Care providers may also find that older individuals can benefit from some coaching on how to seek information themselves, for example, referring to local directories, accessing information from the library, or using the Internet. Many seniors appreciate it when they can find what they need themselves; it facilitates independence.

# Study Findings: Older Adults and Self-Help Support Groups

Lund and Caserta (1992) have conducted longitudinal studies on how self-help bereavement groups help older seniors. Some of the groups that were studied ended after 8 weeks; others continued beyond 8 weeks on a monthly basis for one year. Here are their findings:

- Participants derived help from helping others (the act of giving assistance to another person yields a sense of self-value and makes one feel productive).

- The opportunity to share successes and disappointments provides opportunities for valuable reciprocal emotional and social support.

- Participants stated that entering a group within the first 4 months of bereavement was most beneficial since this was usually a very difficult time.

- Being able to express thoughts and externalize feelings with others as well as keeping busy was very beneficial.

- Participants who were actively involved in each group session attained the best results.

- Participants in the longer-term groups had greater benefits from the group experience than those in the shorter-term groups. However, the idea of attending a group and sitting and talking with strangers can be very daunting to some bereaved persons. Care providers can arrange to have a friend or a current member of the group come with a new participant.

Care providers and family members may need to raise the subject of participation in support groups more than once. Use a "three-time rule": offer to arrange transportation and attend with the bereaved elder three times a few weeks apart. If after 2 or 3 months the senior has not expressed any interest in attending such a group but seems to be in need of one, repeat the three-time offer. If self-help groups don't seem tenable, other social, recreational or educational activities may be feasible. The goal is to minimize isolation and support social connection within reasonable limits.

# Workshops, Lectures, and Other Programs

Workshops and lectures as well as recreational and educational programs such as trips, classes, exercise programs, lunch programs, speakers, and movies, may be sponsored by many of the community organizations listed earlier. Senior centers represent a growing resource in local communities and may be sponsored by an office of aging, a community center, or religious-affiliated organizations. Sometimes, the older bereaved person who attends these activities ultimately decides to seek professional help because the program helped the individual become aware of personal needs that the group setting could not address.

Bereaved senior citizens may be sad and lonely but should never have to be isolated. Those who live in retirement communities, assisted living, or nursing care units can benefit from group programs led by professional staff or individual mental health counseling.

# ☐ Family Caregivers

When we discuss the older grieving person, we must discuss the primary home caregiver. It is estimated that about 80% of caregiving for the elderly is provided by a family member (Beery et al., 1997). Spouses caring for a terminally ill wife or husband living at home make up the majority of home caregivers, though care is also provided by an adult child or sibling. Many of these individuals, although not professionally trained, have typically received some form of instruction from a home care nurse or other professional provider. Many spouses consider mutual care part of their relationship, but they are often surprised by how dramatically and drastically the formerly reciprocal relationship changes after one person suffers a heart attack, stroke, or other life-threatening illness.

## Health Risks for Family Caregivers

Family caregivers may grieve the loss of a once healthy loved one to terminal illness prior to the actual death. They may mourn not only in terms of anticipatory grief for the ultimate death of their spouse but also for all that they have given up to assume the caregiving role. Many show signs of pre-loss grief complications such as depression and anxiety (Beery et al., 1997). (See Chapter 10 for complications of grief.)

Family caregivers frequently resist the term *caregiver* to describe their roles. They portray themselves rather as a wife or husband, a sister or brother, a son or daughter. They often do not adequately credit themselves for performing the critical but often overwhelming tasks associated with providing constant care for a loved one. In spite of this, many describe their role as rewarding. Providers must recognize that they are at high risk for depression, resentment, physical fatigue, and illness. Some family caregivers have been known to treat their depression with tranquilizers and alcohol in an attempt to cope with the demands and stress of their responsibilities.

## Loss of Future

One caregiving spouse lamented that she had lost the future she and her husband had planned for; their dream of spending quality time together as they grew older together was shattered. Some realize this gradually, whereas others feel it as if they walked smack into a devastating wall of reality. The buildup of resentment and frustration can cause the caregiver to have periodic explosions that can seem out of proportion to an outside observer. A visitor may be surprised to hear the anger that pours out, not understanding all the problematic incidents that led up to the emotional release.

## Loss of Freedom

Many caregivers don't notice the limitations on their own mobility because it creeps in subtly and gradually. But in time they notice that they are unable to attend family and other events outside of their homes, or even go for a walk, do the shopping, attend a graduation or a wedding. Their social world has shrunk beyond imagining. As the ill person grows sicker, caretakers become so tethered to the house that they often postpone even their own medical appointments.

Many report feeling as if they are imprisoned in the home, citing the reluctance of the loved one to have anyone else provide care while they are out. Others feel that no one else can adequately care for the ill person. They often deny grief, resentment, or the guilt that is building within. Once they are conscious of these feelings, grief caregivers can help them seek support, respite, spiritual activities, or counseling. These experiences will reduce stress and ward off depression, which are not uncommon in family caregivers. Interestingly, most caregivers are at risk for depression not because they are overly involved with the ill loved one, but because their responsibilities preclude them from engaging in activities that are personally fulfilling and recreational.

# Caregiver Grief

When caretaking an ill family member, family caregivers (spouses, children, siblings, or close friends) grieve for the healthy, functional, and available aspects of the relationship with the care recipient that are now lost. They also grieve for the activities they can no longer engage in; they have lost the freedom to choose how they spend their time. Instead, they are consumed by their caretaking responsibilities, tending to medical, legal, insurance, and financial issues that arise. Their grief reaction is also triggered by anticipation of the actual loss of the loved one to death, dementia, or coma.

Care providers can play an important role in mitigating the risk that family caregivers will burn out by helping these caregivers become aware of the threat to their own physical and emotional health. Caregivers need to have time off; arrangements need to be made for other caregivers to attend the ill person. Engaging professional home health staff or hospice care will give the family caregiver an opportunity to take advantage of much needed downtime. Even a short break can reduce the potential for depression and enable family caregivers to regain their equilibrium.

The provider should also normalize the many reactions that family caregivers have: resentment, guilt, grief, anxiety, fatigue, depression, disorganization, and the feeling of being overwhelmed and of feeling crazy. Caregivers need to take action on their own behalf not only to preserve their physical and emotional health but also to provide the best care for their loved ones. Providers can also refer family caregivers to the various community support groups that are becoming more and more available so that they can share their reactions, hear how others are coping, and know that they are not alone in this difficult role.

# Support Services for Family Caregivers

Support services of various types, including those targeted at specific illnesses or conditions, are proliferating in many communities. Some are specially designed for family members caring for a loved one with cancer, Alzheimer's disease, dementia, Parkinson's, chronic illness, or memory loss; in addition, there are many workshops on how to balance caregiving and careers.

In all communities, the area agency on aging provides education and selected direct services. An important local feature of service for older caretaker adults is Adult Evaluation and Review Services, covering education, health and finances. Assistance is made available according to financial and health needs. Additionally, funding for respite care disseminated by the National Family Caregivers Association is available (V. Liss, personal communication, June 25, 2010).

At some community agencies, nurses train family caregivers in the home. Respite programs allow caregivers to take time off while a competent person cares for the ill family member; or the ill person, if ambulatory, can take part in various community daycare programs, which are frequently run in rehabilitation centers. These services charge a range of fees.

Many publications produced by regional agencies suggest ways that the caregiver can attend to his or her own personal health and emotional care, including stress reduction and ways to balance the caregiving with meeting his or her own needs.

To summarize, too many caregivers are not aware of the risks to their own health when they care for ill family members to the exclusion of their own needs. This can have negative repercussions not only for caregivers but also for the quality of the care they give.

Care providers should remember that family caregivers are knowingly or unknowingly coping with an ongoing bereavement for the loss of their loved one as he or she once was. Care providers also need to make family caregivers aware of the benefits of respite and of the availability of a range of such support services in their local community. Providers need to know about regional agencies for aging adult care that offer support services for family caregivers. (See Appendix A for additional resources.)

## When the Family Caregiver's Loved One Dies

Many family caregivers face a great emptiness when their loved one dies. The grief they feel is not only for the person who is gone but also for the empty space and unfilled time following the death. For help coping, bereaved caregivers can avail themselves of many professionally led bereavement support groups. In time, many people who served as family caregivers find themselves volunteering in a nursing home, hospice, or hospital where they can help others in need as they continue on their own grief journey. To find out about opportunities like this, they should contact the local office on aging's coordinator of caregiver services who may provide individual consultation and a volunteer placement program. As experienced family caregivers begin to help others, they see that the loss of their loved ones ultimately led them to provide care for others.

## ☐ Conclusion

We have reviewed the realities of the various losses the older bereaved adult must cope with as he or she mourns a current death or serves as a caregiver to a loved one. Older persons must not only be able to grieve their losses but also to reclaim life in a world that may appear to be less friendly than it once was.

Providers must also reach out to family caregivers who are truly disenfranchised grievers. (See Chapter 3.) They need help both during the caregiving role and beyond to address their grief and to find new meaning in their post-loss life. Support can come in the form of worship communities, volunteer opportunities, and other support services offered by regional offices on aging.

In Chapter 8, we will look at the issues faced by families and their loved ones who are dying, terminally and/or chronically ill, or have a life-limiting disability. For the family and the dying loved one, the end-of-life experience can be both a tragically devastating and a fulfilling spiritual experience.

> Care providers should help the grieving older adult to obtain the support he or she needs in order to address Worden's four tasks for healing (see Chapter 3), to reach out for social support, to maintain their physical and emotional health, and to connect with spiritual resources where desired.

CHAPTER

8

# Chronic Illness/Disability, Terminality, and Dying

Illness is a family affair.

Richard M. Cohen (2004, p. xiv)

## ☐ Chapter Preview

- Introduction

- Definitions and Statistical Realities

- The Relationship Between the Sick, Dying, or Grieving Person and the Care Provider

- Five Rights That Preserve Patient Dignity

- What to Expect From the Dying Person and Family

- Factors Impacting the Terminally Ill Person and Family

- The Needs of the Patient's Family

- Adapting to Life After a Terminal Illness Diagnosis

- Signs and Symptoms of Approaching Death

- Bedside Guide at the Time of Death: Saying Good-Bye

- Chronic Illness/Disability and the Family

- Medical Dilemmas, Patient Rights, and Bioethical Considerations

- Conclusion

# ☐ Introduction

The story of grief is being written all the time and includes a world of people, invisible to us, who are coping with ongoing loss due to serious illness, chronic physical limitations, and the threat of death.

You never know whether the person walking by you has a loved one at home lying in a bed of pain or if the woman sitting at the next table in the coffee shop has just come from visiting her husband who no longer recognizes her. You may not know that the man buying tickets at the theme park is purchasing them for a child in a wheelchair or that the family in the pew behind you is praying for a loved one who is in a coma and not expected to live much longer.

People who are in the acute phases of grief, who have a loved one who has either recently died or is near death receive a great deal of attention. We tend to pay less attention to those who are dealing with loss due to chronic, life-limiting conditions because these people are still here— eating, breathing, and requiring some level of care, love and attention. For some, *chronic* means, "We have become accustomed to the man in the wheelchair in the house down the street, and don't think about it much anymore." For the family members providing continuing care for the chronically ill, there is no such thing as forgetting about it; they cannot turn their eyes away. They become part of a less visible world of grievers who must cope daily with multiple, accumulating, and anticipated losses.

## The Many Faces of Grief

As we have mentioned earlier, the human grief response is not reserved for death or separation only. Care providers must also be aware of the grief experienced by individuals who are seriously ill, or living with permanent physical or intellectual challenges or a lingering terminal illness. Some are at home; yet many more are in hospitals, hospices, or nursing homes. Teno et al. (2004) found in a study of "last place of care" that about 70% of dying people are in a hospital or a nursing home. Of the remaining 30% who die at home, 36% have no nursing services, 12% have home nursing, and slightly more than 50% receive home hospice services. The climate of grief surrounding these individuals and their families is often less understood and acknowledged than that of those who are bereaved. Consequently, these families may be less supported than those who have already lost a loved one.

From the time of the onset of an illness or disability, many losses flood the family. Grieving has already begun. This is what Elisabeth Kübler-Ross called the "thousand deaths before the final death" (personal communication, 2000). A good example of this is the medical condition known as traumatic brain injury (TBI). Military assaults, sports injuries, vehicle associated trauma, or other physical damage to the head that causes injury to the brain results in TBI. Approximately 1.5 million cases of TBI are diagnosed annually in the United States (Brain Injury Association of America, 2008).

People with a TBI may experience changes in mental abilities, vision, emotions, and behavior. They also may experience headaches, dizziness, and ringing in the ears. Extreme cases can cause paralysis and the inability to communicate. Although the person lives, perhaps in a nursing facility, and participates in holidays or other family events, he or she is no longer available as an active participant in the life of the family. Such families become "invisible grievers." Since the military deployments in Iraq and Afghanistan, thousands of families of returning men and women now fit into this category.

Of the 1.64 million U.S. troops deployed, approximately 320,000 have experienced a TBI and 300,000 suffer from posttraumatic stress disorder (PTSD) or other psychological health issues. Military Health System (MHS) has recorded 43,779 patients who have been diagnosed with a TBI in calendar years 2003 through 2007 (U.S. Department of Defense Report, n.d.). According to the Army Office of the Surgeon General, between September 2001 and January 12, 2009, there were 1,286 amputations ("U.S. Military Casualty Statistics," 2009). In short, many families have been undergoing traumatic, painful, and unrelenting alterations to their lives and will continue to require substantial assistance in order to adjust to the strange new world in which they find themselves.

# The Dying

Tending to the dying requires a different consciousness than tending to the memory of the no-longer living. According to the Teno et al. (2004) study, family perceptions of the quality of end-of-life care differed according to the location of the dying person. Families whose loved one died at home with hospice services reported the greatest overall satisfaction with care. However, about a fourth of all families reported that pain management was inadequate, and roughly another fourth complained of insufficient help with breathing problems. Additionally, "many people dying in institutions have unmet needs for symptom amelioration, physician communication, emotional support, and being treated with respect" (Teno et al., 2004, p. 88).

When we convert the concerns of dying patients and their families into care provider goals, we arrive at five recommendations for providers:

- Be respectful of the patient.

- Provide physical comfort and emotional support.

- Engage the patient and family in decision making.

- Include family members in the information loop and give them emotional support.

- Coordinate the person's care regardless of the care setting.

Wherever the ill or chronically disabled person is in residence, the continuing grief of family members will be affected by medical reports, mood and symptoms of the ill person, reactions of other family members as well as interactions with medical and other care providers. The more effectively care is coordinated, the greater the potential for patient and family well-being. All care providers will need to communicate with other staff members who are concerned with the case: nurses, physicians, aides, pastoral care, mental health staff, and volunteers. For optimal care, it is vital that all care providers involved in the care of a family's loved one have a cooperative team approach and respect the various contributions each team member makes.

# ☐ Definitions and Statistical Realities

## Definitions

### *Palliative Care*

Palliative care has as its primary aim the provision of comfort and enhancement of quality of life for people with advanced life-threatening disease, as well as assistance for their families. Initiating palliative care indicates that the primary medical treatment goals have changed. Medical teams are no longer seeking a cure; instead, they concentrate on providing a broad range of support, comfort, and freedom from pain and debilitating side effects of medicines and procedures. Side effects of illness, symptoms such as pain, weakness, nausea, constipation, and depression, are also treated and managed (National Cancer Institute, Office of Education and Special Initiatives, 2003). Palliative care is described as "patient centered," that is, the focus is on sick or disabled people rather than on disease or medical technology (Institute of Medicine, 1997). The goal is to "address the physical, psychological, social, and spiritual needs of patients with advanced disease and their families" (Addington-Hall, 2002, p. 220). Palliative care can be provided at home, in hospitals, hospices, nursing homes, and other residential settings.

The six skill areas of palliative care are (a) communication, (b) decision making, (c) management of complications, (d) symptom control, (e) psychosocial care of the patient and family, and (f) care of the dying (Institute of Medicine, 2001). These care goals require full communication with the patient and family about the illness and prognosis. The family also needs to be involved in decision making regarding care options.

Further benefits of palliative care were reported by Temel et al. (2010), "Among patients with metastatic non–small-cell lung cancer, early palliative care led to significant improvements in both quality of life and mood" (p. 88). People who had productive discussions with their physicians regarding "their end-of-life preferences were far more likely to die at peace and in control of their situation, and to spare their family anguish" (p. 88).

### *Hospice*

Hospice is a program that offers palliative care for those who are terminally ill (in the United States, this typically means those who have

6 months or less to live) from a multidisciplinary staff. These services are provided at home, in dedicated hospital rooms, assisted-living and nursing facilities, or in freestanding hospice sites.

According to Dame Cicely Saunders (2002), well known for her role establishing the hospice movement in Great Britain, hospice care provides a program of care that affirms a quality of life free from pain, supports the dignity of individuals, helps people to deal with emotional distress, and seeks new ways to understand the quality of life as one is dying. Hospice further supports the completion of end-of-life arrangements and includes the family and friends as an important part of the care.

## Life-Threatening Illness

Life-threatening illnesses may be chronic by virtue of their lingering nature and usually results in an individual's death. Some examples are cancer, AIDS, amyotrophic lateral sclerosis (ALS), multiple sclerosis, cystic fibrosis, emphysema, end-stage renal disease, advanced cardiac illness, Parkinson's, Huntington's, and Alzheimer's disease.

## Chronic Illness and Other Disabling Conditions

Although this category overlaps with life-threatening disease conditions, people who are chronically disabled from illness, injury, or developmental disorders are not necessarily facing immediate threats to their mortality. Their conditions are life-limiting, often requiring long-term care. These situations have a significant impact on the quality of life for the individual as well as for his or her family. A friend whose daughter is developmentally disabled told me, for example, that she mourned a "deathlike" loss when she learned that her child would have profound life limitations. People with a loved one who was born with or develops a severely life-limiting disability often report feeling the "death of their dream." Examples include traumatic brain injury; mental retardation; permanent paralysis; diabetes; hepatitis; dementia; cognitive, intellectual, and developmental disabilities; and certain psychiatric disorders.

## Family

I use *family* in both the conventional sense, referring to people who are related by birth or marriage, and also to those who live together and spend much of their lives in close proximity because of social and occupational needs. Examples include life partners; very closely connected friendship groups; work teams who are dependent on each other, such as fire, police, rescue, and military groups; and close-knit faith communities.

# Statistical Realities

There are an estimated 65 million family caregivers in the United States (National Alliance for Caregiving with American Association of Retired Persons, 2009), and 65 million are grieving for ill and disabled loved ones.

Table 8.1 lists the leading causes of death for 2006 in the United States. Many of these deaths come after varying periods of chronic illness, requiring care for months and in some cases years. To restate the significance of the 1,643,451 deaths reported in Table 8.1, many of the deaths occurred after months and years of families coping with lingering, life-threatening illness. For instance, it is estimated that 9 million persons in the United States have a history of cancer and that in 2002 about 1.3 million people were diagnosed with cancer (National Institutes of Health, 2002). The 58,785 Alzheimer's deaths for 2002 no doubt took place after years of agonizing progressive loss and family caregiving.

Table 8.2 provides estimates of selected newly diagnosed life-threatening conditions. Table 8.2 presents several of the debilitating medical conditions that have an impact on people and their families. The American Brain Injury Association reports that 1.5 million people in the United States sustain a TBI annually and that an estimated 5.3 million people currently live with disabilities resulting from TBI (U.S. CDC, 1999). However, conditions such as developmental, cognitive,

**TABLE 8.1. Leading Causes of Death, 2006, United States**

| | |
|---|---:|
| Diseases of the heart | 631,636 |
| Cancer | 559,888 |
| Stroke | 137,119 |
| Chronic lower respiratory disease | 124,583 |
| Diabetes | 72,449 |
| Alzheimer's | 72,432 |
| Diseases of the kidneys | 45,344 |
| Total | 1,643,451 |

Source: U.S. CDC, *National Vital Statistics Reports*, Vol. 57, No. 14 (2009), p. 5.

TABLE 8.2. Annual Estimates of Newly
Diagnosed Cases of Selected Life-Threatening/
Life-Limiting Conditions

| | |
|---|---|
| Traumatic brain injury | 1,500,000[a] |
| Digestive system cancer | 275,720[b] |
| Respiratory cancer | 236,990[b] |
| Breast cancer | 194,280[b] |
| Spinal cord injury | 11,000[c] |

[a] U.S. Centers for Disease Control, *Traumatic Brain Injury in the United States: A Report to Congress*, http://www.cdc.gov/ncipc/pub-res/tbi_congress/TBI_in_the_US.PDF, 1999.
[b] American Cancer Society, Inc., "Cancer Figures, 2009," retrieved May 17, 2010, from cancer.org.
[c] "Spinal Cord Injury Overview, Types of Spinal Cord Injury," 2006, retrieved May 17, 2010, from Healthcommunities.com.

and emotional impairments and disorders must also be added to the list. The sheer volume of the terminally and chronically ill who require care points to the growing need for family caregivers, professional care providers, and volunteers to work with ill, disabled, and dying persons and their families and to help them with their continuing grief reactions.

## ☐ The Relationship Between the Sick, Dying, or Grieving Person and the Care Provider

Although the care provider can be identified as a professional or volunteer charged with the specific task of helping the sick, dying, or grieving person who is the recipient of this help, the formal distinction between the two can melt away leaving two human beings who are coming together in a relationship. The Exquisite Witness care provider connects with the person in need at a level of one human being to another; it transcends titles. In this way, the helping person can be present in such a way that the sick person feels safe to explore feelings and thoughts regarding his or her life and death.

A friend with whom the dancer Isadora Duncan went to stay with after her two young children drowned demonstrates the essence of this relationship. Her friend encouraged her to repeat all their little sayings and ways. The friend never told her to stop her grieving but grieved with her, and for the first time since their death, Duncan felt she was not alone (Duncan, 1927).

The relationship between the care provider and the grieving person is complex. A sacred trust is developed between two human beings. The trusting nature of the relationship is not based on a care provider's professional degree but rather on the capacity to be present to the person receiving care. I heard a story about a 4-year-old boy who visited his next-door neighbor whose wife had just died. He walked over to the man and climbed up into his lap. When he returned to his mother, she asked him what he said to the man. The boy replied that he didn't say anything. He just "helped him cry." Many grieving people yearn for a helping person who will simply help them cry or feel the feelings of grief without any judgments, time limits, and admonitions to move on with life.

## Working With the Dying

For many care providers, working with dying people is profoundly satisfying and spiritually uplifting. Others are affected in ways that make them view their work as futile and depressing. Sometimes this happens because many ill people do not get well and the effects of their illnesses can be devastating to some care providers. Sick people and their loved ones may be very sad. Further, care providers' own Cowbells (personal loss material) may become overwhelming. Their own unfinished material around grief and loss prevents them from being sufficiently available to those who need care. As a result, care providers may feel burned out, develop physical or emotional problems, and provide less than optimal care for their clients or patients. In most cases, individuals who take the time to identify and discuss their own unfinished business with a trusted friend or colleague are able to provide better care and to be more available. Some care providers, however, are unable to get past a sense of futility and depression. They may say, "I only want to work with people who are going to get well." In such cases, a change of work setting is a good idea. Care providers are needed in all types of health care settings, and those who need to relocate to other venues deserve our support to do so.

Being with a person who is at the very end of life can be an awesome experience. What do you say to a dying person or to the spouse, child, sibling, parent, or best friend of a dying person? How do you offer comfort without crushing hope or raising it unrealistically? What do you ask? What can you do to help?

When I enter the room of a dying person, I feel as if I am entering a sacred place. It may be dark or brightly lit; the television may be blaring or it may be very quiet; it may be hot and have an unpleasant odor. It is not unusual for seriously ill or dying people to confide in me about concerns that they feel they cannot discuss with their families. Often, they want to protect other family members from pain. I may not speak very much; I hope to listen exquisitely.

Family members need to be encouraged to use the final hours or moments to the fullest. I make every effort, within the scope of family and cultural traditions, to support conversation and physical contact, to encourage saying good-bye, and to facilitate forgiveness, in whatever way the family members are willing or able to do. This may also be a time for religious or spiritual practices. The final moments with a dying loved one remain as a "memory photo" throughout a lifetime.

## Visiting the Dying

Before I make a visit, in order to learn as much as possible in advance, I ask:

- What is the nature of the illness or condition that the individual is coping with?

- What is the person's medical condition?

- Who are the primary family or other caregivers?

- What is the family history and current level of functioning?

- How much medical information has already been shared with the person and family?

- What are the cultural background and religious belief system of the ill person and family?

- What kind of external support systems do the person and family have?

Care providers should view the patient's room at home, in the hospital, or nursing facility, as the province of the dying person and his or her family. Permission should always be requested before entering, and providers should make an effort to match their volume of speaking to that of the patient and family members. Suggestions should be offered rather than stated as commands or requirements. Effective listening skills will enable providers to learn what medical information the family knows, the way that people are relating to each other, and how they are interacting with their dying loved one. The care provider's Cowbells must be attended to so that negative energy is not brought into the setting.

# ☐ Five Rights That Preserve Patient Dignity

It is the responsibility of the care provider to help preserve the dignity of the person with a life-threatening illness. Care providers do this by being aware of five patient rights principles (E. Kübler-Ross, personal communication, 1981).

## The Right to Know as Much of the Truth as Can Be Handled

Patients and their families have a right to know about their condition. This information gives them a sense of control and a framework for thinking about the future. Care providers can arrange for members of the medical or nursing staff to deliver health-associated information to a seriously ill or dying person and his or her family. Before arranging for this, it is important to check with the individual and family to determine what has already been conveyed, to get a sense of whether additional information is desired, and to learn if any material needs to be clarified.

It is essential that patients receive only as much information as they really want to know. I once worked with a woman who seemed very eager to more fully understand her prognosis. Yet after the doctor spoke with her, she became distressed and regretted her decision. I realized that I should have spent more time discussing with her what she believed was already happening to her body and how much additional information she truly was seeking. One way to prevent overloading a person with information is to relay it in small increments and stop as soon as verbal or nonverbal cues indicate a negative reaction. We can always gently check with people later to determine if this is what they were looking for or if they have the answers they need at this time.

## The Right to Be Free of Pain and Suffering and Have Hope for Some Quality of Life

Strange as it may seem, hope can always be part of a dying person's worldview. When I work with clients, I always explain that hope exists on a continuum. We begin by hoping we stay healthy. If we receive a terrible diagnosis, we hope there was a mistake. When we know the diagnosis is accurate, we hope for a cure. When a cure is not possible, we hope for long remissions and a quality of life that is pain free, for a life in which we retain control and personal dignity. When the end of life comes, we can hope for a peaceful, pain-free death with our loved ones close by. Finally, we can also hope that our loved ones will heal after we're gone.

## The Right to Participate in Decision Making at One or More Levels of Care

One antidote for depressing and anxiety-producing helplessness that many dying people experience is for the individual to participate in as many decisions as possible. This is an extension of the right that patients

Care providers can ask the person what he or she is thinking about or ask: "Do you have some thoughts about what is happening in your body at this point?" "Have you ever had any thoughts about what may happen when your body just wants to stop working?" The dying person may be very relieved to finally be able to talk about the forbidden topic. If dying people don't want to talk about death in order to protect their families, the care provider can initiate a conversation. Even a short talk can be useful. However, sometimes the dying person does not want to talk about it. This must be respected; no one should be pressured to talk about death. It's important to avoid saying things like, "I'll come back later to see if you've changed your mind." Say instead, "We can talk about whatever you wish, whenever you wish."

have to make decisions about their health care, including the right to refuse treatment and life-support measures. Even though seriously ill or dying people cannot take as active a role in making health-related decisions, they can still maintain some control over their lives. They can decide to raise or lower the bed, how to rearrange their pillows, when to have a bath or be moved, whether the TV should be on or off, what food to eat, whom to see during visiting hours, and what music to listen to.

## The Right to Talk About Death When Ready

Many dying people complain that they never have an opportunity to discuss dying. However, many families do talk about dying—away from the loved one. I've frequently had family members whisper to me, "The doctor said it won't be more than a day or two, but we really haven't talked to Mom about this, and no one wants to be the one to upset her." There is often an unwritten agreement that the family will not bring it up and the dying person will not ask. The care provider can offer an opportunity to talk about this final phase of a person's life with the individual and encourage family members to do so as well when appropriate. Cultural traditions are an important factor to take into consideration regarding information flow.

## The Right to Express Emotional Feelings and Complete Unfinished Business

Dying people who want to express their feelings of grief, rage, and fear should be provided opportunities to do so. In this situation, the care provider becomes an exceptional listener, allowing the dying person the chance to express all feelings. Care providers need to be prepared to stay with the person for as long as needed at a particular session. During this process, the dying person may bring up unfinished material about other relationships.

It is also easy for a very ill person who is in pain and emotional distress to keep his or her feelings locked up inside. The ill person may believe that such feelings are inappropriate or too unpleasant to talk about. He or she may be reluctant to share these feelings with family members in order to protect them from pain. It is also true that families may be uncomfortable hearing the true feelings of their dying loved one, and this may inhibit both parties from expressing themselves honestly. The release of stored grief feelings can help emotional healing before death by allowing the dying person to focus his or her energy on saying good-bye and letting go. In Chapter 9, we will further discuss the externalization of emotional pain and how a skilled care provider can facilitate communication.

## ☐ What to Expect From the Dying Person and Family

The dying person is a grieving person, and the grief begins very early in the process, perhaps as early as the first awareness of troubling and persistent symptoms. Dying people are unique. I have found that some dying people:

- Can be so drained by their disease that they do not have much energy left over for thinking about dying, death, and the consequences for all concerned.

- Are likely to be sick at heart knowing that they will be leaving loved ones, their life activities, and their hopes and dreams for the future. At the same time, they are filled with uncertainty, wondering what's ahead as the reality of their death permeates their conscious awareness.

- May appear to have adapted to the idea of life ending for them and the awareness of their loved ones' grief.

- May be able to understand the ending of their lives into a broader context, whether religious or secular.

- Can be frantic, panicked, depressed, and very frightened at what will happen to them during the active dying process and after death: "Will I be gasping for air?" "Will I be in excruciating pain?" "Will I experience blackness? Oblivion? Heaven? Will I be reincarnated? Reunited with deceased loved ones?"

- May be comatose much of the time and uncommunicative, or wax and wane between alertness and sleep due to a morphine drip or to the effects of such medical conditions as renal or congestive heart failure, encephalopathy, or septicemia.

- Can be withdrawn, fatigued, drained, depressed, and therefore unable to interact very much with their family caregivers and visitors.

All these varied reactions have an effect on family members, friends, and others who are close to the dying person. They are all grieving people, coping with losses due to the illness as well as loss that anticipates the death of the loved one.

## The Final Hours

Sometimes family members will not know what to do in the final hours and minutes of their dying loved one's life. They may sit in the room, nearby, or at a distance, looking at their loved one or trying not to look. Some may congregate outside the room—waiting. They say things like, "He isn't really here anymore," or "She isn't really Mom anymore." Still others may climb right into bed and embrace the dying man or woman. They may hold the person's hand; caress her face or wipe it with a damp cloth; or touch her arm, neck, or shoulders. They may talk to their dying loved one, saying, "I love you." They may express gratitude and find a way to say good-bye. Some ask for or give forgiveness. Ira Byock (2004), a palliative care physician,

Care providers should be aware that not everyone is able to have a close physical and final connection. Providers should educate or even coach family members who are hesitant about staying close by to remain in the room, to talk to the dying loved one, to touch his or her feet and/or hands, and to say whatever they need to say by way of good-bye. Once they see and hear the last breath and know that life is over, they can acknowledge that death has come, though some may want to hear the physician pronounce the loved one dead. They can even touch their loved one or wash his or her hands and feet. Sometimes, people who were unable to be in the room to witness the death wish to come in afterward to say good-bye either silently, out loud, or through some form of physical contact.

People typically find this closeness at the time of death to be not nearly as scary as they imagined it would be. Rather, they experience it as sacred time, an opportunity to make a final emotional and spiritual connection. Others may be unable to be in the room and exercise their right to choose to remain outside the room or in a waiting lounge. Remember though that cultural traditions differ, especially with regard to physical contact at the time of death and afterward. The care provider needs to learn what the family's traditions require at this time.

refers to "the four most important things to say to a loved one *at any time*" and especially with dying patients and their families: "Please forgive me," "I forgive you," "Thank you," and "I love you." These words can begin the process of resolving conflicts between family members, not only at end of life, but whenever the desire to connect is there. They serve as an initial conversation structure, can be adapted to the needs of the speaker, and can lead to cleaning up old unfinished business in the final hours.

For many loved ones, healing begins during the moments of close contact at the time of death and immediately after death. Even though a patient is comatose or has been pronounced dead, it is useful for the loved ones who are willing to say their good-byes. Prayers offered later, at funerals or memorial services, at graveside, or at home are also an important part of the healing process for mourners. For loved ones with a belief that a spiritual connection has been made at the time of death, healing and the beginning of a spiritual bond with the deceased has begun (Bowlby, 1980).

Here is an account of one family's experience with end-of-life bonding.

A young physician on weekend duty was called in to see an elderly woman who was dying on an inpatient medical unit. He was surprised to find only one visitor standing outside of the woman's room. When he inquired as to the whereabouts of the rest of the family, he was informed that a number of others, including the woman's adult children and her grandchildren, had been sent home so Grandma "could die in peace." He immediately had the lone relative phone all of the family members who had been sent away and had them all return. He invited them into the room, had them circle the bed, and for those who wished to do so, told them to make physical contact with the dying woman and say their loving good-byes to her. Later, after the woman died, as they prepared to depart, the family tearfully thanked the doctor for enabling this never-to-be-forgotten gift. This was their memory photo.

I know about this moment because the physician in the story is my son, Dr. Ronald Jeffreys, Steven's older brother.

## ☐ Factors Impacting the Terminally Ill Person and Family

Following are 12 important factors that directly impact the family of a terminally ill loved one.

# The Heartbreak of Remission and Relapse

People undergoing treatment for cancer and other illnesses must have frequent tests to determine the growth of the tumor or the progress of their disease. Their hopes rise and are dashed depending on the outcome of these tests. Life begins to feel like a perpetual roller coaster, continually up and down. As the time for the next blood test, spinal tap, or x-ray gets closer, the whole family can become very tense, their thoughts dwelling on the possible outcome. Sometimes they breathe a long sigh of relief, and at other times they gasp in horror at the diminishing odds for survival.

During long intervals of remission, the family begins to emerge from a period of darkness and have some real hope. The ill loved one may appear to look healthier and act like his or her old self again. Life at home starts to regain a less dread-filled atmosphere. This can continue for a long enough period to be considered a cure. The family and medical staff may then be lulled into an expectation that "It's going to be OKAY!" Then, a follow-up lab report pulls the rug out from under them, and the care provider will need to help the family deal with their renewed grief.

A study of fathers who had children with life-threatening illnesses (Davies et al., 2004) describes the raising and diminishing of their hope for their children's survival. Fathers described this experience as "living in the dragon's shadow." Even when remission occurred or treatment was concluded, the shadow of the underlying illness (the dragon) haunted their thoughts. I still recall the never-ending and recurring fear that would arise during Steven's periods of remission as we awaited the inevitable next blood test or spinal tap. We were never really at peace.

# Grief Reactions

In addition to grief over the loss of remission, grief occurs for losses already incurred during the course of the illness, as well as for the anticipated future loss of the loved one. In other words, the family is bereaved well before the terminally ill person actually dies. This is seen dramatically with people who have ALS (amyotrophic lateral sclerosis; Lou Gehrig's disease), which robs people of their bodily functions one by one, inch by inch, week by week. Each upsetting change may cause additional grief for the person with ALS and for his or her family members and friends.

## Changes in Social Life

Loss of work and other social roles shrink the world of a terminally ill person. As the person moves closer to dying, he or she has to let go of an increasing number of attachments. These include the connections to people outside of their inner circle of family and friends—in the workplace, neighborhood, and social and faith communities. They also lose connections to family members who may live a distance away or who choose to avoid the situation as much as possible. As the illness progresses, the dying individual and his or her loved ones may withdraw more and more from social contact.

## Financial Pressures

Loss of income and the costs of treatment and care may drain financial resources and intensify stress among family members. Even good medical insurance may not cover all charges. Each time financial statements from various specialists, laboratories, and other health care services show up in the mail, the family is reminded what is not being covered by insurance. If the breadwinner becomes ill or if a wage-earning family member becomes a caretaker, financial anxieties increase.

## Physical Pain, Impairment, Disfigurement, and Fatigue

Relentless pain, physical limitations, and upsetting changes in one's appearance can cause the ill person to become depressed. The "face of illness"—how they look to others and to themselves—is very much on the mind of sick people. When my cousin was in the later stages of AIDS, he told me that when he looked in the mirror he saw Auschwitz. During the course of a long-term debilitating illness, multiple losses accumulate (e.g., the loss of strength and mobility; control over hands, fingers, legs, bladder, and bowel) all adding to the individual's and the family's grief.

## Emotional Distress

Many people, whether dying themselves or close to someone who is, experience depression, demoralization, and anxiety that wear away at their ability to sustain hope and to marshal the strength to cope with new medical procedures or changes in medication. This gradual depletion of stamina can contribute to hopelessness.

## Existing Family Dysfunction

Preexisting and newly developed relational conflicts take their toll on the dying person and family members. This may interfere with care and further demoralize the terminally ill loved one. Some families observe a truce during the interval between life and death. Others are simply unable to do so. It is very important that whether the loved one is at home or in a hospice, nursing, or rehabilitation facility, the care provider be aware of such energy-draining issues and help the family resolve conflicts and focus on gathering resources to cope with the health care needs of their ill loved one. When conflict resolution is not possible, it is necessary to keep the negative interactions away from the loved one.

## The Reactions of Others to Progressive Decline

Dying people are often alerted to the reality of their illness by watching the faces of those who come to visit them. Often these faces register the decline in the patient's health since the last visit and remind the patient of the inevitability of approaching death. Some dying people want everything to be above board; they want honesty and openness with everyone. Others are glad to have any negative reactions hidden from them.

## Degree of Information and Uncertainty

Most people I have worked with report that knowing their diagnosis and its implications provides a feeling of control, reduces their anxiety, and enables them to plan for their treatment and care. Lack of knowledge can make people feel uncertain, despairing, and fearful. There are some, however, who appear to be content with little information, and wish to leave all decisions in the hands of their doctors. In some cultures, medical information is given to a designated family member, and the family then determines when, what, and how much information to share with

Care providers can help the family get all of the information they need to make the best choice at any given time. Providers need to help families understand the consequences of decisions regarding care and think through their own issues concerning the aforementioned factors. Families need to be able to draw on other resources, such as clergy, medical, and mental health professionals.

the ill loved one. Care providers must be sensitive to cultural traditions regarding how much information flows to the patient and to others both within and outside the family.

## Dependency

Many dying people, particularly those who have been very independent, are terrified that they will have to depend on others for their basic needs. This kind of dependency is another assault on their self-image. In *Tuesdays With Morrie* (Albom, 1997), Morrie Schwartz, a man with ALS, says that he is horrified by the thought of another person having to wipe his behind. However, when Morrie actually needs this kind of care, he is able to appreciate and accept it. There are many activities of daily living that a seriously ill person or one who is physically limited due to illness or injury has to surrender to another person. For some, this is initially a very difficult loss of personal dignity. Care providers must be sensitive to this shift to dependent status.

## Painful Procedures and Medication Side Effects

Much of the physical and emotional distress of cancer patients and others who are receiving chemotherapy comes from the side effects of medications: hair loss, nausea, vomiting, weakness, itching, and vulnerability to infection. Medical procedures can be uncomfortable at best and very painful at worst. For some, chemotherapy must be discontinued because of the seriousness of the side effects. Other progressive illnesses have their own distressing medication side effects and procedures—spinal taps, mylograms, painful injections, and bed sores—which add to the total suffering of patient and family.

# Difficult Decisions and Upsetting Dilemmas

Having to make decisions regarding treatment and care can create painful and upsetting dilemmas for dying patients and their families. Each treatment has its negative effects. With increased choices, there is the potential for increased anxiety since each option has its advantages and disadvantages. Side effects and potential risks have to be considered. Fathers in the Davies et al. study (2004) commented that they often had to make what seemed like split-second decisions about medical treatments (e.g., whether to transfer a loved one to intensive care, continue or terminate life support, or begin palliative or hospice care), which can place a family in an agonizing position and add to the already existing high stress level. Having advance directives and a health care proxy can ease some of the strain for families. (See Appendix B.)

# ☐ The Needs of the Patient's Family

The family and friends of a very sick and dying loved one may feel as though they are trapped in a nightmare. They may also feel angry and resentful because the illness and impending death has restricted their lives, prevented them from planning for the future, drained their finances, taken them away from other activities, and ravaged them emotionally. The situation can be frightening, draining, painful, unrelenting, and seemingly endless. In reality, there is an end—the death of the very ill person. The conscious acknowledgment of this frequently invokes a guilt reaction in the family member or friend. In sum, the dying person's family has a set of needs, and care providers can play a role in meeting these needs in the following ways.

## Normalizing the Family's Feelings

Many grieving people question whether some of their feelings are disloyal or inappropriate. They are often angry at the dying person and at the intrusion of the illness into their lives. Secretly, they may wish that it were all over, and then experience intense feelings of guilt and shame. People need to know that all of these feelings are simply part of the process. It's what we humans do. One of the benefits of participating in support groups for family of persons with life-threatening conditions is the opportunity to hear that other family caregivers also feel angry, resentful, depressed, or guilty.

## Providing for the Needs of All Members

Some family and extended family members can get overlooked during the course of a loved one's illness. Children, elders, in-laws, classmates, colleagues, and neighbors are among those who may be disenfranchised both during and after the death. Care providers should alert the family in advance to the needs of these important but frequently less noticed members of the dying person's social network. They should be included on lists to receive informational updates, and given the opportunity to organize support services, attend rituals, and visit. Family friends can shop or do other basic chores, keep a fresh supply of flowers in the room, read aloud to the ill person, pray with him or her, relay neighborhood or workplace gossip, or just sit quietly with him or her.

Care providers will let families know, preferably in advance, how normal the reactions of anger, resentment, depression, shame, and guilt are. Family members are typically very relieved to know that they are not bad or disloyal to their loved one if they feel resentful, irritated, or guilty. Family members should also know about local, disease-specific support groups for family members they can attend. (See Appendix A.)

Care providers can include the disenfranchised by giving them information and involving them in some aspects of the caregiving. Children should have an opportunity to spend time with the dying person even if he or she is comatose. They can make cards or other artwork and bring it to the bedside, and be given an opportunity to ask questions or share feelings afterward.

Providers can also arrange for a counselor or nurse to visit a sick child's classroom to relay information about the child and answer questions. Similarly, a care provider can arrange for an employee assistance counselor or human resource staff person to speak to the colleagues of an ill person in the workplace. However, always check to see if the family approves of these outreach activities.

The care provider's interventions regarding denial depend on its nature and effects. Providers need to understand that some denial is healthy, and that each case is unique and should be evaluated individually. For example, a dying woman who was making plans for her funeral decided to purchase a new car. Her family supported this because it gave her a sense of control and made her feel happy. In this case, the care provider did not intervene to prevent the car's purchase. However, in another case, a care provider did intervene when a couple decided to spend all of their savings on buying an expensive new home even though the husband had terminal AIDS. This decision, rooted in denial, was a potential financial disaster for the wife. When the couple reevaluated and discussed the purchase with their accountant, they dropped the plans.

## Helping to Balance Denial and Acceptance

During the end-of-life period and after the death of the loved one, family members may react with varying degrees of denial to cope with grief. At the beginning of the process, the care provider may need to help family members balance their desire to avoid the reality of the terminal illness with their need to accept it. Families can be helped to acknowledge the true nature of the medical condition if they are encouraged to obtain accurate medical information; share their feelings with each other (if this behavior is appropriate for this family's traditions); and organize caregiving activities such as gathering medical, financial, spiritual, and logistical resources.

## Facilitating Accurate, Clear, and Open Communication

Each family has its own unique way of understanding and communicating medical information. Many families use the language of medical technology as fluently as their doctors and are familiar with treatment options and the statistical realities of survival. Other families—because of education or linguistic barriers, family communication styles, or by choice—appear to know little about medical options and treatment plans. Often, one family member serves as the communication bridge between the dying person and the rest of the family, and sometimes to the various providers on the health team as well. This person needs to be present when medical or nursing providers are supplying medical information.

The care provider must determine how much information the family really requires, what's preventing the information that they want from getting through, and which medical professional should communicate the information so it will be understood. A good way to initiate a conversation about this is for the physician or nurse to ask a general question regarding what the family already knows about the patient's medical condition and proceed from there. For example, the nurse can ask, "Are there any gaps in the medical information you wish to have filled in?" "What is your understanding of his or her medical status as of now?"

Providers working with the family should obtain parental permission before speaking with children, who should be given an opportunity to express their concerns and their needs. The conversation should be confidential unless health or safety issues arise.

If appropriate, he or she can plan to meet with the family or schedule a telephone conference call to share information.

Children should also be included in family-wide discussions when appropriate or at least be given appropriate information arising from such discussions. They need to be told how to reply when others ask about the ill family member, which includes saying that they don't want to talk about it. I have found it useful to talk to children when they are away from their families so that they can express feelings and raise questions more freely.

## Continuing to Relate to the Dying Person as a Member of the Family

My wife was visiting her mother in a nursing home when the physician stopped in. He checked my mother-in-law's vital signs and started to relate his findings to my wife. "Talk to *me*!" my mother-in-law told him in a voice more powerful than she had used since her condition began to deteriorate.

It's so easy for care providers or family members to forget to honor the dignity of an ill or dying person. Some people simply talk to each other about the dying person as if he or she were not in the room. You can easily imagine how irrelevant the dying person must feel. Although some cultures view medical decisions as the family's responsibility and not the patient's, care providers should make every effort to encourage the dying person to stay involved as much as possible and to the extent that this does not conflict with family or cultural traditions. Always ask if you are not sure.

Care providers can also help families sustain their relationship with the dying person. Many times, families withdraw prematurely; they stop visiting comatose Grandpa on sunny days, and then stop visiting altogether. In these cases the family needs to be reminded not to abandon the dying person. It's not always satisfying to spend time with people who are drifting in and out of a coma or who have dementia, but it is important for family to be there in case the fog does lift—if only for a few moments—and provide the dying loved one with the opportunity to talk to the family and say whatever still needs to be said.

Care providers can remind families to accord dying loved ones the respect they are due. Even patients who have regressed mentally or emotionally need to be treated with respect.

Ill people are also discounted when they are treated like infants. I heard a health care worker say to an older ill gentleman, "Are we going to be a good boy and make all gone our dinner today?" The old man spit the food out, cursed, and said, "The only thing I want all gone today is you! Just who do you think you are talking to, a 1-year-old?" Infantilizing very sick persons robs them of their dignity. Even those who are not as verbally emphatic as this man most likely feel the same way. In fact, many people who don't want to speak up quietly confided to me their unhappiness at being patronized. Some find ingenious ways of conveying their feelings. One older dying woman, for example, kept firing her home health aides. It was her way of letting everyone know she was still lucid and in charge of her care.

## Balancing the Person's Increasing Dependency With Autonomy

Care providers need to find ways to maintain an ill or dying person's autonomy as much as possible. As mentioned earlier, one way to do this is to keep him or her involved in making decisions about health care and treatment options. For example, if a patient were no longer able to go to the toilet, the next step would be to offer him or her the use of a bedside commode rather than use a bedpan. In this way, the person still feels some control over care.

Care providers can help the family caregiver identify other inter-mediary steps that would help the individual bathe, eat, and per-form daily functions. The goal is to preserve the individual's dignity and provide opportunities for the person to be independent as long as possible.

Care providers can help family members to understand the grief reactions that occur long before a loved one has died. Explaining and normalizing the grief response may ease any guilt and remorse that may arise when a family member engages in fantasies of the loved one's death. Care providers should help family members understand that they may be grieving over what has already been lost as well as anticipating what is yet to be lost.

## Helping With Grief, Anticipatory Grief, and Guilt

A family who has a dying loved one is already grieving. They have had to cope with multiple losses as the loved one's condition worsens and his or her appearance changes before their eyes. There are also losses due to changes in the family system. Things the family can no longer do and things that they now must do will alter normal family patterns. Family members are learning to let go. At the same time, the family is also envi-sioning what's to come: the death, the funeral, and life without their loved one. This is anticipatory mourning. The care provider can help a family move through this process by encouraging them to talk about their thoughts and feelings.

## Helping Family Members Say Good-Bye

Saying good-bye may occur at every step of the journey from terminal diagnosis to the moment of death. I find it useful to ask family members what they feel they need to say in order to say good-bye. Good-byes can be said silently or out loud, and at any point in the process. People will usually have a sense of what they want to say even if the person has slipped into a coma.

# Assisting With the Event of Dying and After-Death Rituals

We come into the world with a single breath, and we leave after a single breath. As life has begun, so it is finished. Most medical personnel at hospitals or hospice describe to families what may occur during the moments of death. Knowing this in advance is very useful and allows the family members to stay in physical and verbal contact with the dying loved one as he or she slips away. Saying final words and touching the person, as life is suddenly no more, can help them experience the sacredness of dying as well as the pain of grief.

Care providers can suggest some general ideas of what to say and then let people fill in their own details. Family members can be invited to touch their deceased loved one, wash their face, hold hands, and let their good-byes flow from their hearts.

Care providers need to be prepared for a variety of emotional reactions on the part of the survivors; some become agitated, some cry and sob, some withdraw into silence. Unless requested or if it is obvious that a loved one is in extreme distress and agitation, there is no need for the care provider to be other than an observing Exquisite Witness at this very important time.

The question of whether the provider should attend the funeral often comes up, a subject for which no detailed set of criteria exist. In general, I am in favor of care providers attending the funeral. However, time constraints on the provider and the wishes of the family need to be considered. Some loved ones look upon the providers as part of their own family and even request that they attend their funeral. Attendance enables the provider to say his or her own good-byes and lets the family know of the provider's continued support and concern for them and their loss. However, the presence of the provider may remind the family of what they see as the failure of medical science, the hospital, and the provider to keep their now deceased loved one alive.

# ☐ Adapting to Life After a Terminal Illness Diagnosis

Although every family adapts to the diagnosis and progression of a terminal illness in its own way, a pattern of behavior often emerges. The care provider can assist family members as they journey through the three phases of this process.

## Phase 1: The Beginning

The grief process can begin immediately, as early as the first occurrence of troubling symptoms or as late as the final diagnosis of a fatal illness. When the patient receives a prognosis and treatment plan, some families rapidly circle the wagons to strengthen their connection and keep the terrible news inside the family. Others actively seek all of the resources they can marshal—members of the extended family, neighbors, health care providers, clergy, community services, the Internet, library, and others who have experienced the same or similar diagnoses.

The initial grief responses may include fear, anger, denial, panic, and disorganization. Some family members may withdraw or seek some form of distraction. Those who have a strong faith belief system may embrace prayer and seek the prayers of others. Denial of the seriousness of the illness or its ultimate consequences may soften the horror of a terrible diagnosis, and can be expected from some of the family members. Some people experience absolute panic; others exercise seemingly impossible emotional control. Some family members may pursue information seeking on-line or from other medical resources. There is no single right way to grieve.

## Phase 2: Living With a Fatally Ill Loved One

The family begins to organize the caregiving responsibilities. They become familiar with medications, medical procedures, various therapies—respiratory, physical, radiation—and establish routines. They confront the daily challenges of caring for the loved one both physically and emotionally, but at a cost. Care exacts a toll. The relentless cycle of good days–bad days, and the heartbreak of remission and relapse drain energy and hope.

Care providers should be aware of all three phases after a terminal illness diagnosis. Each family will present many variations on this theme. Normalizing reactions can help family members recognize that they are coping as many others in their situation do; this knowledge is often comforting. Families should also be informed of how they can use the time in the latter phase of the journey to complete unfinished business, engage in forgiveness when appropriate, and say good-bye.

Some family members (frequently children and elders) may be left out of the caregiving process. If so, they need to be attended to. During this time, it's not unusual for existing family conflicts to go underground or become aggravated by the stress and anxiety. Failure to express these inner stresses and tensions can impact on caregiving and the quality of life of all involved. Families need to secure outside support (including hospice, when appropriate) to help in caregiving routines.

## Phase 3: Ending Phase

Much of the denial concerning the terminal nature of the illness usually melts away by this time. Now, the question is "when" rather than "if" the loved one dies. Underground conflicts may burst into the open if the temporary "truce" has been shattered. The family may circle the wagons even closer. Sometimes a "bunker" mentality emerges as the end approaches. Family members may need to discuss issues of abandonment that they are experiencing as well as begin to make plans for the actual death.

## ☐ Signs and Symptoms of Approaching Death

Health care providers are in the best position to guide the family with regard to what to expect from a dying person. It is important preparation for family caregivers and other persons close to the family who may be present at the time of active dying. Although every individual dies in his or her own way, some general information on what to expect in terms of signs and symptoms is presented in the following. (Clinical medical material in the following sections has been drawn from information provided by Dr. R. Jeffreys [personal communication, May 24, 2010].)

# The Process of Dying

To help the family be prepared as death approaches, the following signs and symptoms are included and should be reviewed with the family by a medical or nursing health care provider.

## *Prior to the Final Dying Period*

Three weeks before death, the following symptoms occur (most often because the body can no longer clear toxins):

- Diminished eating and drinking

- Restlessness

- Withdrawal

- Confusion and/or agitation

- Increased periods of sleep

- Persistence of wounds and infections

- Swelling of bodily extremities

Nurses frequently report that dying persons claim to see deceased persons and repeatedly say that they are dying. It is also usual for many dying people to seek completion of unfinished business and make financial arrangements. (See earlier section "Helping Family Members Say Good-Bye.")

## *Final Phase of Dying*

Three days prior to death, these symptoms occur:

- Periods of lethargy alternating with extreme agitation

- Inability to swallow fluids or ingest food

- Urinary and/or bowel incontinence and decreased urine output

- Swelling and puffiness

- Cold extremities (hands and feet may turn blue)

- Drop in blood pressure

In the later stages, dying people may slip into a coma or become very hard to arouse; they may be reluctant to speak even if not comatose. Change in breathing patterns include breathing through open mouth, very shallow breathing, and lengthening intervals between breaths with periods of no breathing extending from 5 to 30 seconds and up to a full minute (Cheyne–Stokes breathing). As fluid builds up in the lungs, crackling sounds are heard in the chest. Dying people often repeat that they are dying. They may also complain of being very cold and maintain a rigid body position. Toward the end, however, they may experience a sudden resurgence of energy and appetite, as if miraculously returned to life for one or more days of well being. This typically is followed by rapid deterioration and death.

## The Signs at Death

Although family members may be prepared for the process leading up to death, they may not be equipped for the actual moment of death. Care providers can be helpful by ensuring that family members know the signs that indicate that death has occurred. These include no breathing, no heartbeat, release of bowel and bladder functioning, and no response to sensory stimuli. The eyes of dead people remain slightly open and enlarged pupils fixate on one spot; there is no blinking. The jaw is relaxed and mouth slightly open. When they believe that death has occurred, family members should notify the appropriate medical or nursing provider.

## Spiritual and Emotional Changes

In addition to the physical signs of approaching death, spiritual and emotional changes, which are interrelated and interdependent, are taking place. Some dying people seem to let go of their agitation and become calm and accepting of the inevitable. They may seem to possess great wisdom about the meaning of life and seek to pass this on to loved ones. One couple I worked with became fascinated with the literature about life after death and read voraciously about those who claimed to have had near-death experiences. Other dying patients may withdraw from family members who are present and seem to be in conversation with others who are unseen. Still others desire to say good-bye to as many of their

Care providers and family members can help the dying person, after ensuring that all activities are in accordance with family traditions, by enhancing physical comfort, supporting the release of emotions, meeting his or her spiritual and religious needs, encouraging letting go of attachments, and moving toward the transition.

Providers should coordinate care for the family but need to know the family's wishes. Each family moves at its own pace. Some family members may stay to wash or touch the body, say good-bye, or simply be present at their final time together before the formal death rituals begin. Some families wish to spend extended time with the body of the deceased. In these cases, care providers can attempt to arrange for the body to be moved to another location in the hospital, nursing home, or hospice so the family can have the uninterrupted time they desire. The provision of time after death with the loved one enables the family to begin the process of letting go of the body.

Providers should also find out if a postmortem is necessary so that they can prepare the family for this. If decisions regarding organ donation have not yet taken place, which is optimal, they need to take place now. This may also be the time to contact the funeral director, clergy, family, and friends who may be needed for support and to handle details of arrangements. Care providers need to give the family the opportunity to do as much of the planning and preparation of after-death rituals as they desire. Continued teamwork and communication are in the best interest of the deceased patient, the family, and the care providers. Working together is a gift care providers can give the family.

family, friends, and colleagues as possible before they die. Even people who have never put much stock in prayer and worship may embrace this transition as a final connection to the mystery of life and death.

## ☐ Bedside Guide at the Time of Death: Saying Good-Bye

Many family members have their first experience with dying when a loved one dies. Often, in a hospital room, nursing home, or at home, a family at the bedside will not know what to do as the final breaths are taken. If care providers are present, they can help the family have a healing experience; if they are unable to be present, they can prepare the family to deal with the final moments on their own. (The following guide has been adapted from material prepared by Patricia Wudel, Director of Joseph's House Hospice, Washington, DC, and her staff. Personal communication, 2002.)

> Take several breaths and turn off the TV. You are on holy ground. Quietly pull a chair close to the head of the bed. It is natural to feel anxious or afraid. Be patient with yourself. Take the hand of the dying person and give thanks for the opportunity to be together during the last minutes and seconds of his or her life.
>
> Assume that even in the last moments the dying person is able to hear. If you are a family member or have been especially close to the person who is dying, this is the time to say your good-byes. Where appropriate, let the person know that he or she is loved and will be missed, but that you will be all right and that you want him or her to be in peace. If your tears come, that is okay. If no tears come, that is okay, too. *There is no one right way to be or one right thing to say.*
>
> Respect the dying person as a full human being as long as he or she is alive. Use the person's name when talking. If you need to talk about the dying person to someone, step outside of the room and close the door. If you forget, be gentle with yourself but keep practicing deep respect.
>
> If the dying person is a person of religious faith and you feel comfortable talking about this, do so. You may want to read from the Bible or other spiritual books, or any passages that may have special meaning. You may be inspired to sing hymns, lullabies, or songs of comfort that communicate love and care.
>
> Keep distraction to a minimum. If others in the room appear overcome with grief, comfort them, or step outside of the room with them for a few minutes so you can gently care for them.
>
> The moment of death is different for each person. As you watch, keep your heart soft and open. Take a moment to sit quietly in the room to honor the passing and sense the world with his or her living, physical presence no longer in it. Allow your feelings to come out—tears, sighs, sobs. Have mercy on yourself. You have just shared an awesome moment with someone dear to you.

The following story of spiritual transition made a lasting impression on me. A man who was losing his battle with cancer had been telling his close friends, who visited regularly, that he saw visitors whom he did not know. As he grew weaker and weaker, he continued to talk about the strangers. When he was barely able to talk, he asked one close friend how his wife and daughters were doing. When the friend said they were doing fine, the dying man said, "Then I can go home with the visitors." He died very shortly afterward. During the eulogy for him, a friend who is a priest related this story and then led the congregation in "Swing low, sweet chariot ... a band of angels, coming for to carry me home."

Care providers must be aware of the fact that not every death experience may be filled with awe and spiritual significance. In some cases, the end comes as family watch breathing cease and track critical changes in vital sign monitors. Some report an unreal feeling as the loved one breathes in and then out, but the next breath never comes. Some deaths are very upsetting to witness. The loved one may be struggling for breath or calling out to be saved from death before lapsing into a final, irreversible coma. Every opportunity must be taken to allow as peaceful a death as possible, and providers must be sensitive to the effects of upsetting deaths on some family members.

# ☐ Chronic Illness/Disability and the Family

Some chronic, life-limiting illnesses or injuries that do not have a mortality risk may linger for many years creating the potential for other medical problems to arise, conditions such as chronic bed sores, infections, depression, demoralization, and an array of emotional disorders.

## Effects of Life-Threatening Illness

Living with a family member who has a life-threatening illness alters the psychosocial climate. Family members will need to adapt to new ways to view their family unit and the way they relate to the outside world.

I know this from personal experience. During the 3 years from the time of our son Steven was diagnosed with cancer until his death at age 8, we were a family living with a chronic, life-threatening illness. He actually had about 11 months of remission: His hair grew back, he returned to school, and he even rejoined his soccer team. When we received the crushing news of his relapse just before spring break, we decided, with his physician's approval, that the five of us would take a trip to Disney World. That's when we truly saw how different we were from other families. Steven, weak and not able to enjoy many of the rides or wait in line, was in a wheelchair. My wife and I were uncomfortably aware of other people looking at us, especially when we overheard some young children ask their parents, "Mommy, why is that boy in a wheelchair?" Even when people didn't say anything about Steven, we detected subtle reactions to the fact that our family was "different."

The oral chemotherapy medications made Steven sick some of the time, and we had to cut outings short so that he could get back to the hotel and rest. I worried that Steven's siblings resented this. We worked hard to make sure that our other two children were having a good time. Yet we were always aware of Steven's schedule and of our overriding need to care for him. We were also very aware of the other families there—carefree, active, and happy, whose only worries appeared to be which ride to go on, which exhibit to enter, and where to have lunch. Gradually, we began to notice other family groups who were different: a mother in a wheelchair, a child in braces up on her father's shoulders, a teenager with a portable oxygen tank and nasal tube, and several families with Down's syndrome children. As I mentally reviewed these other families, I felt an unspoken connection to them—a sense of community with family groups who were different.

We all experienced the frustration of living amid so many restrictions, especially the limitations on socializing at home or away from home. Siblings of the ill child are sometimes reluctant to have friends over; a handicapped parent or a bald sister or brother may embarrass them. Many people experience chronic sorrow with only a few periods of well-being. Fortunate families find ways to have some fun or enjoy a good quality of life between the periods of great pain. Family life is different. Life itself is different.

Here is another illustration of how families adapt to chronic illness. I visited Sue (not her real name), 35, in the nursing home where she has lived for the past 14 years, a victim of traumatic brain injury suffered as a result of a motor vehicle accident. Sue was in a reclining wheelchair, and her hair was neatly pulled back with a pink ribbon. She receives nourishment through a gastric tube, has no control over her environment, and is totally dependent. She is unable to speak or to communicate through gestures. While we were together, her mother maintained constant physical contact with her.

Sue didn't react to my talking to her although she did move her head and appeared to be looking around. Her parents told me, however, that Sue smiles when she recognizes her aide's voice and moves her body closer to her mother when her mother gets into bed with her. These reactions make her parents feel connected to her, and their faces are happy when they tell me this. Sue's parents visit her twice daily, and she comes home on holidays because they want her to spend time with the family. They feel that she is getting good care at this facility and have special praise for her aide.

I asked both parents what they believe constitutes good provider care. They recommended that people who are training to work with the chronically physically impaired would benefit from spending time in a wheelchair with their hands bound to get a sense of the loss of control and the experience of total dependency. They also suggested that good care providers:

- Have good skills in physical care—feeding, bathing, moving, and dressing.

- Are compassionate and empathic.

- Treat the care recipient with respect by:

  - Telling the person they are caring for what they are going to do: "I'm going to bathe you now; feed you now; turn the TV off so you can get some sleep."

  - Talking to the person; telling him or her what is going on around them.

  - Never assuming that people who cannot express their needs have no feelings.

  - Providing auditory stimulation that is especially significant to the patient—music, singing, cheerful talking.

  - Touching, massaging, and maintaining physical contact with loved ones.

  - Providing opportunities for the impaired to exert some level of control over their environment whenever possible: "Do you want the TV on now? Your lunch now? Bed adjusted up or down? Vanilla or chocolate ice cream?"

  - Sharing stories from the care provider's own life that can be appreciated by family members.

## Consequences of Chronic Illness and Conditions on the Family

Families who have a loved one with chronic illness or other disabling physical or mental conditions may be affected in one or more of the following significant ways:

- They are always aware that they are different from other families.

- They live with ongoing concerns for the health and well-being of the ill or handicapped loved one and always need to balance these concerns with the needs of other members of the family.

- They experience various levels of resentment and anger at the limits and restrictions imposed by the situation, and the consequent guilt and shame that frequently follow.

- They may despair at the "no end in sight" nature of the chronic condition, and at the uncertainty of life with a chronically ill or disabled person in the family.

- They undergo grief reactions regarding their past and anticipated losses.

- They may feel angry at other relatives, friends, and neighbors who are happy and seemingly unaware of the continued impact of chronic illness on "our family."

- They often feel tired of caregiving and are emotionally drained.

- They may express the desire to withdraw into themselves and spend increasing time away from the family.

- They are proud of their ability to reframe the way the family thinks of itself. They may consider themselves a family unit composed of independent, caring members who can adapt to one of life's most challenging situations: coping with chronic illness and exceptional conditions.

## Family Caregivers

Family caregivers are family, friends, and neighbors who serve those they love in the face of terminal and chronic illness, disability, and dying (McLeod, 2002). "They may bathe, feed, dress, shop for, listen to, and transport frail parents, spouses, children, friends, relatives, neighbors, and even strangers" (McLeod, 1999, p. 3). Family caregivers require special attention. They are subject to their own grief reactions, which may include depression, burnout, physical breakdown, and substance abuse; they may have difficulties with work and nonwork relationships. When a spouse cares for a chronically ill life partner of many years, the losses are

Care providers need to let families coping with chronic illness know that they are not alone and that their frustrations and other reactions are normal. They can direct families to specific support groups that include other families coping with similar illnesses or disabilities. Care providers can help family caregivers assess their level of burnout to determine if they need to seek respite services. Family caregivers must maintain their own physical and emotional health so that they can continue to be available to their loved one.

many and continuous. The loss of the "way we were" is an ever-present reality as the loved one's physical and mental condition deteriorates and the caregiver strives to provide the care that will keep him or her at home. Parents caring for a chronically ill or disabled child must cope with the "way we will never be."

The strong desire to care for the loved one can lead to a form of stress called *compassion fatigue.* This is the decreasing ability to continue care at the level that the caregiver feels he or she must provide (McLeod, 1999). "Competing demands on time and energy ... fears for the future ... lead to distress such as loneliness, exhaustion, anxiety, and sadness" (McLeod, 1999, p. 103). In addition to the direct care services that must be addressed, there are medical, financial, and legal issues as well. If the caregiver also experiences guilt, depression, and resentment, he or she may no longer be able to care at home for the loved one.

If home care is no longer possible, a range of alternatives exists. Many regional agencies for aging have caregiver support groups. Local family and children service agencies offer training programs specifically for family caregivers, and a new specialty in *geriatric care management* (McLeod, 2002) has emerged to assist the family in managing care for their loved one. (See Appendix A for resources from the National Alliance for Caregiving, the Family Caregiver Alliance, the National Association of Professional Geriatric Care Managers, and other various support organizations devoted to people with specific diseases and disabilities.)

## ☐ Medical Dilemmas, Patient Rights, and Bioethical Considerations

With the growing capacity of medical science to extend the life of terminally ill and critically injured persons, and as more patients and their families become aware of their right to participate in medical decisions, the potential for conflict over decision making has increased. Conflicts about treatment and end-of-life decisions may arise between the patient/ family and the health care staff, and also among family members themselves, including the patient. In this next section, I will focus on the bioethical considerations and dilemmas associated with medical and general care decisions and patient autonomy that can arise in hospitals, hospices, long-term care facilities, and in the home.

## Family Dilemmas

Dilemmas can occur when a shift from curative treatment to palliative or hospice care is being considered. Patients and family may feel that this shift implies that their medical providers are giving up on them. Family members may disagree with one another regarding the cessation of active, aggressive treatment in favor of comfort care. A sick and weak person may be overlooked in the decision-making process.

For example, an older widow with advanced metastatic cancer was being cared for by her daughter who lived nearby. The daughter's two brothers, both of whom live out of town, had been minimally involved in their mother's care. The oncologist, the mother, and her caregiving daughter agreed that it was time to shift to palliative care, and a referral to hospice was made. When the brothers learned of this, they immediately came home and attempted to take over their mother's care. Sidelining the caregiving sister, they attempted to convince the mother that she would be well again, and had her admitted to another hospital against medical advice and the wishes of their sister who felt anguished over this decision. Within a day, the new hospital staff affirmed the original decision for a hospice referral. The two brothers reluctantly agreed and home hospice care was arranged for. The mother lived for 2 more weeks, the brothers departed, and the caregiving sister was left emotionally distraught and estranged from her brothers.

I've found that it is not unusual for out-of-town family members to show up late in the course of an illness and attempt to impose their wishes for the dying loved one to "hang in there and we'll get you well." This is upsetting for the person who has been the continuing caregiver, who may experience doubts, guilt, and anger. It is also very human for adult children who have been involved in a parent's daily care picture to seek intense involvement as a way of holding on to their parent. These efforts exemplify John Bowlby's (1980) "protest phase" and a struggle with reality that is characteristic of early grief. (See Chapter 3.)

In the aforementioned case, the sons' decision to overrule their sister and the physician was also a function of old, unfinished sibling issues as well as the fact that they were in a different part of the grief process than their sister. The mother, confused, and extremely weak, was unable to participate in medical care decisions. She typically had left these medical decisions to her physicians and her daughter. Sadly, the flaring up of old family struggles—in this case, a long history of sibling conflict—erupted and continued after the mother's death. Typically, the resentment siblings feel toward each other does not begin at the time of a health crisis but rather has its roots in past relationship issues. In many conflicted families, discord may continue after the parent has died when inheritance and property disposition issues are considered.

## Treatment Choice Dilemmas

Patients and their families must make decisions about treatment options. Sometimes, these decisions may conflict with medical staff recommendations, which creates a very unpleasant situation for all concerned.

Disagreements can occur over when to move the patient to the intensive care unit (ICU); whether to initiate or maintain aggressive treatment, such as the use of a respirator, gastric tube, or antibiotics to fight infections; whether to resuscitate; and how to assess the extent of patient pain and discomfort. Patients and family must be given a clear picture of the implications of these treatments. For example, many patients suffer cracked ribs during aggressive resuscitation procedures or may have their hands tied down to prevent them from interfering with vital lines and tubes. Medical care providers should discuss a clear and understandable plan with the patient and family before initiating a move to intensive care. This will reduce any mistaken expectations on the part of the family about what should be done to help a person survive. It will also

Care providers can help a family examine options based on medical information and consider the consequences for each option available. However, a clear resolution of all dilemmas may not be possible. Medical staff and other resources may need to be called in to resolve conflicting positions. Hospitals and other health care facilities have established ethics boards to advise those with difficult decisions to make. In some cases, the institution's legal department may need to be consulted.

help to clarify what procedures they do not want done. Sometimes staff will feel that certain heroic measures are futile and view the family's request for these procedures as evidence of denial or false hopes. Yet the decision rests with the family. Another area of potential conflict opens when care shifts from aggressive, curative treatment to palliative care or a hospice program. Care providers must give families clear and understandable information and allow them to participate fully in what can be a traumatic and guilt-producing decision. The family needs to know that their loved one will be kept as comfortable and pain-free as possible, and that any concerns about pain need to be responded to promptly.

One way to reduce confusion at this stage is to make sure the patient's chart contains an up-to-date advance directive and that it is also available to family members.

## Advance Directives

Advance directives are documents signed by an individual and witnessed. In the event that a person becomes too disabled to act on his or her own behalf, this document accomplishes two important things. First, it *identifies a health agent* or proxy who will make medical decisions (a backup person may also be appointed in the event that the proxy is not able to perform this role). Second, it *delineates the lifesaving or life-preserving procedures* that may be used in the event of a medical crisis. For example, it spells out whether the patient requests a DNR (do not resuscitate) or a DNI (do not intubate). It also specifies whether the patient wants a feeding tube, dialysis, blood transfusions, or the administration of antibiotics. Some advanced directives stipulate that life-preserving measures will be used only for a period of 72 hours and then terminated if no improvement is determined. Most states require that all patients entering a hospital have a signed copy in their medical records. The purpose of advance directives is "to define a level of intolerable indignity at which death becomes, for them, preferable to continued existence" (Cantor, 1998, p. 630). (See Appendix B.)

Advance directives are most helpful when family members have discussed them early on. Family members who have never discussed what each would want done (or not done) are at a disadvantage when a medical crisis occurs and an unconscious loved one cannot articulate his or her desires. Even in the best of circumstances, problems arise. Some ill patients clearly stipulate their wishes to avoid life-prolonging measures, yet, at the moment of decision, families may be unwilling to enforce the DNR. It's as if they suddenly realize, "Sure, Dad wanted it this way, but if we do so, we'll be killing him!" In short, advance directives are only as good as the designated health agent and the physician who are responsible for carrying them out.

In a study of cognitively normal seniors over age 65 by Gjerdingen, Neff, Wang, and Chaloner (1999), most respondents did not desire life-sustaining procedures such as CPR, ventilatory support, or artificial nutrition if they were to develop any level of dementia. Further, most said they would not want to be hospitalized or given antibiotics if they were no longer able to recognize their loved ones or care for themselves. As dementia is a condition common to many deteriorating illnesses, it is important that families have a conversation about desired life-prolonging measures while loved ones are capable of making decisions for themselves. The decisions should be part of the advance directive, including specifics regarding the point of discontinuing life support.

Other problems can arise. Sometimes the advance directive document is vague and too general. If, for example, the siblings and the spouse of a comatose patient don't agree on the level of DNR, it's possible to suggest a compromise. Try one resuscitation before the DNR goes into effect. This may or may not be what the patient wanted, but it resolves the family conflict.

Treating for illness other than the primary disease also involves a shaky judgment call. Should an antibiotic be administered if a dying person spikes a fever? Should the person be placed on a ventilator and run the risk of developing pneumonia from the aspiration of fluids? Should a feeding tube or a line for fluids be inserted? Many areas of decision making are not provided for in the standard advance directive document. The family should be in communication with the physician regarding these concerns.

In addition, the patient may change his or her mind. I have seen this happen frequently in inpatient medical units. A patient who is frightened may suddenly terminate the original "do nots." The care provider needs to be aware of this tendency to revise one's wishes as death draws near as well as the likelihood that family members' wishes may conflict. For example, an 89-year-old woman is transferred to a hospital from a nursing home. She is incoherent, very sleepy, and unresponsive. Her advance directives only indicate that her four children will serve as her health agents if she is unable to make decisions for herself. Two daughters and a son meet with their mother's attending physician to review her medical history and assess her present condition. The doctor, seeking direction in terms of taking heroic, life-saving measures, asks the children which life-saving procedures and treatments they want placed in their mother's medical chart. The children decide that she will receive resuscitation and antibiotics for any disease whose course could be reversed. At one

The care provider must be aware of the potential difficulties that arise because a medical directive cannot cover all of the possible medical scenarios. This is why it is so important for the family to have prior conversations with their loved one and with the physician as well about the multiple provisions of an advance directive document.

point the mother becomes alert just long enough to refuse any artificial breathing procedures. She continues to survive for another week: sleeping, breathing on her own, and receiving fluids and small amounts of food orally. One day, she opens her eyes and says, "Where am I and what is happening?"

The woman spends the next 6 months at home with health aides, wishing she had died and never returned home. She's very angry with her children for enabling her to live. She can't walk, hates having "strangers" in her home, and fires and rehires her home aides every other day. After a brief period of being clouded, noncommunicative, and completely bedridden, the family meets and decides to add "DNR, no feeding, and no antibiotics" to the life support orders. However, a week after the family meets, she dies peacefully in her sleep.

Further problems with advance directives, cited by Cantor (1998), include the low percentage of patients completing the document, and the use of terms that are not sufficiently specific (terminal condition, significant recovery, and personal dignity). Studies reported by Cantor found that 598 of 688 advanced directive documents were uninformative and lacked descriptive elements that spelled out which life-sustaining measures will be withdrawn or not initiated as well as how this would be determined. An increasing number of advance directive documents provide the specificity lacking in earlier forms.

To help families decide what to do, Cantor (1998) offers an advance medical directive model which contains five categories of concern. (See Appendix B.) His model enables a person to "identify crucial personal values or considerations to be used in end-of-life decisions" (pp. 648–652). The profile provides the individual with a list of conditions and a rating for level of intolerability at which they do not desire to be kept alive. It helps people determine the levels at which feeding and hydration will be provided or discontinued. Additionally, each of the five conditions includes a description of circumstances under which the person wishes to be kept alive.

The five conditions for ranking the level of "intolerable indignity" from "intolerable" to "unimportant" are:

- Pain and suffering

- Mental incapacity

- Physical immobility

- Physical helplessness

- Interests of loved ones

This model also allows people to designate primary and secondary health care representatives, other family members to be consulted, living arrangements desired or rejected, and medical interventions accepted or rejected. Signatures are required from the patient, health care representatives, and witnesses. There is also a provision for periodic review. Although this model will not necessarily resolve all of the difficult decision-making problems that occur at the end of life, it is much more specific than earlier versions. For example, many advance directives now include the provision to terminate all life-support measures if the patient doesn't improve after 72 hours.

Creating an advance directive is a continuing process that begins when a patient's status first begins to change and continues along a continuum, adapting to patient circumstances and needs, until death.

In his discussion of the responsibility for end-of-life communication, Goodman (1998) states "the overarching goal of advance directives is to inform caregivers, family members, and others about preferences for end-of-life care" (p. 722). Goodman urges medical providers to initiate a discussion of options, values, concerns, and decisions rather than leaving the task to other staff members or expecting the patient to bring it up. He concludes that those professionals who resist these conversations have not had sufficient training in the areas of death, dying, and communication skills.

As discussed in Chapter 2, not all cultures view the decision-making process in the same way as many middle-class, Western families do. As Koenig (1997) points out, bioethics as taught in the United States stresses the Western values of patient autonomy. She indicates that discussions regarding the continuation or cessation of aggressive treatment with a patient and family may require a translator who is sensitive to the ethnic and cultural mores of that family.

In some cultural traditions, family members do not share the extent of the disease and the fatal nature of the diagnosis with their loved one. Either family members make the decisions for the loved one or the decisions are left up to the medical staff, with the assumption that all will be

Care providers must familiarize themselves with advance directives; ascertain whether the dying person has completed an advance directive, whether the family is aware of its existence, and if the document is up to date and still viable. If family traditions allow, a frank discussion of these issues should take place. The family communication process is of paramount importance. The advance directive should never supplant this needed interaction (Goodman, 1998).

Care providers working with such families must facilitate the sharing of diagnoses, prognoses, and treatment options within a dual context: best ethical practices and the patient's cultural traditions. Advance directives, in concert with family traditions, may need to be written in both English and in the patient's native language.

Care providers can help families with a dying loved one by understanding the family issues and dynamics, being sure that the needs of all family members are being considered, and helping all to maintain the dignity of the ill person.

done to prolong the life of the patient. In these cases, medical information is not easily conveyed because of language and communication barriers.

# ☐ Conclusion

We have discussed chronic and terminal illness, the nature of the dying process, the needs of the dying patient and family, bioethical considerations, and ways to say good-bye. We maintain that the dying person is a bereaved person as are his or her loved ones. The losses that occur daily cause the family to rewrite the narrative of their lives constantly. Terminal and chronic life-limiting illnesses and disabilities have an extraordinary effect on family members who view themselves as different from other families and in some cases restricted in their lifestyle options.

In Chapter 9 we will focus on the hands dimension of the Exquisite Witness care provider by furnishing a review of both general supportive and specific clinical interventions for helping grieving people.

# CHAPTER 9

# Helping Grieving People
## A Continuum of Care for Healing

Bereavement is choiceless, but grieving is not.

Thomas Attig (1996, p. 32)

## ☐ Chapter Preview

- Introduction

- General Support Guidelines for All Care Providers

- Interventions for Helping Grieving People

- Clinical Tools for Trained Mental Health Professionals

- Clinical Tools for the Care Provider

- A Care Provider's Grief and Cowbells

- Provider Self-Assessment: The Four Tasks of Healing Exercise

- Conclusion

# ☐ Introduction

Thus far we have focused on the "heart" and "head" dimensions of the Exquisite Witness grief care provider: understanding both personal loss material and the human grief response. This chapter will concentrate on the "hands" dimension, that is, on general guidelines and the specific skills or interventions the Exquisite Witness grief care provider can supply. The interventions fall into three categories: (a) general supportive behaviors, (b) facilitating work on the four tasks of mourning, and (c) clinical tools. These overlapping categories of helping actions form a continuum of care for grieving people.

# ☐ General Support Guidelines for All Care Providers

How can we, as unique human beings possessing our own backgrounds, culture, and skills, help grieving people? Let's first look at some general suggestions for providing care that can be used whether you are feeding a dying grandma ice chips, listening to a widow's pain, or helping a bereaved father express his rage.

• Offer yourself.

• Be respectful.

• Become comfortable with silence.

• Be a skilled listener.

• Normalize practically everything.

• Avoid judgment.

• Take action! (Don't do "nothing.")

• Don't do everything by yourself.

• Keep your promises.

• Teach the "side by side" or the intermittent approach to grieving.

- Be sensitive to cultural, ethnic, and family traditions.

- "Bracket" your own Cowbells when they surface.

- Be aware of and respond to your own compassion fatigue.

## Offer Yourself

Remember that you want to make a caring connection with the person who is grieving. The amount of time that you spend with him or her is less important than the quality of time. Don't appear rushed; avoid looking at your watch. Be fully present—look at the person and listen attentively. Let the grieving person know that he or she has been heard. Know that there will be times, however, when there will be no conversation and you will simply be present in the silence. Never underestimate the value of human presence. Be sure that you have allowed appropriate time for the interaction. Stay aware of your own personal Cowbells that may have already been triggered by the person or the loss situation.

If appropriate, offer to perform a simple task, like picking up some dry cleaning, buying some groceries, or changing television stations. Even the smallest offer to help will be appreciated. This is a golden opportunity to connect with the grieving person. A little caring goes a long way.

Loyola

22

1.5

## Be Respectful

Let an ill person know that despite the circumstances, he or she is still a unique and valuable human being. Don't talk down to an ill person even if the behavior you observe has become childlike. If another person is in the room, look at and talk directly to the ill person when the conversation refers to him or her.

## Become Comfortable With Silence

Quiet time together can be golden. There is no need to fill up every moment with conversation. You can light a candle, set some flowers in a vase, listen to some music, or simply sit relaxed and wait for the person to speak.

## Be a Skilled Listener

To be truly effective as a listener, you will need to focus and give the grieving individual your complete attention. True listening connects the care provider to the grieving person in a way that can bring a sense of acceptance and healing into the process. Make eye contact, maintain an attentive posture, and match the volume and speed of your voice to the person you are addressing. Refrain from asking too many questions; let him or her steer the conversation. Nod and affirm, saying words of encouragement: "Uh, huh," "Yes," "Go on." Provide a sounding board by reflecting back to them the meanings or feelings you hear them saying. Grieving people will then be more willing to share their stories and express their feelings to you. People in grief and distress from illness want to be heard. They may need to tell their story over and over again, and sometimes the care provider is the only one who is always willing to listen.

## Normalize Practically Everything

Grieving people experience a wide range of emotions and thoughts: confusion, helplessness, hopelessness, a sense of dread, and a feeling of being stuck in a nightmare that never ends. They worry that they are going crazy. Often, they lose their appetite for food, sex, or entertainment. These reactions are all normal, and care providers need to normalize them. Normalizing is never done in a patronizing or belittling way. It is never intended to minimize or discredit a person's feelings or thoughts. It is used to assure people that what they are feeling is distressing but a usual part of the grieving process—it's what we humans do—and that the need to talk about the loss is something we all experience. Say things like, "It's okay to feel this way," "Of course you're angry," "Many people feel this way too," and "It's good to let those tears out." Grieving people need to be able to express themselves without worrying that they are burdening the care provider.

## Avoid Judgment

Try to keep the why or shoulds out of the conversation. If the person receiving care says, "It's hopeless," don't respond by saying, "You shouldn't feel that way." Instead, say, "It's not unusual to feel this way." Also, don't allow your facial expressions, body language, or gestures to give away any negative thoughts. For instance, be careful of the telltale raised eyebrow, which signals judgment. Instead, acknowledge the person's expressions of helplessness and continue to listen. Counselors may wish to gracefully and gently introduce a "let's count our blessings" conversation when the time is appropriate to do so. Keep in mind that we are entitled to every feeling we have; don't judge the person if he or she says something that strikes you as strange or provocative.

## Take Action! (Don't Do "Nothing")

Help people who are bereaved to become active. They can write obituaries, plan the funeral, create other mourning rituals, block out daily schedules, send acknowledgment cards, fill a vase with flowers on Mother's Day, invite special friends over to reminisce, make a donation in honor of the deceased, get into an exercise routine, or take a class. People grieving due to a serious or life-threatening diagnosis can go online to research the latest developments concerning their illness, make a list of all the medical specialists who are conducting studies or research on their disease or condition, and locate local support groups related to their illness or loss.

   Doing something gives us a sense of control and purpose; it's a perfect antidote for feelings of helpless despair. (Keep in mind, though, that there are times when grieving people welcome inactivity as a respite from being overextended.) In the case of perinatal loss, nurses in hospital obstetric units have increasingly "provided opportunities for parents to see, name, and embrace their deceased babies" (Leon, 1992, p. 7). Having an extended period of time to sing, hold, dress, and grieve before leaving the child gives parents a sense that they are saying good-bye to a physical being. Parents frequently will take a thumb-, foot-, or handprint; blanket; or identification bracelet as a needed connection to the deceased infant.

## Don't Do Everything by Yourself

Avoid making care a one-person show. Widen the circle of support. Identify social, spiritual, and health care resources. Locate family, friends, clergy, neighbors, colleagues, other care providers, and community services that can become part of the team. Clergy and congregational members can be invaluable sources of support during the grieving–healing process. If an individual experiences physical symptoms as a result of grief, a referral to the primary care physician is advisable. Don't try to fix everything; some issues may not require fixing whereas others can be put on hold. For example, it is not necessary to respond immediately to condolence cards. When the grieving person has both energy and inclination, writing cards can be both absorbing and a productive way to expend emotional energy. If the person is exhausted, the care provider can help to legitimize putting off this task until the individual is physically and mentally ready to do so.

## Keep Your Promises

If you make a commitment to visit, run errands, prepare a meal, or even make phone calls, do everything possible to keep that promise. This builds trust. People who are confined to bed usually look forward to visits from family and friends. When the anticipated visit does not materialize, the confined or ill person may feel sad, depressed, forgotten, or not important.

## Teach the "Side by Side" or the Intermittent Approach to Grieving

Few bereaved people can maintain grieving behaviors on a continuous basis. I encourage time-outs from grieving and prescribe activities such as taking a walk outdoors, working out at a health club, taking time out for a hobby, watching a funny video or television show, scrubbing the kitchen floor, and even "retail therapy" at a nearby shopping mall to temporarily distract the grieving person. Sometimes people need permission not to grieve—to do or think about something else. Most grieving people can learn to take brief time-outs before returning to their grieving. I have found that even those bereaved people who state that their grief is a measure of loyalty to their deceased loved one can gradually allow themselves brief time-out periods. These can become gradually longer intervals, so that the bereaved become increasingly adjusted to the realities of the post-loss world. (See the section in Chapter 3, "Margaret Stroebe and Henk Schut: Dual Process Model of Grief.")

# Be Sensitive to Cultural, Ethnic, and Family Traditions

An individual's cultural and family background influences the way grief is expressed, the way family members communicate their thoughts and feelings about dying and death, how one plans for end-of-life rituals, and how one makes decisions. It also affects expectations for the care provider's role. Care providers need to learn how each family interprets its own cultural, religious, and ethnic traditions. Sometimes all it takes is asking someone in the family. Don't be surprised to learn that a particular family does not follow the presumed pattern for their cultural group or that some family members do not agree with each other. The more information obtained, the better equipped the care provider will be to intervene appropriately to avoid making unproductive interventions that impede establishing rapport with the family.

# "Bracket" Your Own Cowbells When They Surface

"Ask not for whom the Cowbells toll, they toll for thee—and for me." Everyone grieves at some point in his or her life, and it is not unusual for our own Cowbells to suddenly surface—often when you least expect them. You may be in the middle of a conversation with a bereaved or a dying person and suddenly feel the urge to cry. This may be an empathic reaction to the other person's situation, or it may be your own Cowbells ringing. At moments like this, care providers should remember that they have the capacity to put personal feelings to the side, to bracket them. We do this by consciously assuring ourselves that we will address our own issues as soon as we are finished talking to the person we are working with. The next step is vital: We must talk to a colleague, friend, or someone to whom we can express our bracketed feelings. If we don't discuss and acknowledge our unfinished loss material, we may hear Cowbells ring the next time we're working with people who are grieving, and run the risk that our Cowbells may drown them out.

Students frequently ask if it is okay to cry when they are with a grieving person. This is very individual and should be based on the provider's comfort with sharing his or her feelings at a time of sadness. I have, at times, shed a tear when I was saddened by what was being said, and simply told the person that I was very moved by what he or she was telling me. A care provider should not overly emote to the point of making the other person uncomfortable. In these situations, strong emotions should be bracketed.

## Be Aware of and Respond to Your Own Compassion Fatigue

If providers find their own Cowbells ringing frequently, they may have reached a point of compassion fatigue or burnout. Accept that you have your own issues to deal with; that you may feel resentful or angry with a loved one, client, or with the situation; and that you may need someone to give you some loving care. This is normal, but it is also a signal that you need a break and some outside social or spiritual support or personal counseling.

# ☐ Interventions for Helping Grieving People

Interventions undertaken on behalf of grieving people can range from sitting silently with ill or bereaved people, listening and responding to them, offering specific suggestions, making referrals to various specialists, or engaging in clinical actions taken by professionally trained care providers. In the following, these interventions are grouped to correspond to the three roles a caregiver may assume: being supportive, helping with the four tasks of mourning, and using clinical tools.

## General Supportive Interventions for Family Caregivers

General supportive caregiving functions, sometimes referred to as the "chicken soup component of care," can be initiated by a person who desires to help an individual in grief. Activities may include taking care of everyday needs (shopping, cooking, cleaning house, running errands), listening, adjusting the television, reading out loud, and arranging for family and community resources. Family members, friends, and neighbors typically perform these care functions in addition to performing certain nursing activities as instructed by a physician, nurse, or other health professional, such as administering medications, providing massages, and assisting with bathing.

### *Family Caregivers Are Grieving People Caring for Loved Ones*

"When one is sick—two need help" (Well Spouse Association, 2009). Based on census data, over 50 million people (over a fourth of the adult population) serve as family caregivers for a loved one (National Family

Caregivers Association, 2002), providing about 80% of all home health services, estimated at a value of $257 billion annually (Arno, Levine, & Memmott, 1999).

Family caregivers include family members, friends, and neighbors who provide care to someone who is ill, incapacitated, in need of help, or may be dying. Family caregivers, whether serving as the primary (full-time) or as a secondary (part-time) caregiver, may also be grieving themselves, coping with physical and mental fatigue. Often they can feel depressed; overburdened by financial, legal, and medical concerns; unhappy to be relinquishing their own lives; and overwhelmed. Sometimes they may feel taken for granted. They, perhaps more than most, experience the "thousand deaths that occur before the actual death" (E. Kübler-Ross, personal communication, November 20, 1981).

Family caregivers also assist the ill with toileting, bathing, feeding, medicating, and other activities for daily living. They answer phones; greet visitors; cook; clean; shop; handle finances, insurance, and other business matters; interface with medical and other care providers; and worry, love, and grieve for what once was and what is still yet to be lost. They are nurse, counselor, and at times spiritual advisor. Their most critical role is not that of a "fixer" but rather one who will be there for the long-term, and will honor the individual and his or her illness and needs.

Caregivers must also be careful to talk and treat their loved one with respect and dignity. Talking in a patronizing way can be hurtful and reinforce behavior that is unnecessarily dependent and childlike. When loved ones are talking about their feelings, stay focused on their agenda and hold back your own for a while. Cultivate the art of just being there, in silence with no obligation to keep a conversation going. Practice the "ministry of presence" (Doka, 2010).

Affirm the ill loved one and give yourself permission to be able to sit with them and accept them if they cry or express anger, fear, guilt, or

To most effectively engage the loved one, the family caregivers may wish to enhance their own communication skills. Effective listening techniques can ease the flow of conversation and help ill people express their needs. Questions using the word "why" should be posed sparingly as this can be taken as judgment on the part of the loved one. Reflecting feelings ("It sounds like you are upset, or angry, or sad"), rather than asking, "Why are you so angry?" implies care and respect rather than criticism.

shame. These are all normal grief reactions, particularly if the medical condition causes physical deterioration. For many caregivers, the role can become a spiritual practice in which a level of connection with the loved one reaches deeply into their own awareness of life and its meanings. Being aware of the ever-present changes due to illness makes denial recede, which makes it possible for the care provider and ill person to talk at a very deep and honest level. When the end of life does come, the caregiver often feels as if he or she has not only survived a difficult, draining, and grief-filled experience but has also embarked on a spiritual journey that will forever change his or her own meaning of life in the post-loss world. One woman, a member of the Well Spouse Association, wrote that at some point after her man died, she realized that "supping from the table of his harsh life had the miraculous effect of flipping a switch, turning everything on its heels, and relighting all the colors of the universe in each bit of nature that surrounds me now" (Bekele, 2009, p. 1). (See Appendix A, Well Spouse Association.)

To be available as a family caregiver in the healthiest way for both the loved one and for oneself, family caregivers need to maintain their own physical health and psychological equilibrium.

## Guidelines for Maintaining Caregiver Physical and Emotional Health

- Avoid making decisions that can be made by the person being cared for; whenever possible, offer him or her choices. This not only reduces decision-making stress but also keeps the ill person involved in the process of care.

- Avoid doing things for the ill person that he or she can do now without help. Individuals being cared for may be able to feed themselves, use the bathroom, and adjust the TV on their own. This helps give them a sense of control and independence.

- Take care of yourself every day: eat regularly, exercise, rest, and get enough sleep. Take care of your own spiritual needs, attend religious services or have them at your home if possible, attend a workshop on a topic of interest, take a nature walk.

- Make sure the home is safe: Check any hazards regarding electrical appliances; secure medications, poisons, and household chemicals; and make sure bathing areas have grab bars.

- Have emergency phone numbers and important resources (legal, insurance, medical, financial, home repair) readily available.

- Encourage the drafting of a living will or advance directives. If the ill person isn't willing to do this, talk about what specific life-saving or life-preserving measures he or she wants and under what conditions should they be discontinued. Seek assistance from a nurse, hospice staff, or others who have experience with these issues.

- Anticipate future needs so that you will not be caught by surprise when health care or household needs change; learn about hospice or other available home health care services.

  - Don't do it all alone. Connect with social support systems, including other family, friends, clergy, hospice staff, and other local community services. Let people know specifically what you need done—shopping, repairs, transportation, housecleaning, a prescription picked up, other errands run, and visits with the loved one—so you can have a time-out.

  - Don't let your loved one's illness or disability overshadow your entire life. Honor and value yourself by finding ways to pay attention to yourself. Become your own advocate as well as that of your loved one. If your loved one is an older adult, check with your local office on aging for nationally funded respite programs.

## Guidelines for Visitors

Family caregivers play an important role in educating and managing visitor behavior. Many people who come to visit an ill or dying person are unsure of how to act; sometimes they irritate rather than soothe. To make visits more helpful, visitors should be apprised of all of the interventions for helping grieving people listed earlier, and need to be aware of the following specific guidelines for visitors, listed and explained next.

## Simply by Visiting, You Are Making a Commitment

Whether this is an ongoing activity or a one-time visit, you are devoting time to support the person you are visiting. The agenda belongs to the ill person being visited. If you are too absorbed with "doing a good deed" or putting in obligatory time, the person you are visiting may resent rather than welcome your presence.

## Look at the Person You Are Visiting

If you avoid eye contact, the person may conclude, "I must be too terrible to look at" or "I'm worse off than I thought." In addition to feeling insecure about one's physical appearance, the ill person may feel embarrassed. Stay focused on the person you are visiting and refrain from allowing every sound outside to pull your gaze away from him or her. This does not imply staring so intensely that the other is made to feel uncomfortable. Look away from time to time and then look back.

## Talk Directly to the Individual

Talking to another person in the room about the person whom you are visiting is discounting and hurtful. Additionally, using the "Royal We" (How are we today? Would we like our meds now? Are we ready for lunch?") is hurtful. Just converse normally.

## Make Physical Contact

Approach the person, whether he or she is in bed or in a chair, then, asking first to make sure that the person would welcome your gesture, ask to hold a hand, wipe a forehead, or massage a foot. Offer to bring a drink or food, rearrange pillows, take a walk, or take a wheelchair stroll.

## Bring Something as a Connecting Activity

Anything that interests you or that you know interests the other person can be used as a good ice breaker: a novel, magazine article, prayer book or book of psalms, scriptures, cards, checkers, chess, or other games to play. You can also pray or reminisce together.

## Do Not Persist in Probing for Medical Information or Express Concerns for the Person's Condition

Allow the person you are visiting to determine whether the conversation will include his or her medical information. Share your concerns with and get additional medical information from the family caregiver.

## Bring News of the Outside World

Talking about the neighborhood, larger community, or workplace gives the person a sense of ongoing connection with the outside world.

## Use Humor When Appropriate

Some people will appreciate hearing new jokes; others will want to read humorous books or watch funny videos or DVDs together.

## Keep Advice Out of the Conversation Unless Asked For

If you want to make a suggestion or give advice, speak to the family caregiver. Advice is not always met with enthusiasm; be prepared for this.

## Be Aware of Your Own Feelings and Respect Them

Visiting a very ill, disabled, or dying person can be a profoundly sad and possibly a scary experience. If you begin to feel overwhelmed by these feelings, say good-bye and promise to return. If possible, give a specific time when you will come back.

## Do Not Overstay Your Visit

Be sensitive to the person's level of fatigue and need for privacy. Keep your visit short and plan on returning soon.

# The Four Tasks of Mourning/Healing

*There are interventions listed in the following that require professional skills training. These are noted with an asterisk (\*).*

Worden's (2009) four tasks of mourning will be used as a structure for organizing care provider interventions that help the grieving person address each task for healing grief. A detailed explanation of the four tasks appears in Chapter 3. Trained volunteers, professional health and pastoral care providers, educators, workplace human resources and employee assistance personnel, funeral directors, school counselors, and police/fire/rescue workers can address the tasks. Worden's four tasks have also been adapted for application to workplace change and grief (Jeffreys, 2005).

Care providers should adapt the suggestions listed under each of the four tasks of mourning or in the clinical tools section to their own background and training as well as to the needs of the grieving person.

## Task I: Accepting the Reality of the Loss

As we discussed in Chapter 3, relying on denial enables people to absorb the reality of their loss and its consequences at different rates. When grieving people are ready to confront their loss as reality, providers must be particularly sensitive to their continuing need to strike some balance between facing the loss and avoiding it. Also, be prepared for the head–heart split: Some people intellectually recall loss events with little or no accompanying physical or emotional reactions because the head knows the terrible truth but the heart has still not registered it. Thus, the grieving person may act as though the loss had not occurred. The activities that follow are designed to reconnect the grieving person with the reality of the loss and facilitate intellectual acceptance of its irreversibility.

## Listening: The First Provider Action

Exquisite Witnesses will listen first and provide ample opportunity for the grieving person to tell the story of the loss. This is the beginning of a long process of registering the awful truth of a death, a diagnosis, a paralysis, or a layoff. If the grieving person doesn't want to talk, suggest that he or she write thoughts down in a journal or speak them into a recording device, or write a new eulogy and bring it to the next appointment to share with the care provider.

## Facilitating Insights Regarding a Terminal Illness Diagnosis*

When a terminally ill person addresses this task, the care provider can review, clarify, or summarize the patient's current medical information by asking some of the following questions: What is your understanding of your current medical condition? What specifically has the doctor or nurse told you? What do you believe your body is telling you? Who was with you when the doctor told you the diagnosis? What is the effect of this information on you? What do you believe the next steps are? Do you need clarification from a medical provider? Who do you believe would be most helpful for you to talk to regarding your diagnosis at this point?

## Revisiting the Time of Death*

To help a grieving client reintroduce the reality of the death or other loss condition, ask some of the following questions: How did you find out about the death? Where were you when you found out? What happened then? Who did you speak to next? Who made the funeral arrangements? Was there a viewing? How was that for you? Were you there when (he or she) died? Can you describe what happened? What was that like for you? Who else was in the room? Were you able to say good-bye? What did he or she look like?

## Recalling Rituals

Asking questions about the death-associated rituals can also help to reintroduce the reality of loss. You can ask: What was the funeral like? Where was it held? Who officiated at the service? What can you remember about the eulogies? Who gave them? Did you say anything at the service? At the graveside? What was the casket like? What was the burial like for you? Were you satisfied with the service? What did you like or dislike?

Here are some additional ways to help people cope with the reality of loss:

- Review the medical examiner's report,* death certificate,* or newspaper story.

- Review the guest book, condolence cards, memorabilia items, funeral expense invoice, and a catalog with a picture of the casket.

- Create a ritual on paper for a missed funeral; script the details from beginning to end.

- Create a guided imagery exercise* to recall a loss event, funeral, memorial, or burial. This can also be used if the mourner was unable to attend the funeral.

## Identify Changes in Life

To help a grieving person to gain a sense of what has changed as a result of the loss, ask these questions: What is different in your life now? What do you miss the most? When is the worst time for you? In what way does your body feel different now? What are some next steps for you now? How has life been different since you lost your job (or changed jobs or survived downsizing)?

## Summary of Task I

Grieving people who reconnect with the reality of the loss may experience an emotional release. This is normal grief reaction, and the griever should be told that his or her behavior is acceptable and appropriate. Note: Grievers who either do not appear to grieve or have a muted emotional release may be adapting to the loss more cognitively than emotionally (see Bonanno, 2004; Doka & Martin, 2010).

## Task II: Experiencing the Feelings of Grief

If you are a care provider seeing a grieving person for a counseling session, make sure that the room you are using is private, quiet, and soundproof. Have one or two boxes of tissues within easy reach. Allow ample time for the session so that you are not tempted to look at the clock or your watch; do not become internally preoccupied with what time it is.

The goal of the care provider is to accept whatever emotions at whatever level the grieving person is willing or able to express. To facilitate the further expression of grief, the care provider can make the following suggestions (see also "Externalizing the Feelings of Emotional Pain" section later):

- *Look at photos*—Photos are a good source of background information. Old photos can also provide opportunities for grieving people to talk about older losses and the childhood messages they received about the acceptability of expressing such feelings as sadness, anger, and fear.

- *Write letters**—Grieving people can be encouraged to write a letter to the deceased loved one, "Death," their cancer, their loved ones, the old job, the old home, the beloved pet, their doctor, or their body. The letter can be read aloud to the provider if desirable.

- *Write a history*—Some people have a better grasp of the reality of their loss after they put it in some kind of historical perspective. I have found that writing the history of a relationship that has ended or some other significant loss can help individuals express feelings they are unable to verbalize.

- *Write stories**—The grieving person can write a fictional account of his or her grief if this will help elicit feelings of loss.

- *Reading published stories can also help a person express feelings of grief*—I have found the booklet *Love You Forever* (Munsch, 1986) useful.

- *Drawings**—Grieving people who are more comfortable with images than words can be encouraged to draw about the loss and their life now. If the care provider has no training in the interpretation of drawings, then the grieving person can simply be asked to talk about the drawing. They can also describe how it feels to draw images representing the loss. Often, this allows them to verbally express grief feelings.

• *Create memory books*—Many grieving people want to collect photos, letters, travel, and other memorabilia belonging or pertaining to the loved one or loss. To remember and share feelings in this way almost always involves that others participate. Families can work on these together and share feelings while creating the album.

• *Read books about the expression of feelings*—Many books have been written for grieving people. *When Going to Pieces Keeps You Together* (Miller, 1976) is an especially good resource because it demonstrates how some people can heal if they allow themselves to express their most painful emotions.

## Task III: Adjusting to a Life Changed; Creating New Meanings in the Post-Loss World

### Acknowledging the Changes

Moving from couplehood to single status or parent to bereaved parent will require a reconfigured self-picture and a new way to be seen by others. Attig (2004) discusses grief not as a passive life process but rather as active and engaging. The assumptions and meanings of the pre-loss world need to be rewritten, and the provider can assist the grieving person with this activity (Neimeyer, 2001). Grieving people will typically experience pain as they adjust to their new circumstances. To help grievers clarify the extent of their losses and gain insight into the cognitive restructuring that must be accomplished, care providers can suggest the following: Compile a loss book* that will describe the post-loss world. Care providers can assist families to establish new traditions—especially associated with holidays and other significant times. Include answers to the questions:

1. What's different now?

2. Who am I now that I am no longer (part of a couple, the mother of a newborn baby, a worker in my old job, able to walk or breathe without life support, etc.)? The list can go on and on.

3. What do I need to learn or get help with in order to make my life work now? This list will help to identify new skills required for life in the post-loss world.

4. How are others doing it? Support groups composed of people with similar losses can offer comfort, acceptance, and an opportunity to learn from others how to handle many of the concerns that are part of their new identity. Surrounded by people coping with similar challenges, grievers can feel a sense of normalcy. (See Appendix A for a listing of support organizations.)

## Care Provider as Coach and as Teacher in the Post-Loss World

Care providers need to help grieving people become functional in the post-loss world directly or by finding appropriate resources to help with the task. This might entail:

1. Explaining the nature of the grieving process to grieving people.*

2. Acknowledging and normalizing feelings and behaviors that take place in difficult situations. Widows, for instance, often report that they don't feel welcome when they are with married friends. People who have lost their jobs may withdraw from social situations to avoid painful and embarrassing questions and conversation.*

3. Providing decision-making support for newly widowed parents. For example, advising a widow on managing her teenagers or making financial decisions. Other consultants, such as school or medical personnel, or members of the clergy can be useful additional resources.*

4. Facilitating bereaved siblings to reenter social activities. For example, encourage a boy who has lost an older sibling to join a little league team, Boy Scout troop, or school club or sports team.

5. Supporting people who have lost a mate to begin socializing. For example, coach a widowed man who wants to call a woman he knows to ask her for a date or provide contacts for "single again" support groups.

Grieving people who have lost a loved one may need the care provider's assistance as they develop a new picture of themselves in the post-loss world. Dennis Klass (2001) sees the development of a new way of being with other people as an important part of healing. Bereaved people may be very fearful and hesitant to leave their social safety net. When they do venture out into new settings, the care provider can help such persons by setting up "length-of-stay time limits" and a "back door" arrangement for easy departure if needed. For example, the care provider can suggest that a widow sit at the back of a religious service near an exit, or that she go to a party for only an hour, or take her own car so that she can leave when she wants to. Remember to respect people's own timing when they begin to reenter social life. For example, I have counseled bereaved older widowed persons for several months before they were ready to join an adult community program. Once they joined, they became active participants in the program; some found partners and even remarried.

Care providers may also seek out other resources—faith communities, educational and recreational programs—to help with the transition.

Some men and women desiring to reenter the social dating world may need fashion advice, information about activities, or opportunities for meeting others. The road back to social functioning in the post-loss world may be slow with many stops, starts, and regressions. Grieving people are creating a new narrative for living and this takes time. For many, a gradual reentry to outer society beyond the safety and comfort of their inner social support circle is the least threatening approach.

## Additional Resources

- Books can be a great source of help for grieving people as they struggle with relearning the world and reinventing themselves. I particularly recommend *A Grief Observed* by C. S. Lewis (1961). This nonfictional account of untimely death recounts how the author and his wife were able to foresee his life without her and how he could bring their happiness together into his future after she died. In *When Bad Things Happen to Good People*, by Rabbi Harold Kushner (1981), the author tries to reconcile his earlier concepts of God with a new notion of God's role in tragedy.

- Drawings* can help a grieving person envision his or her new life. I suggest the "past, present, future" drawing. Ask the person to divide a piece of paper into thirds. Panel one depicts life before the loss occurred. Panel two depicts life now since the loss occurred. Panel three represents the life the person desires in the future. Another helpful activity is to make a drawing of what steps the person feels he or she needs to take to achieve their desired future. Whatever form of artwork is used, have the person describe what it is he or she has drawn, how they feel about the material, and how the drawings contribute to a sense of how they would like their life to be in the post-loss world.

- Spiritual resources that come from a grieving person's faith can help that person place a tragic loss experience in a spiritual context, and give it meaning which that person can then carry into the post-loss world. When appropriate to the client's spiritual beliefs, care providers can refer a grieving person to a member of the clergy or a spiritual director for additional help.

- Setting goals for the future can help a grieving person focus some energy on what's ahead rather than on what's behind. If a person is unable to generate goals, suggest meditation, relaxation, guided imagery, and story-making exercises, such as creating a fairy tale of your own life. These techniques can help a griever visualize and generate a sense of life's future possibilities.

- Training and education can help a grieving person who feels ready to move on. There are many workshops on grief, loss, trauma, and bereavement open to the public sponsored by hospice, Bereaved Parents of the USA, The Compassionate Friends, AARP, religious organizations, funeral establishments, the Red Cross, regional offices on aging, and other community organizations. Having an intellectual understanding of human grief can provide a grieving person with a sense of control and demystify his or her own grief reaction.

## Task IV: Reconfiguring the Bond With the Lost Person or Other Loss

The goal of this Task IV is to learn how to maintain a bond with a deceased loved one while reclaiming life in the post-loss world. This involves realizing that the bond must be altered to fit the new reality, but that it can still exist. A grieving person needs to think, "Though the image of my loved one is always with me and while I hold on to the legacy of values we shared, I don't expect him or her to be physically present as a living bond-mate."

I suggest that most people who are grieving create a new kind of bond with their deceased loved one—a spiritual bond—or one that creates a new image of the deceased loved one. This new bond should define the loved one as gone but still available internally to the grieving person in his or her thoughts. In this way, the griever can feel a continued connection to the loved one in the post-loss world. Care providers can help to facilitate this transition by:

1. Asking questions* to uncover the grieving person's relationship to the ill or deceased loved one:

   • "How do you relate to your loved one now?"

   • "Do you ever find yourself talking to her or him?"

   • "When or under what circumstances do you talk to her or him?"

   • "How do you feel about doing this?"

   • "How does this affect your life?"

   • "What gets in the way of being able to have an inner conversation?"

   • "What rituals or ceremonial activities can help you feel connected to your lost loved one or to whatever you have lost?"

2. Dealing with unfinished business* with the deceased loved one that may prevent the formation of a continuing bond. The provider can help the griever recall memories—both positive and negative—concerning the deceased.

   To elicit positive memories, use family photo albums, have the person write an autobiography, or create an annotated timeline highlighting key moments in the deceased person's life. Help the grieving person to verbalize what he or she wants to thank the loved one for, and to articulate what legacy or values will be carried forward into the postloss world.

   Negative memory recall* may also need to take place to achieve a sense of catharsis. To help grieving people identify the hurt or angry feelings, upsetting events, or other unfinished or unpleasant business, suggest that they write a letter, make a list on a chalkboard or flip chart, draw a picture, talk out loud to the deceased (empty chair), or use guided imagery.*

**Note:** The grieving person may find it traumatic to relive unpleasant memories associated with the deceased individual. The care provider should be prepared for the possibility of a strong emotional release and must be especially careful with individuals who are too fragile to handle traumatic memories. Some grieving people may need additional time to feel safe enough to recall negative memories and some may lack sufficient mental health. *Individuals who show features of posttrauma stress should be referred to a professional skilled in this area.*

Care providers will need to be skilled in such externalization techniques* as the "empty chair," role-playing, or psychodrama. (The following section on "Externalizing the Feelings of Emotional Pain" provides further details.) They can also ask questions such as "What is still left over?" "If your loved one were in that chair, what might you say to her?" "What might she say to you?" If the grieving person feels awkward about having a conversation with someone who is not there, the care provider can ask, "What would you say to him or her in a letter?" or "Would you feel comfortable sharing this letter with me?" It can also help to have the grieving client imagine and say what he or she believes the deceased loved one might say in response to the letter.

1. Help the grieving person(s) say good-bye.* If a good-bye never took place or if it was insufficient, this lack of closure could block the formation of an altered (spiritual) bond with the loved one. In saying good-bye, the grieving person can incorporate into his or her own life, special traits or values that the deceased held dear. (See Exercise 5, "Saying Good-Bye" later in this chapter.)

2. Discuss the ways that the loved one continues or could continue to be mentioned in family rituals, conversations with family and friends, religious services, memorials, tree and garden plantings as well as memorialized through donations to charity.

3. Help the grieving person envision the future through drawing.* Using the "past, present, future" drawing technique, encourage the person to depict in the future panel the type of spiritual bond he or she would like to establish with the deceased. When people have difficulty imagining such a bond, I sometimes simply ask the individual to say whatever comes up about the deceased.*

The work of addressing each of the four tasks may continue throughout life. Some people need far less of one area than another; others may address multiple areas simultaneously. When individuals seek and obtain grief counseling or grief therapy from mental health professionals, clinical tools exist that can be used as part of the practitioner's tool kit. These are explained next.

# ☐ Clinical Tools for Trained Mental Health Professionals*

Sometimes grieving individuals need to receive grief counseling or therapy from mental health professionals who employ a variety of clinical interventions. These are behaviors that require (a) either technical training for volunteers from a sponsoring organization, for example, hospice, hospital pastoral care department, community crisis center; or (b) professional provider training or continuing education programs for physicians, nurses, mental health professionals, funeral directors, or clergy. The following clinical tools* include methods for gathering needed information and techniques for trained care providers engaging in counseling or therapy. These can be used with individuals who are having difficulties with normal grieving and with those experiencing complicated grief.

## Grief Assessment*

Part of the information gathering process should include an assessment of the level and nature of grief. This can be done very informally by simply using the following grief assessment.

### Death Inquiry*

Learn the circumstances of the death

- "Tell me what happened."

- "How did you find out?"

- "Was this death expected?"

- "Were you there at the time of death? Describe what that was like for you."

- "Tell me about the funeral. How was this for you?"

- "Did you get a chance to say anything before he or she died?"

- "Did you see the body? The burial? Cremation ashes?"

## *History of the Relationship With the Deceased\**

Determine the level of ambivalence and dependence the person had with the deceased:

- "How would you describe life with your loved one?"

- "What were the positive aspects of the relationship? What were negative aspects?"

Determine the nature and extent of unfinished business with the deceased: "What about this relationship remains unfinished?"

**Note:** See caution about negative memory recall in the previous section concerning Task IV.

Postdeath History**\***

- "What has been happening since the death?"

- "How have things been between you and your family?"

- "How have people been reacting to you since the loss?"

- "How have things been at work, at school, and so forth?"

Nature and Extent of the Current Grief*

- "How would you describe your grief?"

- "Are there times when you cannot stop thinking about your loss?"

- "When is the hardest time for you?"

- "To what extent have you been able to return to usual activities?"

- "What physical symptoms are you experiencing?"

- "How have you been sleeping?"

- "What has your appetite been like?"

- "How would you describe your energy level?"

- "Have you been having any difficulty in concentrating?"

- "Are you experiencing memory difficulties?"

- "What helps you feel better?"

- "How do you feel about yourself?"

- "Have you had any suicidal or homicidal thoughts?"

- "Do you ever have hallucinations—see, hear, feel or smell things that are not here?"

Available Support System and Resources

- "Who in your family or social network can you turn to?"

- "What organizations or community groups can you turn to for support?"

- "Do you have a religious or spiritual community to support you?"

- "In what way does your own religious belief system or life philosophy help you at this time?"

## *Cultural and Traditional Background Information*

The care provider needs to learn as much as possible about the grieving person's religious, spiritual, and cultural background so that the provider can minimize any of his or her behaviors that may conflict with this information. Insight into the family's traditions may be obtained during the assessment session or from family, friends, and neighbors.

Special Considerations Regarding Ethnicity, Religion, and Culture

- "Tell me about religious, ethnic, cultural beliefs or traditions and how these influence funeral, memorials, burial/cremation, or other rituals."

- "To what extent does your family observe these rituals?"

- "Can you identify some books I can read that will educate me about the cultural requirements of your tradition?"

- "Who can I speak with to learn more about your traditions to facilitate our work together?"

- "What are your beliefs regarding an afterlife?"

- "How does this affect the way you maintain a continuing relationship with your loved one?"

Loss History*

- "What other losses have you thought about since you sustained this loss?"

- "Is there unfinished business or other issues from these previous losses that need to be addressed? What are these issues?"

- "How did you and your family address each of these prior losses?"

- "May we make a list of these losses and any other issues in your past history?"

- "If you think of old losses after you leave today, please jot them down and bring them in next time."

## Suicide Risk Assessment*

Care providers usually develop their own individual methods for eliciting information on suicide risk. The goal is to determine the extent of the suicidal ideation and the specificity of the plans for self-destruction. Does the survivor have a history of prior attempts or a diagnosis of major depression or bipolar disorder? The existence of prior attempts or major depression can elevate the risk factor for suicide. (You can adapt the following assessment items to your own style of inquiry.) Take every comment related to killing oneself, not wanting to live, and reunion ideation (wanting to die to be reunited with deceased loved one) seriously.

- Ask how often this thought comes up.

- Ask if they ever think about how they would do this.

- If they have no current plan or ideas about methods, let them know that you take this very seriously and you wish to stay informed about these thoughts.

- If they indicate that this is a serious option, you can set up a contract according to which you will be immediately notified should they feel the impulse to attempt suicide or harm themselves. However, there is no real evidence for this as a deterrent to suicidal ideation or attempts (Jobes, 2006).

- If they refuse or if you doubt their sincerity, notify a family member.

- If you believe that their acting on suicidal impulse is likely, detain the person and call 911 or other predetermined emergency support.

- Once a person has given some indication of suicidal ideation, the provider should keep current regarding any changes in the risk level. Note: Jobes (2006) proposes a collaborative assessment and management of suicide approach in which a suicide assessment form is used for tracking and working with the suicidal person.

- Determine to what extent the person is engaging in substance abuse; overdosing is frequently used in suicide attempts.

- If you have limited experience dealing with suicidal risk situations, refer the person to a mental health professional who has the requisite experience.

# Externalizing the Feelings of Emotional Pain*

## *Externalization Defined*

Externalization, a process developed for use in workshops conducted by the Elisabeth Kübler-Ross Center, is an emotionally expressive modality designed to facilitate the emotional release of stored unfinished business (Cowbells). Generally, people externalize to the extent that they feel safe in their environment and with the provider facilitating this process. It has theoretical origins in such analytic concepts as regression and abreaction, and uses aspects of techniques used in psychodrama, gestalt psychology, primal scream therapy, affirmations, saying good-bye, inner child work, and physical exercise release.

**Note:** The externalization techniques used in the former Kübler-Ross Center's Life, Death and Transition workshops require specialized training by experienced facilitators. Licensed mental health professionals can do the limited version of this process described next.

The care provider needs to feel comfortable with the information expressed by the grieving person; otherwise, the grieving person will feel inhibited. Providers working with grieving or dying people and their families must pay attention to their own personal unfinished business to be able to attend to their griever's agenda rather than to their own. The grieving person needs to know that the provider can handle his or her anguish and won't be judgmental or flee from the distress of hearing emotional pain.

Care providers also need to keep in mind cultural variations that affect how comfortable a person may be when sharing intimate feelings. The provider should find out as much information as possible regarding cultural norms before offering the grieving person an opportunity to externalize feelings. When in doubt, consult with a colleague or another resource person. Again, providers are cautioned with regard to ensuring the safety of persons who may be retraumatized by the recall of negative material. In my years of using externalization with grieving people, I have avoided using these procedures with individuals who have DSM Axis I diagnoses—thought, mood, and anxiety disorders. (See note in Task IV regarding negative memory recall.) When in doubt, seek consultation. (See also S. M. Johnson, 2002.)

## Grieving People Want to Be Heard

Grieving people want to know that you know how hurt they are. They need to know it's okay to feel and express all of their thoughts to you, even the ones they consider crazy. Your comfortable self, your good listener self, and your interest in their hurt and thoughts create the foundation for a caring, safe, and healing environment.

Here are specific suggestions for helping grieving people externalize feelings of emotional pain:

- *Be self-aware*—Care providers need to be aware of their own Cowbells and be available to help the grieving person release his or her emotions. This communicates trust and safety.

- *Secure the environment*—Make sure that the work area is private, soundproof, and that the risk of interruptions is minimized. Cell phones and pagers should be turned off.

- *Establish confidentiality*—Assure the grieving person that what he or she says is private and confidential, and will not be shared unless it poses a risk to the safety or life of the grieving person or of another person.

- *Time boundaries*—Clearly state the time boundaries of the session by saying at the outset, "We have one hour to be together this morning; if we need more time, we can schedule it." Avoid obvious checking of the clock or your watch.

- *Communicate permission to grieve*—Let the person know that this is a safe place and any feelings that come out are okay. You can say, "This is a place where people cry, express anger, and fears all the time." Make sure that tissue boxes and a waste can are placed within reach.

- *Be a skilled listener*—First listen, then listen some more. Never interrupt the flow of feelings or thoughts. From time to time, paraphrase the content of what the person has said and then reflect back the feelings you hear: "What I hear you saying is ..." "It sounds like what this means to you is ..." "This is so very sad for you." "It sounds like you have so much pain." "I hear the pain behind those tears." This way, the person knows that he or she has been heard and feels acknowledged.

- *Going further\**—Once the professional mental health care provider has established a good rapport with the grieving person, offer the grieving person an opportunity to express additional feelings by asking questions like, "What is still left over for you?" or "What would you still like to tell your loved one?" If words fail, ask the person to put his or her thoughts into a letter to the deceased, or begin to keep a daily "feelings journal," which can be brought into the session to discuss with the care provider.

These techniques can help address Worden's Task II, which is concerned with the release of the emotional pain of grief. However, it is the combination of affective release and cognitive restructuring (making new meanings for the post-loss world) that provides the basis for healing grief.

## Cognitive and Behavioral Approaches*

Once people begin to release their feelings through *externalization*, they need to address two critical cognitive issues: (a) to reconfigure their sense of identity, and (b) create new meanings and new assumptions for their new life. In other words, they need to answer the question: How do I make sense of this strange, new post-loss world and who am I in this world? The process of reinventing self and relearning the world is a major step in the healing process. It is through this process that the grieving person comes to a new understanding not only about the person who died but also about his or her prior assumptions concerning life that have been violated.

The point at which these cognitive issues are raised varies, and the care provider should take cues from the client's communication. When appropriate, the care provider can suggest that the grieving person begin to compare the realities of life before and after the loss. How the person made sense of the pre-loss world may not fit the post-loss world. The creation of a new self and new world meanings do not usually happen without some pain. For example, I worked with a bereaved mother who sobbed every time she took out the trash. "Am I going crazy?" she asked me. "All I'm doing is taking out the garbage, and I can't stop sobbing as I do this." I soon learned that this had been one of her dead son's chores. She wasn't going crazy. She was simply externalizing emotional pain while at the same time adapting to a new responsibility in her post-loss world.

When helping a grieving person adapt to the post-loss world by relearning his or her identity, the care provider can use the following questions: "How are people reacting to you now?" "What is this like for you?" Focus on discussions of how grieving people perceive other people's reaction to them. Locate the points of discomfort in the interactions. For example, friends and colleagues who are uncomfortable may change the topic, stay away, become very anxious and stumble for words, say hurtful things, press for too much information, or give unwanted and inappropriate advice. Assure grieving people that such reactions are typical, and help them create some responses to use in these different scenarios as well as how to avoid the situation. For example, if someone said to a widow or widower, "You should start dating," he or she can learn to say, "Thanks, I'll think about that," "I'll work on it," "I know you're trying to help, but I'm just not there," or "I really can't talk now, see you another time." Some grieving people just walk away and firmly say, "That's not helpful!"

A care provider's questions about the details of social interactions can also help a widow or widower establish a new identity as a single person. A griever's new identity can unfold in conversations with others. Seeing people in our lives react to us after a loss helps us realize that our self-picture is shaped by social interactions. People who have lost a life partner have a major investment in the identity of being part of a couple. What is it like to go to family and other social events as a single and not part of a couple? What is it like to attend a school function as the mother of a child whose father is dying? What is it like for a child whose parents are engulfed in caring for a dying sibling? When a significant relationship that helps us to define who we are is lost or is threatened, part of our self-picture is open to change.

To help in this process, care providers can ask:

- "What plans do you have for the house, the business, your daughter's wedding, or your family's vacation?"

- Ask the grieving person to talk about potential short- and long-term changes. These questions can help a bereaved person begin to think about how he or she will function without the loved one.

- "What's different for you now?" This question can initiate a discussion of how the post-loss world is changed and how the grieving person is adapting to some of the changes and not to others. All of these activities and discussions give the person an opportunity to talk about the new circumstances. Naturally, these discussions may be painful. One widow was calmly outlining the new skills she needed and the ways she would compensate for the emptiness she felt since her husband's death. Suddenly she began to sob and cried out, "No! No! I won't have him dead. I won't!" This is an opportunity for the care provider to facilitate additional emotional release.

- "Who was I? Who am I now? Who will I be?" The answers to these questions can be worked out over a period of weeks through drawings (past, present, and future) or writing exercises ("My Goals for the Future"; "My Autobiography Five Years from Now"; "The Fairy Tale of My Life"). Wherever possible, ask the grieving persons to include desired values and traits of their deceased loved one that will be helpful to them as they develop their new identity (Who will I be?). Often a discussion of the completed activities will help grieving people gain insight into the process of slowly adapting to the post-loss world and healing. A meeting of family members can be held to review a memory book, share feelings of grief, and discuss the deceased and the survivors' hopes for the future.

## Assistance for Further Facing the Post-Loss Reality

When grieving people are ready, they can be given various assignments to help them integrate their new understanding of what they have lost.

Some appropriate assignments include visiting the gravesite, obtaining family photos since the death, listing items of the deceased to be given away to family and friends, creating a memory book, including funeral memorabilia, gathering notes about the deceased from friends and family, and making plans to modify the loved one's room or closets.

A care provider can also suggest the following cognitive/behavioral activities:

- Write a letter to yourself about who you are now.

- Find examples in films and novels of people who experienced a similar loss and study how they coped in their post-loss world.

- Create a list of ideal beliefs about yourself that you want to make a reality one day.

- Complete the past, present, future drawing.

- Find a new hobby or activity that you enjoy that is not dependent on another person.

- Keep a record of positive experiences throughout the week.

- Schedule as many of the positive experiences listed above as possible.

- Make a list of tasks that must be accomplished that were formerly the responsibility of the deceased. See how many of these tasks you can do.

- Develop a list of organizations and people who can help support completion of the four tasks of mourning.

- Rehearse responses to people who are unaware of the loss.

- Learn to use relaxation and meditation techniques.

- Compose a list of things to be grateful for.

## Dealing With Guilt

Elements of "guilt are typically present in each mourner's bereavement experience" (Rando, 1993b, p. 479). Family caregivers and other family and friends of ill and dying people also commonly experience guilt. In certain situations, guilt may be so intense and complex that it becomes debilitating, contributing to a level of dysfunction that complicates the mourning process. This will be addressed further in Chapter 10.

Often, bereavement guilt is related to the grieving person's care-giving role. People say, "I should have brought hospice in sooner and reduced his or her suffering," "I never should have put Mom in that nursing home," "We should have gotten another medical opinion," "I didn't visit her enough," "I wasn't there when he died," and "I didn't call 911 soon enough." Other comments about guilt relate to the relationship or activities taking place just prior to the death: "I wasn't such a good son," "I failed my parental job description," "I was so mean to my brother," "I never should have allowed her to go out that night," "We fought all the time and now ..."

## *Regrets, Recriminations, and Self-Condemnation\**

Typically, regrets, recriminations, self-condemnation, and many should haves and shouldn't haves are part of the typical guilt conversations grieving people have. What they have in common is the feeling that "I didn't do it right; I wasn't good enough." Many times, guilt is a way of trying to extract some meaning from a situation that resists meaning making. By engaging in self-attacks for the perceived or real failures, the grieving person has a basis for explaining why this terrible thing happened. Some mourners feel strongly that the death or other loss is part of their own punishment for past misdeeds or sins. Some guilty feelings can arise simply because the grieving person survived although another person died.

The care provider needs to be aware of the pervasiveness of guilty thoughts and comments, and allow them to be expressed at least initially without challenge. However, although guilty feelings should not be aggressively confronted, they should not be minimized or validated. I have found that guilt often dissipates over time if the care provider is a skilled listener and can normalize the feelings. For example, a care provider can say, "Guilt is something I hear a lot of the time. I hear what you are saying and want you to know that for many people this is part of the grieving process."

If the grieving person was actually involved in the cause of death through negligence or poor judgment (failure to adequately supervise a child, reckless driving, etc.), they may need special help from a qualified mental health professional.

Here are some general guidelines for dealing with grieving people who feel guilty*:

- Listen and respect the need for expressing these feelings. Let the guilty feelings be expressed fully.

- Normalize the feelings when appropriate.

- Do a reality test if guilt persists by asking: Do the medical facts support your beliefs? Does the police report support them? Does a review of the positive aspects of the relationship support your guilt?

- Use self-forgiveness as a way of enabling a grieving person to acknowledge the imperfection of being human. This will also allow the grieving person to see that he or she can coexist with the sad memories of the cause of death. (See the next section "Forgiveness as a Healing Tool.")

- Offer the possibility of spiritual and religious guidance in order to confess, do penance, or achieve atonement for perceived failings.

## Forgiveness as a Healing Tool*

"We ask for and offer forgiveness ... because we no longer wish to carry the load of our resentments and guilt" (Levine, 1987, p. 90). Asking for and granting forgiveness frees the grieving person from negative material that has resisted release. The act of forgiveness is a way to alter the ties to a living or spiritual bond. It is an important part of saying good-bye and letting go of what was. Any unfinished business—resentments, frustrations, hurts, and other negative material—can be released like an "unfinished symphony" through the practice of forgiveness. According to Byock (1997), "The resolution of unfinished business can form the basis of new beginnings and a continued bond with the loved one" (p. 160).

According to a recent study, a 4-week forgiveness therapy program "demonstrated psychological benefits for elderly terminally ill cancer patients and thus may be an appropriate addition to the treatment plan for terminal cancer patient" (Hanson, Enright, Baskin, & Klatt, 2009). Anger was reduced, hopefulness returned, and the quality of life improved. These changes complement the goals of palliative care. In some cases, old hurts from family conflicts that had been carried for years were released.

Forgiveness allows the individual to move from a position of resentment to one of diminished anger toward the perceived wrongdoer (Cosgrove & Konstam, 2008) on his or her own terms. In their study comparing forgiveness interventions using Worthington's REACH model with a muscle relaxation stress reduction exercise, Wade, Worthington, and Haake (2009) found "no discernable differences among the several treatments" (p. 149). However, all of the interventions did promote a reduction in nonforgiveness. The clinical recommendations support the use of clinicians' existing skills to help clients work toward forgiveness rather than use only a structured forgiveness program (Wade et al., 2009, p. 150).

Eckstein, Sperber, and Shanon (2009) point out that forgiveness is an important theme in many religious belief systems. They cite material from the Christian Bible, Jewish Rabbinic texts, the Koran, and the Bhagavad Gita as containing forgiveness as a recurring theme for raising spiritual consciousness, releasing sin, and expressing love.

Candace Pert (2006) has described the neurobiological consequences of nonforgiveness—holding on to resentment, hurt, anger, and its other toxic features—stating, "Once you forgive someone, that shift penetrates all the way down to the cells of your immune system" (p. 146). She believes that *positive affirmations* can relieve guilt and depression, and promote self-forgiveness (p. 147). This is an important clinical procedure for working with grieving people who are dealing with guilt, regret, and self-blame for a loved one's death.

The openness to and initiation of forgiveness does not condone the negative behavior that has caused pain and damage. Forgiveness is directed to the actor but not the act. The wording is personal and can be descriptive or general: "I forgive you or I ask forgiveness for any negative acts that have had a toxic effect," or "I forgive you or I ask forgiveness for (insert specific negative acts)." Forgiveness can be granted for either acts of commission or omission in each category. The wrongdoer does not even have to be present for forgiveness to be granted. In addition, there are three conditions under which forgiveness can be granted. It can:

1. Be given to another person who has caused pain or injury.

2. Be requested from another to whom we may have caused pain or damage.

3. Be given to oneself.

The notion of forgiving oneself should not be overlooked. People who cling to guilt and are unable to heal can lighten their load by forgiving themselves and allowing love to flow to the self. As the Hebrew sage Hillel said, "If I am not for myself, who will be for me? If I am only for myself, what am I?" The Buddha said, "There is no one in the universe more deserving of love than oneself."

## Saying Good-Bye as a Healing Tool*

Many people believe that the ideal time to say good-bye is while the dying person can still acknowledge his or her loved one. Good-byes can be said immediately after a person has been pronounced dead or a week, a month, or even years later. The uttering of the word *good-bye* directed to the loved one who has died is the mourner's way of taking a step into the grieving–healing journey. I have often heard people say that good-bye is a shortened version of "God be with you."

Here's my story.

My friend had just slipped into a coma. He was dying after a long battle with lung cancer. His children were grown. His wife and children were sad and yet realistic about his imminent death. He had provided very well for them, both emotionally and financially, and they stood by his bedside waiting for him to stop breathing. About a half-hour later, after he'd lost consciousness, his daughter arrived at the hospital. She briefly visited his room before returning to the waiting area. She was terribly upset to learn that she had "missed" Dad in his precoma state.

I suggested that she say, silently or out loud, whatever she wished she had been able to say to him before he lost consciousness. She hesitated, looked at me inquiringly, and I said, "You can assume that Dad can hear you." That was all she needed me to say before she walked back into his room. About 20 minutes later she emerged significantly relieved that she had been able to say good-bye.

Since I had to leave, I stopped in my friend's room to say one more good-bye. He lay on his back, unconscious, breathing with great effort. I told him silently that he had done a great job for his family and that, because of the way he had handled his end-of-life phase, they were in good shape—very sad but all right. I said good-bye and told him that he didn't have to worry about his family and that he could leave anytime he needed to.

My office is 5 minutes from the hospital. As I came through the front door, the phone was ringing. His son-in-law told me my friend had just died.

Some grieving people may reject saying good-bye for their own reasons—they don't want to let go yet or simply feel it is unnecessary. This decision must be respected without any admonitions. Some grieving people reject the idea of saying good-bye because it sounds too final. Care providers can let them know that any phrase, such as "So long for now," can be used instead. The care provider can also suggest, "Say anything you want your loved one to hear from you now as a form of good-bye, as a way of completion for now. There may be other things to say to your loved one at another time (before or after death); saying good-bye does not have to happen just once."

When we say good-bye, it is a time to share what you have learned from the dying person and will use in your life. You can remember some pleasant times together and, if appropriate, offer or request forgiveness. Think of it as an opportunity to clear and free the heart so that both the dying person and the survivor can take the next steps in their journey feeling less encumbered. This can be done in person, or through meditation or prayer when a loved one is many miles away.

Saying good-bye is especially useful when family or other intimates have come after the person has died and are feeling guilty and regretful at having missed the last opportunity to talk to the deceased. Byock (1997) suggests a four-part good-bye message that contains giving forgiveness, asking for forgiveness, expressing love, and saying good-bye. Actually, this conversation can be held at any time. In this way, we begin or continue a process of coping with the reality of the loss or imminent loss, and initiate a continuing connection to the loved one.

As discussed earlier, care providers can also help family members at this time by suggesting ways to say good-bye and ways to give permission to the dying loved one to leave. This is often difficult. Many times, the family does not want to let go, and dying people are reluctant to say good-bye even if they are in pain, wanting to stay and protect those who will be left behind. If death is imminent and the family is willing, care providers can help the family understand that they can assist the dying loved one by saying things like, "It's all right to go whenever you are ready. I love you and we'll be okay." If the dying person has expressed guilt over leaving, such a statement by family members can ease the loved one's release and serve as a final gift.

## Saying Good-Bye Exercise*

Use Exercise 5 to experience saying good-bye in preparation for helping people who have a loved one who is going to die, has lapsed into a coma, or has already died. The activity itself can evoke strong emotions and is best done with another trusted person present. I usually recommend that students and trainees do as much as they are comfortable with and note in their journal the areas of discomfort, which should be discussed or worked through as part of developing the heart dimension of the Exquisite Witness care provider.

### EXERCISE 5: SAYING GOOD-BYE

1. Directions: Write the name of someone who you would want to say good-bye to if he or she were going to die or move away forever; or someone who has already died to whom you would have wanted to say good-bye.
2. Indicate any special times you shared together.
3. Think of this person's legacy in terms of the values or ideals you have received from him, or her and what you would wish to say by way of "thank you," "good-bye," or "so long for now."
4. Think of what you can say to forgive him or her for any left-over negative material if applicable.
5. Consider whether you'd like to ask this person for forgiveness.
6. What else might you want to ask or say to this person?
7. In what way do you need to forgive yourself for any unfinished issues?

With this person in mind, take some time to sit and meditate on whatever you're feeling and thinking. Then do some journaling, listing areas of discomfort, unfinished material that may require additional attention, and material that brings a smile to your face. The more a care provider can be open to this personal material, the less energy he will have to expend repressing it, freeing him to devote more energy to grieving people and to living in general. This material can be discussed with a trusted friend or colleague, spiritual advisor, or counselor.

## The Use of Rituals for Healing

Technically, "a ritual is a specific behavior or activity that gives symbolic expression to certain feelings and thoughts ... individually or as a group" (Rando, 1984, p. 105). Rituals are taking place all around us all the time. Rituals can be a one-time occurrence (a moment of silence) or a repeated event (memorial candle lighting); they can be as simple as observing a moment of silence before a meal. We frequently hear a wedding officiant acknowledge deceased individuals who will be "part of this special time as we bring them into our minds and hearts." At other times, we light a candle, plant a tree, place flowers at a grave, place a highway religious symbol, make a donation in someone's name, place a notice of remembrance in the newspaper, create a memorial foundation or scholarship fund, have a fundraiser for a special cause, organize a food drive, or have a benefit performance "in the name of ...." We tell grieving people "don't do nothing." Doing nothing invites helplessness and despair.

Some death- and mourning-related rituals are already in place thanks to our culture and religious traditions. Clergy members, funeral directors, the military, and organizations such as unions, societies, and other groups all follow proscribed rituals. Ceremonial activities at funerals and memorials, and the burial and disposal of cremation ashes may be preordained by custom and religious and legal requirements.

All of these rituals are designed to acknowledge and honor the death of a loved one, to maintain connection with them, and to give us a reason to undertake a useful action at a time when we feel most helpless. Although not everyone who is grieving finds rituals useful, most people depend on them as a lifeline in the early weeks and months of mourning.

## Holidays and Special Calendar Days

Special days such as Mother's Day, Father's Day, and anniversaries are appropriate and natural times for bereaved people to acknowledge their lost loved ones and maintain their continued bonds. Care providers can help individuals and families to plan for some ritual or ceremonial observance of this acknowledgment. Families can create artwork, letters of remembrance, memory albums, and collage posters.

When I was a child, Mother's Day was celebrated in part by dressing up in our best spring clothes and promenading on a broad avenue where we bought sweets from vendors. Adults wore a red carnation to signify that their mothers were still living. Those people whose mothers were dead wore a white carnation. Everyone had a carnation to wear and everyone acknowledged his or her mother's existence. Many of my clients mourning the loss of their mother found this simple ritual extremely useful when observing the first post-loss Mother's Day.

A holiday like Thanksgiving offers many opportunities for remembrance. This may not be as difficult as it may seem at first. Before the holiday, people attending the meal can be told that they will have an opportunity to talk about their blessings and to name whomever they are missing. A deceased loved one's favorite food can be served, a candle can be lit in remembrance, and a vase of flowers can be placed on the table in honor of the deceased. Sharing will help people recall the loved one's special role in the family. Remembrance, acknowledgment, and celebration of legacy are important ingredients in rituals. Each family will be able to create these to meet their own needs.

In addition to holidays, families have to cope with life-cycle events—graduations, weddings, and birthdays. These can be very intimidating. Some grieving people commemorate these occasions by visiting the grave, urn, or site of scattered ashes; singing hymns and other meaningful songs; and recalling and reminiscing about the loved one.

Here is a personal story:

"Happy Steven's Birthday," I heard my son Ronald say into the telephone. His brother Steven would have been 35 years old today, October 23rd. His older sister, Deborah, called earlier. Each year on his birthday, my wife and our two surviving children see or call each other to acknowledge the day. We repeat this ritual on November 23, the anniversary of his death. It is a simple ritual that acknowledges we are the family that lived through his illness and death. It makes me feel good to mark this special connection on these important days.

However, some grieving people avoid any overt rituals concerning their loved one. This is their decision and must be respected. In truth, the deceased loved one will probably be on the minds of those attending a life-cycle event such as a family meal, wedding, or graduation whether the person's name is mentioned or not. Some cultures revere and maintain contact with ancestors and find ways to bring the wisdom of those who went before into their lives. In this vein, we can acknowledge the values we have inherited from the deceased loved one by private meditation, prayer or through remembrances at a family gathering. Journal keepers can record this wisdom in their journals. None of these activities requires much time to plan or implement, yet they all maintain the continuing bond and bring the loved one into the post-loss world.

## Spontaneous Rituals and Memorials

Spontaneous rituals and memorials can be seen where a vehicle crash has taken a life. Crosses with flowers or ribbons dot highway median strips and roadways. Outpourings of flowers, cards, drawings, and photos covered the sides of fences, buildings, and sidewalks in lower Manhattan where the World Trade Center towers were brought down by terrorists. The Royal Palace and many other areas in Britain were deluged with flowers after the death of Princess Diana.

Many treasures and cards are left at the base of the Vietnam Memorial in Washington, DC. The wall is visited every day, and on Memorial Day hundreds of people attend the ceremonies. When I attended, I noticed that most of those surrounding me were middle-aged men in various uniforms identifying their branch of service and unit. Parents, wives, children, and friends of the men and women whose names were on the wall were there in great numbers, some silently moving through the postceremony throngs. Others, with red and tearing eyes, looked slightly dazed as they touched and stared at the patterns of names on the black granite surface—a surface shining with death. Piled at the wall were flowers and assorted other items. I saw boots, medals, letters, poems, pictures, and other articles of clothing and battle gear. Many of the surviving veterans of "Nam" greeted each other, caught up on back-home news, and parted with promises to "see you next year." Just before the ceremony ended, our attention was directed to the bugler, which led me to write this poem.

TAPS AT THE WALL: A RITUAL

Taps at The Wall
It tears into our hearts
And brings us into the memory.
I see men and women in various uniforms
With hands saluting the black granite tribute.
Gnarled, arthritic hands
And blotchy, wrinkled hands,
And young, sinewy hands,
Saluting the thousands who are not physically here.
But maybe, as we hear the final notes
Of that bugler's Taps,
I feel the Thousands from The Wall ...
Saluting back.
November 11, 2002

(© 2002, J. Shep Jeffreys)

## ☐ A Care Provider's Grief and Cowbells

As a final word, I want to remind care providers to consider their own unfinished business, which I call Cowbells and which psychologists refer to as countertransferential material. They need to address this so that it does not distract them from hearing and being available to the people they are trying to help.

I once worked with a woman in an abuse workshop who, as a child, had been repeatedly beaten by her mentally ill mother. In our session, she allowed herself to regress to that very young age and cried out, "Mommy, Mommy, I didn't do anything." This caught me in the heart and throat, paralyzing me. Fighting back tears and the desire to cry, I helped the woman return to her present age and, after drawing the session to a close, left the workshop area. As soon as I was alone, I cried and cried without any clear idea why this was happening. As I began to calm down, her little child screams tore through me again. This time, I recognized those painful, shrieking cries. It was Steven's crying out in pain as he underwent a bone marrow aspiration or a particularly painful lumbar puncture. I had swallowed my cries at the time, and for all the intervening years they were crying for release. I could not have continued serving as a facilitator in that workshop if I had not been able to work with a colleague and let the stored, suppressed pain out.

The Exquisite Witness care provider must be aware of personal material that has the potential for drowning out the person being helped. So much of our stored, unfinished business lurks below our level of awareness and manifests itself in camouflaged ways. If you find yourself unusually fatigued, sad, depressed, unmotivated, impatient or irritable with others, or reluctant to approach certain patients or make a home visit to certain families, you need to pay attention. If you keep sweeping these feelings under the rug you can run out of room and be on the road to developing a condition known variously as *compassion fatigue, secondary trauma, or burnout*. One of the best remedies is to seek out a colleague or another person who understands the work of providing care to bereaved, ill, or dying people, who can listen and be supportive.

When I work with health care staff that is vulnerable to provider grief, as I did for 12 years as the consulting psychologist at the Johns Hopkins AIDS service, I encourage care providers to have a staff buddy—someone who can be called when needed during or after the workday. At Hopkins, I also scheduled regular staff support groups, consulted with individual staff members as needed, we held quarterly memorial services for deceased patients, and scheduled several retreats. People working in settings in which people are always dying have their own denial systems penetrated repeatedly. Having a designated staff support person available on a regular basis for group support or individual consultation is well worth the expenditure for both patients and staff.

## ☐ Provider Self-Assessment: The Four Tasks of Healing Exercise

The next exercise will help you become aware of any current Cowbells in your life.

**EXERCISE 6: SELF-ASSESSMENT**

Choose an important loss in your life, possibly one you listed in the Past Loss Survey in Chapter 3. How would you assess your level of completion of each of the four tasks of grief (with regard to a personal loss)? Place an X in the appropriate location between 10 and 0 to indicate the degree of completion. (This can be done on a separate sheet.)

**Identify Loss:** _____

1. How real does the loss feel to you now?

   Very real; no doubt that it          Still mostly unreal
   happened

   10 ————————————————————————————— 0

2. To what extent have you expressed your feelings about this loss?

   Many feelings have been              Little or no feelings have
   expressed                            been expressed

   10 ————————————————————————————— 0

3. Rate your level of adjustment to life regarding the loss.

   Pretty used to life without          Not used to life without
   deceased (or other loss)             deceased (or other loss)

   10 ————————————————————————————— 0

4. How much of your inner picture of the deceased or other loss object is still the way it was before the loss occurred?

   My connection with deceased          Still can't let go of him/her
   continues as a new inner             or other loss as it used to
   image or spiritual bond, and         be; have difficulty forming
   this fits with my new life           new interests

   10 ————————————————————————————— 0

This exercise reflects how you feel about a particular loss now. It is not a clinical tool for diagnostic or any other clinical assessment purpose; it is simply a way of looking at yourself and beginning to think about what, if anything, is surfacing at a particular time about a specific loss. Use it to begin a conversation with yourself or another person. Give it some time and journal whatever comes up. You can revisit the loss and your ratings on the self-assessment at a later time to see what changes, if any, have occurred.

# ☐ Conclusion

I hope that you, as care providers and providers-in-training, will use the suggested interventions and adjust them to meet your clinical skills and needs as well as the needs of the grieving person. Add to them and share them with your colleagues. With this repertoire of activities, you will be a healing support for those who need your help, and you will experience a satisfying level of comfort as you do this sacred work.

While presenting the keynote address at the National Convention of the Employee Assistance Professionals Association in Baltimore, W. Mitchell, author and motivational speaker, pointed to his wheelchair with his fire-scarred hand and said, "It's not what happens to you; it's what you do about it." Sometimes, the grieving-healing process goes painfully off course. Care for people with special needs and those with significant grief complications will be addressed in Chapter 10. This will be followed by a series of case studies for practical application of assessment and intervention skills in Chapter 11.

CHAPTER

# 10

# Complications of the Human Grief Process

## ☐ Chapter Preview

- Behaviors That Signal Complicated Grief or Psychiatric Disorders in Bereaved Parents

- Conclusion

*Although this chapter is intended primarily for use by care providers with mental health training, all care providers can obtain some general benefit from the material for referral purposes, especially the section on the signs and symptoms suggesting complicated grief.*

# ☐ Introduction

This chapter will discuss how care providers can identify and address the complications of grief. It will also describe the various traditional categories of complicated grief and consider specific mourner conditions and loss circumstances that are likely to result in complicated grief reactions. Additionally, research identifying criteria for determining specific criteria for a diagnosis of prolonged grief disorder will be presented. This will be followed by a discussion of psychiatric disorders commonly associated with complicated grief. In its final section, the chapter will consider people who are coping with such traumatic death as suicide and the death of a child.

Most of the time, the human grief reaction is predictable: People's thoughts, feelings and behavior follow certain patterns. People who are grieving a loss can be expected to cry and be sad, angry, frightened, confused, or apathetic. They talk about their loss, yearn and sigh often, and may engage in various rituals connected to the loss. Grieving people can also be expected to be preoccupied with their distress during this period; they may have difficulty concentrating, remembering, and organizing their activities. They may avoid others or may need much constant social contact. They may be viewed as not being themselves, or of having many physical complaints beyond what they usually experience or express. Some may reject spiritual traditions; others will seek religiosity as an important source of healing. With time, most grieving people gradually heal and reclaim a life—not the same life, but perhaps a reasonable and functional life. Sadly though, not all grieving follows this pattern.

# ☐ Definition: What Is Complicated Grief?

Many terms have been used to describe grieving people whose grief is considered atypical, beyond the usual and customary boundaries of mental health within a specific culture. Atypical grief has been referred to variously as abnormal, pathological, complicated, traumatic, and prolonged; it is also known as complicated mourning. I will use the term *complicated grief* to describe the clients I have seen who present with grief that has gone on *too long*, with symptoms so *severe in effects* that *significant dysfunction* is created in the life of the grieving person.

Researchers estimate that about 80% of bereaved people are functioning reasonably well 6 months after sustaining a significant loss (Prigerson et al., 1997). This leaves roughly 20% who continue to suffer severe grief responses and extreme levels of dysfunction in various areas of their lives. These are people who are identified as having complicated grief (CG) or prolonged grief disorder (PGD) (Bonanno et al., 2002; Prigerson, Vanderwerker, & Maciejewski, 2008). If there are over 2.4 million deaths in the United States annually, and we estimate that each of these deaths leaves 5 bereaved people behind, then roughly 10 to 12 million newly grieving people are added to the ranks of the bereaved, which means that 2 million people are potentially at risk for complications of grief each year.

Grief reactions ripple through social groups, beginning with the deceased person's most intimate family members and moving into the extended family, the community, and sometimes to national and international communities as well. Think of high-impact tragedies such as the deaths of President Kennedy or Princess Diana, and of natural and human-made disasters such as the 9/11 terrorist attacks, tsunamis, floods, and earthquakes. People who witness these incidents or view media coverage may be at risk for complications of grief as well as for physical and psychiatric disorders (Zinner & Williams, 1999).

Although complicated grief occurs most often after the death of a person, I have counseled people who presented features of complicated grief due to separation or divorce, loss of a career or business, loss of their home, or the realization that they would never have their own biological children.

# ☐ Signs and Symptoms Suggesting Complications of Grief

Because research about the criteria for determining the presence of complicated grief is ongoing, care providers need to stay current in their reading.

How do we know when the ship of grief has been blown off course into complicated waters? Most signs and symptoms of complicated grief appear along a continuum from less severe to very severe (Bowlby, 1980). A recent study investigating the underlying structure of grief concluded that "pathological reactions might be best defined as a continuum with

Care providers need to use the paradigm for diagnosing the presence of complicated grief or prolonged grief disorder with the same caution that they bring to any diagnosis. There is no one-size-fits-all template. Nothing takes the place of a full, complete history, including a loss history. Clinicians should also seek consultation from specialists who work with grieving people, and "When in doubt—give a shout."

the most severe grief symptoms persisting for 6 months or longer at one end and with *normal* [emphasis added] grief at the other end" (Holland, Neimeyer, Boelen, & Prigerson, 2008, p. 190). I italicized "normal" to underscore the difficulty of saying, "This is definitely a case of complicated or prolonged grief disorder." Although there are specific criteria to identify and assess the presence of complicated grief (Jacobs, 1999), I have found that the distinction between uncomplicated grief and complicated grief is not always clear. Many variables, such as the nature of the death, the mental health history of the grieving client, the relationship with the deceased, the level of support as well as other unique circumstances can combine to produce what may be clinically viewed as "normal" grief reactions, and these may occur well beyond the 6-month interval.

Grief, complicated or not, comes in waves, more severe at times and less at others. When the bad times exceed the better times, when the griever finds little relief from deep distress or continues to behave in ways that cause concern to family and friends, care providers can suspect complications in the grief process. It is also not uncommon that people who seek non-grief-related help from a medical or mental health professional learn that their physical complaint or emotional disorder has its roots in or is being aggravated by unresolved grief material.

# ☐ Danger Signals for Complicated Grief

I have compiled a list of the most commonly agreed-upon signs and symptoms of complicated grief from several sources (Horowitz et al., 1997; Jacobs, 1993, 1999; Parkes & Weiss, 1983; Prigerson, Frank, et al., 1995; Raphael, 1983; Rando, 1993; Worden, 2009) as well as from my own clinical experience. When I see three or more of these signs, I am alerted to the possibility that there may be complications of grief. Seven of these signals, marked with an asterisk, should be considered *serious alerts*.

The care provider should gather this information when taking a history, by clinical observation or from reports of family, friends and/or other providers.

## Emotional Signals

- Continued irritability or outbursts of rage with violent implications.*

- Deep feelings of guilt, regret, and a self-picture significantly more negative than the predeath level.*

- Episodes of severe emotional yearning, pining, and mental searching for the lost person.

- Intense acute grief triggered by visual cues, musical sounds, and even smells that recall the person or loss event.

- High anxiety about the safety, health, and possible death of self and loved ones.

- Feelings of despair, hopelessness, and apathy about the future, which are verbalized as, "What's the use?" "Life will always be empty, meaningless, and lonely."

- High levels of stress and anxiety about day-to-day or future tasks.

- Frequent panic attacks, and intensifying or expanding phobic reactions to leaving the house, having visitors, talking about the loss, or being with others who knew the lost loved one.

- Deep depression and inability to function in daily life.

- Lack of any emotional expression regarding the loss.

- Inability to express any sense of feelings.

## Cognitive Signals

- Suicidal thoughts and/or plans to act upon the thoughts.*

- Severe mental disorganization including inability to concentrate or learn new information, and inability to recall previously known information.*

- Intrusive, distressing memories and thoughts about the deceased or lost relationship.

- Avoidance of discussion of the loss, and of all signs, symbols, and mention of death and death-associated activities.

- Rigid retention of lost person's space and all belongings, or immediate removal of all traces of the lost relationship.

- Feeling stunned, dazed, or disoriented.

- A sense of being dead or of not functioning.

- Major shift in personality style—introvert to extrovert or vice versa.

- Experience of ongoing numbness, alienation, and detachment from self and others.

## Behavioral Signals

- Self-destructive behaviors including self-cutting, substance abuse, workplace failure, burning of social bridges, and constant self-defeating comments.*

- Radical and sudden changes in lifestyle, shocking family and friends, such as relocating, changing jobs, dropping out of school, or divorcing.*

- Compulsive sets of repeated behaviors that interfere with daily living.

- Imitating the speech, dress, and behaviors of the lost person.

- Engaging in compulsive post-loss caregiving and/or replacement relationships.

## Physical Signals

- Physical symptoms that imitate those of the deceased.*

- Chronic physical complaints, such as gastrointestinal disturbance, muscular aches, headaches.

- Major disturbances in sleeping and eating—either too much or too little.

**SERIOUS ALERTS AT A GLANCE**
- Suicidal thoughts and/or plans to act upon the thoughts.
- Self-destructive behaviors including self-cutting, substance abuse, workplace failure, burning of social bridges, and constant self-defeating comments.
- Severe mental disorganization including inability to concentrate or learn new information, and inability to recall previously known information.
- Deep feelings of guilt, regrets, and a very low self-picture.
- Continued irritability or outbursts of rage with violent implications.
- Radical and sudden changes in lifestyle, shocking family and friends, such as relocating, changing jobs, dropping out of school, or divorcing.
- Physical symptoms that imitate those of the deceased.

# ☐ Measures for Determining the Presence of Complicated Grief

Problematic signals and symptoms alone may not necessarily indicate the presence of complicated grief. Deeply distressing and immobilizing grief may be quite normal immediately after the traumatizing loss of a loved one or the diagnosis of a terminal illness. To make a determination of *when* grief is complicated, three measures must be applied to the grief reaction (Jacobs, 1999).

1. The degree of *severe and devastating symptoms* reported by others or assessed by the survivor.

2. The *length of time* the symptoms have persisted.

3. The extent of profound and widespread *dysfunction* in the grieving person's life.

A mental health care provider typically makes this assessment, knowing that clear-cut answers are difficult to achieve. Providers need to weigh all factors that impinge on how a person grieves: cultural issues; personality features; and nature of the loss, loss history, and mental status. Care providers should always seek consultation from another professional if there is any doubt as to whether an individual is experiencing grief complications.

1. *Severity of devastating symptoms.* There is no simple formula for determining when grief becomes complicated. Behavior can vacillate between okay and not okay. The person can report having good days and bad days. Be on the alert for:

   - Profound immobilization

   - Disorientation as to time, place, and person

   - Failure to eat or otherwise take the necessary steps for maintaining health

   - Persistent, unrelenting, and severely distressing intrusive thoughts about the loss

   - Active suicidal thoughts and plans for completing suicide

   - Homicidal ideation and/or actions or threats of violence to others

   - Psychotic episodes during which the person is not in touch with reality

2. *The length of time of severe symptoms.* Severe symptoms alone do not necessarily indicate complicated grief. In some cases, signs and symptoms may persist for many months and even years; intermittent waves of acute grief triggered by internal memories, external cues, or for no apparent explanation at all can still be viewed as "normal" reactions. If the grief is uncomplicated, then over time, these waves occur less often and last for shorter periods of time.

   Immobility, disorientation, lack of self-care, and even some psychotic features (hallucinations, delusions) can be considered part of the normal grief reaction for days and even some weeks after a loss has occurred. If these persist, or if the bereaved cannot be left alone for fear that he or she will do harm to his- or herself or another person, then complications are present and medical assessment or hospitalization should be considered.

3. *The extent of life dysfunction.* The grieving person's dysfunction needs to be assessed in terms of his or her family and home life, workplace, community, and other social settings. Is the grieving person handling the customary activities of daily living, maintaining normal household

routines, and functioning in his or her occupation and in other social roles? Some people function better at certain times of the day and less well at others, a natural fluctuation that needs to be taken into account when determining dysfunction.

# ☐ Prolonged Grief Disorder

The concepts associated with atypically aggravated grief flow from the research and rich clinical commentary of Lindemann (1944), Bowlby (1980), Parkes and Weiss (1983), Raphael (1983), Rando (1993), Jacobs (1993, 1994), and Worden (2009). Over the past 15 years, a profile of criteria using some of the concepts presented by these writers has developed into a diagnostic syndrome called *prolonged grief disorder*.

Jacobs, Mazur, and Prigerson (2000) presented a set of symptom criteria for diagnosing a person with what was then termed *traumatic grief disorder* due to a death that partially overlapped with the criteria Horowitz et al. (1997) used. Prigerson (personal communication, October 2, 2004) has indicated that these criteria may be adapted by clinicians for use with other traumatic loss events such as terminal diagnosis and other life-limiting medical conditions.

Prigerson and her colleagues determined two categories of symptoms: (a) *separation distress symptoms*—yearning, searching, and excessive loneliness; and (b) *cognitive, behavioral, and emotional symptoms*—intrusive thoughts and feelings, numbness, disbelief, and loss of trust. The criteria include a 6-month interval since time of death (Jacobs, 1999; Jacobs et al., 2000; Prigerson & Jacobs, 2001; Prigerson et al., 1995, 1996, 1999, 2009). Impairment in functioning in various life spheres is included in the evolving criteria, which follow next.

---

## CRITERIA FOR PROLONGED GRIEF DISORDER

| Category | Definitions |
| --- | --- |
| A | Bereavement—Loss of a significant other |
| B | Separation distress—Yearning, longing, pining for deceased; physical and emotional suffering due to unfulfilled desire for reunion daily or to a disabling degree |

*(Continued)*

## CRITERIA FOR PROLONGED GRIEF DISORDER (Continued)

| Category | Definitions |
| --- | --- |
| C | Cognitive, behavioral and emotional symptoms—At least five of the following symptoms daily or to a disabling degree: |
|  | 1. Role in life confusion or diminished sense of self |
|  | 2. Difficulty accepting the loss |
|  | 3. Avoidance of reminders of the reality of the loss |
|  | 4. Inability to trust others since the loss |
|  | 5. Bitterness or anger related to the loss |
|  | 6. Difficulty moving on with life (pursuing new interests, friends) |
|  | 7. Numbness since the loss |
|  | 8. Feeling that life is empty, unfulfilling, or meaningless since the loss |
|  | 9. Feeling stunned, dazed or shocked by the loss |
| D | Timing—6 months should have elapsed since the loss |
| E | Impairment—Clinically significant impairment in social, occupational, or other important areas of functioning (domestic responsibilities) |
| F | The disturbance is not better accounted for by major depressive disorder, generalized anxiety disorder, or posttraumatic stress disorder |

*Source:* Prigerson, H. G., Horowitz, M. J., Jacobs, S. C., Parkes, C. M., Aslan, M., Goodkin, K., ... Maciejewski, P. K. (2009), Prolonged Grief Disorder: Psychometric Validation of Criteria Proposed for *DSM-V* and *ICD-11*, *PLoS Medicine* 6(8): e1000121. doi:10.1371/journal.pmed.1000121.

An "issue that remains under debate is whether this condition [complicated grief] can be clearly distinguished from other psychiatric disorders, such as major depression and posttraumatic stress disorder, with which CG frequently coexists" (Simon et al., 2007, p. 395). Another study found that the similarities between bereavement-related depression and

It is essential that *all* care providers be familiar with the signs and symptoms of complicated grief so that they can take proper clinical actions or make appropriate referrals.

depression related to other stressful life events substantially outweigh their differences (Kendler, Myers, & Zisook, 2008).

In my clinical practice, I have found bereaved people who also have a history of major depression, dysthymia, general and posttrauma anxiety disorders, phobias, personality disorders, and chronic medical conditions typically have significantly problematic grief responses. "Comorbid complicated grief appears to contribute to greater severity and poorer functioning in unipolar depressed patients and should be specifically addressed in psychotherapeutic treatment" (Kersting et al., 2009). However, some studies demonstrate clear separation between grief responses and depressive responses (Bonanno et al., 2007; Ogrodniczuk et al., 2003; Prigerson, Frank, et al., 1995). From a clinical standpoint, I find it useful to view these prior psychiatric and medical conditions as existing simultaneously or as a comorbid diagnosis along with prolonged grief disorder. Treatment planning must take both diagnoses into consideration and provide clinical attention to the preexisting condition as well as prolonged grief.

## ☐ Working With Complicated Grief Syndromes

Grief turns out to be a place none of us know until we reach it.

Joan Didion (2006, p. 188)

## Introduction

Clients typically do not present themselves as suffering from complicated grief. They are more likely to say: "I just can't seem to stop crying and thinking about my husband and it has been two years since he died." "I never have cried for my brother and he was my best friend. Is there something wrong with me?" "I have no interest in life anymore since my child died. I can't even enjoy my other children or my husband." "My neck aches and I am sure there is a problem with my stomach but my physician finds nothing wrong with me."

Complications of grief, as originally discussed by Bowlby (1980), Lindemann (1944), Parkes and Weiss (1983), Raphael (1983), and

Worden (2009) are divided here into three syndromes or categories seen in my clinical practice. The descriptions are general and should be modified to the unique needs of each grieving person. (See Chapter 9 for additional clinical tools and interventions.)

## Syndromes of Complicated Grief

### Chronic or Prolonged Grief

> I know why we try to keep the dead alive: we try to keep them alive in order to keep them with us.
>
> Joan Didion (2006, p. 225)

### Separation Distress

I define chronic or prolonged grief as an intense and persistent grief reaction that fails to reach some desired level of healing and adaptation to the post-loss world. This syndrome is characterized by sadness, ongoing sorrow, and preoccupation with and yearning for the lost person or condition, continued crying, depression, regrets, disorganized life, anxiety, inability to complete or address the process of saying good-bye, and a persistent sense that the loss has just occurred. People who have chronic grief reactions are unable to make any sense or meaning of the loss as it applies to their new post-loss life. They may be unwilling or unable to disconnect from the image of the lost loved one as a living and available human attachment. They yearn to reconnect, to overcome the separation gap. This keeps them in a pattern of intense grieving behavior that impedes their moving adaptively into the post-loss world. For some, the level of depression becomes so severe that a major affective disorder diagnosis needs to be considered.

### Additional Explanations for Chronic Grieving

Care providers must understand that, in the end, all the behaviors composing the human grief response— regardless how extreme they are judged to be—are efforts to cope with tragedies that may be impossible to cope with. For example, some people exhibit agitated behaviors that are associated with the protest and searching reminiscent of early childhood attachment behavior (Bowlby, 1980). This can be characterized as a *never-ending separation anxiety*. The struggle to reunite with the lost person or condition (relationship, job, role) continues and dominates the life of the grieving person. The refusal to accept the reality of the loss or the recognition that the loss is irreversible causes the individual to remain in a state of agitation (Rando, 1993; Worden, 2002).

In some situations, a form of denial called "magical thinking" may be employed to keep the painful reality from being perceived. In Joan Didion's 2006 book *The Year of Magical Thinking,* she describes how she used stories to tell herself why her husband was not there in order to make his death "to not have happened." She went in and out of these intervals of magical thinking during the first year until she was gradually able to take in the tragic truth of his death. People with terminal or nonrecoverable long-term illness or permanent life-limiting disabilities (and their families) may present with chronic grief because of "the way we were" and will never be again. Those with life-threatening conditions may forlornly go along with the medical procedures that promise some extension of life, hoping that the painful, disruptive, and sickening side effects of the treatments will prolong their lives. Grief over the "thousand losses" they have already experienced and the threat of loss looming in the future is ongoing. Its nature and duration is affected by many factors including: lab and other medical test results, how they are feeling, how they look to themselves and to others, their ability to sleep, their appetite, how much weight they have gained or lost, the nature of their emotional support, religiosity, and longevity assessments. Grief may be chronic or variable as the illness progresses.

## Attachment Styles and Chronic Grief

In some cases, chronic grief may be the product of a dependent or a possessive, anxious-insecure relationship that precludes the grieving person's ability to adapt to the post-loss world without the lost loved one. The anxious-insecure attachment style is characterized by distress and preoccupation with the pre-loss relationship (Fraley & Shaver, 1999). I believe it is also characterized by fear of loss of the relationship, possessiveness, and dependency. Prolonging grief maintains the attachment to the loved one and continues a familiar level of distress. It also causes the bereaved to feel as if he or she will never be able to form a new relationship. (See Chapter 3.)

## Chronic Grief as Stress

The prolongation of grief is also viewed as "a stress response syndrome" caused by the griever's inability to integrate the absence of the deceased loved one into the new reality of the post-loss world (Shear, Monk, & Houk, 2007). A lack of adequate coping skills and resources for adaptive problem solving may also contribute to the extended state of severe grief reactions. People who are limited in their general ability to cope with new situations, who lack confidence, and who have been emotionally unstable may find that healing into the post-loss world is a formidable task (Bonanno & Kaltman, 1999; W. Stroebe & Stroebe, 1987). Bonanno et al. (2002) suggest that people who have seen the world as a negative (e.g., unjust or uncontrollable) place may find their loss "may confirm their negative world view and contribute to their spiraling distress" (p. 8).

In these cases, useful clinical interventions include stress coping techniques and cognitive restructuring approaches.

## Reactions of Others to Chronic Grieving

As if stress, separation distress, attachment difficulties, and negative world and self views are not bad enough, grieving people frequently hear many unhelpful comments and questions such as: "When are you going to move on?" "You're *still* crying?" "It's such a downer to be with you these days." "You can't sit in the house forever!" "You're going to lose your job!" "Going to the grave *again*?" "Why are you having a birthday cake for a dead child?"

A mother who had been grieving intensely for her son for over 2 years sought help in achieving some respite. She maintained that her acute grieving was her only connection to her son and that moving away from grieving would represent moving away from him. As she explained, "As long as the pain is there, so is he." Her agitated sadness, anxiety-laden protesting, and searching behaviors were very problematic; however, she desperately needed this form of "contact."

"How long will it take?" people ask. My answer is always the same: "As long as it takes." As we have stated earlier, persistent grief is not necessarily complicated grief. Many grieving persons may experience 10 months

The care provider should not be misled by the occurrence of ongoing grief reactions. These do not always represent complicated grief but rather a continuation of grieving that requires more time than is generally believed to be acceptable. This is particularly the case with bereaved parents who usually have more intense and continued grief that is not viewed as complicated but reflects the unique nature of parental grief (Klass, 1988). On the other hand, some people who show no obvious signs of mourning behavior have other overwhelming issues that are masking their unresolved grief. (See "Distorted Grief" section later in this chapter.)

or a year or more of painful, disruptive mourning before they are able to regulate the periods of acute grieving. Many factors determine the nature of grief (see "Grief Assessment" in Chapter 9) and they all contribute to the length of the grieving period and its impact on daily functioning.

## Suggestions for the Care Provider for Chronic Grief

### Reframing the Nature of the Attachment Bond

Help the grieving person find other ways to achieve the goal he or she now accomplishes through prolonged and profound grieving. For example, survivors holding on to the deceased through mourning can be helped to reconfigure the bond with the deceased so that they can continue to feel connected. Rituals are useful in constructing new ways of maintaining the connection in a spiritual or symbolic way. For example, mourners can plant a remembrance garden or tree; organize a memorial scholarship fund; take on or be involved in a cause that the loved one supported, such as a charity or medical research that is connected with his or her illness or other cause of death; donate money to an organization of which the deceased was a member; or create a memory album with collected memorabilia from friends and family. One parent of a teenager killed in a drunk driving incident frequently participates in regional high school highway safety programs. This keeps her connected to her child while helping others. Activities like these help the bereaved liberate themselves and reclaim their lives in the post-loss world.

### Affective Release and Conflict Resolution

If the relationship was characterized by an anxious or ambivalent attachment, the grieving person can be helped to identify, process, and ultimately let go of leftover ambivalent feelings. The caregiver can suggest statements of closure such as "What do you need to say to your loved one as a way of letting go of unfinished business?" and "What can you say to him as a good-bye?" Forgiveness exercises also help bereaved people let go of negative material and move forward in the post-loss world while maintaining a connection to or relationship with the deceased.

### Redefining Self in the Post-Loss World

Helping the grieving person to focus on ways to redefine him- or herself in the post-loss world without the loved one's physical presence can also support separation from the deceased person as the only source of identity and validation. By identifying the positive characteristics and values of the deceased person he or she desires to carry forward into the post-loss life, the grieving person can form a new, continuing bond with the deceased and relinquish the need to hold on to grief as a chronic and disabling connection.

For example, a young man can be asked to recall or imagine sitting at his father's deathbed where he lists those traits of his father that he admired and which he will use in his own life. A mother can be asked to reflect on the courage and determination her son showed in the course of his illness and dying from AIDS. She can promise herself that she will carry these attributes with her into the post-loss world. A man in the depths of chronic and disabling grief over his adult daughter's sudden death can begin to view her gentle way of interacting with others as a trait he will carry with him into his new life.

Whenever possible, the care provider should help the grieving person identify and reinforce his or her own positive features. Providers should also help chronically grieving people obtain further validation in other ways—from friends and relatives, and through work, hobbies, and community service.

Care providers can initiate conversations about the bereaved's relationship with the deceased, reviewing both its positive and negative features. Similarly, journaling thoughts about the deceased or writing a letter to the lost loved one about what the grieving person seeks for him- or herself in the future can help to validate feelings of grief and alter the old internal self-image while creating new goals. Saying good-bye and forgiveness exercises, as well as the past, present, and future drawings described in Chapter 9, can also help bereaved people let go of old pictures and see new possibilities. Activities can be repeated over time as needed; they can be given as homework or intermingled with other therapies.

## Learning New Skills

If a death or separation represents the loss of an extremely dependent relationship resulting in chronic grieving, the individual should be helped to identify the secondary consequences of the death and develop plans to adjust to the absence of the deceased loved one, and to the roles he or she fulfilled. For example, if the lost loved one did the cooking and shopping, was the primary breadwinner, and was responsible for home repairs, the grieving person needs to compensate for the loss of these functions by either learning new skills or obtaining outside help. If the deceased or separated loved one provided a crucial source of identity and validation, the bereaved may need counseling to help reconfigure her self-picture as an autonomous being.

## Resistance to Saying Good-Bye or Letting Go of the Way We Were

Care providers can use the saying good-bye exercise detailed in Chapter 9 as a way to develop ways for the grieving person to say good-bye or so long for now. If the mourner resists this activity, talk about the resistance: "I see that you don't want to do this. Let's take a few minutes to look at how your reluctance is serving you. What do you think would happen if you did say goodbye? How else can you meet that goal? Let's make a list."

## Comorbidity With a Psychiatric Disorder

In my experience, complicated grief is most likely to be present if the bereaved has borderline personality disorder, major depression, general anxiety disorder, posttraumatic stress disorder, agoraphobia, or is a substance abuser. The most common condition for comorbidity was major depression. However, Melham et al. (2001) found that outpatients who presented with traumatic grief had comorbid major depression and posttraumatic stress disorder. When the complication of chronic grief is a result of a preexisting psychiatric problem such as pre-loss depression or anxiety disorder, treatment for the disorder, including antidepressant or antianxiety medication, may be indicated before the grief issues are engaged. I have worked with borderline personality disordered individuals who, having experienced a traumatic loss, become very depressed, possibly suicidal and fall into a state of chronic mourning requiring intensive treatment, medication, and on occasion hospitalization.

People with severe and chronic grief and a pre-loss history of major depression may already be under treatment for the depression. A thorough history should reveal patterns of affective disturbance, names of treating physicians, hospitalizations, and any medications taken. The pre-loss emotional disorder has a major impact on the course of the person's grief and vice versa. Each of these emotional difficulties aggravates the other and becomes further complicated should alcohol abuse be part of the mix of problems. I have found that the bereaved's mood level must be raised before much therapeutic work on complicated grief can be accomplished. Nonphysician care providers must refer those people with grief complications who show symptoms of clinical depression to a psychiatrist for a medication evaluation. (See the section in this chapter, "Psychiatric Disorders Associated With Complicated Grief" for diagnostic criteria.)

# Delayed or Inhibited Grief

## Situational and Problematic Inhibited Grief

Rando (1993a) reiterates Bowlby's formulation and writes that the person afflicted with complicated grief seeks either to:

- Avoid aspects of the loss, its pain, and the full realization of its implications

- Hold on to and avoid relinquishing the lost loved one

When a bereaved person doesn't express grief, he or she also avoids the pain of the reality of the loss. Raphael (1983) states that grief is typically inhibited to "avoid the pain of the loss" (p. 60). Grief may be inhibited because the grieving person is unwilling to open up to the painful aspects of the relationship with the deceased because it evokes negative feelings and terrible memories. A woman in a workshop I attended made it clear that she would never grieve the person she had selected to use in the "Saying Good-Bye" exercise because, "He was a terrible and hurtful person. I mourned the positive parts of the relationship," she explained, "but since that constituted only a small part of who he was to me, I didn't have much grieving to do."

There are bereaved people who appear to postpone the onset of their grief reaction for weeks, months, or years. In some cases, their attention and energy is absorbed by other more immediate requirements that preclude personal grieving. For example, a man whose wife was killed in a car crash in which his daughter was severely injured spent months caring for her and arranging for educational placement. He was too preoccupied with caregiving and advocating for his daughter to allow himself to feel any grief. He was aware that his "time for grieving would come." For some grieving people, preoccupation with nongrieving activities serves as a socially acceptable means to avoid the expression of grief.

The intentional or unintentional lack of observable grieving behaviors has been interpreted in the past in various ways. Some observers conclude, "You are so brave," "She's doing so well," "What a survivor you are." Others conclude that this lack indicates a degree of pathology. Clinically, the lack of grief, inhibited grief, or delayed grief may have a number of possible causes. A man brought his two young children to see me because he was concerned that one showed no evidence of mourning for her dead mother. After some tender questioning, I learned that she grieved privately at night because it "upsets Daddy too much when I cry." There are situations in which a mourner has responsibilities and obligations that either override grief reactions or consume the energy that would have been devoted to grieving. Further, early childhood messages restricting tears, anger, or any expression of feelings can continue to inhibit the expression of grief. Some individuals have so strongly embraced a religious belief system based on accepting God's will that grief behaviors are minimized or even nonobservable.

Mourning may also be postponed because the individual does not feel safe enough or entitled to release his or her feelings of grief. This can be due to family pressure arising from old childhood messages (stiff upper lip), social pressure to get on with life as quickly as possible, or the lack of social support for mourning. Some cultures encourage delaying or inhibiting grief. In these cases, some individuals express their grief privately when they are away from their families. Still other grieving persons may have physical conditions that preclude their grieving until such time as they are strong enough to mourn. For instance, they may have been seriously injured in an accident in which a loved one was killed. Psychiatric disorders can also overwhelm and displace the grief response until the person's mental health is restored. Many war veterans with severe brain injuries, for instance, become suicidally grief stricken after they have recovered sufficiently to learn of their condition and the crippling limitations it imposes on them.

## Resilient Grievers

As discussed earlier, a growing literature identifies and explains why a minority of grievers exhibit few typical signs or feelings of grief agitation or sadness. These "resilient" mourners may have some inner adaptive skills or other personality features that preclude them from experiencing usual grieving patterns. Some may have been viewed as having inhibited or delayed grief complications (Bonanno, 2004; Bonanno et al., 2002). However, the blanket assumption that minimal grief is a sign of maladaptation has been challenged by a growing number of investigators who argue that people who do not show overt signs of distress after loss may do so because of either the capacity for quick adjustment (Stroebe, Hansson, & Stroebe, 1993) or because of adaptation styles that promote an inherent resilience to loss. Individuals who indicate little in the way of overt, acute grieving behaviors and have apparent rapid adjustment to the post-loss world fall into the category of *instrumental grievers*. That is, they are more focused on active problem solving than expressing their feelings (*intuitive grievers*) (Doka & Martin, 2010). (See Chapter 3.)

## Additional Explanations for Inhibited Grief

Mourning can also be delayed when loved ones die during wars, terrorist attacks, or disasters, and especially in situations in which there is no body to view and never will be. If the cause of death is stigmatized (due to AIDS, suicide, abortion), or the nature of the relationship to the deceased is socially ambiguous (the deceased is a gay partner, ex-spouse, secret lover), or the mourner is considered disenfranchised (as older people and children are), then social support may not be forthcoming; this may cause mourners to withhold their expressions of grief. Without permission to grieve, the grief may be inhibited and stored away, only to emerge later in an indirect or distorted way. Grief has to go somewhere; otherwise, it gets stored as unfinished business that can eventually present as physical or psychiatric symptoms.

### Suggestions for the Care Provider for Delayed or Inhibited Grief

### Lack of a Body or Other Physical Evidence of the Deceased, Ambiguous Loss

(See Chapter 4.) If the delay is related to lack of a body or other physical evidence (clothing or other effects of the missing loved one), then the care provider can suggest that mourners gather evidence and data related to the circumstance of the death that will help fill in some of the missing details regarding the facts of the loss. Memorial rituals, reviewing photographs of the accident or disaster site, newspaper accounts, and eyewitness statements can help to provide some closure. Military families of missing-in-action loved ones have had burials with empty caskets at Arlington Cemetery; this helps them attain closure after many years of delaying their grief in the hope that some remains would be recovered.

### Other Factors Delaying Grief Reaction

When other reasons for the delay are related to physical injury, illness, or emotional shock, the care provider can help the mourner accept the need for the delay and understand that grieving is a long-term process. The care provider can engage in psychoeducational discussions with the bereaved until he or she understands how the human grief process unfolds over time.

## Children

Children can postpone active grieving for weeks and, in some cases, months. This can alarm parents. Care providers can help parents and other adults in the child's life to understand the nature of children's grief and how it differs from adult grief.

## Unfinished Relationship Business

If the lack of grieving results from residual relational issues, the care provider can ask the griever to review the relationship with the deceased to determine the negative and positive aspects of the loss. The grieving person can be given the opportunity to forgive the deceased for whatever was negative or unfinished in the relationship and to say good-bye, thus clearing the way for the release of grief.

## Disenfranchised Grief

Care providers can assist disenfranchised grievers who need permission to grieve (see "Additional Explanations for Inhibited Grief"). Begin the process by asking them to review and retell the story, review the consequences of the loss, and support any tears and feelings that arise.

Providers can help mourners who fear the pain and anguish of giving in to grief by giving them time and permission to grieve in small steps. Reluctant mourners can be helped to grieve by doing artwork or engaging in guided imagery, journaling incidents of grief, and describing what they fear might happen if they did allow the grief to come forward. A provider can ask people to describe what might happen if they give voice to the grief they fear.

The care provider can be most helpful to a grieving person when he or she understands how a particular complication serves the person.

# Distorted Grief

The three most common forms of distorted grief are (a) extreme anger, (b) unremitting guilt, and (c) persistent problematic physical symptoms. Often, people suffering from distorted grief seek help for any of the three conditions without mentioning that they are also grieving. This underscores the need for care providers to take a comprehensive loss history with all clients.

In my experience, seldom do these distortions of underlying grief—rage, guilt, or physical symptoms (whether pychosomatic or of organic etiology)—originate solely with the issues of loss. Often they predate the loss event, are related to other life experiences, or are evidence of the grieving person's psychological development and coping styles.

Here are three examples:

1. A bereaved father was in therapy for persistent rage and interpersonal conflicts. He reported that he was merely reacting to slights and hurts that he received. Eventually he realized that he was displacing the rage he felt toward himself for not being able to keep his child alive. He felt that he had failed his "parental job description." He was angry that his child was dead and grieved this loss with rage and bitterness. An older, buried issue regarding anger toward his own father for being cold and distant surfaced during therapy. Subsequent treatment focused on his unfinished business with a father he felt had failed his parental job description. Once this issue was clarified, the man stopped reprimanding himself and experienced a softening in his relationships with others.

2. A woman who had been the family caregiver for her now deceased father presented with severe and unremitting guilt, remorse, and very low self-picture. She also reported escalating family conflicts and significant symptoms of depression. She explained that she felt guilty that she had not been able to take better care of her dad who had suffered several strokes that left him unable to walk and increasingly demented. Although her supportive and caring friends told her that she had taken excellent care of her father, she continued to feel depressed. Only when she began to talk about her earlier conflicted relationships with her parents and her older siblings regarding self-identity and entitlement within her family of origin did her depressive symptoms ease.

3. A widower with two young school-aged children had been referred by his physician for various physical complaints that the doctor believed to be stress related. His wife had died of cancer 6 months earlier. His outward expression of grief for his wife was limited. He was extremely preoccupied with other issues such as providing childcare for his children, his declining work performance, fears that he would lose his job, and various undiagnosed aches and pains that

he researched extensively on the Internet. When one set of symptoms abated, another arose. He was concerned that he had cancer and would be unable to care for his children. Though each medical test and examination proved negative, the man's fears were unalleviated. Occasionally he was able to admit that his physical symptoms were related to the stress of caring for his wife during the many months of her illness.

Therapy was focused first on reducing his stress level using relaxation exercises and journaling episodes of anxiety. He started taking anti-anxiety medication and later explored several new childcare options as well as ways to improve his work output. When his anxiety stabilized, he was able to review his relationship with his deceased wife, which eventually led him to focus on his mother whom he described as a "worrying nervous wreck."

With relaxation exercises and goal setting, the man was able to reconfigure his own self-picture in his therapy. He ultimately found a new job that was more interesting and closer to home. He later indicated that he was thinking of dating. His physical symptoms were significantly diminished, but he planned to check in with his physician regularly—just in case.

## Suggestions for the Care Provider for Distorted Grief

### Initial Focus on Presenting Symptoms

Initially, the care provider will need to focus on the presenting symptoms and complaints. These may require medical attention, especially if medication for depression, anxiety, or sleep disorder is indicated. To deal with rage and guilt, care providers can initially use relaxation techniques, hypnotherapy, and guided imagery. For some explosive rage disorders, medication will need to be considered. Rage has also been reduced with regular physical exercise. Guilt can be eased through reality testing, that is, through confronting the actual events, facts, and information. (See Chapter 9 for details on working with people experiencing rage and guilt.)

### Resolving Relational Issues

Care providers can review the relationship with the deceased, especially during the period of illness, and examine the nature and duration of the caregiving role. People need to be assured that experiencing resentful feelings is normal. The pre-illness relationship should also be explored and any unfinished business should be identified and processed through discussion, externalization of feelings, and the creation of a continuing or spiritual bond with the deceased loved one. Rituals, memorials, and creating eulogies can help establish a continuing bond.

It is always useful to determine the source of anger and assist the grieving person in externalizing this material. If the anger cannot be reduced through review, processing, or reframing, the care provider can use good-bye and forgiveness exercises to help establish a sense of closure or partial completion for the grieving person.

To alleviate unremitting guilt and low self-concept, care providers can focus on the initial source of the person's sense of unworthiness. Other areas to explore are early attachment history and the sense of self in the relationship. The cognitive restructuring of self-picture can enable the grieving person to move into the post-loss world free from the sense of unworthiness that is typically associated with the distortions presented as guilt. The provider can reinforce positive self-statements and help the grieving person to see the loving role he or she had while serving as the loved one's caregiver. Counseling for developing or enhancing self-empowerment has been a major part of therapy for such individuals in my practice. Should the person slip into a depressive state, referral for antidepressant medication evaluation will be necessary.

# ☐ Four Predisposing Risk Factors: Circumstances and Conditions

Depending on the negative characteristics of each of these four circumstances, the care provider may begin to either suspect the presence of grief complications or rule them out. After identifying the existence of potentially predisposing criteria, the care provider must carefully assess for the presence of complications in the grief process according to the following criteria: severity of the symptoms, length of time the symptoms are present, and extent of dysfunction. Additionally, the presence of the various danger signals detailed earlier in this chapter can also be helpful in determining the presence of grief complications.

# Conditions That May Affect the Risk for Complicated Grief

Four circumstances potentially influence or affect a complicated grief reaction (Jacobs, 1999; Rando, 1993a,b; Raphael, 1983; Worden, 2002):

1. The nature of the death or other loss.

2. The nature of the relationship to the deceased or separated person.

3. The psychological characteristics of the grieving person.

4. Social issues associated with the death or other loss.

## The Nature of the Loss/Death Event

• Sudden, unexpected death for which no one was prepared

• Violent, mutilating, or abusive homicide

• Suicide

• Occurrence of multiple deaths

• Death from a catastrophic disaster

• Death viewed as preventable

• Grieving person witnessed the violent death

• Grieving person played some role in cause of death

• No body or other evidence of death recovered

- Grieving person not informed of the death for some time and missed death-associated rituals

- Death of child

- Death following very lengthy illness

## The Nature of the Relationship With the Lost Loved One

- An attachment disturbance in the form of an ambivalent, dependent, or otherwise insecure relationship.

- A history of being sexually, physically, or emotionally abused by the deceased.

- A preponderance of unfinished business with deceased at time of death.

- Overidentification with the deceased.

## Psychological Characteristics of the Grieving Person

- Extremely dependent personality.

- Severely limited ability to express feelings.

- Intense feelings of inadequacy and guilt regarding relationship with deceased, especially during period of illness.

- History of depressive illness or personality disorders.

- History of past complicated grief reactions.

- Loss of parents or other significant loss during childhood resulting in inadequate nurturing.

- History of life crisis and unaccommodated multiple losses.

- View of grief as the only way to maintain contact with deceased.

## Social Issues Associated With the Death or Other Loss

- Cause of death is stigmatized by society (those who die as a result of suicide, AIDS, substance abuse, abortion, or criminal activity).

- Griever feels disenfranchised by society; for example, the mourner is elderly, or is grieving a gay partner or miscarriage.

- Lack of adequate social support for the grieving person and/or family may encourage a premature end to mourning.

- Griever socially isolated and hesitant to express grief for fear of others' reactions.

- Additional concurrent major life crises: financial, occupational, physical, familial, or spiritual.

Grieving persons who meet any of these conditions may experience complicated grief. Some may also exhibit symptoms of a psychiatric disorder associated with problematic grief. If these factors are present, care providers should assess the presence of complicated grief using the criteria described earlier in this chapter (see "Danger Signals for Complicated Grief").

## ☐ Psychiatric Disorders Associated With Complicated Grief

Death or other traumatic loss can result in a psychiatric condition or can aggravate an existing one. The following psychiatric disorders are associated with complications of the grief reaction.

## Affective Disorders

Affective disorders are disturbances of mood and include major depression, bipolar disorder, and dysthymia. Affective disorders "are the category most often diagnosed in individuals experiencing either uncomplicated or complicated mourning" (Rando, 1993b, p. 199). It is believed that the psychiatric designation of depressive illness coexists with many of the grief reactions we have described as complicated grief (Jacobs, 1999).

Care providers should assess for clinical depression when any features of complicated grief are present. Indicators include the presence and worsening of the following conditions: recurrent thoughts of death; suicidal ideation or plans; flat emotional expression; loss of energy and interests; guilt; feelings of worthlessness; sleep and eating disturbances; slowed down thinking and moving; difficulty concentrating; and statements about feeling sad, hopeless, and discouraged (American Psychiatric Association, 1994, p. 317).

## Differentiating Chronic Grief From Depression

It is often difficult to tease out an easy and simple formula for diagnosing depression in a chronically grieving person. People who are clinically depressed look and sound very much like deeply grieving people. However, some researchers formulate a distinction. According to Jacobs (1999), depression is distinguished by "pervasive, depressed mood disturbance, depressive cognitive schemata, and a disturbance of self-esteem" (p. 37). Grief is more episodic and lacks the "feelings of worthlessness and pervasive feelings of guilt" associated with depression (p. 37). Rando (1993b) cites the "damage to self-esteem created by depression as much greater, more global, and more associated with an unrealistic sense of worthlessness and guilt" (p. 204). Extended duration of a depressed state for 6 months or more is seen as another indicator of depression.

## Clinical History

In my experience, most grieving people who develop a depressive disorder have had a history of depression prior to the loss or death event that is aggravated by the trauma of loss. A history of past treatment for depression or a family history of depression will further indicate the need for psychiatric support in order for grief therapy to proceed. Nonphysician care providers should refer clients to the primary care physician or to a psychiatrist for medication assessment and management when significant depression persists.

# Anxiety Disorders

## Traumatic Death

Anxiety is a common feature of acute grief. Those psychiatric disorders that are initiated by a death or other traumatic loss are more likely to fall into the anxiety disorders category. Posttraumatic stress disorder (PTSD), general anxiety, and panic disorders are typically found among people with complicated grief. If the death was traumatic—that is, sudden, violent or mutilating, or the result of suicide or homicide—the grieving person is at risk for PTSD. If the survivor witnessed or was involved in the events leading up to the death, there is a greater likelihood of PTSD developing (American Psychiatric Association, 1994).

### Separation Anxiety

The role played by anxiety in the initial period of acute grief may alter the nature of the grief reaction. The bereaved person may exhibit a full range of agitated and distressing behaviors associated with separation anxiety (e.g., searching, yearning, pining) or may control these through avoidance and denial.

### Other Manifestations of Anxiety

Anxiety disorders associated with complicated grief include (a) *general anxiety* regarding survival in the post-loss world—"How will I ever survive without her or him?"; (b) *social anxiety* associated with loss of a loved one that may take the form of agoraphobia or the fear of leaving the home (this usually arises from a fear of running into people, places, or signs that trigger memories of the deceased or of the traumatic event); and (c) *panic disorders* as related to the physical health of themselves or of surviving loved ones. Usually, anxiety needs to be treated before grief issues can be fully addressed. Treatment may involve the use of anti-anxiety medications, relaxation exercises, hypnotherapy, and cognitive/behavioral techniques. Treatment for PTSD symptoms associated with mourning—hyperarousal reactions, sleep disturbance including nightmares, and flashbacks of the traumatic event—may require a medical referral for anti-anxiety or sleep medication.

## Adjustment Disorders

Depression, anxiety, or mixed depression and anxiety may present as transitory adjustment disorders "in response to a psychosocial stressor" that are not as severe as major depression or the anxiety disorders discussed earlier but exceed the expected reaction to a death or other loss (American Psychiatric Association, 1994, p. 623). Many people suffering chronic grief are given a diagnosis of adjustment disorder with depression. This designation is justified because the depressive symptoms are related to a specific life stressor, the condition is transitory, and it has a negative impact on the quality of the grieving person's life. If the death created ongoing medical, legal, or financial issues, or family disruption (separation or divorce), the diagnosis for adjustment disorder can be made (American Psychiatric Association, 1994).

# ☐ Traumatic Death

*How Could God?*

(Doka, 2002b, p. 49)

Extremely traumatic deaths such as violent or mutilating deaths; the death of a child; and deaths due to war, suicide, or homicide leave survivors who are at high risk for complications of grief and associated psychiatric disorders. Traumatic deaths can leave the mourner with posttraumatic stress and agitation. As indicated earlier, these include hyperarousal, disturbed sleep, high anxiety, and the intrusion of disturbing images. This agitated and anxious state is diagnosed as posttraumatic stress disorder should it last more than 1 month (American Psychiatric Association, 1994). Trauma symptoms need to be treated—processed, reviewed, and neutralized—before grief can be addressed (T. Rando, personal communication, May 5, 2004).

# ☐ Suicide Death

"The person who commits suicide puts their psychological skeletons in the survivors' emotional closet" (Shneidman, 1972, p. x). I have been at funerals for persons who completed suicide and heard eulogies filled with anger, questions, shame, and fear. When a loved one has taken his or her own life, the survivors face complex issues and difficult barriers to healing, including:

1. *Social stigmatization*—Mourners are typically left with a legacy of shame, blame, and a desire to hide from the world. Grollman (1988) calls these grieving people suicide victims.

2. *Guilt*—Many mourners also feel guilty and plagued by failure, saying to themselves, "I should have known" and "How did I miss the clues?"

3. *Anger*—This may take the form of blaming God, the physician, clergy member, therapist, other family members, hospital staff, self, and the deceased. Anger is often particularly strong when the person who committed suicide left children behind.

4. *Search for meaning*—Mourners struggle to make sense of the suicide asking, " Why? How do I make sense of this?" "How does this fit in with my sense of the world?" "Nothing makes sense anymore."

5. *Social awkwardness*—Many people simply do not know what to say to someone grieving a suicide. The griever may have to cope with intrusive and clumsy questions.

6. *Fears*—Some survivors of suicide become concerned that they or other loved ones will succumb to suicide.

7. *Emotional distress*—Suicide leaves many questions left unanswered, and grievers often suffer by having to deal with the deceased's unfinished business.

The care provider should provide the survivors with information about the nature of grieving a suicide death and normalize their reactions of guilt, rage, or profound despair. Grievers also need to be provided with opportunities to share their feelings with other family members to achieve a level of honesty with each other. Children in particular must have their questions answered and be included in discussions and family mourning activities in age-appropriate ways. Various rituals, religious or nonreligious, can be used to help the family come together, share thoughts and feelings, and find ways to recall positive memories of the deceased loved one. Survivors should be urged to get proper rest, exercise, and regular meals. "Saying good-bye" exercises, forgiveness practices, and continued family discussions regarding the positive attributes of the deceased loved one can begin the process of healing.

Several community support groups may be useful to family and friends: Survivors of Suicide and SEASONS; and for parents, Bereaved Parents of the USA and The Compassionate Friends. (See Appendix A.)

The care provider can also help friends of the family support those who are grieving a suicide death.

8. *Desire to deny the truth*—Mourners will frequently fail to tell the truth about the real cause of death, thus creating more tension in the family system.

9. *Medical, legal, and insurance investigations*—These necessary but intrusive processes may create additional stress and shame.

10. *Physical distress*—Mourners may feel like they are "going crazy" and experience somatic symptoms such as aches, pains, and psychosomatic illnesses.

In addition to these issues, the "victim-survivors of suicide" may experience inhibited grief and also are at risk for agitated depression.

## Supporting Suicide Survivors

- Share their own memories of the deceased

- Share what they learned from the deceased to use in their lives

- Accept survivors' feelings without argument

- Invite survivors to go on outings, for a walk, or shopping

- Share significant anniversaries and other dates

- Run errands for survivors

- Bring food, and help with cooking and cleaning

- Invite survivors to their homes

Care providers can also encourage the family to view the life of the deceased loved one as having been productive and loving, and even recall humorous incidents to help the mourning proceed toward a healing resolution.

# ☐ The Death of a Child and Complicated Grief: A Review

(See also Chapter 6.) Many factors cause those who mourn the death of a child to be at high risk for complicated grief:

1. *The nature of the attachment.* Parents see themselves in their child and view the child as part of them, as their stake in the future. Thus, the death of a child is also the death of a part of the parent. It also severs parents' link to the future via this child. The loss looms as a catastrophic failure in the natural cycle of life as we commonly experience it.

2. *Tearing asunder of the parental identity.* Parents who lose a child lose a major part of their personal identity. They also lose an important aspect of their social identity since being a parent is a label of pride and status. After a child's death, they ask themselves: "Who am I now? I was someone's father (or mother) but now I am diminished."

3. *Failure.* Parents feel, often irrationally, as if they have failed at their primary role of protecting their child. This adds to their stress and anxiety.

4. *Violation of assumptions.* The death of a child represents the end of an age of innocence. Parents naturally assume that their children will outlive them. When they don't, the shock waves are concussive. Families experiencing the death of a child will never be the same, and they grieve for this fact as well as for the loss of their child.

5. *Loss of a future caregiver and resource.* Older parents may also grieve not only the loss of a child but also the person they were counting on to provide care for them as they age. This theme is heard frequently from older bereaved parents at The Compassionate Friends and Bereaved Parents of the USA support group meetings.

6. *Ambivalent social support.* Though you would think that society would generously support families that have lost a child, this is not always the case. Recall the "Safeway Samba" story in Chapter 3 in which the bereaved father noticed friends dodging him in the supermarket aisles. Because the loss is so painful, others may need to keep away lest contact with the bereaved parent brings up one's own fears of shattered assumptions about the world.

7. *Marital issues.* Surviving parents may grieve and heal differently and at different rates. Additionally, each parent experiences unique secondary losses since each had a unique relationship with the child. Parents or partners also may withhold their grief from each other to protect each other or themselves; however, this shuts down communication and can lead to feelings of isolation. Couples may also disagree about when to resume sexual relations. If one partner seems unavailable or impatient, communication may further break down, and the relationship will begin to deteriorate. Marital distress is a secondary loss and requires special attention from a skilled mental health provider.

8. *Sibling issues.* The siblings of a deceased child are often forgotten during mourning. If the deceased child had a lingering illness, siblings may have been overlooked by parents and others even before the death occurred; afterward, the parents may be so grief stricken that the surviving siblings still receive very little attention. These children are at risk for acting out, and becoming depressed and physically ill. (See "Siblings Speak," Chapter 6.)

9. *Suicide death of a child.* The death of a child by suicide raises the level of risk and the severity of grief complications for parents. These grieving parents may have reactions ranging from barely containable rage to uncontrollable anguish and anxiety.

A man whose son had died as a result of suicide was left with what felt like a volcano of rage. To vent, he bought second-hand china and spent many hours at the county dump flinging the dishes into huge trash containers. He did this several times a week, and over several months his massive rage began to diminish. For many, the release of rage and other feelings associated with a child's suicide death represents an early phase of treatment. Once the initial stage of rage has been externalized, other grief issues can rise to the surface.

The care provider will need to explore relationship issues with the child's parents and siblings so that they can begin to understand the suicide, and gather positive aspects of the child's life that they can take with them into their postdeath world. Providers must help family members work on forgiving the child and themselves, and facilitate saying good-bye. Families can seek comfort in faith-based rituals if appropriate.

# ☐ Behaviors That Signal Complicated Grief or Psychiatric Disorders in Bereaved Parents

This list of signals of complicated grief or psychiatric disorders can help care providers identify and help bereaved parents.

1. Persistent rage and explosive episodes that may erupt in violent attacks on others, or cause the person to become even more angry, bitter, and unhappy.

2. A terrible sense of parental inadequacy which affects other areas of life; statements of low self-worth: "I failed my job description as parent," "I dread the future and fear what else can go wrong."

3. Significant areas of life dysfunction as being increasingly demanding and difficult at home with spouse and surviving children, with friends, at work, when engaged in community activities, and in one's spiritual life.

4. Denial extremes—Delusional thoughts and actions that view the child is still alive; these thoughts and actions are beyond the usual use of linking objects and remembrance rituals.

5. Overidentification—Frequently imitates dress, speech, and other behaviors of the dead child.

6. Histrionic and excessive overprotection of surviving children; obsessively watchful and smothering, protective behavior.

7. Phobias—Avoids any reminders of child's death; flees any connection and will not discuss any aspect of the child's life.

8. Signs and symptoms of major depression, suicidal ideation, or anxiety disorder.

9. Continued disorientation, hallucinations, delusions, and dissociations.

10. Abandonment of family—Parent takes no responsibility for other children or for tasks of daily living.

Care providers can help bereaved parents by:

- Educating them about the grief process, and helping them to focus on the needs of the surviving siblings and other family members
- Counseling couples to enhance their communication and help them respect their different grieving styles
- Giving them opportunities to tell their story and cry over and over again
- Working to alleviate guilt when possible; use of forgiveness exercises
- Locating support groups such as the The Compassionate Friends, Bereaved Parents of the USA, and Mothers Against Drunk Driving for social support (see Appendix A for additional resources)
- Helping them address each of the four tasks of mourning and offering help as indicated under the appropriate complicated grief syndrome rubric (see Chapter 9)
- Referring them for psychiatric assessment if depression or anxiety overwhelms the psychotherapy or if cognitive functioning rapidly deteriorates
- Referral to a trained mental health professional

# ☐ Conclusion

This chapter has summarized the identification, nature, and treatment of complicated or prolonged grief and associated psychiatric disorders, which requires careful attention to presenting symptoms. If care providers have questions or are uncertain about the diagnosis of complicated or prolonged grief, they should refer the person to a mental health professional or seek consultation with a mental health colleague experienced with complications of grief and associated psychiatric disorders.

Care providers have a responsibility to ensure that grieving people do not see their natural responses to loss as pathological. What may be normal and natural in terms of symptoms and their duration with some grieving individuals may be seen as complicated or prolonged in others. Further, some clinicians and patients will argue against the generalization that most grief is healed within 6 months. For certain types of death, in certain life settings, for certain mourners of various cultural backgrounds who have varying levels of support, 6 months is just the first step in a long grief journey.

On the other hand, it may also be fair to say that *all grief is complicated* because a life has been derailed and normal human functioning is distorted (Rubin & Malkinson, 2001). I approach all grief reactions as a complication in the life of the individual who seeks help. We travel life's roadway and suddenly, around the bend, without any warning, we learn that the bridge is out. A death, a life-threatening diagnosis, an accident, a layoff notice, or other traumatic change has painfully altered the course of our journey and requires us to look at life in a new way. The process of grieving represents a disruption in life. We have to alter our direction, our plans, and how we identify ourselves in the post-loss and changed world.

Normal grief presents many complications and deserves the help of a care provider who is an Exquisite Witness. People who are grieving deserve care at whatever level their grief requires—whether we call it complicated or prolonged. At all times, individual differences must be taken into consideration when determining how we as care providers will serve them. In Chapter 11, several case studies are presented that will provide the reader an opportunity to review, consider, and respond.

# Case Studies

## ☐ Chapter Preview

- Explanation of Case Studies

- Seven Case Studies

- Conclusion

Following are case presentations that will give you an opportunity to do some assessment and indicate some possible interventions for immediate help in each of the situations involving grieving people.

Trainers/instructors may wish to assign separate cases to small groups and have them compare responses in a general discussion. The cases can also be used in online, distance education programs, and as a pre- and postassessment of theoretical and clinical learning. These cases can be developed more fully for clinical-training purposes, either as written exercises or as role-play exercises.

## ☐ Explanation of Case Studies

The purpose of the following loss and grief case presentations is to give you an opportunity to:

- *Assess the needs* of the grieving individual(s).

- Determine what *additional information* may be necessary.

- Provide some *initial help and recommendations* for long-term assistance.

We are not seeking to develop a comprehensive treatment plan in each case but rather to help you get a sense of how to start the process of helping a grieving person. The first five case responses have been provided as an example of what we are asking you the reader to do on your own for the sixth and seventh cases. Please add to the provided responses whatever else you feel you would want to know and do.

Although all chapters in the book may provide guidance for responding to a particular case, those chapters that discuss material particularly relevant to each case are indicated after each case title.

After reviewing the case material, think about what the person needs from you or someone else at that particular point in the process. Check the assessment material questions in Chapter 9 for suggestions on what you may want to be looking for. Ask yourself:

- How can I be of most help right now?

- Can I do this alone or do I need somebody else to be part of the action?

- What family and other support people are available for the grieving person?

- What long-term assistance can I provide or refer to another provider?

# ☐ Seven Case Studies

## Case 1: Perinatal Loss—When Dreams Are Crushed (Review Chapters 6 and 8)

A young couple is in the hospital delivery room. This has been a difficult and disturbing pregnancy and the mother, who had spent much of the pregnancy in bed, has gone into premature labor. As the mother is being prepared for delivery, the doctor is unable to detect the baby's heartbeat. The physician listens again and again but to no avail. She has a colleague confirm her finding: the baby is dead. The man and woman are shocked and devastated, as are the doctors and nurses.

1. What do you see as the couple's immediate needs?

2. What additional information do you need (spiritual/religious needs, support system, background)?

3. What other steps would you take with the couple and/or with the medical and nursing staff?

4. What additional recommendations do you have for them?

5. What (if anything) would you do additionally at this point?

## Suggested Responses

1. *Immediate needs*—The couple needs a safe space to express their feelings. They may want to do this alone or with another person present. They can choose from several possibilities: family member, friend, chaplain staff, social worker, nurse, or personal clergy. One or both of the couple may need to know what happened, to have sufficient medical information to understand why their baby died.

2. *Additional information needed*—Information needed by care provider: physical/medical status of mother; pre-loss emotional functioning of husband and wife; identification of available support system; other losses or crises in their lives; spiritual/religious preferences.

3. *Short-term help*—Offer opportunities for them to hold and dress the baby, choose a name, take a picture, get a hand- and/or footprint, say good-bye to the baby, and whatever else they need to say. Help them obtain whatever medical information from the doctors they may need in order to make some sense of what has happened. Get an okay from the nursing staff to let them remain in a room with the baby for a while and even have some of their family with them.

Facilitate the beginning of the notification process and any arrangements they wish to initiate regarding pastoral care, religious rituals, funeral, memorial, burial, cremation, or family gathering.

4. *Long-term help*—When timing is appropriate, the couple or a supporting family member should be made aware of available resources, including the following: The Compassionate Friends or Bereaved Parents of the USA self-help support groups, availability of reading material and

other sources of medical information about neonatal loss, and where to get grief counseling should they desire it.

5. *What (if anything) would you do additionally at this point?*

## Case 2: Advanced Cancer—Balancing Hope With Medical Reality (Review Chapters 8 and 9)

A man with advanced cancer is seen at a pastoral counseling office at the insistence of his wife. She is concerned because he has unrealistic hopes for a new experimental chemotherapy. She and their young adult children know that there is very little possibility that he will benefit from any additional treatment. They do not discuss this with him for fear of dashing his hopes and upsetting him. He has made no arrangements about finances or advance directives, nor has he had any other discussions with the family.

1. What do you see as the family's immediate needs?

2. What additional information do you need?

3. What other steps would you take with the family?

4. What additional recommendations do you have for them?

5. What (if anything) would you do additionally at this point?

### Suggested Responses

1. *Immediate needs*—The family should have an opportunity to voice their concerns both as individuals and as a group, and separately from the patient in order to respect their desire not to upset him. It is important that the wife and children have the same up-to-date medical information. Where there is either superficial or outdated information, a meeting with a medical provider should be arranged.

   A home visit can be very helpful to get an indication of how they communicate and how the man responds to them. A separate meeting should be held with the man to ascertain how much of the medical realities he really is aware. Also, he can be offered an opportunity to become updated by his oncologist. It is important that he get only as much information as he truly wants and not what he thinks you or the family want him to have. Gently inquire as to what he thinks he may need to do for or with his family in the event that the new treatment does not work. Ask him what he may have done differently had the new chemotherapy not been available.

2. *Additional information needed*—Additional information regarding the status of arrangements, financial, legal, advance health directives, and concerns about personal unfinished business should also be explored. Availability of spiritual or religious resources, and external support should also be explored. The emotional functioning of the wife and children should also be determined in the event that a mental health referral is required.

3. *Short-term help*—At the appropriate time, the family should be made aware of ongoing support groups in the community, for example, widow support programs and general bereavement support groups for the children as well. Resources for obtaining future family or individual counseling should be provided. The family should also be given the opportunity to meet and determine how each person is faring emotionally in the face of the deterioration of their father/husband. Cancer support groups should be offered.

4. *Long-term help*—Discussion with family members of the use of rituals and family activities to honor the man represents a way of looking ahead and taking positive action. Also, offer the possibility of thinking about how they would say good-bye or what they would say to him at the very end. Any faith resources they might have can also be reinforced if desired by the family. A clergy or spiritual advisor can be called in for this assistance.

5. *What (if anything) would you do additionally at this point?*

## Case 3: Sudden Death of a Young Child (Review Chapters 6, 9, and 10)

A child was killed instantly when a car, being driven by his mother, slips on a wet surface and hits a tree. Both parents and an older child were moderately injured. They frequently express regret that they did not die in the accident. Father is depressed 6 months later and can't work.

Mother keeps very busy. They are seen as a couple by a mental health professional because of husband's depression, and its effect on their marriage and his work.

1. What do you see as the couple's immediate needs?

2. What additional information do you need?

3. What other steps would you take with the couple?

4. What additional recommendations do you have for them?

5. What (if anything) would you do additionally at this point?

## Suggested Responses

1. *Immediate needs*—The couple can be encouraged to express initially what they see as their needs from the care provider. This can form the basis of a plan for helping them. Unless they are too fragile, they should be given an opportunity to tell and retell the story of the tragic event and hear how this has been affecting each of them individually and as a couple. They need a safe place to release their feelings and especially any guilt and regrets they desire to express.

2. *Additional information needed*—Additional information is needed about the emotional functioning of each, both within and external to the relationship. What support is being provided for the older child? What support is available from family, friends, faith, or other community sources? Are they able to grieve together? How do they support each other? What are the details of workplace difficulties initially mentioned in the referral intake? Obtain a history and background on each of them and on their relationship.

3. *Short-term help*—Facilitate communication skills development and provide psychoeducation regarding the nature and differences of the human grief response. Also, coach them on understanding and dealing with the grief of their other child. At some later point help them to say good-bye to the deceased child and ask for his forgiveness as well as seek self-forgiveness.

4. *Long-term help*—Refer them to the local The Compassionate Friends or Bereaved Parents of the USA self-help group. Provide continued couple's sessions. Also, assess the level of the husband's depression and

determine the need for individual treatment or referral for antidepressant medication evaluation. Offer them the opportunity to explore connection with their faith community or a spiritual advisor.

5. *What (if anything) would you do additionally at this point?*

# Case 4: Elder Grief (Review Chapters 7, 9, and 10)

A 75-year-old woman, newly widowed, has stopped coming to the senior center activities. She had attended intermittently for the month since her husband of 50 years died after a long battle with ALS (amyotrophic lateral sclerosis; Lou Gehrig's disease). You are a trained volunteer from the Office of Aging who has met this woman in the past. You have phoned her and are now meeting with her at her home. The woman looked and sounded physically well but her energy appeared much lower than before. She says that since her husband died she feels lost and unsure of what to do and how to be. She has some friends and neighbors to talk with but says "I have such an empty place in my body, and my home suddenly feels so big."

1. What does this woman need right now?

2. What other information do you want to obtain in order to help her?

3. What do you plan to do to help her in the short-term?

4. What long-term recommendations do you have for her?

5. What (if anything) would you do additionally at this point?

## *Suggested Responses*

1. *Immediate needs*—This woman needs some hope and a sense of self-worth in her strange, new post-loss world. She has lost her primary attachment figure and a productive, rewarding activity—her caregiving job—as well as her role as spouse. Initially, we want to hear all we can hear about what it was like to be a caregiver all that time and the difficulty of seeing your loved one literally "die by inches." We also want to encourage the telling of how it has been since he died.

In addition, when a bereaved spouse can have some understanding of the multiplicity of his or her losses, that knowledge can give him or her a sense of control of the situation. Not all persons want or can handle too much information. Communicating information can be done as an offer of clarification of why she feels as she does and to "normalize" her grief responses. If the offer is turned down, we want to continue to listen and then offer some action-oriented program possibilities. These can be community-based programs for seniors, religious programs, or volunteering in various local service facilities.

2. *Additional information needed*—Additional information in this case would be to determine the level of support available from family, friends, and community resources (e.g., faith community, neighbors, senior centers, and widow support groups). Also, you would want to know how she learned to be a home caregiver and what she liked about doing this work. As a fairly new widow living alone, you would also want to make some determination as to her self-destructive impulses. This is especially important if she has no family support and is seeking to withdraw from social contacts.

3. *Short-term help*—Offer her opportunities to attend the senior center's activities, even providing a "buddy" to pick her up so that they can attend together. There are other activity-oriented programs sponsored by faith communities, AARP, recreation departments, and other service organizations. If she rejects group activities, she may be interested in having a friend or family member visit her at home or call daily. If she wishes little or no contact, she may be content to have a family member check in on her at some agreed upon interval.

4. *Long-term help*—For a long-term recommendation, offer her a way to use her considerable home caregiving skills and knowledge. Many volunteer programs in nursing homes, hospitals, and other rehabilitation facilities would benefit from even a few hours a week from a person who has such caregiving experience. This would also benefit her in that she once again would feel productively engaged in a rewarding experience. The antidote to loneliness and depression often is found in providing care and service to others. Other possibilities could be connected to her spiritual pathway, and, if needed, individual mental health counseling. Also, offer her the opportunity to say good-bye or make any other statement she would like to have her husband hear from her.

5. *What (if anything) would you do additionally at this point?*

# Case 5: Young Adult Suicide
# (Review Chapters 4, 6, 9, and 10)

A 24-year-old single woman has been found dead in her apartment by her neighbor. She was taken by ambulance to the hospital emergency room and pronounced dead of an overdose of medications. No suicide note was found. The family has gathered in the hospital chapel. You are the on-call psychiatric resident and have been requested to meet with the family. When you enter, the mother is in shock, not speaking, and the father is barely controlling his rage. One brother and sister, both younger and still living at home, are quietly weeping. A chaplain's assistant is sitting silently near the parents and being an exquisite listener.

A police investigator is waiting outside to ask some routine questions. The emergency room supervisor has requested a psychiatric consultation because of the mother's state of shock and concern for the father's brimming rage.

1. What do you see as the family's immediate needs (psychiatric, medical, spiritual, or other support)?

2. What additional information do you need?

3. What other steps would you take for short-term help?

4. What additional longer-term mental health recommendations do you have for them?

5. What (if anything) would you do additionally at this point?

## Suggested Responses

1. *Immediate needs*—The concussive shock of a suicide is a devastatingly unique loss. No two situations are ever the same. People in shock need to be made to feel safe and able to say and ask whatever they need to. The chapel is a good place for them to be as long as others will not disturb the family. You would want to assess the emotional condition of each family member by informal observation and some casual questions: "How did you find out about this?" "What did you do then?"

"Who besides the people here have you called?" The mother and father may need to scream, moan, and express their sorrow and rage they are feeling. This is the externalization of deep anguish, and, when it starts to come out, the care provider must be able to be there with this explosive material and allow it to flow. The parents must be kept safe and as an Exquisite Witness care provider, you are able to be with them and provide a sense of stability and security. When needed, medication for anxiety and distress can be provided.

2. *Additional information needed*—It would also be useful to obtain the specific observations from the emergency room supervisor regarding the reasons for requesting the consultation, and also to have a few moments with the chaplain's assistant to get his or her impressions. In a situation that feels chaotic and out of control, providing some structure in the form of appropriate and innocuous questions can help to restore some sense of balance and caring. If the family members have many questions, take out a pad and write them all down and indicate that every effort will be made to get the answers. It is important that no emotion that comes up is judged as unacceptable or wrong.

3. *Short-term help*—The variety of reactions can also include self-destructive threats or threats to others. There should be a follow-up on such statements and an assessment made to determine the risk level for acting on such thoughts and the need for medical intervention or hospitalization. If this is not warranted, some form of very close observation by a family member or friend of the family should be arranged. In some cases, the resident may prescribe medication for anxiety or for sleep.

Additionally, referral to an outpatient mental health resource may also be beneficial so that family members can feel the security of a safety net. The mother may simply be in shock, or she may have shut down to the point that she requires treatment. The father's barely controlled rage can be very appropriate to the situation, even if he releases it into the room. However, it can be indicative of other explosive issues and require professional help. You could also indicate that the chaplain's assistant is available for them right now as well. They should leave when they feel they are able to. Where it has been determined that family members are not safe to drive, transportation should be arranged.

The family should leave with phone numbers of whom they can call day or night should they feel out of control and in crisis. They should also be prepared for the routine questions the police may need to ask and any other required legal procedures. This is a difficult and sometimes time-consuming process, and at times results in delay in the releasing of the body.

4. *Long-term help*—For long-term recommendations, give the family the contact numbers for The Compassionate Friends, Bereaved Parents of the USA, Survivors of Suicide, and the SEASONS suicide support groups. (See Appendix A.) If the topic of faith-based resources has come up, the family should contact its clergy or spiritual advisor when ready. Family members to be seen in therapy could be offered the opportunity to say good-bye to and forgive their deceased loved one and themselves.

5. *What would you do additionally at this point?*

For the next two cases please read the presenting summary, consult the suggested chapters, and answer the four questions for each case.

# Case 6: Death of a Spouse
# (Review Chapters 3, 4, 9, and 10)

A 59-year-old man has been widowed for 3 months after 35 years of marriage. He complains of concentration problems at work, difficulty sleeping, and finds himself drinking in excess of a six-pack of beer on weekends. The latter is unusual behavior for him. He admits to intermittent crying daily and calls his married daughter five to six times a week. Occasionally, he believes that he hears his wife calling him from some distant place in the house, usually at night. He admits to some anxiety regarding the possibility that he is going crazy. He denies suicidal ideation but wonders if he will see her again someday.

His daughter has suggested that he talk to his clergy about his questions regarding his bewilderment as to why his wife died so unexpectedly. The clergy has referred him to you for an assessment to decide whether he needs grief counseling.

1. What are some immediate suggestions that you can offer to give him some comfort and stability?

2. What additional information do you need in order to make an assessment?

3. What other steps would you take for short-term help?

4. What additional longer-term recommendations do you have for him?

## Case 7: Dying Child and Siblings (Review Chapters 4, 5, and 6)

A 10-year-old girl is in her second round of chemotherapy for leukemia. She had been in remission for several months but is now weak, nauseous, and bald again. She has a younger sister, age 8, and an older brother, age 12. Her parents are heartsick over the reoccurrence of her tumor cells. The girl is very devoted to her parents and siblings, and feels very badly that her illness has caused so much pain and disruption to their lives.

Her older brother has much ambivalence about his sick younger sister. He fears that she will die and yet makes angry comments about all of the attention she gets from Mom and Dad—especially Dad. People come to the house and all of their time is spent with his sister and she gets "so many cool things." When you talk to him alone, he says that he has a very bad sinus problem, "but I guess that's not bad enough." He thinks leukemia may be some kind of cancer but is "not sure how serious this is." He says that his parents do not talk much about his sister's illness, only about how tired they are and how "they can't do stuff with him anymore."

The younger sister idolizes her big sister and is not quite sure of how sick she is. She knows her parents are worried and always running to the doctor, the hospital, or the pharmacy. All of this frightens her, but no one will talk to her about her sister's illness.

The parents are dedicated to "beating this thing!" They get other medical opinions, search the Internet, and do everything they can to keep things normal in their home. They are asking for help because the school has reported that their son is acting out and his grades are falling. In addition, the younger sister's teacher has called with concerns that she is becoming increasingly withdrawn.

1. How can you be of most help right now?

2. Can you do this alone or do you need somebody else to be part of the action? (Who?)

3. What short-term external support can you suggest?

4. What long-term assistance can you provide or refer to another provider for?

# ☐ **Conclusion**

The cases studies represent just a sampling of situations that will come to your attention as a provider of service to grieving people. The amount of information supplied just scratches the surface of what you must obtain for any long-term help planning. Please add any ideas to those provided in response to the questions. Always seek the combined wisdom of colleagues whenever you can.

The "Epilogue" that follows will provide an ending to our heart, head, and hands journey together. It is my hope that you will be an Exquisite Witness for the grieving people who so very much need you to be there to help them when their tears are not enough.

# EPILOGUE

Two roads diverged in a wood, and I—
I took the one less traveled by,
And that has made all the difference.

Robert Frost, "The Road Not Taken"

## ☐ Life, Loss, and Grief

… And the painful losses I experienced have made more obvious the precious blessings I still retain in life.

As I conclude the writing of this book, I am more than ever convinced of the importance of communicating a simple message to all care providers and to all grieving people blessed by their care: Most grief is normal and has a function in healing through a loss. We need to learn to manage grief and to live with it side by side.

Imagine what the world might be like if all 6 billion people on this planet truly grasped the nature of normal grief and accepted without judgment, the variety of means for healing—using the griever's own time schedule. People may need to talk and talk and talk out grief, cry it out, scream it out, write it out, exercise it out, draw it out, creatively express it out, and find the means to somehow re-create self and life meanings in the post-loss world. Friends, family, and acquaintances must further accept that grieving people are subject to reoccurrences of grief reaction as life continues.

Additionally, those in the social world of people who grieve must also recognize the multiple effects of a person's loss and grief reactions on those around them. This includes the effect on care providers. Writing this book has been a healing, yet at times, painful experience for me. I continue to marvel at the grief that surfaces each time I write about my personal experience or when clinical work triggers a painful memory. We as care providers are vulnerable to the effects of the work we do—the supporting, the helping, the being there. Each time new grief announces itself we are again challenged and entitled to take care of ourselves.

# ☐ Those Who Do Not Turn Their Eyes Away

Writer Brad Lemley wrote a story for *Washington Post Magazine* (1986) about his very sick newborn son. One day he observed the nurse try, yet again, to find an accessible vein for intravenous feeding. She found a vein and successfully inserted the needle. Lemley had turned his eyes away but the nurse did not turn her eyes away from her task with this baby. There are so many other people in our society who do not turn their eyes away from jobs that most of us are happy to let them do: preparing bodies for viewings; emptying bedpans; recovering drowning victims; working the emergency rooms; and providing care to the dying, bereaved, and very ill. These individuals do not, cannot, turn their eyes away from what has to be done to serve society's shadowy side.

Exquisite Witness grief care providers at all levels of training and experience will learn to stay focused on the task at hand, and this is facilitated by not turning their eyes away from their own current or old loss material. Our service in helping grieving people can become informed by our own Cowbells. When in doubt, seek consultation.

As this book draws to a close, I want to assure you who are newly entering this work that while there are some tough and at times painful situations we face with grieving people, there are many gifts that we receive. Some of the treasures come in the form of being with sick and dying people who have reordered their priorities to such bottom-line goals as being pain free, being clean, and giving and receiving love. Other gifts come from the recognition of our own Cowbells, our personal unfinished grief which, when effectively managed, will not diminish our availability to those we are serving.

Finally, while dying and death is a topic so many wish to turn their eyes away from, you as an Exquisite Witness provider will be shining your light into that darkness because you will not turn your eyes away. The nurse who did not turn her eyes away knew what to do and how to do it. Your joy as a grief care provider will come from the confidence in your knowledge and skills, as well as your comfort in knowing that you will be available to help grieving people heal when tears are not enough.

# APPENDIX A: ORGANIZATION RESOURCES

**AARP**
800-687-2277
http://www.aarp.org

**Alzheimer's Association**
866-AFA-8484
http://www.alz.org

**American Academy of Hospice and Palliative Medicine**
847-375-4712
http://www.aahpm.org

**American Association of Suicidology**
800-237-TALK (8255)
http://www.suicidology.org

**American Childhood Cancer Organization**
800-366-CCCF (2223)
http://www.candlelighters.org

**American Foundation for Suicide Prevention**
888-333-2377
http://www.afsp.org

**American SIDS Institute**
239-431-5425
http://www.sids.org

**ARCH National Respite Network**
703-256-2084
http://www.archrespite.org

## Bereaved Parents of the USA
708-748-7866
http://www.bereavedparentsusa.org

## Brain Injury Association of America
1-888-333-AFSP (2377)
http://www.afsp.org

## The Compassionate Friends
877-969-0010
http://www.compassionatefriends.org

## The Dougy Center: National Center for Grieving Children & Families
866-775-5683
http://www.dougy.org

## Eldercare Locator
1-800-677-1116

## Family Caregiver Alliance
Camps for Caring for Alzheimer's patients
800-445-8106
http://www.caregiver.org

## Funeral Consumers Alliance
800-765-0107
http://www.funerals.org

## GriefNet.org
http://www.griefnet.org
http://www.kidsaid.com

## Helping Grieving People
J. Shep Jeffreys
http://www.GriefCareProvider.com

## Hospice Foundation of America
1-800-854-3402
http://www.hospicefoundation.org

## Mothers Against Drunk Driving
800-GET-MADD (438-6233)
http://www.madd.org

**National Alliance for Caregiving**
800-366-2223
http://www.caregiving.org

**National Association of Professional Geriatric Care Managers**
520-881-8008
http://www.caremanager.org

**National Cancer Institute, National Institutes of Health**
800-4-CANCER (800-422-6237)
http://www.cancer.gov

**National Center for Post-Traumatic Stress Disorder (PTSD)**
United States Department of Veterans Affairs
802-296-6300
http://www.ptsd.va.org

**National Council on Disability**
202-272-2004
TTY: 202-272-2074
http://www.ncd.gov

**National Family Caregivers Association**
1-800-896-3650
http://www.nfcacares.org

**National Hospice and Palliative Care Organization**
703-837-1500
http://www.nhpco.org

**National Organization of Parents of Murdered Children, Inc.**
888-818-POMC (7662)
http://www.pomc.org

**National Sudden and Unexpected Infant/Child Death & Pregnancy Loss**
866-866-7437
http://www.sidscenter.org

**National Suicide Prevention Hotline**
800-273-TALK (8255)
http://www.suicidepreventionlifeline.org

**Red Cross**
800-366-2223
http://www.redcross.org

**Survivors of Suicide**
800-273-8255
http://www.survivorsofsuicide.com

**Tragedy Assistance Program for Survivors**
800-959-TAPS (8277)
http://www.taps.org

# APPENDIX B: ADVANCE MEDICAL DIRECTIVE

Norman L. Cantor

*Rutgers Law School*

## ☐ Part I: Introduction

The following material is designed to guide my medical treatment after I have become incompetent—that is, unable to understand the nature and consequences of important medical decisions. The object is to appoint a decision maker on my behalf (to be known as my health care representative) and to instruct that decision maker concerning the level of deterioration that would warrant ending life-sustaining medical intervention. I assume that comfort care (care intended to keep me pain free, clean, and comfortable) will always be provided.

# ☐  Part II: Designation of a Health Care Representative

## A. Primary Designation

I, _____, hereby designate the following individual as my health care representative to act on my behalf, in the event of my incompetence, with respect to any and all health care decisions. These include decisions to provide, withhold, or withdraw life-sustaining measures, to hire and fire health care providers, or to transfer my care to another physician or institution.

Primary Health Care Representative:

Name _____

Address _____

City _____ State _____

Telephone _____

## B. Alternate Designation(s) (Naming of Alternate(s) Is Recommended, But Not Required)

In the event the individual named above is unavailable, or is unable or unwilling to serve as my health care representative, I hereby designate the following individual(s) to act as alternate(s):

First Alternate:

Name _____

Address _____

City _____ State _____

Telephone _____

Second Alternate:

Name _____

Address _____

City _____ State _____

Telephone _____

## C. Consultation

To the extent feasible in the circumstances, I direct my health care representative to confer with the following individuals prior to making any health care decisions on my behalf. These individuals may provide advice to be considered by the health care representative, but they shall not have veto power over the health care representative's decisions. (Check all that apply, and provide names and telephone numbers if not specified above):

_____ (a) Family member(s):

_____ (b) My physician or physicians:

_____ (c) My attorney:

_____ (d) My priest, minister, rabbi, or other clergy person:

_____ (e) Others:

## ☐ Part III: General Instructions for Care

To inform those responsible for my care, I declare that there are circumstances in which I would not want my life to be prolonged by further medical treatment. In such circumstances (as described below), life-sustaining measures should not be initiated and, if they have been initiated, they should be discontinued. I recognize that this is likely to hasten my death.

If I become stricken with a serious illness or condition, with no reasonable expectation of cure or recovery to a competent state, I do not want life-sustaining treatment to be provided or continued after my health care representative determines that the burdens of my continued existence outweigh the benefits or that my condition has permanently deteriorated to a point of intolerable indignity. In making these judgments, I want my health care representative to consider my suffering and my diminished quality of life, with particular attention to the elements of indignity noted in my values profile in Part IV. In the event my wishes are not clear, or if a situation arises that I did not anticipate, my health care representative is authorized to use his/her best judgment about what I would want done, keeping in mind my conceptions of indignity sketched in Part IV.

# ☐ Part IV: Values Profile Introduction

Like many people, I am concerned about medical prolongation of my life upon reaching an intolerably deteriorated condition. Below I have given my reactions to various factors which many people consider important in shaping postcompetence medical care. To the extent that I am concerned about such factors, I have indicated conditions that, for me, are intolerable.

## A. Pain and Suffering

In my postcompetency state, I am concerned about extreme pain and would expect to receive pain medication to make me as comfortable as possible. My attitude toward being in a permanent condition in which pain can be controlled only by substances that leave me unconscious all or most of the time:

___ intolerable; I prefer to be allowed to die, even if that means withholding or withdrawal of artificial nutrition and hydration in my unconscious condition

___ intolerable; I prefer to be allowed to die, but I want artificial nutrition and hydration

___ a very negative factor, to be weighed with other factors in determining intolerable indignity

___ unimportant; I prefer that I be kept alive even if pain medication leaves me unconscious

My attitude toward being in a permanent condition in which pain or suffering can be controlled only by substances that leave me disoriented and confused all or most of the time:

___ intolerable; I prefer to be allowed to die, even if that means withholding or withdrawal of artificial nutrition and hydration in my disoriented condition

___ intolerable; I prefer to be allowed to die, but I want artificial nutrition and hydration

___ a very negative factor, to be weighed with other factors in determining intolerable indignity

___ unimportant; I prefer that I be kept alive even if pain medication leaves me disoriented

## B. Mental Incapacity

In my postcompetency state, I am concerned about the level of my mental deterioration to the following extent:

___ a very critical factor

___ important, but not determinative by itself; a factor to be weighed with other factors in determining intolerable indignity

___ unimportant

My attitude toward a permanently unconscious state, confirmed by up-to-date medical tests, showing no hope of ever regaining consciousness:

___ intolerable; I prefer death

___ tolerable

___ tolerable, so long as insurance or other nonfamily sources are paying the bills

My reaction to profound dementia to the point where I can no longer recognize my loved ones and interact with them in a coherent fashion:

___ intolerable; I prefer death

___ a very negative factor, to be weighed with other factors in determining intolerable indignity

___ tolerable

My reaction to dementia to the point where I can no longer read and understand written material such as a newspaper:

___ intolerable; I prefer death

___ a very negative factor, to be weighed with other factors in determining intolerable indignity

___ tolerable

My reaction to moderate dementia (such as Alzheimer's disease) characterized by frequent confusion and loss of short-term memory, though I am still able to experience pleasant feelings and emotions and to interact with people:

___ intolerable; I prefer to be allowed to die, even if this means nontreatment of curable conditions such as pneumonia or infections

___ a very negative factor, to be weighed with other factors in determining intolerable indignity

___ tolerable

## C. Physical Immobility

In my incompetent state, I am concerned about physical immobility to the following extent:

___ important

___ unimportant

My reaction to being permanently bed-ridden:

___ intolerable; I prefer death

___ a very negative factor, to be weighed with other factors in determining intolerable indignity

___ tolerable

My reaction to being nonambulatory, meaning that I can leave my bed but can only move around if others transport me in a wheelchair:

___ intolerable; I prefer death

___ a very negative factor, to be weighed with other factors in determining intolerable indignity

___ tolerable

## D.  Physical Helplessness

In my incompetent state, I am concerned about my independence and ability to tend to my own physical needs to the following extent:

___ important

___ unimportant

My reaction to being incapable of feeding myself:

___ intolerable; I prefer death

___ a very negative factor, to be weighed with other factors in determining intolerable indignity

___ tolerable

My reaction to being incapable of dressing myself:

___ intolerable; I prefer death

___ a very negative factor, to be weighed with other factors in determining intolerable indignity

___ tolerable

My reaction to being incontinent:

___ intolerable; I prefer death

___ a very negative factor, to be weighed with other factors in determining intolerable indignity

___ tolerable

## E. Interests of Loved Ones

In my incompetent state, the emotional and financial burdens imposed on my loved ones are of concern to the following extent:

___ a critical factor

___ an important factor, depending on degree of burden

___ unimportant

My reaction to emotional strain posed for my spouse or other loved ones surrounding me during my incompetency:

___ an important factor

___ a somewhat important factor

___ unimportant; although I care about my loved ones, I want my treatment decisions to be based on my own circumstances

My reaction to a heavy financial burden being imposed on my spouse or other loved ones:

___ an important factor

___ a somewhat important factor

___ unimportant; although I care about my loved ones, I want my treatment decisions to be based on my own circumstances

My reaction to my assets being depleted by heavy medical expenses for my care:

___ an important factor

___ unimportant

## F. Living Arrangements

In my incompetent state, I am concerned about my living arrangements to the following extent:

___ not important; I want my care to be determined by my personal condition rather than the surroundings

___ some living arrangements would be intolerable (if so, proceed to the next question)

I would find any of the following living arrangements intolerable, so that if there were no alternative I would prefer cessation or withdrawal of life-sustaining medical care:

___ living at home, but with need for full-time help

___ living permanently in the home of one of my children or other relative

___ living permanently in a nursing home or other long-term care facility

___ being confined to a hospital with little or no hope of ever leaving

# G. Types of Medical Intervention

My attitude toward artificially provided fluids and nutrition, such as feeding tubes or intravenous infusion:

___ to be handled in the same way as other medical interventions (guided by my instructions above)

___ to be provided at all times, regardless of my condition

I understand decisions as to all types of medical intervention will be governed by my instructions as indicated in this document. However, I feel an especially strong aversion to certain form(s) of intervention. *(Indicate here any special aversions, such as to a respirator, a blood transfusion, or CPR):*

_____

_____

_____

My attitude toward hand- or spoon-feeding in the event that I have reached a level of deterioration that I have defined as intolerably undignified:

___ I wish to receive oral nutrition only so long as I am willingly taking what is offered, and I do not want to be force-fed or to receive artificial nutrition or hydration in the event I am resisting oral nutrition.

___ I wish to receive oral nutrition only so long as I am willingly taking what is offered, but I would expect artificial nutrition or hydration in the event I am resisting oral nutrition.

# ☐ Part V: Signature and Witnesses

## A. Signature

By writing this directive, I intend to ease the burdens of decision making on those entrusted with my health care decisions. I understand the purpose and effect of this document and sign it knowingly, voluntarily, and after careful deliberation.

Signed this _____ day of _____, 20 _____

Printed Name _____

Address _____

City _____ State _____

Signature _____

## B. Signature of Witnesses

I declare that the person who signed this document, or asked another to sign this document on his or her behalf, did so in my presence, that he or she is personally known to me, and that he or she appears to be of sound mind and free of duress or undue influence. I am 18 years of age or older and am not designated by this or any other document as the person's health care representative, nor as an alternate health care representative.

Witness's Printed Name _____

Address _____

City _____ State _____

Signature _____

Witness's Printed Name _____

Address _____

City _____ State _____

Signature _____

## C. Signature of Health Care Representatives and Alternates (Optional, but Strongly Encouraged)

I have read this document and agree to act as health care representative, or as an alternate health care representative.

_____

Signature of Primary Health Care Representative

_____

Signature of First Alternate

_____

Signature of Second Alternate

## D. Periodic Review

**You may cancel or change this document at any time. You should review it every so often. Each time you review it, place your initials and the date here:

Cantor, N. L. (1998). Making advance directives meaningful. *Psychology, Public Policy and Law, 4,* 629–652.

# REFERENCES

Addington-Hall, J. (2002). Research sensitivities to palliative care patients. *European Journal of Cancer Care, 11*, 220–224.

Ainsworth, M. (1973). The development of infant–mother attachment. In B. Caldwell & H. Ricciuti (Eds.), *Review of child development research* (Vol. 3). Chicago, IL: University of Chicago Press.

Ainsworth, M., Blehar, M. C., Waters, E., & Wall, S. (1978). *Patterns of attachment: A psychological study of the strange situation.* Hillsdale, NJ: Erlbaum.

Ainsworth, M., & Bowlby, J. (1991). An ethological approach to personality development. *American Psychologist, 45*, 333–341.

Albom, M. (1997). *Tuesdays with Morrie.* New York: Doubleday.

Ambrose Video Publishing, Inc. (Producer). (1993). *Death: The trip of a lifetime* [VHS]. Discontinued and possibly available via intercollegiate loan.

American Cancer Society, Inc. (1999). *Cancer facts and figures, 1999, selected cancers.* Retrieved from www.cancer.org/statisticscff99selectedcancers.html

American Psychiatric Association. (1994). *Diagnostic and statistical manual of mental disorders* (4th ed.). Washington, DC: Author.

American Psychological Association. (2003). Guidelines on multicultural education, training, research, practice, and organizational change for psychologists. *American Psychologist, 58*, 377–402. Washington, DC: Author.

Archer, J. (1999). *The nature of grief: The evolution and psychology of reactions to loss.* London, England: Routledge.

Arno, P. S., Levine, D., & Memmott, M. M. (1999). The economic value of informal caregiving. *Health Affairs, 2*, 182–188.

Ashenburg, K. (2002). *The mourner's dance.* New York: North Point Press.

Attig, T. (1996). *How we grieve: Relearning the world.* New York: Oxford University Press.

Attig, T. (2001). Relearning the world: Making and finding meanings. In R. A. Neimeyer (Ed.), *Meaning reconstruction & the experience of loss* (pp. 33–53). Washington, DC: American Psychological Association.

Attig, T. (2004). Meanings of death seen through the lens of grieving. *Death Studies, 28*, 341–360.

Barrera, M., O'Connor, K., D'Agostino, N. M., Spencer, L., Nicholas, D., Jovcevska, V., … Schneiderman, G. (2009). Early parental adjustment and bereavement after childhood cancer death. *Death Studies, 33*(6), 497–520. doi:10.1080/07481180902961153.

Bartholomew, K., & Horowitz, L. (1991). Attachment styles among young adults: A test of a Four-Category Model. *Journal of Personality and Social Psychology, 61*(2), 226–244.

Baumeister, R. F. (1991). *Meanings of life.* New York: Guilford.

Beery, L. D., Prigerson, H. G., Bierhals, A. J., Santucci, L. M., Newsom, J. T., Maciejewski, P. K., ... Reynolds, C. F. (1997). Traumatic grief, depression and caregiving in elderly spouses of the terminally ill. *Omega, 35,* 261–279.

Bekele, S. (2009, Summer). Broken cowboy. *Mainstay* (Issue No. 93). Freehold, NJ: Well Spouse Association.

Bernstein, P. P., & Gavin, L. A. (1996). The death of a child: Implications for marital and family therapy. In J. Lonsdale, *The Hatherleigh guide to marriage and family therapy* (pp. 147–167). New York: Hatherleigh Press.

Bloombaum, M., Yamamoto, J., & James, Q. (1968). Cultural stereotyping among psychotherapists. *Journal of Consulting and Clinical Psychology, 32,* 99.

Bonanno, G. (2004). Loss, trauma and human resiliency. *American Psychologist, 59,* 2–28.

Bonanno, G., & Kaltman, S. (1999). Toward an integrative perspective on bereavement. *Psychological Bulletin, 125,* 760–776.

Bonanno, G., Neria, Y., Mancini, A., Coifman, K., Litz, B., & Insel, B. (2007). Is there more to complicated grief than depression and posttraumatic stress disorder? A test of incremental validity. *Journal of Abnormal Psychology, 116*(2), 342–351.

Bonanno, G., Wortman, C., Lehman, D., Tweed, R., Haring, M., Sonnega, J., ... Nesse, R. (2002). Resilience to loss and chronic grief: A prospective study from preloss to 18 months postloss. *Journal of Personality and Social Psychology, 83,* 1150–1164.

Boss, P. (2004). Ambiguous loss. In F. Walsh & M. McGoldrick (Eds.), *Living beyond loss: Death in the family* (2nd ed., pp. 237–246). New York: Norton.

Bowen, M. (1991). Family reactions to death. In F. Walsh & M. McGoldrick (Eds.), *Living beyond loss: Death in the family* (pp. 79–92). New York: Norton.

Bowlby, J. (1973). *Attachment and loss, Vol. 2. Separation: Anxiety and anger.* New York: Basic Books.

Bowlby, J. (1979). *The making and breaking of affectional bonds.* London, England: Tavistock.

Bowlby, J. (1980). *Attachment and loss, Vol. 3. Loss: Sadness and depression:* New York: Basic Books.

Bowlby, J. (1982). *Attachment and loss, Vol. 1. Attachment* (2nd ed.). New York: Basic Books.

Brain Injury Association of America. (2008, October). *Types of brain injury.* Retrieved from http://www.biausa.org/Pages/types_of_brain_injury.html#tbi.

Byock, I. (1997). *Dying well: The prospect for growth at the end of life.* New York: Riverhead Books.

Byock, I. (2004). *The four things that matter most.* New York: Simon and Schuster/ Free Press.

Byrne, G. J. A., & Raphael, B. (1997). The psychological symptoms of conjugal bereavement in elderly men over the first 13 months. *International Journal of Geriatric Psychiatry, 12,* 241–251.

Cantor, N. L. (1998). Making advanced directives meaningful. *Psychology, Public Policy, and Law, 4,* 629–652.

Carr, D. (2008). Factors that influence late-life bereavement: Considering data from the Changing Lives of Older Couples study. In M. S. Stroebe, R. O. Hannson, H. Schut, & W. Stroebe (Eds.), *Handbook of bereavement research and practice: Advances in theory and interventions* (pp. 417–440). Washington, DC: American Psychological Association.

Carr, D., & Jeffreys, J. S. (in press). Spousal bereavement in later life. In R. Neimeyer, H. Winokuer, D. Harris, & G. Thornton (Eds.), *Grief and bereavement in contemporary society: Bridging research and practice.* New York: Routledge.

Cohen, R. (2004). *Blindsided: A reluctant memoir.* New York: HarperCollins.

Coor, C., Nabe, C., & Coor, D. (2006). *Death and dying, life and living* (5th ed.). Belmont, CA: Thomson.

Cosgrove, L., & Konstam, V. (2008). Forgiveness and forgetting: Clinical implications for mental health counselors. *Journal of Mental Health Counseling, 30,* 1–13.

Crawley, L., Marshall, P., Bernard, L., & Koenig, B. (2002). Strategies for effective end-of-life care. *Annals of Internal Medicine, 136*(9), 673–679.

Crawley, L., Marshall, P., Bernard, L., & Koenig, C. M. (1996). *Bereavement studies of grief in adult life.* New York: International Universities Press. (Original work published 1972.)

Davies, B., Gudmundsottir, M., Worden, W., Orloff, S., Sumner, L., & Brenner, P. (2004). Living in the dragon's shadow: Fathers' experience of a child's life-limiting illness. *Death Studies, 28,* 111–135.

Davis, C. G., Nolen-Hoeksema, S., & Larson, J. (1998). Making sense of loss and benefiting from the experience: Two construals of meaning. *Journal of Personality and Social Psychology, 75,* 561–574.

Didion, J. (2006). *The year of magical thinking.* New York: Alfred A. Knopf.

Doka, K. J. (Ed.). (1989). *Disenfranchised grief: Recognizing hidden sorrow.* Lexington, MA: Lexington.

Doka, K. J. (Ed.). (2002a). *Disenfranchised grief: New direction, challenges and strategies for practice.* Champaign, IL: Research Press.

Doka, K. J. (2002b). How could God? Loss and the spiritual assumptive world. In J. Kauffman (Ed.), *Loss of the assumptive world: A theory of traumatic loss* (pp. 49–54). New York: Brunner-Routledge/Taylor & Francis.

Doka, K. J. (2010). *Living with grief: Cancer and end-of-life care.* Hospice Foundation of America, 17th Annual Living with Grief Teleconference. Televised at Johns Hopkins Medical Institutions, Baltimore, MD.

Doka, K. J., & Martin, T. L. (Eds.). (2010). *Grieving beyond gender: Understanding the ways men and women mourn* (rev. ed.). New York: Routledge.

Duncan, I. (1927). *My life.* New York: Boni and Liverright.

Eckstein, D., Sperber, M., & Shanon, M. (2009). Forgiveness: Another relationship "F" word. *The Family Journal, 17,* 256–262.

Elison, J., & McGonigle, C. (2003). *Liberating losses: When death brings relief.* Cambridge, MA: Da Capo Lifelong Books.

Fanos, J. H. (1996). *Sibling loss.* Mahwah, NJ: Lawrence Erlbaum.

Fears, D. (2002, July 15). America—the sweet hereafter: Tradition minded Asians bring ancestors' ashes to U.S. *The Washington Post,* p. A1.

Feeney, J. A. (1998). Adult attachment and relationship-centered anxiety: Responses to physical and emotional distancing. In J. A. Simpson & W. S. Rholes (Eds.), *Attachment theory and close relationships* (pp. 189–218). New York: Guilford.

Fenchuk, G. W. (Ed.). (1994). *Timeless wisdom* (p. 2). Midlothian, VA: Cake Eaters, Inc.

Field, N. P., Gao, B., & Paderna, L. (2005). Continuing bonds in bereavement: An attachment theory based perspective. *Death Studies, 29*(4), 277–299.

Field, T. (1985). Attachment as psychobiological attunement: Being on the same wavelength. In M. Reite & T. Field (Eds.), *The psychobiology of attachment and separation* (pp. 415–454). New York: Academic Press.

Fischer, R., Norberg, A., & Lundman, B. (2008). Embracing opposites: Meanings of growing old: As narrated by people aged 85. *Aging and Human Development, 67*, 259–271.

Fraley, R. C. (2002). Attachment stability from infancy to adulthood: Meta-analysis and dynamic modeling of developmental mechanisms. *Personality and Social Psychology Review, 6*, 123–151.

Fraley, R. C., Davis, K. E., & Shaver, P. R. (1998). Dismissing-avoidance and the defensive organization of emotion, cognition, and behavior. In J. A. Simpson & W. S. Rhodes (Eds.), *Attachment theory and close relationships* (pp. 249–279). New York: Guilford.

Fraley, R. C., & Shaver, P. R. (1999). Loss and bereavement: Attachment theory and recent controversies concerning "grief work" and the nature of detachment. In J. Cassidy & P. R. Shaver (Eds.), *Handbook of attachment: Theory, research, and clinical applications* (pp. 735–759). New York: Guilford.

Frankl, V. E. (1977). *Man's search for meaning.* New York: Pocket Books.

Frantz, T., Trolley, B., & Johll, M. (1996). Religious aspects of bereavement. *Pastoral Psychology, 44*(3), 151–164.

Freud, S. (1957). Mourning and melancholia. In J. Strachey (Ed. & Trans.), *The standard edition of the complete psychological works of Sigmund Freud* (Vol. 14). London, England: Hogarth. (Original work published 1917.)

Galinsky, N. (2003, January/February). The death of a grandchild: A complex grief. *The Forum Newsletter, Association for Death Education and Counseling, 29*, 6–7.

Gjerdingen, D. K., Neff, J. A., Wang, M., & Chaloner, K. (1999). Older persons' opinions about life-sustaining procedures in the face of dementia. *Archives of Family Medicine, 8*, 421–425.

Godwin, G. (2002). *Father melancholy's daughter.* New York: William Morrow.

Goldman, L. (1996). We can help children grieve: A child-oriented model for memorializing. *Young Children, 57*, 69–73.

Goldman, L. (2000). *Life and loss: A guide to help grieving children* (2nd ed.). New York: Taylor & Francis.

Goldman, L. (2002). The assumptive world of children. In J. Kauffman (Ed.), *Loss of the assumptive world: A theory of traumatic loss. The series in trauma and loss* (pp. 193–202). New York: Brunner-Routledge.

Goldman, L. (2005). Family bereavement and the experience of a bereavement camp. *Dissertation Abstracts International: Section B: The Sciences and Engineering, 66*(5-B), 2820.

Goodman, K. W. (1998). End-of-life algorithms. *Psychology, Public Policy, and Law, 4,* 719–727.

Grollman, E. A. (1988). *Suicide: Prevention, intervention postvention* (2nd ed.). Boston, MA: Beacon Press.

Hall, C. I. (1997). Cultural malpractice: The growing obsolescence of psychology with the changing U.S. population. *American Psychologist, 52,* 642–651.

Hanson, M., Enright, R., Baskin, T., & Klatt, J. (2009). A palliative care intervention in forgiveness therapy for elderly terminally ill cancer patients. *Journal of Palliative Care, 25,* 51–62.

Hansson, R., & Stroebe, M. (2007). *Bereavement in later life: Coping, adaptation, and developmental influences.* Washington, DC: American Psychological Association.

Hazen, C., & Shaver, P. (1990). Love and work: An attachment-theoretical perspective. *Journal of Personality and Social Psychology, 59,* 270–280.

Heron, M. P., Hoyert, D. L., Murphy, S. L., Xu, J. Q., Kochanek, K. D., & Tejada-Vera, B. (2009). Deaths: Final data for 2006. *National Vital Statistics Reports, 57*(14). Hyattsville, MD: National Center for Health Statistics.

Hirsch, J., Hofer, M., & Holland, J. (1984). Toward a Biology of Grieving. In M. Osterweis, F. Solomon & M. Green (Eds.), *Bereavement: Reactions, consequences, and care* (pp. 145–175). Washington, DC: National Academy Press.

Hoar, J. (2006, April). *For almost all Americans, there is a God: CBS News poll: 82 percent believe in God; fewer pray.* Retrieved from http://www.cbsnews.com/stories/2006/04/13/opinion/polls/main1498219.shtml.

Hogan, N. S., & DeSantis, L. D. (1996). Adolescent sibling bereavement: Toward a new theory. In C. Corr & D. B. Balk (Eds.), *Helping adolescents cope with death and bereavement* (pp. 173–195). Philadelphia, PA: Springer.

Holland, J., Neimeyer, R., Boelen, P., & Prigerson, H. (2008). The underlying structure of grief: A taxometric investigation of prolonged and normal reactions to loss. *Journal of Psychopathology and Behavioral Assessment, 31*(3), 190–201, doi:10.1007/s10862-008-9113-1.

Horowitz, M. J., Siegel, B., Holen, A., Bonanno, G. A., Milbrath, C., & Stinson, C. H. (1997). Diagnostic criteria for complicated grief disorder. *American Journal of Psychiatry, 157,* 904–910.

Insel, T. R. (2000). Toward a neurobiology of attachment. *Review of General Psychology, 4,* 176–185.

Institute of Medicine. (1997). *Approaching death: Improving care at the end of life* (M. J. Field & C. K. Cassel, Eds.). Washington, DC: National Academy Press.

Institute of Medicine (2001). *Improving palliative care for cancer* (K. M. Foley & H. Gelband, Eds.). Washington, DC: National Academy Press.

Irish, D. P. (1993). Introduction: Multiculturalism and the majority population. In D. Irish, K. Lundquist, & V. Nelsen (Eds.), *Ethnic variations in dying, death, and grief: Diversity in universality* (pp. 1–10). Philadelphia, PA: Taylor & Francis.

Jacobs, S. (1993). *Pathologic grief: Maladaption to loss.* Washington, DC: American Psychiatric Press.

Jacobs, S. (1999). *Traumatic grief: Diagnosis, treatment, and prevention.* Philadelphia, PA: Brunner/Mazel.

Jacobs, S., Mazur, C., & Prigerson, H. (2000). Diagnostic criteria for traumatic grief. *Death Studies, 24,* 185–199.

Jeffreys, J. S. (2005). *Coping with workplace grief: Dealing with loss, trauma, and change* (rev. ed.). Boston, MA: Thomson Learning (Axzo Press).

Jobes, D. (2006). *Managing suicidal risk: A collaborative approach*. New York: Guilford Press.

Johnson, S. E. (1987). *After a child dies: Counseling bereaved families*. New York: Springer.

Johnson, S. M. (2002). *Emotionally focused couple therapy with trauma survivors: Strengthening attachment bonds*. New York: Guilford Press.

Johnson, S. M. (2004). *The practice of emotionally focused couples therapy: Creating connection* (2nd ed.). New York: Routledge.

Katz, R., & Johnson, T. (2006). *When professionals weep: Emotional and countertransference responses in end-of-life care*. New York: Routledge.

Kendler, K. S., Myers, J., & Zisook, S. (2008). Does bereavement-related major depression differ from major depression associated with other stressful life events? *American Journal of Psychiatry, 165*(11), 1449–1455.

Kersting, A., Kroker, K., Horstmann, J., Ohrmann, P., Baune, B. T., Arolt, V., & Suslow, T. (2009). Complicated grief in patients with unipolar depression. *Journal of Affective Disorders, 118*(1–3), 201–204.

Kissane, D. W., Bloch, S., Onghena, P., McKenzie, D. P., Snyder, R. D., & Dowe, D. L. (1996). The Melbourne family grief study, II: Psychosocial morbidity and grief in bereaved families. *American Journal of Psychiatry, 153*, 659–666.

Klass, D. (1988). *Parental grief: Solace and resolution*. New York: Springer.

Klass, D. (1996). The deceased child in the psychic and social worlds of bereaved parents during the resolution of grief. In D. Klass, P. R. Silverman, & S. L. Nickman (Eds.), *Continuing bonds: New understanding of grief* (pp. 199–215). Washington, DC: Taylor & Francis.

Klass, D. (1997). The deceased child in the psychic and social worlds of bereaved parents during the resolution of grief. *Death Studies, 21*, 147–175.

Klass, D. (1999). *Spiritual lives of bereaved parents*. Philadelphia, PA: Brunner/Mazel.

Klass, D. (2001). The inner representation of the dead child in the psychic and social narratives of bereaved parents (pp. 77–94). In R. Neimeyer (Ed.), *Meaning reconstruction and the experience of loss*. Washington, DC: American Psychological Association.

Klass, D., & Goss, R. (1999). Spiritual bonds to the dead in cross-cultural and historical perspective: Comparative religion and modern grief. *Death Studies, 23*(6), 547–567.

Klerman, G. L., & Clayton, P. (1984). Epidemiologic perspectives on the health consequences of bereavement. In M. Osterweis, F. Solomon, & M. Green (Eds.), *Bereavement: Reactions, consequences, and care* (pp. 15–44). Washington, DC: National Academy Press.

Kochanek, K. D., & Smith B. L. (2004, February 11). Deaths: Preliminary data for 2002. *National Vital Statistics Reports, 52*(13).

Koenig, B. A. (1997). Cultural diversity in decision making about care at the end of life. In M. Field & C. Cassel (Eds.), *Approaching death: Improving care at the end of life* (pp. 362–382). Washington, DC: National Academy Press.

Kroeber, A. L., & Kluckhohn, C. (1952). Culture: A critical review of concepts and definitions. Papers. *Peabody Museum of Archaeology & Ethnology, Harvard University, 47*(1), 223.

Kübler-Ross, E. (1969). *On death and dying: What the dying have to teach doctors, nurses, clergy and their own families.* New York: Macmillan.

Kübler-Ross, E. (1978). *To live until we say goodbye.* Englewood Cliffs, NJ: Prentice-Hall.

Kübler-Ross, E. (1981). *Living with death and dying.* New York: Macmillan.

Kushner, H. (1981). *When bad things happen to good people.* New York: Schocken Books.

La Guardia, J. G., Ryan, R. M., Couchman, C. E., & Deci, E. L. (2000). Within-person variation in security of attachment: A self-determination theory perspective on attachment, need fulfillment, and well-being. *Journal of Personality and Social Psychology, 79,* 367–384.

Lemley, B. (1986). "My baby is very sick but I can't pray for him." *Washington Post Magazine,* December 14, 1986.

Leon, I. G. (1992). Perinatal loss: Choreographing grief on the obstetric unit. *American Journal of Orthopsychiatry, 62,* 7.

Levine, S. (1987). *Healing into life and death.* New York: Doubleday.

Lewis, C. S. (1961). *A grief observed.* San Francisco, CA: Harper.

Lindemann, E. (1944). Symptomology and management of acute grief. *American Journal of Psychiatry, 101,* 141–148.

Lund, D. A., & Caserta, M. S. (1992). Older bereaved spouses participation in self-help groups. *Omega, 25,* 47–61.

MacLean, P. D. (1952). Some psychiatric implications of physiological studies on frontotemporal portions of limbic system ("visceral brain"). *Electroencephalography & Clinical Neurophysiology, 4,* 407–418.

MacLean, P. D. (1955a). The limbic system ("visceral brain") and emotional behavior. *Archives of Neurology & Psychiatry (Chicago), 73,* 130–134.

MacLean, P. D. (1955b). The limbic system ("visceral brain") in relation to central gray and reticulum of the brain stem; evidence in emotional process. *Psychosomatic Medicine, 17,* 355–366.

MacLean, P. D. (1973). *A triune concept of the brain and behavior.* Toronto, ON: University of Toronto Press.

MacLean, P. D. (1985). Brain evolution relating to family, play, and the separation call. *Archives of General Psychiatry, 42,* 405–417.

MacLean, P. D., & Pribram, K. H. (1953). The neuronographic analysis of medial and basilcerebral cortex. *Journal of Neurophysiology, 26,* 312–323.

Mancini, A., Robinaugh, D., Shear, K., & Bonanno, G. (2009). Does attachment avoidance help people cope with loss? The moderating effects of relationship quality. *Journal of Clinical Psychology, 65*(10), 1127–1136.

Marshall, V. W. (1996). Death, bereavement, and the social psychology of aging and dying. In J. D. Morgan (Ed.), *The ethical issues in the care of the dying and bereaved aged* (pp. 57–73). Amityville, NY: Baywood.

Mayo Foundation for Medical Education. *Attachment styles.* Retrieved July 16, 2009 from www.MayoClinic.com

McGoldrick, M. (1991). Echoes from the past: Helping families mourn their losses. In F. Walsh & M. McGoldrick (Eds.), *Living beyond loss: Death in the family* (pp. 50–78). New York: Norton.

McGoldrick, M., & Gerson, R. (1985). *Genograms in family assessment.* New York: Norton.

McGoldrick, M., & Walsh, F. (1991a). A time to mourn: Death and the family life cycle. In F. Walsh & M. McGoldrick (Eds.), *Living beyond loss: Death in the family* (pp. 30–49). New York: Norton.

McIntosh, D. N., Silver, R. C., & Wortman, C. B. (1993). Religion's role in adjustment to a negative life event: Coping with the loss of a child. *Journal of Personality and Social Psychology, 65,* 812–821.

McLeod, B.W. (1999). *Caregiving: The spiritual journey of love, loss and renewal.* New York: John Wiley & Sons.

McLeod, B.W. (Ed.). (2002). *And thou shalt honor: The caregiver's companion.* Emmaus, PA: Rodale.

Melham, N. M., Rosales, C., Karageorge, J., Reynolds, C., Frank, E., & Shear, M. (2001). Comorbidity of Axis I disorders in patients with traumatic grief. *Journal of Clinical Psychiatry, 62,* 884–887.

Mikulincer, M., Shaver, P. R., Bar-On, M., & Ein-Dor, T. (2010). The pushes and pulls of close relationships: Attachment insecurities and relational ambivalence. *Journal of Personality and Social Psychology, 98*(3), 450–468.

Miller, J. S., Segal, D. L., & Coolidge, F. L. (2001). The comparison of suicidal thinking and reasons for living among younger and older adults. *Death Studies, 25,* 357–365.

Miller, W. (1976). *When going to pieces holds you together.* Minneapolis, MN: Augsburg Publications.

Mitford, J. (1963). *American way of death.* New York: Simon & Schuster.

Morgan, J. D. (1995). Living our dying and our grieving: Historical and cultural attitudes. In H. Wass & R. A. Neimeyer (Eds.), *Dying: Facing the facts* (pp. 25–45). Washington, DC: Taylor & Francis.

Moss, M. S., Moss, S. Z., & Hansson, R. O. (2001). Bereavement and old age. In M. S. Stroebe, R. O. Hansson, W. Stroebe, & H. Schut (Eds.), *Handbook of bereavement research: Consequences, coping, and care* (pp. 241–260). Washington, DC: American Psychological Association.

Munsch, R. (1986). *Love you forever.* Willowdale, Ontario, Canada: Firefly Books.

Nadeau, J. W. (2001). Meaning making in family bereavement: A family systems approach. In M. S. Stroebe, R. O. Hansson, W. Stroebe, & H. Schut (Eds.), *Handbook of bereavement research: Consequences, coping, and care* (pp. 329–347). Washington, DC: American Psychological Association.

National Cancer Institute, Office of Education and Special Initiatives. (2003). *Palliative care: A review of the literature.* Special Report to Office of Special Initiatives No. 263-01-D-0174.

National Center for Health Statistics. (2001). Births, marriages, divorces, and deaths: Provisional data for January–December 2000. *National Vital Statistics Reports, 49*(6). Hyattsville, MD: NVSR Staff.

National Institutes of Health. (2002). *Symptom management in cancer: Pain, depression, and fatigue.* State-of-the-Science Conference Statement, October 26, 2002.

National Institutes of Health. (2009). *Suicide in the U.S.: Statistics and prevention.* Retrieved from Centers for Disease Control and Prevention, National Center for Injury Prevention and Control, Web-Based Injury Statistics Query and Reporting System (WISQARS), www.cdc.gov/ncipc/wisqars.

*National Vital Statistics Reports,* 2004.

*National Vital Statistics Reports,* Vol. 59(2), December 9, 2010, Author: Minino et al.

Neimeyer, R. A. (1998). *Lessons of loss: A guide to coping.* New York: McGraw-Hill.

Neimeyer, R. (2000). Searching for the meaning of meaning: Grief therapy and the process of reconstruction. *Death Studies, 24,* 541–558.

Neimeyer, R. A. (2001). The language of loss: Grief therapy as a process of meaning reconstruction. In R. A. Neimeyer (Ed.), *Meaning reconstruction & the experience of loss* (pp. 261–292). Washington, DC: American Psychological Association.

Neimeyer, R. A. (2004). Research on grief and bereavement: Evolution and revolution. *Death Studies, 28,* 529–530.

Newman, J. (2002). At your disposal: The funeral industry prepares for boom times. In G. E. Dickinson & M. R. Leming (Eds.), *Dying, death and bereavement* (6th ed., pp. 18–27). Guilford, CT: McGraw-Hill/Dushkin. (Original in *Harpers,* November 1997.)

Nickerson, K., Helms, J., & Terrell, F. (1994). Culture mistrust, opinions about mental illness, and black student attitudes toward seeking psychological help from white counselors. *Journal of Counseling Psychology, 41,* 378–385.

Nouwen, H. (1972). *The wounded healer: Ministry in contemporary society.* New York: Doubleday.

Ogrodniczuk, J. S., Piper, W. E., Joyce, A. S., Weidman, R., McCallum, M., Azim, H., & Rosie, J. S. (2003). Differentiating symptoms of complicated grief and depression among psychiatric outpatients. *Canadian Journal of Psychiatry, 48,* 87–93.

Oliver, L. E. (1999). Effects of a child's death on the marital relationship: A review. *Omega, 39,* 197–227.

Oman, D., & Thorensen, C. E. (2005). Do religion and spirituality influence health? In A. D. Ong & M. H. M van Dulmen (Eds.), *Oxford handbook of methods in positive psychology* (pp. 435–459). Oxford, England: Oxford University Press.

Ortega y Casset, J. (1957). *The revolt of the masses.* New York: Norton.

Pargament, K. I. (2002). Is religion nothing but …? Explaining religion versus explaining religion away. *Psychological Inquiry, 13*(3), 239–244.

Pargament, K. I., & Park, C. L. (1997). In times of stress: The religion—coping connection. In B. Spilka & D. N. McIntosh (Eds.), *The psychology of religion: Theoretical approaches* (pp. 43–53). Boulder, CO: Westview Press.

Park, C. L. (2005). Religion and meaning. In R. F. Paloutzian & C. L. Park (Eds.), *Handbook of the psychology of religion and spirituality* (pp. 295–314). New York: Guilford Press.

Parkes, C. M. (1996). *Bereavement studies of grief in adult life.* New York: International Universities Press. (Original work published 1972.)

Parkes, C. M., Laungani, P., & Young, B. (Eds.). (1997). *Death and bereavement across cultures.* London, England: Routledge.

Parkes, C. M., & Prigerson, H. (2010). *Bereavement: Studies of grief in adult life* (4th ed.). London, England: Routledge.

Parkes, C. M., & Weiss, R. S. (1983). *Recovery from bereavement.* Northvale, NJ: Jason Aronson.

Pert, C. (2006). *Everything you need to know to feel go(o)d.* New York: Hay House.

Peters, N. (2008). *The interrelationship of grief and adult attachment prior to and following the death of a partner* (Doctoral dissertation) [Abstract]. Retrieved from ProQuest Information and Learning Cos.

Pew Forum on Religion & Public Life. (2010). *Religious knowledge survey.* Retrieved from http://pewforum.org/.

Ponzetti, J. (1992). Bereaved families: A comparison of parents' and grandparents' reactions to the death of a child. *Omega, 25,* 63–71.

Prigerson, H. G., Bierhals, A. J., Kasl, S. V., Reynolds, C. F., III, Shear, M. K., Day, N., ... Jacobs, S. (1997). Traumatic grief as a risk factor for mental and physical morbidity. *American Journal of Psychiatry, 154,* 616–623.

Prigerson, H. G., Frank, E., Kasl, S. V., Reynolds, C. F. III, Anderson, B., Zubenko, G.S., ... Kupfer, D. J. (1995). Traumatic grief and bereaved-related depression as distinct disorders: Preliminary empirical validation in elderly bereaved spouses. *American Journal of Psychiatry, 152,* 22–30.

Prigerson, H. G., Horowitz, M. J., Jacobs, S. C., Parkes, C. M., Aslan, M., Goodkin, K., ... Maciejewski, P. K. (2009). Prolonged grief disorder: Psychometric validation of criteria proposed for *DSM-V* and *ICD-11. PLoS Medicine* 6(8): e1000121, doi:10.1371/journal.pmed.1000121.

Prigerson, H. G., & Jacobs, S. C. (2001). Traumatic grief as a distinct disorder: A rationale, consensus criteria, and a preliminary empirical test. In M. S. Stroebe, R. O. Hansson, W. Stroebe, & H. Schut (Eds.), *Handbook of bereavement research: Consequences, coping, and care* (pp. 613–637). Washington, DC: American Psychological Association.

Prigerson, H. G., Maciejewski, P. K., Reynolds, C. F. III, Bierhals, E. J., Newsom, J. T., Fasiczka, A., ... Miller, M. (1995). The inventory of complicated grief: A scale to measure certain maladaptive symptoms of loss. *Psychiatry Research, 59,* 65–79.

Prigerson, H. G., Shear, M. K., Jacobs, S. C., Reynolds, C. F. III, Maciejewski, P. K., Davidson, J.R.T., ... Zisook, S. (1999). Consensus criteria for traumatic grief: A preliminary empirical test. *British Journal of Psychiatry, 174,* 67–73.

Prigerson, H. G., Shear, M. K., Newsom, J. T., Frank, E., Reynolds, C. F. III, Maciejewski, P. K., ... Kupfer, D. J. (1996). Anxiety among widowed elders: Is it distinct from depression and grief? *Anxiety, 2,* 1–12.

Prigerson, H. G., Vanderwerker, L. C., Maciejewski, P. K. (2008). A case for inclusion of prolonged grief disorder in DSM-V. In M. S. Stroebe, R. O. Hannson, H. Schut, & W. Stroebe (Eds.), *Handbook of bereavement research and practice: Advances in theory and interventions* (pp. 165–186). Washington, DC: American Psychological Association.

Rando, T. A. (1984). *Grief, dying and death: Clinical interventions for caregivers.* Champaign, IL: Research Press.

Rando, T. A. (1986). The unique issues and impact of the death of a child. In T. A. Rando (Ed.), *Parental loss of a child* (pp. 5–43). Champaign, IL: Research Press.

Rando, T. A. (1993a). The increasing prevalence of complicated mourning: The onslaught is just beginning. *Omega, 26,* 43–59.

Rando, T. A. (1993b). *The treatment of complicated mourning.* Champaign, IL: Research Press.

Raphael, B. (1983). *The anatomy of bereavement.* New York: Basic Books.

Raphael, B., Minkov, C., & Dobson, M. (2001). Psychotherapeutic and pharmacological intervention for bereaved persons. In M. S. Stroebe, R. O. Hansson, W. Strobe, & H. Schut (Eds.), *Handbook of bereavement research: Consequences, coping, and care* (pp. 587–612). Washington, DC: American Psychological Association.

Reed, M. L. (2003, January/February). Grandparents' grief—Who is listening? *The Forum Newsletter, Association for Death Education and Counseling, 29*, 1–3.

Repole, M. J. (1996). The death of a sibling: Theories of attachment and loss. *Dissertation Abstracts International: Section B: The Sciences & Engineering, 57*(3-B), 2181.

Rholes, W. S., & Simpson, J. A. (2004). Attachment theory: Basic concepts and contemporary questions. In W. S. Rholes & J. A. Simpson (Eds.), *Adult attachment: Theory, research, and clinical implications* (pp. 3–14). New York: Guilford Press.

Rosen, E. (1990). *Families facing death: Family dynamics of terminal illness.* Lexington, MA: Lexington Books.

Rosenberg, H. M., Ventura, S. J., Maurer, J. D., Heuser, R. L., & Freedman, M. A. (1996). Births and deaths: United States, 1995. *Monthly Vital Statistics Report,* 45(3, supp 2). Hyattsville, MD: National Center for Health Statistics.

Rosenblatt, P. C. (1993). Cross-cultural variation in the experience, expression, and understanding of grief. In D. Irish, K. Lundquist, & V. Nelsen (Eds.), *Ethnic variations in dying, death, and grief: Diversity in universality* (pp. 13–19). Philadelphia, PA: Taylor & Francis.

Rosenblatt, P. C. (2000a). *Help your marriage survive the death of a child.* Philadelphia, PA: Temple University Press.

Rosenblatt, P. C. (2000b). *Parent grief: Narratives of loss and relationship.* Philadelphia, PA: Brunner/Mazel.

Rothman, J. C. (1997). *The bereaved parents survival guide.* New York: Continuum.

Rubin, S. (1996). The wounded family: Bereaved parents and the impact of adult child loss. In D. Klass, P. R. Silverman, & S. Nickman (Eds.), *Continuing bonds: Understanding the resolution of grief* (pp. 217–232). Washington, DC: Taylor & Francis.

Rubin, S., & Malkinson, R. (2001). Parental response to child loss across the life cycle: Clinical and research perspectives. In M. S. Stroebe, R. O. Hansson, W. Stroebe, & H. Schut (Eds.), *Handbook of bereavement research: Consequences, coping, and care* (pp. 219–240). Washington, DC: American Psychological Association.

Sakalauskas, P. (1992). Understanding the spiritual and cultural influences on the attitudes of the bereaved. In G. R. Cox & R. J. Fundis (Eds.), *Spiritual, ethical and pastoral aspects of death and bereavement* (pp. 81–91). Amityville, NY: Baywood.

Saunders, C. (2002). The philosophy of hospice. In N. Thompson (Ed.), *Loss and grief: A guide for human services practitioners* (pp. 23–33). New York: Palgrave.

Scherago, M. (1987). *Sibling grief.* Redmond, WA: Medic Publishing Company.

Schultz, R., Boerner, K., & Herbert, R. (2008). Caregiving and bereavement. In M. S. Stroebe, R. O. Hannson, H. Schut, & W. Stroebe, (Eds.). *Handbook of bereavement research and practice: Advances in theory and interventions* (pp. 265–285). Washington, DC: American Psychological Association.

Schwab, R. (1998). A child's death and divorce: Dispelling the myth. *Death Studies, 22*, 445–468.

Shear, K., Monk, T., & Houk, P. (2007). An attachment-based model of complicated grief including the role of avoidance. *European Archives of Psychiatry and Clinical Neuroscience, 257*(8), 453–461, doi:10.1007/s00406-007-0745-z.

Shneidman, E. S. (1972). Foreword. In A. C. Cain (Ed.), *Survivors of suicide* (pp. ix–xi). Springfield, IL: Thomas.

Simon, N. M., Shear, K. M., Thompson, E. H., Zalta, A. K., Perlman, C., Reynolds, C. F., ... Silowash, R. (2007). The prevalence and correlates of psychiatric comorbidity in individuals with complicated grief. *Comprehensive Psychiatry, 48*(5), 395–399.

Simpson, J. A., & Rholes, W. S. (1998). Attachment in adulthood. In J. A. Simpson & W. S. Rholes (Eds.), *Attachment theory and close relationships.* New York: Guilford.

Smilansky, S. (1987). *On death: Helping children understand and cope.* New York: Peter Lang.

Smith, S. A. (2002). *Hospice concepts: A guide to palliative care in terminal illness.* Champaign, IL: Research Press.

Solsberry, M. S. W. (1984). Reacting to particular types of bereavement: Death of a child. In M. Osterweis, F. Solomon, & M. Green (Eds.), *Bereavement: Reactions, consequences, and care* (pp. 47–68). Washington, DC: National Academy Press.

"Spinal Cord Injury Overview, Types of Spinal Cord Injury." (2006). Retrieved May 17, 2010, from www.healthcommunities.com.

Spiritual Care Work Group of the International Work Group on Death, Dying and Bereavement. (1990). *Death Studies, 14*, 75–81.

Stroebe, M. S., Hansson, R., Stroebe, W. (1993). Contemporary themes and controversies in bereavement research. In M. S. Stroebe, W. Stroebe, & R. O. Hansson (Eds.), *Handbook of bereavement research: Theory, research, and intervention* (pp. 457–476). Cambridge, UK: Cambridge University Press.

Stroebe, M. S., & Schut, H. (1999). The dual process model of coping with bereavement: Rationale and description. *Death Studies. 23*(3), 197–224, doi: 10.1080/074811899201046.

Stroebe, M. S., & Schut, H. (2001a). Meaning making in the dual process model of coping with bereavement. In R. A. Neimeyer (Ed.), *Meaning reconstruction & the experience of loss* (55–73). Washington, DC: American Psychological Association.

Stroebe, M. S., & Schut, H. (2001b). Models of coping with bereavement: A review. In M. S. Stroebe, R. O. Hansson, W. Stroebe, & H. Schut (Eds.), *Handbook of bereavement research: Consequences, coping, and care* (pp. 375–403). Washington, DC: American Psychological Association.

Stroebe, M. S., & Stroebe, W. (1991). Does "griefwork" work? *Journal of Consulting and Clinical Psychology, 59*, 479–482.

Stroebe, W., & Stroebe, M. (1987). *Bereavement and health.* New York: Cambridge University Press.

Sue, S. W., & Sue, D. (2003). *Counseling the culturally diverse: Theory and practice* (4th ed.). New York: Wiley.

Talamantes, M. A., & Aranda, M. P. (2004). *Cultural competency in working with Latino family caregivers.* National Caregivers Alliance monograph. Retrieved from http://www.caregiver.org.

Temel, J., Greer, J., Muzikansky, A., Gallagher, E., Admane, S., Jackson, V., … Lynch, T., (2010). Early palliative care for patients with metastatic non–small-cell lung cancer. *The New England Journal of Medicine, 363,* 733–742.

Teno, J. M., Clarridge, B. R., Casey, V., Welch, L. C., Wetle, T., Shield, R., & Mor, V. (2004). Family perspectives on end-of-life care at the last place of care. *Journal of the American Medical Association, 291,* 88–93.

The Compassionate Friends. (1999). When a child dies: A survey of bereaved parents. *The Forum Newsletter, Association for Death Education and Counseling, 25,* 1/10–11.

Triesman, G., & Angelo, A. (2004). *Psychiatry and AIDS: Guide to diagnosis and treatment.* Baltimore, MD: Johns Hopkins Press.

U.S. Census Bureau. (2009). *Decennial census, populations estimates and projections.*

U.S. Centers for Disease Control and Prevention. (1999). *Traumatic Brain Injury in the United States: A report to Congress.* Retrieved from http://www.cdc.gov/ncipc/tbi/tbi_congress/TBI_in_the_US.PDF.

U.S. Centers for Disease Control and Prevention. (2001a). *HIV/AIDS surveillance report, US HIV and AIDS cases reported through December 1999, Year End Edition, 11*(2). Retrieved from http://www.cdc.gov/hiv/stats/hasr1102.pdf.

U.S. Centers for Disease Control and Prevention. (2001b). *Safe USA—What you should know about spinal cord injury.* Retrieved from http://www.cdc.gov/safeusahome/home/sci.htm.

U.S. Department of Defense Report. (n.d.). *Report to Congress in accordance with Section 1634 (b) of the National Defense Authorization Act for Fiscal Year 2008.* Retrieved from http://www.biausa.org/aboutbi.htm.

U.S. Department of Health and Human Services. (1998). *Family caregiver alliance fact sheet.*

"U.S. Military Casualty Statistics," CRS Report for Congress. (2009, March 25). Retrieved from http://www.defenselink.mil/news/casualty.pdf.

Ventura, S. J., Anderson, R. N., Martin, J. A., and Smith, B. L. (1998). Births and deaths: Preliminary data for 1997. *National Vital Statistics Reports, 47*(4). Hyattsville, MD: National Center for Health Statistics.

Wade, N., Worthington, E., & Haake, S. (2009). Comparison of explicit forgiveness interventions with an alternative treatment: A randomized clinical trial. *Journal of Counseling and Development, 87,* 143–151.

Walsh, F. (2004). Spirituality, death and loss. In F. Walsh, & M. McGoldrick (Eds.), *Living beyond loss: Death in the family* (2nd ed., pp. 182–210). New York: Norton.

Walsh, F., & McGoldrick, M. (1991). Loss and the family: A systemic perspective. In F. Walsh & M. McGoldrick (Eds.), *Living beyond loss: Death in the family* (pp. 1–29). New York: Norton.

Walsh, F., & McGoldrick, M. (1998). A family systems perspective on loss, recovery and resilience. In P. Sutcliffe, G. Tufnell, & U. Cornish, *Working with the dying and bereaved: Systemic approaches to therapeutic work* (pp. 1–26). New York: Routledge.

Walsh, F., & McGoldrick, M. (Eds.). (2004). *Living beyond loss: Death in the family* (2nd ed.). New York: Norton and Co.

Wayment, H. A., & Vierthaler, J. (2002). Attachment style and bereavement reactions. *Journal of Loss and Trauma, 7,* 129–149.

Weaver, A. J., & Koenig, H. G. (1996). Elderly suicide, mental health professionals and the clergy. *Death Studies, 20,* 495–508.

Weeks, O. D. (2004). Comfort and healing death ceremonies that work. *Illness, Crisis & Loss, 12,* 113–125.

Well Spouse Association. (2009, Summer). *Mainstay.*

Wicks, R. J. (1995). *Seeds of sensitivity.* Notre Dame, IN: Ave Maria Press.

Worden, J. W. (1996). *Children and grief.* New York: Guilford.

Worden, J. W. (2002). *Grief counseling and grief therapy: A handbook for the mental health practitioner* (3rd ed.). New York: Springer.

Worden, J. W. (2009). *Grief counseling and grief therapy* (4th ed.). New York: Springer.

Wortman, C. B., & Silver, R. C. (1989). The myths of coping with loss. *Journal of Consulting and Clinical Psychology, 57,* 349–357.

Wortmann, J., & Park, C. (2008). Religion and spirituality in adjustment following bereavement: An integrative review. *Death Studies, 32,* 703–736.

Yalom, I. (2008). *Staring at the Sun: Overcoming the Terror of Death.* San Francisco, CA: Jossey-Bass.

Zinner, E. S. (2002). Incorporating disenfranchised grief in the death education classroom. In K. J. Doka (Ed.), *Disenfranchised grief: New direction, challenges and strategies for practice* (pp. 389–404). Champaign, IL: Research Press.

Zinner, E. S., & Williams, M. B. (1999). *When a community weeps.* New York: Brunner/Mazel.

# INDEX

"f" indicates material in figures. "t" indicates material in tables.

Morphine, 31
Moss, M. & S., 191, 192, 193
Mother
  attachment to, 50–54
  case study on death of child
    accidental, 337–339
    perinatal, 334–336
  children and death of, 125–132, 134
  distress cry and, 40, 50–51, 125
  environment and grief of, 163
  miscarriage by, 68, 89, 107, 149, 161,
    321
  pregnancy termination by, 91, 314, 321
  psychobiological attunement with, 51
  self-esteem of, 149
  sexual needs of, 167, 328
  style of grieving by, 41, 76–77, 163–166
Mothers Against Drunk Driving (MADD),
  197, 330, 350
Mother's Day, 289
Motor vehicles, 13t
Mourning, 43
Multiple sclerosis, 210
Munsch, R., 266
Muscle relaxation, 285
Muslims, 28, 33–34
Myers, J., 304–305

**N**

Nabe, C., 184
Nadeau, J. W., 104
National Alliance for Caregiving, 211, 351
National Association of Professional
    Geriatric Care Managers, 351
National Cancer Institute, 209, 351
National Caregivers Alliance, 21
National Caregivers Association, 197
National Center for Grieving Children &
    Families, 350
National Center for Post-Traumatic Stress
    Disorder, 351
National Council on Disability, 351
National Family Caregivers Association,
    202, 258–259, 351
National Hospice and Palliative Care
    Organization, 351
National Institutes of Health, 159, 211, 351
National Organization of Parents of
    Murdered Children, Inc., 351
National Sudden and Unexpected Infant/
    Child Death & Pregnancy Loss,
    351
National Suicide Prevention Hotline, 351

*National Vital Statistics Reports*, 13t–14t, 16,
  88, 211t
Native Americans, 29, 34
Neff, J. A., 246
Neimeyer, Robert, 25, 77–78, 155, 267,
  297–298
Newman, J., 28
Nickerson, K., 22
Nightmares, 134
Nolen-Hoeksema, S., 25
Nondeath losses
  about, 92
  disability; *See* Disability
  families and, 108
  illness; *See* Chronic illness
  of older adults, 184
  sadness for, 59
  support after, 92–93
  work-related; *See* Work-related loss
Norbeerg, A., 195
Nouwen, Henri, 4

**O**

Obituaries, 18, 88, 103
O'Connor, Carroll, 145
Ogrodniczuk, J. S., 305
Older adults
  activities of, 188, 199
  anxiety of, 191, 194
  caring for, 199–202
  case study on death of spouse, 339–
    340, 343–345
  cognitive functions of, 187
  complicated grief of, 327
  culture on, 188–189
  death of, 89, 203
  on dementia, 246
  disenfranchisement of, 188, 314
  emotions of, 46
  during end-of-life care, 233
  in family life-cycle, 96t
  grandparents; *See* Grandparents
  help for grieving, 195–199
  isolation of, 97, 187–188, 199
  losses of, 18–19, 98, 184–195
  "passage of time" grief, 19
  physical health of, 186–187
  realities faced by, 18–19, 183–185
  rites, rituals, and, 29, 189
  same-sex couples, 192
  sibling grief of, 193
  social factors affecting, 187–189
  suicide by, 194–195